The Electoral Challenge

The Electoral Challenge

Theory Meets Practice

SECOND EDITION

Edited by

Stephen C. Craig
University of Florida

David B. Hill
Auburn University and Hill Research Consultants

CQ PRESS

A Division of SAGE
Washington, D.C.

CQ Press
2300 N Street, NW, Suite 800
Washington, DC 20037

Phone, 202-729-1900; toll-free, 1-866-427-7737 (1-866-4CQ-PRESS)

Web: www.cqpress.com

Cover design: Anne Kerns, Anne Likes Red Inc.
Composition: C&M Digitals (P) Ltd.

♾ The paper used in this publication exceeds the requirements of the American National Standard for Information Sciences—Permanence of Paper for Printed Library Materials, ANSI Z39.48-1992.

Printed and bound in the United States of America

14   13   12   11   10   1   2   3   4   5

Library of Congress Cataloging-in-Publication Data

The electoral challenge : theory meets practice / edited by Stephen C. Craig, David B. Hill. — 2nd ed.
    p. cm.
Includes bibliographical references.
ISBN 978-1-60426-636-8 (alk. paper)
    1. Presidents—United States—Election. 2. Political campaigns—United States. 3. Voting—United States. I. Craig, Stephen C. II. Hill, David B. III. Title.

JK524.E366 2010
324.70973—dc22

                                                    2010011805

Dedicated to:

Bill Hamilton, superpollster and good friend, without whom the University of Florida's Graduate Program in Political Campaigning would not be what it is today.

—Stephen C. Craig

Roger Ailes, John Deardourff, and Bob Goodman, three pioneering political consultants who taught me what it means to be a political professional.

—David B. Hill

Contents

❖ = The Political Professionals Respond text box.

❖ = The Political Professionals Respond text box.

Preface

Do campaigns really matter? A good bit of academic literature suggests that they do not—or at least not as much as politicians and the media tend to think they do. It has now been more than half a century since James Farley, President Franklin Roosevelt's campaign manager, offered what is known as Farley's Law: most elections are decided before the campaign even begins. More recently, in an analysis of the 1984, 1988, and 1992 presidential elections, Thomas Holbrook (1996) concluded that the *general* level of support for candidates during a campaign season is a function of national conditions (which vary primarily from one election to the next), whereas *fluctuations* in candidate support over the course of a single election year are in response to campaign-specific events. Although Holbrook acknowledged that these events (for example, the so-called convention bump, candidate debates, and blunders by one of the candidates) have an impact, national conditions—measured in terms of *consumer sentiment* and *presidential job approval*, both factors that are in place before the general election campaign begins in earnest—ultimately matter a great deal more in determining who wins and who loses.

Similarly, James Campbell (2000) conceded that *nonsystematic* campaign events, or those that are idiosyncratic to a particular election—for example, Harry Truman's relentless attacks on the "do-nothing" Republican Congress in 1948, John F. Kennedy's strong performance in the first-ever televised presidential debates in 1960, the violent clashes between police and anti–Vietnam War protesters during the 1968 Democratic National Convention in Chicago, and Gerald Ford's apparent mis-statement about Soviet domination of Eastern Europe in a 1976 debate—can have significant, and even decisive, effects on the outcome of an extremely close contest. Yet Campbell argued that these events were important precisely *because* the elections in question were close. In most instances (according to Campbell and others), nothing that happens during the campaign is likely to have more than a marginal impact, with the great majority of votes falling into place very early (because of the effects of partisan attachments, incumbent evaluations, the national economy, incumbency, and selective perception and overall indifference on the part of voters) and one candidate often running clearly ahead of the other(s).

Analyses such as those provided by Holbrook and Campbell apply specifically to the top of the ticket, but there are reasons to suspect that short-term forces such as issues, candidate traits, and campaign events may have even less impact on lower-level races in which voter attention is typically even more limited and factors such as partisanship and incumbency often appear to be overwhelmingly decisive, regardless of what does or does not happen over the course of the campaign (Jacobson 2009). Overall, then, the conventional wisdom within the academic community is that campaign events and the decisions made by candidates and their advisors matter relatively little, except under the most unusual of circumstances. That wisdom has changed a bit, especially after the spectacular failure of forecasting models to predict accurately the outcome of the 2000 presidential election (see the symposium in *PS: Political Science and Politics,* March 2001). Nevertheless, the weight of the evidence seems to indicate that most campaigns at all levels are over, or almost over, before they even begin.

Candidates and political operatives would, of course, disagree. Indeed, industry journals (most notably *Politics,* formerly known as *Campaigns & Elections*) and a number of trade books (for example, Bailey et al. 2000; Watson and Campbell 2003)[1] seek to illustrate the importance of the various strategic and tactical decisions made both in advance of the campaign and during the heat of battle. Unfortunately, these accounts provide little more than anecdotal evidence bearing on the larger question: Do campaigns matter? Candidate A is said to have won because of an effective communications strategy, including just the right mix of positive and negative advertising (and of communications media, electronic versus direct mail). Candidate B's winning edge is thought to have resulted from an effective targeting of potential supporters and a strong get-out-the-vote effort on election day. Candidates C, D, and E were able to defeat their opponents because of newspaper endorsements, innovative use of the Internet, and better money management, respectively, and so on. The problem is not that the conclusions drawn from case studies such as these are wrong. It is that broad conclusions cannot be drawn from case studies, period. What works for one candidate in one type of situation may not (and often does not) work for another candidate who faces a different opponent and an entirely different set of circumstances.

---

[1]From the academic world, readers might also want to peruse Magleby and Patterson (2008), Thurber and Nelson (2010), Adkins and Dulio (2010), and Medvic (2010).

At the same time, a considerable amount of academic research has been produced in recent years that bears directly on many of the claims made by political practitioners. Scholars have, for example, tried to determine whether

- negative ads drive turnout rates up or down and whether they are more effective than positive ads at shaping voter preferences;
- party and candidate mobilization efforts make enough of a difference to justify the effort and expense required to mount them;
- personal appearances by a candidate in a state or local area help to generate support for that candidate on election day;
- increased spending by a candidate results in higher vote totals;
- the Internet is more effective than other communications channels; and
- elections are shaped by factors such as candidate debates, scandals, external events, or the hiring of professional consultants.

The literature has not yet provided definitive answers to these (and many other) questions, but there is little doubt that we are better informed today about the factors shaping election outcomes than was the case fifteen or twenty years ago.

The first edition of this book emerged from a workshop hosted by the Graduate Program in Political Campaigning at the University of Florida in February 2005. At that workshop, we brought together two groups of individuals that typically do not interact with each other on a regular basis: academics and campaign consultants. Most professionals seem to believe that the academic literature on campaigns and elections is either obvious (it tells you what everyone already knows anyway) or wrong—though they are often too busy with their work to follow that literature closely. For their part, many academics take the position that campaign consultants operate by the seat of their pants— that is, promoting the latest folk wisdom about which strategies and tactics work and which ones do not, without knowing for sure until it is too late. A problem here, at least in the past, has been that too many academics study campaigns and elections without ever talking directly to those on the front lines, getting involved in a campaign, or otherwise taking the time to learn about the latest developments in the increasingly professionalized field of campaign management.

Without necessarily resolving these issues, the 2005 workshop provided a unique opportunity for the two sides to get together and hear what the other had to say. The first edition of *The Electoral Challenge* was the product of that exchange, offering a series of essays that reviewed existing research on such topics as campaign strategy, campaign spending, political advertising, voter mobilization, and the Internet, as well as occasional comments (based on their remarks at the workshop) from practitioners who shared their views about the strengths and weaknesses of the academic approach. The format is pretty much the same this time around, except that each review essay is followed by a written response by one or more political professionals who have experience in the area covered by that chapter. Although these professionals do not always see the world of campaigns and elections the same way their academic counterparts do, the level of outright disagreement between the two groups is not nearly as high as some might expect.

The Graduate Program in Political Campaigning was created in 1985 in response to complaints from students that the political science department at the University of Florida did not offer enough classes dealing with the nuts and bolts of everyday politics. It was then, and is still today, one of the few practical politics programs in the country (especially at the graduate level), not because few young people are interested in such studies, but, in large measure, because of the difficulty of blending two worlds that do not always see eye to eye. Although neither the Campaigning Program nor this book will fundamentally change that, we hope that our efforts represent a step in the right direction. Academics and political consultants have much to learn from one another, and for that to happen the lines of communication must remain open.

We are indebted to reviewers of the first edition who gave us feedback on how to improve on the first iteration of this volume: Randall Adkins, University of Nebraska–Omaha; Michael Brogan, Rider University; Daniel Coffey, University of Akron; John McNulty, Binghamton University, SUNY; Paul Mueller, University of Notre Dame; and Zoe Oxley, Union College.

Contributors

About the Editors

STEPHEN C. CRAIG is professor of political science at the University of Florida. He is author of *The Malevolent Leaders: Popular Discontent in America* (1993); editor of five books, including *Broken Contract? Changing Relationships Between Citizens and Their Government in the United States* (1996), *After the Boom: The Politics of Generation X* (1997), and *Ambivalence and the Structure of Political Opinion* (2005); and has published numerous book chapters and articles in professional journals. His research deals with attitude measurement, campaign effects, and various other aspects of contemporary public opinion and political behavior in the United States. Craig is director of the University of Florida's Graduate Program in Political Campaigning. He has worked extensively with both academic and political surveys in Florida and nationwide.

DAVID B. HILL is director of Hill Research Consultants and a member of the research faculty at Auburn University, where he is associate director of the Center for Governmental Services. As a political pollster, he has advised more than fifty candidates for governor and Congress across the nation; he also frequently serves as pollster and strategist for initiative and referenda campaigns in Florida, Colorado, Michigan, and California. Prior to becoming a consultant, he was director of the Public Policy Resources Laboratory at Texas A&M University.

About the Chapter Authors

MICHAEL JOHN BURTON is associate professor of political science at Ohio University. He worked in the White House office of Vice President Al Gore (1993–1998) as special assistant to the chief of staff and assistant political director. With Daniel M. Shea, he has coauthored *Campaign Craft: The Strategies, Tactics, and Art of Political Campaign Management* (2010) and *Campaign Mode: Strategic Vision in Congressional Elections* (2003).

MARIAN L. CURRINDER is senior fellow at Georgetown University's Government Affairs Institute; she previously was assistant professor of political science at the College of Charleston. Her research focuses mainly on Congress, campaign finance, and congressional party organizations. Currinder has published in *Legislative Studies Quarterly* and *State and Local Government Review* and is author of *Money in the House: Campaign Funds and Congressional Party Politics* (2008). She was an American Political Science Association Congressional Fellow in 2003–2004.

DAVID A. DULIO is associate professor of political science at Oakland University, where he teaches courses on campaigns and elections, Congress, political parties, interest groups, and other aspects of American politics. Dulio has published seven books, including *Cases in Congressional Campaigns: Incumbents Playing Defense in 2008* (2010), *Vital Signs: Perspectives on the Health of American Campaigning* (2005), and *For Better or Worse? How Professional Political Consultants Are Changing Elections in the United States* (2004). He has written dozens of articles and book chapters on subjects ranging from the role of professional consultants in U.S. elections to campaign finance. During 2001–2002, Dulio served as an American Political Science Congressional Fellow, working in the House Republican Conference for Rep. J. C. Watts Jr. (Okla.).

MICHAEL M. FRANZ is associate professor of government at Bowdoin College. His research interests include interest groups, parties, elections, and campaign advertising. He has published articles in *American Journal of Political Science, Journal of Politics, Political Behavior, Political Analysis,* and *Social Science Quarterly* and is coauthor of *Campaign Advertising and American Democracy* (2008) and author of *Choices and Changes: Interest Groups in the Electoral Process* (2008). Franz received the E. E. Schattschneider Award in 2007 from the American Political Science Association for the best dissertation on American politics during the previous year. He is currently working on a book that explores the effects of campaign advertising on voter evaluations of candidates.

JOHN C. GREEN is distinguished professor of political science and director of the Ray C. Bliss Institute of Applied Politics at the University of Akron. He is coauthor of *The Financiers of Congressional Elections: Investors, Ideologues, and Intimates* (2003) and coeditor of *The State of the Parties* (2006) and *The Faith Factor: How Religion Influences American Elections* (2007). Green has published numerous journal articles and book chapters dealing with campaign finance, political parties, and religion and politics.

MICHAEL T. HEANEY is assistant professor of organizational studies and political science at the University of Michigan. His research focuses on social networks and the intersections among interest groups, political parties, and social movements in the United States. Heaney was an American Political Science Association Congressional Fellow in 2007–2008. He has published numerous book chapters and articles in such professional journals as *American Political Science Review, American Politics Research,* and *Perspectives on Politics.*

THOMAS M. HOLBROOK is Wilder Crane Professor of Government at the University of Wisconsin–Milwaukee. He is former editor of *American Politics Research* and author of *Do Campaigns Matter?* (1996). He also has published extensively in leading journals on topics related to public opinion and elections, with an emphasis on the impact of presidential campaigns on voting behavior and election outcomes. Holbrook is currently working on a National Science Foundation–funded project that studies urban mayoral elections and is a sometimes accurate forecaster of presidential election outcomes.

THOMAS A. HOLLIHAN is a professor in the Annenberg School for Communication and Journalism at the University of Southern California. He is author of *Uncivil Wars: Political Campaigns in a Media Age* (2009), *Arguments and Arguing: The Products and Process of Human Decision Making* (2004), and *Argument at Century's End: Remembering the Past and Envisioning the Future* (2000) and has published numerous book chapters and articles in *Quarterly Journal of Speech, Communication Quarterly, Western Journal of Communication, Argumentation and Advocacy,* and other professional journals. Hollihan has served as president of the American Forensics Association, chaired the board of trustees of the National Debate Tournament, and chaired the National Debate Tournament Committee.

MICHAEL D. MARTINEZ is professor and chair of the Department of Political Science at the University of Florida. He is coeditor of *Ambivalence and the Structure of Political Opinion* (2005) and *Ambivalence, Politics, and Public Policy* (2005). Martinez has published numerous book chapters and articles in professional journals on such topics as attitudinal ambivalence, voter turnout, partisanship, voting behavior, and political ideology. He has received research support from the Canadian Embassy Faculty Research Support Program and was a Fulbright Scholar at the University of Calgary.

WILLIAM G. MAYER is associate professor of political science at Northeastern University. His research interests are in American politics, public opinion, and media and politics. He is author or editor of several books, including *The Divided Democrats: Ideological Unity, Party Reform, and Presidential Elections* (1996) and *The Swing Voter in American Politics* (2008).

WILLIAM J. MILLER is assistant professor of political science at Southeast Missouri State University. He received his Ph.D. from the University of Akron in public administration and urban studies and has previously served in visiting positions at Ohio University and Notre Dame College. His research focuses primarily on public attitudes toward various domestic and international policies and institutions, with an emphasis on the European Union. Miller's work can be found in *Journal of Political Science Education, Journal of Common Market Studies*, and *Studies in Conflict & Terrorism*.

MATTHEW E. NEWMAN is an undergraduate student majoring in political science at the University of Florida, where he has participated in the University Scholars Program (a program that allows students to work one-on-one with faculty members to complete a scholarly research project). He plans to write his senior honors thesis on the use of social networking sites in U.S. congressional campaigns.

BETH A. ROSENSON is associate professor of political science at the University of Florida. A former journalist, she conducts research primarily on the politics of ethics regulation, corruption, political reform, and legislative behavior. She is author of *The Shadowlands of Conduct: Ethics and State Politics* (2005) and has published articles in numerous academic journals, including *Legislative Studies Quarterly, Political Research Quarterly*, and *Public Choice*.

DANIEL M. SHEA is professor of political science and director of the Center for Political Participation at Allegheny College. He has worked as a political strategist in some of New York's most challenging races and has written widely on campaign strategy and political parties. He is author or editor of numerous books, including *Mass Politics: The Politics of Entertainment* (1999), *Contemplating the People's Branch: Legislative Dynamics in the Twenty-first Century* (2001), *Campaign Mode* (2002), *New Party Politics: From Hamilton and Jefferson to the Information Age* (2000/2003), and *The Fountain of Youth* (2007).

DANIEL A. SMITH is professor of political science and director of the Graduate Program in Political Campaigning at the University of Florida. He is author of *Tax Crusaders and the Politics of Direct Democracy* (1998) and coauthor of *Educated by Initiative: The Effects of Direct Democracy on Citizens and Political Organizations in the American States* (2004) and *State and Local Politics: Institutions and Reform* (2009/2011). Smith has written more than forty scholarly articles and book chapters on the politics and process of direct democracy. He serves on the board of directors of the Ballot Initiative Strategy

Center Foundation and as a member of the board of scholars of the Initiative and Referendum Institute.

DARI E. SYLVESTER is assistant professor of political science and senior research fellow with the Jacoby Center for Public Service and Civic Leadership at the University of the Pacific. Her research interests include state and local government, educating for political involvement, and volunteerism; she recently coauthored an article, "The Digital Divide, Political Participation and Place," that appeared in the *Social Science Computer Review*. Working with the San Joaquin County, California, Registrar of Voters in 2008, Sylvester helped to lead a voter education project aimed at increasing vote-by-mail ballots and turnout rates and reducing voter error.

PETER W. WIELHOUWER is associate professor of political science at Western Michigan University; his research deals mainly with mobilization politics, campaign strategy, religion and politics, and racial politics. He is an occasional political consultant, former director of a graduate program in campaign management, and regular speaker on elections and faith and politics. His research has appeared in such journals as *American Journal of Political Science* and *Journal of Politics* and in *The Oxford Handbook of Religion and American Politics* (2010). Wielhouwer currently serves as executive director of the Southwestern Social Science Association (which publishes *Social Science Quarterly*).

About the Professionals

WHIT AYRES is president of the American Association of Political Consultants and president of Ayres, McHenry, and Associates, Inc., a public opinion research firm. Before establishing his firm, he was a tenured faculty member in the Department of Government and International Studies at the University of South Carolina. He holds a Ph.D. in political science from the University of North Carolina at Chapel Hill.

CHARLIE BLACK is chair of Prime Policy Group, a Washington-based public affairs and government relations firm. He has been involved in every Republican presidential campaign since 1976, as well as the election of a dozen U.S. senators and more than a dozen members of the U.S. House. In March 2010, he was inducted into the American Association of Political Consultants Hall of Fame.

MARK M. BLUMENTHAL is editor and publisher of Pollster.com, a Web site that publishes poll results and a daily running commentary on political polling. Launched in 2006, Pollster.com builds on Blumenthal's Mystery Pollster blog, started in 2004. Blumenthal also writes a weekly column on polling for NationalJournal.com. Previously, he gained more than twenty years of experience as a Democratic campaign pollster.

CHRIS CASEY is vice president of online campaigns at NGP Software, a political technology firm that serves Democrats and progressive organizations. The Online Campaigns team provides award-winning Web design and development and strategic support to campaigns at every level. Casey's involvement in online politics began while he was working in the office of Sen. Edward Kennedy. In 1994, he helped Kennedy become the first member of Congress to have a Web site. He is author of *The Hill on the Net: Congress Enters the Information Age* (1996).

SUSAN B. CASEY has been an organizer, strategist, manager, and advisor in five presidential campaigns. In 1986, she authored *Hart and Soul: Gary Hart's New Hampshire Odyssey ... and Beyond*, an insider look at the 1984 New Hampshire primary campaign. Casey, a former Denver city councilwoman, continues to provide strategic and management advice to candidates and elected leaders, and has been an adjunct professor at the University of Colorado Graduate School of Public Affairs and elsewhere.

RON FAUCHEUX is president of Clarus Research Group, a nonpartisan polling firm based in Washington, D.C. A former two-term Louisiana state legislator and publisher of *Campaigns & Elections* magazine, he has a B.S.F.S. from Georgetown University, a Juris Doctor degree from the Louisiana State University Law Center, and a Ph.D. in political science from the University of New Orleans. As a political consultant, he has worked in 124 issue and candidate campaigns throughout the country. Dr. Faucheux teaches courses in political and advocacy campaigning at Georgetown University's Public Policy Institute and George Washington University's Graduate School of Political Management. He has written or edited numerous books on politics, including *Running for Office: The Strategies, Techniques, and Messages Modern Political Candidates Need to Win Elections* (2002) and *Winning Elections: Political Campaign Management, Strategy, and Tactics* (2003).

DANIEL GOTOFF heads Lake Research Partners New York office. Since joining the firm in 1996, he has worked for candidates at all levels of the electoral process as well as on a wide range of issues, including the economy, national security, regulation, and government accountability. Gotoff's tenure at LRP has included extensive research for progressive clients, including presidential, senatorial, congressional, gubernatorial, and mayoral candidates, as well as the Democratic National Committeee, the Democratic Congressional Campaign Committee, and the NAACP National Voter Fund.

CELINDA LAKE, the president of Lake Research Partners, is a pollster and political strategist for Democrats and progressives. Her advice helped candidates such as Sen. Jon Tester (Montana), Rep. Tim Walz (Minnesota), and Gov. Bob Wise (West Virginia) defeat incumbent Republicans and made Mark Begich the first Senate candidate in Alaska to oust an incumbent in fifty years. She has focused especially on women candidates and women's concerns, working for House Speaker Nancy Pelosi, Gov. Janet Napolitano (Arizona), and Sen. Debbie Stabenow (Michigan). Lake also was a key player in campaigns launched by progressive groups such as the AFL-CIO, Sierra Club, Planned Parenthood, EMILY's List, and others. Additionally, she recently helped elect Annise Parker as the first openly gay mayor of a major U.S. city (Houston) and served as pollster for Joe Biden's presidential bid in 2008. Lake is coauthor (with Republican pollster Kellyanne Conway) of *What Women Really Want*, which examines how women are changing the political landscape in America.

MIKE MURPHY has handled campaigns for Jeb Bush, Arnold Schwarzenegger, Mitt Romney, John Engler, and many other Republican senators and governors. In 2000, he was senior strategist for John McCain's first presidential campaign. He has been a fellow at the John F. Kennedy School's Institute of Politics at Harvard University and serves as a frequent panelist on NBC's *Meet the Press* and occasional columnist for *Time* magazine. Murphy attended Georgetown University's Walsh School of Foreign Service.

STUART ROTHENBERG is editor and publisher of the *Rothenberg Political Report*, a nonpartisan newsletter (see http://rothenbergpoliticalreport.blog spot.com) that reports on and handicaps U.S. House and Senate races. He holds a B.A. from Colby College and a Ph.D. from the University of Connecticut. A columnist for *Roll Call* newspaper, he has served as a political analyst for various media organizations, including CNN, CBS News, and the *NewsHour* on PBS.

ADAM SMITH has been with the *St. Petersburg Times* since 1992, serving as political editor since 2001. He has won numerous awards for investigative and political reporting; created *The Buzz* (http://blogs.tampabay.com/buzz), a popular Florida political blog; and cohosts a Sunday public affairs show on Bay News 9 in Tampa Bay. He attended the University of Edinburgh and graduated from Kenyon College with a degree in political science.

JACK ST. MARTIN has served as director of grassroots development, regional political director, and coalitions director for the Republican National Committee. He also has managed a number of statewide campaigns, run three national nonprofit grassroots organizations, and been senior vice president at the Direct Impact Company (which does national grassroots lobbying). He currently is a partner at the Orange Hat Group, a new media mobilization firm.

V. LANCE TARRANCE JR. is a leading Republican pollster. He recently served as a senior strategist for John McCain's Straight Talk America political action committee and for the senator's 2008 presidential campaign. Tarrance was previously involved in the presidential campaigns of Barry Goldwater, Richard Nixon, Ronald Reagan, John Connally, Jack Kemp, and George H. W. Bush. He served on the board of directors of the Gallup Organization (1987–1992), as first managing director and president of Gallup China in Beijing (1993–1995), and as a president and founder of Tarrance & Associates, a Houston-based national survey research company (1977–1992).

1 Do Campaigns Really Matter?

Thomas M. Holbrook

It has been more than a dozen years since the publication of *Do Campaigns Matter?* (Holbrook 1996), in which I argued against the general sentiment among scholars that presidential campaigns have, at best, minimal effects on election outcomes. Four additional presidential elections have now come and gone, and the number of scholarly articles and books on campaign effects has grown accordingly. In this chapter, which serves as a backdrop for the more narrowly focused essays that follow, I return to the question of whether campaigns matter by reviewing recent developments in the academic literature and by revisiting and broadening the way in which the question itself is conceived. First, I examine early research that helped to define the "minimal effects" perspective. Second, I briefly review my own arguments and findings from *Do Campaigns Matter?*, along with those of a number of other studies that have dealt primarily with the persuasive effects of presidential campaigns. Third, I discuss the unnecessarily narrow framework used by most scholars working in this area and review research on nonpersuasion effects that appear to be associated with political campaigns. Finally, I suggest that the presidential arena might not be the best place to look for evidence of campaign effects.

Setting the Stage: Early Work and Minimal Effects

Modern election research originated with two studies conducted by members of the so-called Columbia school (reflecting the authors' institutional affiliation). The first of these was Lazarsfeld, Berelson, and Gaudet's *The People's Choice* (1944), which looked at residents of Erie County, Ohio, over the course of the 1940 presidential race between Franklin Roosevelt and Wendell Willkie; this was followed by Berelson, Lazarsfeld, and McPhee's *Voting* (1954), a study of Elmira, New York, during the 1948 contest between Harry Truman and Thomas Dewey. Even by contemporary standards, the design of the Columbia studies was quite sophisticated in that both used panel surveys, interviewing the same group of voters throughout the summer and fall of the election year. This approach was particularly well suited for detecting campaign effects and, indeed, the authors anticipated that what people experienced during the campaign season would influence how they voted—a seemingly plausible expectation.

Lazarsfeld and his colleagues (1944) focused mainly on the influence of media exposure (radio and newspaper) during the campaign and, in the end, concluded that what voters read or heard about the candidates had surprisingly little impact on how they voted. Instead, it appeared that there was a strong social dimension to the vote. Specifically, various groups in society were predisposed to supporting one party or the other; to the extent that there was any movement in candidate preferences during the campaign, it usually resulted from wayward voters returning to their group's historical voting pattern.[1] This phenomenon led to the creation of something called the "index of political predisposition" (a precursor to the concept of party identification, discussed later in this chapter), which emphasized the group-based aspects of voting.

Looking at changes that took place during the time period covered by their surveys, Lazarsfeld and his colleagues (1944, 102) found that a mere 8 percent of all voters could be described as having been "converted" by the campaign. The rest either exhibited no change from their original vote intention (69 percent), initially planned to cross over or were undecided but ended up voting in a manner consistent with their social group characteristics (17 percent), or changed from expressing a vote preference to "undecided" (6 percent).[2] This, to the authors, was evidence of the relative inefficacy of the campaign. In a separate essay that summarized many of the findings from *The People's Choice*, Lazarsfeld, Berelson, and Gaudet (1944) made a pointed assessment of the importance of campaigns, concluding that "[i]n an important sense, modern Presidential campaigns are over before they begin" (317), and that "elections are decided by the events occurring in the entire period between two Presidential elections and not by the campaign" (330).

The Elmira study followed up on many of the key findings from *The People's Choice* but also placed a greater emphasis on the degree to which issues and interpersonal communications can affect vote choice (Berelson, Lazarsfeld, and McPhee 1954). As before, Berelson and his colleagues learned that a relatively modest share of the electorate changed their minds during the campaign—and that those who did usually returned to the predictable voting pattern of their social group(s). The authors concluded that the principal effect of campaigns is to pressure people toward consistency and that "as time goes on . . . we find that people abandon deviant opinions on specific issues to agree with the position taken by their party" (285). In other words, even voters who initially take issue positions contrary to those of their preferred party are more likely to change those positions than to use them as grounds for supporting the other party's candidate.

Although some scholars took exception (for example, see Gosnell 1950), the results of these early studies stood essentially unchallenged for many years. With the conventional wisdom asserting that campaigns didn't count for very much, the academic study of presidential campaigns lay largely dormant and untouched until the 1990s. In the 1960s, the *American Voter* model (A. Campbell, Converse, Miller, and Stokes 1960) gained currency among scholars. This model identified party identification—an orientation typically learned during childhood, from one's parents—as the decisive factor shaping vote choice. Later, as various examinations of issue-based voting gained prominence,[3] and especially as the literature on economic voting took off,[4] little attention was paid to the potential importance of campaigns in shaping election outcomes. If anything, the predictability of individuals' votes based on their partisan loyalties and a handful of retrospective evaluations, and of election outcomes based on macroeconomic conditions and presidential approval scores, contributed to a general sense in the academic community that if campaigns did matter, they mattered only at the margins.[5]

Renewed Interest in Campaigns

After several decades of relative neglect, political campaigns began to draw increased scholarly attention in the late 1980s and early 1990s. A few studies began to focus on changes in public opinion that took place during campaigns and on the impact of specific campaign events on both partisanship (Allsop and Weisberg 1988) and candidate preference (J. Campbell, Cherry, and Wink 1992; Geer 1988). This line of research signaled a renewed interest in campaigns that was fueled further by several articles that appeared in print almost simultaneously (Bartels 1993; Finkel 1993; Gelman and King 1993). Finkel (1993), who harkened back to earlier work done by the Columbia group, examined changes in vote intention over the course of the 1980 campaign season. Finkel's main finding was that very few people (fewer than 5 percent) changed their minds during the campaign, and that vote intention in the early summer was a very strong predictor of how a person voted on election day. Given these results, Finkel argued that campaign effects would have to be much more substantial to be considered nonminimal (19).

Bartels (1993) also focused on changes in vote intention during the 1980 presidential campaign and found that, although candidate support was highly stable over time, exposure to the campaign via mass media was an important predictor of the changes that occurred. Among Bartels's conclusions was that exposure to the media is likely to be most important when people have relatively weak ties to the candidates, and when one of the candidates is relatively unknown. Finally, Gelman and King (1993) provided an innovative and provocative analysis of more than sixty-seven thousand survey respondents from dozens of surveys that were conducted during the summer and fall of the 1988 presidential contest. The authors maintained, among other things, that campaigns (and the media's coverage of them) tend to make elections more predictable by helping bring voters to "enlightened" decisions based on "fundamentals" such as performance evaluations and party cues.

Do Campaigns Matter?

These studies helped to form my own ideas about whether and how campaigns might matter (Holbrook 1994, 1996). One particularly troublesome aspect of the earlier work was the implication that, in order to "matter," campaigns had to be not just *a* determinant of election outcomes but *the* determinant. Take the estimates from Lazarsfeld, Berelson, and Gaudet (1944) and from Finkel (1993), for example, that roughly 8 percent and 5 percent of voters were converted by the campaigns in 1940 and 1980, respectively. Although effects of this magnitude may not have been decisive to the outcomes of those two elections, they could be consequential in years when the final result is much closer. More to the point, when researchers examine changes in vote intention among respondents who have already made up their minds, it is not too surprising to find that the rates of conversion are fairly low. In fact, when Finkel's "conversion" category is expanded to include those who were undecided in June and ultimately voted contrary to their predispositions in November, it grows to almost 16 percent of the electorate. Moreover, the proportion of voters who were "activated" (that is, moved from the undecided column to vote in line with their predispositions) is substantial in both the Lazarsfeld et al. and Finkel studies (14 percent and 44 percent, respectively).[6] Surely these findings represent campaign effects of some consequence. I argue elsewhere (Holbrook and McClurg 2005) that the ability of parties to activate (or reactivate) their partisans is an important asset that may well be determinative in some cases. In fairness, Finkel (1993, 19) acknowledged that activation and other sources of indirect influence can also be an important function of campaigns. But because the judgment of what constitutes minimal versus nonminimal effects seems to be made on the basis of changing voters' minds, there is a tendency to dismiss these effects as trivial.

In *Do Campaigns Matter?* (Holbrook 1996), I developed a model of campaign effects and tested it using trial-heat polling data from the 1984, 1988, and 1992 presidential elections. I acknowledged that the ability of campaigns to influence public opinion was constrained by such things as voters' long-term partisan predispositions and the political and economic context of the election, while showing that, given those constraints, campaign events could nevertheless exert considerable sway over people's preferences. The model was based on several different propositions, three of which warrant emphasis here:

- First, there exists for each election cycle an equilibrium level of support for the candidates, and that equilibrium reflects the political and economic context of the election.
- Second, public support for the candidates during the campaign season fluctuates, sometimes widely, around the equilibrium, and those fluctuations are in response to campaign events.
- Third, the magnitude of the impact of campaign events depends partly on the disparity between relative candidate support in the polls and the expected (equilibrium) level of support. In other words, candidates running far behind their expected level of support can expect greater increases in support in response to favorable campaign events compared with candidates running ahead of their expected level.

Among my major empirical findings were that (1) economic conditions and presidential approval determine the equilibrium level of support during a campaign; (2) campaign events do a fair job of explaining fluctuations around that equilibrium level; and (3) among these events, nominating conventions are particularly important (though their impact is stronger for the challenging party candidate and is constrained by the equilibrium level of support for the candidates), presidential debates are usually associated with relatively small shifts in candidate support, and day-to-day campaign events also have a modest impact.

Overall, my analysis indicated that what went on during the campaign generally was not as important to the ultimate outcome as was the context of the campaign. By far the most important determinants of the outcomes of the three elections I examined were the national economy and presidential approval. In this sense, my results were consistent with Lazarsfeld's (1944) conclusion that what goes on between elections is more important than what goes on during the campaign. This is not to say that the campaigns didn't matter, however. Indeed, a set of "counterfactuals" showed that switching net campaign effects from one election to another could easily have changed two of the three outcomes (nothing, it seems, could have produced a different result in 1984).[7] In the end, I took the influence of campaign events on fluctuations in candidate support to represent meaningful and theoretically interesting campaign effects, even if those effects cannot be said to have "caused" the outcome.

There have been two notable book-length treatments of the impact of campaigns since the publication of *Do Campaigns Matter?* James Campbell's *The American Campaign* (2000) used a number of different types of data to examine presidential elections from 1952 to 1996. Campbell's main findings were that campaigns usually follow certain predictable patterns, chief among them a "narrowing" effect in which the trailing candidate draws closer to the front-runner as the race nears its climax.[8] In Campbell's model, which focuses on the general election, the predictability of *campaigns* helps to make *elections* predictable. In some ways, his research supports the view of Gelman and King (1993), specifically, that campaigns help bring voters the information they need to make "enlightened" decisions—information that reflects the fundamental aspects of the political and economic context, which are the things that make elections predictable in the first place. While Campbell's approach differs from mine on many of the particulars, his point about the role of information is consistent with the underlying logic of my own model of campaign effects. In terms of actual vote changes, Campbell estimated that fall campaigns account for shifts of about four percentage points on average. A more recent analysis that considered elections from 1948 to 2000 directly addressed the question of whether campaigns mattered enough to determine the final outcome (J. Campbell 2001b). Campbell concluded that they had a major impact in 1948 and 1960, and probably affected the outcomes in 1976, 1980, and 2000 as well. This interpretation of the term *impact*—the potential to change the election result—sets a pretty tough standard.

A second major treatment of campaign effects is *The 2000 Presidential Election and the Foundations of Party Politics* (R. Johnston, Hagen, and Jamieson 2004). This innovative study built on existing work on campaigns from the perspective of both political science and communications. What makes the book exciting—and what permits a detailed analysis of many different aspects of the 2000 campaign—is the design of the 2000 National Annenberg Election Study (NAES). The NAES conducted a massive, rolling cross-sectional public opinion survey (N = 37,000) that went into the field in December 1999 and continued until mid-January 2001. Using data collected from July through election day, Richard Johnston and his colleagues were able to capture campaign dynamics in a way that had previously not been possible. Also, in addition to the NAES, the authors incorporated data from the Campaign Media Analysis Group detailing the tone and volume of campaign advertising in specific media markets, as well as the content of network news and newspaper coverage of the campaign. By attaching media and advertising information to individual respondents' survey records, Johnston and his colleagues were able to see how voters reacted to specific campaign information as that information was produced. This approach represented real progress over analyses such as my own that gauged the impact of campaign events based on the assumption that those events produce certain types of information.[9]

Findings from Johnston, Hagen, and Jamieson (2004) are far too numerous to detail here, but a few merit inclusion as they speak most directly to the issue of the campaign's overall impact. First, the authors found convention bumps (increases in candidate support) similar to those that James Campbell (2000) and I (Holbrook 1996) identified; the bumps coincided with the naming of vice-presidential candidates just days prior to the major parties' conventions. Second, the final two debates had important, offsetting effects that influenced the tenor of the campaign; at the same time, both the first and final debates had significant short-term priming effects that increased the salience of Social Security as an issue in the presidential race.[10] Third, media coverage of the campaign was influential; it appears, for example, that the media were responsible for Democratic nominee Al Gore's decline in the polls during late September and early October, as well as for his recovery in the last couple of weeks of the campaign. Of particular interest, at least from the standpoint of the efficacy of campaigns, is that media content was influenced by the activities and strategies of the candidates. For example, the authors attributed Gore's media advantage in the late stages of the campaign to his decision to emphasize the importance of Social Security. Fourth, the impact of advertising was decidedly one-sided. Support for Gore was highly susceptible to the influence of advertising, while support for Republican nominee George W. Bush was relatively immune to it. This asymmetry enabled the Republicans to use advertising to dilute Gore's advantage in media coverage during the closing days of the campaign. Finally—and this runs counter to some prior research (Jones 1998; D. R. Shaw 1999b)—the authors found that candidate campaign appearances had no discernible, theoretically plausible influence on voter choice. In fact, the only statistically significant influence identified was a rather implausible negative effect on Bush's standing in the polls in the wake of a Bush-Cheney appearance.

A number of other scholars have examined the impact of presidential campaigns on votes and election outcomes. These inquiries can be classified broadly into one of three categories: (1) aggregate-level national events models; (2) individual-level events models; or (3) aggregate-level, state campaign activities models.[11] Daron Shaw's work in the first category focused on the same types of events that I considered in *Do Campaigns Matter?*, though his measures were in many ways much more refined. The principal contribution of Shaw's approach was in distinguishing among categories of events and incorporating measures of media coverage as a conditioning influence on the impact of events. Shaw acknowledged that efforts to measure the impact of campaign events have in some instances succeeded in detecting interesting influences, but noted that on the whole these models are likely to be misspecified because they usually employ measures that combine seemingly dissimilar events into single variables. In an analysis of campaign events from 1952 to 1992, Shaw (1999a) demonstrated that some types of events (national conventions, candidate blunders, party unity activities, presidential debates) have stronger and more lasting effects on candidate support than do others (most speeches, external events not related to the campaign). In a more detailed study of the 1992 and 1996 campaigns, Shaw (1999c) found that the influence of events (this time measured using broader, catch-all variables) was conditioned by media coverage at the time of the event; that is, the impact of an event expected to favor one party tended to be exacerbated by positive media coverage and dampened by negative media coverage for that party at the time of the event.

Two other national aggregate-level studies have looked at how events influence the contours of candidate support during campaigns. Wlezien and Erikson (2002) was perhaps the most exhaustive analysis of trial-heat results, with data amassed from more than 1,400 polls conducted during fifteen presidential campaigns from 1944 to 2000. In an elegant essay, the authors examined the statistical properties of what they called the "bump and wiggle" of public opinion during these campaigns. Essentially, their interest was in how voter preferences evolve over time and the degree to which observed changes in candidate support that might be attributed to campaign effects represent real, sustained opinion shifts rather than transient effects that dissipate quickly over time. They found that changes that occur early in the campaign (the hundred days prior to the conventions), while sometimes quite substantial, are generally transitory and do not represent genuine changes in candidate support. In contrast, the relatively smaller shifts that take place during the last hundred days of the campaign are usually both real and permanent. Somewhat ironically, then, the wider swings in public opinion that might normally be assumed the most important turn out to be considerably less meaningful than the smaller "bumps and wiggles" that occur later in the campaign.

James Stimson's *Tides of Consent,* which is a broader treatise on macro-opinion in the United States, includes an interesting analysis of the impact of presidential campaigns from 1960 to 2000 (Stimson 2004, see chap. 4). Like a number of others, Stimson examined changes in trial-heat polls during the campaign season, with a specific emphasis on the impact of party nominating conventions and candidate debates.[12] His findings were similar to those reported in *Do Campaigns Matter?* First, he found that conventions create substantial and durable shifts in opinion. This finding appears to be at odds with James Campbell (2000), who concludes that about 50 percent of the effect of the convention bump dissipates by election day. In fairness, the focus in Stimson's work was on the second convention because the bump from the first would no doubt be affected by the second. Stimson estimated that the average effect of the second convention is a bump of five percentage points in the convening party's favor, an amount that could have an important impact on the eventual outcome. In addition, Stimson found that debates have relatively slight effects and are probably of little consequence to the ultimate outcome—except, of course, for extremely close contests when almost any event is potentially decisive.

Hillygus and Jackman (2003) also focused on the role played by conventions and debates, but their study differed from others in a couple of important respects. Although the authors addressed aggregate shifts, most of their analysis attempted to gauge the impact of conventions and debates on individual voters (compare, for example, R. Johnston, Hagen, and Jamieson 2004). In addition, they used panel data from a survey conducted by Knowledge Networks during the 2000 presidential campaign that enabled them to control for prior predispositions when measuring the impact of events—an extremely important advantage.[13] Absent panel data, the interpretation of observed changes in public opinion following campaign events must be limited to statements like the following: "The level of support for a candidate was higher (or lower) after an event than before the event." The implication here is that the event changed people's minds, or perhaps activated some predisposition, and yet such a conclusion can be reached with confidence only if one knows what each individual's opinion was prior to the event. Due to the large size of the overall sample (29,000), Hillygus and Jackman were able to use 2,588 panel respondents for their convention analysis and 3,102 panel respondents for their debate analysis.

Hillygus and Jackman introduced their study (2003) by saying that they assumed the question of "do campaigns matter?" had been answered in the affirmative by prior research, and that they were more interested in determining how and for whom campaigns matter. The ensuing analysis was quite sophisticated and provided a detailed account of the process by which conventions and debates influence the public. First, the results indicated that conventions and debates do influence how people intend to vote, although the former tend to have a decidedly larger impact. Second (and this is where the panel design really bears fruit), Hillygus and Jackman concluded that the effects are strongest among mismatched partisans (those who initially favored the other party's candidate), undecided voters, and independents. Although the observed pattern was somewhat different for Democrats and Republicans, overall it appears that individuals with these characteristics are most likely to change their vote intention in response to the conventions and debates.

The third major group of studies dealing with campaign effects considers the impact of activities below the national level, which seems appropriate given that presidential races are all about putting together the right combination of states in the quest for a majority in the Electoral College.[14] Research in this area is mixed but generally points to the existence of some important effects. Daron Shaw's analysis of the 1988–1996 campaigns in the states (1999b), which was one of the first comprehensive efforts in this area, assessed the impact of both candidate visits and campaign media expenditures. Results showed that each variable has a significant effect on state-level vote distributions, especially in places where higher numbers of citizens are undecided about which candidate they will support. Shaw (2006) later studied the same kinds of influences in 2000 and 2004 and found somewhat weaker effects, especially for candidate visits. Examining the impact of candidate visits on turnout (more on this later) and vote percentages (within media markets rather than states), Jones (1998) also found interesting conditional effects: candidate visits had a significant impact on voting, although the magnitude of that impact was much greater for visits occurring later in the campaign than for those occurring earlier.

In an analysis of campaign appearances in the 1996 election, Herr (2002) reported mixed results, with only appearances by President Bill Clinton in the month of October shaping the ultimate distribution of votes. Finally, my own work in this area also has been somewhat inconsistent. An examination of Harry Truman's whistle-stop campaign in 1948 indicated that the president's state-level campaign strategy, along with opponent Thomas Dewey's lack of the same,[15] played a key role in Truman's successful bid for reelection (Holbrook 2002a). My work with Scott McClurg, however, suggests that although candidate visits and media expenditures did not affect state-level results in presidential campaigns from 1992 to 2000, national party monetary transfers to the state parties had a significant impact (Holbrook and McClurg 2005).

Do Predictable Elections Mean Weak Campaign Effects?

It may strike some that there is an inherent conflict between the literature on presidential campaigns and the literature on forecasting presidential elections, which generally finds that national aggregate outcomes can be predicted fairly accurately, sometimes using indicators measured well before the fall campaign period begins.[16] Most forecasting models incorporate some aspect of retrospective voting, such as presidential approval and economic performance, and none of them explicitly model outcomes as a function of campaign activity. The accuracy of forecasts varies across models and across years, but they virtually always predict the winner of the popular vote and, on average, come within a few percentage points of the actual vote share. For example, in the 2008 election cycle the average absolute error for twelve of the most prominent forecasting models was 2.86 percentage points, which was close to the average error in 2004 (2.96) and much smaller than the error in 2000 (5.26; see Holbrook 2010).

The apparent conflict between the forecasting literature and the finding of important campaign effects stems from the flawed assumption that predictable outcomes are in some way preordained and completely disconnected from events that occur during the campaign period. Nothing could be further from the truth. In fact, recall that part of the renewed interest in campaigns during the early 1990s came out of Gelman and King's (1993) supposition that campaigns help to make election outcomes more predictable by informing voters of the current conditions and important issues of the day. This conclusion played a prominent role in shaping my own ideas about the existence of an equilibrium outcome and the important role that campaigns play in pushing the electorate toward that point (Holbrook 1996). James Campbell's research (2000) led him to a similar conclusion, specifically, that it is the predictability of election *campaigns* that helps make predictable election *outcomes*. It is worth noting that blame for the relatively large forecasting error in 2000 has been attributed by some to Democratic nominee Al Gore's campaign (J. Campbell 2001a; Holbrook 2001; Wlezien 2001). In effect, following the logic of Gelman and King, there is an assumption that elections are predictable in part because candidates behave in a predictable fashion and take advantage of issues and conditions (such as the economy) that favor them. The perception in 2000 was that Gore failed to exploit positive economic conditions and high levels of presidential approval; as a result, the election outcome was otherwise than expected.

This idea was examined more rigorously by Vavreck (2009), who artfully connected campaign activity to voting behavior and election outcomes. Looking at campaigns from 1952–2000, she concluded that when candidates exploit the political and economic environment in predictable ways (the candidate favored by economic conditions runs a "clarifying" campaign that focuses on those conditions; the candidate who is hurt runs an "insurgent" campaign that seeks to shift attention away from economic conditions), election outcomes are fairly predictable. Interestingly, Vavreck identified the 2000 campaign as one in which the predicted clarifying candidate (Gore) did little to take advantage of prevailing conditions, whereas his opponent (Bush) ran the predicted insurgent campaign that helped him overcome a distinct contextual disadvantage. A result of these actions was the greater error of forecasting models in 2000—a result springing from *campaign activities*. Vavreck's work vividly illustrates the intertwining of significant campaign effects and predictable election outcomes. The two clearly are inextricably linked.

Presidential Campaigns Matter

Although the "modern" study of political campaigns began more than sixty years ago with Lazarsfeld, Berelson, and Gaudet (1944), almost all of the studies cited in the preceding section have been published since 1990. This renewed interest in campaigns was, to a large degree, sparked by the emerging academic consensus that campaigns didn't in fact matter. The newer threads of research clearly suggest otherwise, at least at the presidential level. National nominating conventions are prime opportunities to get out a message in a relatively uncontested format, something that is particularly important for the lesser-known (challenging-party) candidate. The public's response is usually a substantial shift in support toward the convening party,[17] although some disagreement exists among scholars over the extent to which this convention bump dissipates over time. And although presidential debates generally lead to fairly small shifts in candidate support,[18] some evidence indicates that specific debates can alter the tenor of the campaign in a more substantial way (R. Johnston, Hagen, and Jamieson 2004).

Moreover, day-to-day campaign events appear to have a cumulative effect on the candidates' relative standing in the polls (Holbrook 1996; D. R. Shaw 1999a), depending on the content of media coverage of the campaign at the time of the event (D. R. Shaw 1999c). Evidence also indicates that campaign activities in the states play an important role in shaping state-level results,[19] although some activities weigh more heavily than others and their overall impact may be influenced to some degree by when they occur. Finally, Richard Johnston, Hagen, and Jamieson (2004) presented evidence that illustrates the role played by campaign advertising and media coverage of the campaign (see also chapters 6 and 7 in this volume), not just in terms of changing minds but also in priming voters to place more emphasis on some criteria than on others (see note 10).

There can be little doubt, then, that campaign activities influence the levels of candidate support exhibited by voters. In this sense, campaigns clearly matter, and they matter quite a lot. But do campaigns *determine* election outcomes? This is a tricky, and perhaps unfair, question. In a given election any number of factors *influence* the outcome; but these factors could not necessarily be said to *determine* the outcome. Certainly, in close races such as those that occurred in 1960, 1968, 1976, 2000, and 2004 the outcomes might have been different had the respective campaigns been waged differently. In contrast, the contexts surrounding the elections in 1972 and 1984 likely would have required Herculean effort on the part of the challengers, George McGovern and Walter Mondale (combined with the total collapse of the incumbents, Richard Nixon and Ronald Reagan, respectively), to alter the final result. But this argument misses an important point: campaigns don't need to be the primary determinant of election outcomes in order to matter. They matter by being among the factors that shape the public's overall evaluations of the candidates and that ultimately, in combination, help to explain election outcomes. It also is important to remember that even when elections turn out as expected given national conditions (for example, the Democrats winning in 2008), part of the explanation for that result can be found in how the campaigns were run (Vavreck 2009).

A Broader View of How Campaigns Matter

In the remainder of this chapter I propose that scholars may underestimate the extent to which campaigns matter by focusing too narrowly on a campaign's role in shaping *presidential* election outcomes. First, I argue that the entire discussion has been distorted by an overemphasis on the competitive, horse-race aspect of elections. Second, I suggest that the presidential perspective is unnecessarily restrictive and probably biases our findings in a manner that prevents us from seeing the full impact of campaigns.

The Civic Functions of Campaigns

It is easy to comprehend why academic research on, and casual discussions of, whether campaigns matter tend to focus on election outcomes. After all, it is the final result, and the relentless march toward it, that most people care about and that dominate coverage in the media. Yet campaigns serve other important functions—civic functions—that, while less glamorous and certainly less visible than the head-on competition between candidates, are still important and might help to shape the eventual outcome in any event. Broadly speaking, the civic functions of campaigns are voter education and voter mobilization.

Voter Education. In earlier work (Holbrook 1996), I maintained that campaigns are nothing if not large-scale efforts to generate information with the express purpose of persuading voters. Campaigns seek to "educate" voters about why they should support one candidate over others. The assumption put forth in Gelman and King (1993) was probably correct: that the information generated by campaigns serves to "enlighten" voters regarding the issues of the day while reinforcing the importance of fundamental considerations such as partisanship, ideology, and presidential performance. Yet even if this account isn't exactly right, we should not underestimate the potential importance of information acquisition during the campaign and the consequences it can have for both voters and the election outcome.

The existing literature on voter learning during presidential campaigns suggests that even though voters may not live up to the civic ideal of being fully informed, learning nevertheless does take place, with the nature of that learning varying with different types of campaign events. Thomas Patterson, in *The Vanishing Voter* (2002, 125), reported that just prior to election day in 2000, "[o]n the average issue, 38 percent correctly identified the candidate's position, 16 percent incorrectly identified it . . . and 46 percent said they did not know it." Although this may be taken as a sign that the campaigns that year did not do a good job of educating voters, Patterson pointed to distinct periods of intense voter learning: the contested primary season, the convention period, and the debates. During these periods voters absorbed about 80 percent of what they learned as a whole in the 2000 campaign (127). What went on during the remainder of the campaign appears to have accomplished relatively little in the way of conveying information about the candidates' policy stands.

Although little academic research has been done on the role of conventions in voter education (a topic ripe for future investigation), numerous scholars have examined the role of debates as sources of information.[20] Most recently, a meta-analysis of the literature on presidential debates indicated that they tend to increase citizens' issue knowledge while also influencing the salience of some of the issues discussed (Benoit, Hansen, and Verser 2003).[21] Some evidence indicates that debates may be of particular benefit to those who possess relatively low levels of preexisting information. My analysis of trends in six elections (1976–1996) revealed that the gap in candidate information between low- and high-education respondents generally widened over the course of the general election campaign but was sometimes reduced in size by the presidential debates (Holbrook 2002b).

Several studies suggest that campaign advertising also contributes to voter education. Brians and Wattenberg (1996), for example, found that voter recall of campaign ads in the 1992 presidential contest was positively associated with knowledge of candidate issue stands, and that this relationship was stronger among respondents who were interviewed in October as opposed to September (that is, later in the campaign rather than earlier). Freedman, Franz, and Goldstein (2004) provided an interesting take on this topic, with an innovative look at the 2000 presidential election. Unlike Brians and Wattenberg, who relied on respondents' (not always reliable) recollections of what they had seen during the campaign, Freedman and colleagues used data from a satellite tracking system to calibrate the level of advertising in the media market in which a voter resided. Integrating this information with data from the National Election Study survey,[22] the authors showed that exposure to advertising had a significant, if modest, effect on knowledge of candidates' issue positions—but a much more pronounced impact on respondents' ability to articulate reasons for voting for or (especially) against Bush and Gore. In addition, some evidence indicated that the individuals who benefited most from campaign advertising were those who needed information the most, specifically, voters with relatively low levels of preexisting information.[23]

As noted earlier, one of the biggest holes in our understanding of how campaigns affect citizen competence stems from the lack of research on the impact of conventions. I tend to agree with Stimson (2004) that the convention period is probably a period of very intense learning, a period that can help to frame and establish the parameters of the fall campaign. At the same time, however, we know very little about how much and what kind of learning takes place during the nominating conventions. Given that these are the only occasions when parties and candidates are able to control the flow of information, thereby ensuring that the information stream is clearly biased in their favor, relatively rapid learning might be expected.

Voter Mobilization and Turnout. The other civic function of campaigns is that of mobilizing the electorate to turn out on election day. As in the case of voter education, campaigns perform this function in their selfish pursuit of votes. But the end result is voter mobilization. One group of academic studies has examined the impact of party contacting on participation in elections.[24] Most of these analyses focus on party contacting during both presidential and congressional election cycles, and the general conclusion is that contacting motivates people to get out and vote. This effect is fairly robust even when researchers take into account the increasing tendency for campaigns to target voters who are already predisposed toward voting.[25] An early read on the impact of personal contacting in 2004 was provided by *The Vanishing Voter* project, the results of which suggested that get-out-the-vote efforts by organized groups, along with encouragement from friends and family, played an important role in convincing young people to participate.[26]

A handful of studies have looked exclusively at the impact of presidential campaign activities on mobilization and turnout, producing decidedly mixed results. Both Jones (1998) and Herr (2002) assessed the impact of campaign appearances on turnout, the latter in 1996 and the former in elections from 1980 to 1992. Using media markets as his unit of analysis, Jones observed that candidate visits exerted a significant influence, with the impact growing stronger as election day approached. The Herr study, however, found no connection between candidate appearances and turnout in the 1996 election. To be fair, Herr considered only the thirty-seven states that candidates visited in 1996, thus limiting variation on the primary independent variable in his analysis. McClurg and I examined the relative mobilization effects of campaign appearances, candidate media expenditures, and national party monetary transfers to the states in the 1992, 1996, and 2000 elections (Holbrook and McClurg 2005). We discovered that campaign appearances and media expenditures had no discernible impact on turnout in these races. We did, however, find a significant and robust impact resulting from national party monetary transfers to the states; even when controlling for previous levels of turnout, more party money led to higher levels of turnout. Party money, we concluded, was used effectively to target core constituency groups and encourage them to get to the polls on election day. Finally, the general impact of campaign activities in the states emerged as an important determinant of voter engagement in Thomas Patterson's study of the 2000 election. Patterson's results indicated that residents of so-called battleground states (where the race was competitive and candidates invested the bulk of their resources) were more likely than others to report having thought and talked about the campaign; to be able to recall campaign news stories; and, ultimately (though very slightly), to have voted (T. Patterson 2002, 143; see also Hill and McKee 2005; Wolak 2006; Gimpel, Kaufmann, and Pearson-Merkowitz 2007).

A heated and seemingly endless debate continues among political scientists concerning the effects of negative advertising, specifically, whether or not its effect is to demobilize the electorate.[27] Given the extensive literature on this topic, it is not surprising that different studies have occasionally produced conflicting results. In a meta-analysis of fifty-two empirical studies (Lau et al. 1999; see also Lau, Sigelman, and Rovner 2007), the authors concluded that there simply was no consistent pattern of findings concerning the mobilizing or demobilizing effects of negative advertising.[28] However, more recent scholarship suggests that negative ads may actually have a positive impact. Djupe and Peterson (2002), for example, found that negative campaigning leads to increased turnout in U.S. Senate primaries, while Lau and Pomper (2001) observed a positive relationship between overall negativity and turnout in Senate general elections—but only among strong partisans; a demobilizing effect was in evidence among independents. Goldstein and Freedman (2002a) took advantage of new technology and were able to match respondents with the ads to which they could have been exposed during the 1996 presidential election (see also, note 22); they found strong evidence that negative ads stimulated turnout. Clinton and Lapinski's analysis (2004) of a Knowledge Networks sample (see note 13) four years later provided at least modest support for the proposition that negative ads can stimulate turnout among targeted populations. Finally, Freedman, Franz, and Goldstein (2004) examined the impact of advertising in general (regardless of tone) in the 2000 presidential race and found that exposure to ads had a positive influence on both political interest (especially among low-information voters) and turnout.[29]

Looking for Campaign Effects in the Least Likely Place

Although the academic research cited in this chapter clearly illustrates that presidential campaigns do indeed "matter," our perspective is nonetheless distorted by the fact that scholars have tended to look for campaign effects in many of the wrong places. Certain characteristics of presidential campaigns make them the most obvious place to look for campaign effects—and yet they remain an arena that is particularly inhospitable to such effects. Given that presidential campaigns usually involve two extremely well-known (at least by the fall) candidates possessing relatively equal resources, and given that both sides are staffed with experienced professionals who can be counted on to do their jobs effectively, it is somewhat surprising to find presidential campaign effects of the magnitude reported in the literature. In fact, the ideal electoral contexts for detecting campaign effects are those in which voters' preexisting levels of information are relatively low and an asymmetry exists in the competing streams of information (Zaller 1996). This is certainly not an accurate description of modern presidential elections.

The information environment most likely to produce strong campaign effects is that found in elections for state and local offices. Notwithstanding the fact that our empirical work has sometimes uncovered impressive effects, we are unnecessarily biasing our estimate of the impact of campaigns by focusing so much of our attention on the race for the presidency. Although presidential elections, and especially presidential election outcomes, are higher profile and no doubt of greater interest to most observers, they represent only one level at which campaigns can be evaluated. If we are interested in answering the question "Do campaigns matter?" then the influence of contests taking place elsewhere on the ballot surely warrants scrutiny, because that is where effects are likely to be most pronounced.

One consistent message from research on nonpresidential elections has been the importance of two key elements in any campaign: the candidates themselves and campaign resources. The literature on congressional campaigns points to a huge information advantage for most incumbents—an advantage that can usually be overcome only by experienced, well-funded challengers. In open-seat contests the political experience of the candidates and the amount of money they can raise become even more important.[30] Similar effects are found in state legislative, gubernatorial, local, and initiative elections.[31] Research conducted at these different levels of government has also contributed to a better understanding of how campaigns act to mobilize and inform voters.[32]

Together, the studies cited in the notes to this section identify a host of important and interesting campaign effects, most of which cannot be examined at the presidential level due to the relative parity of candidate exposure and campaign resources characteristic of national elections. Thus, if we broaden the scope of our inquiry when we ask, "Do campaigns matter?" the answer—already in the affirmative—becomes a resounding *Yes!* This point has been made elsewhere (Finkel 1993; Holbrook 1996), of course, but the time has come to take it more seriously when assessing how campaigns influence voters.

Moving Beyond the Candidates' Campaigns

Finally, I believe that the study of presidential campaigns needs to be more holistic in approach. Although this is beginning to change, most research on the topic has looked mainly at the effect of actors associated with the formal campaign. Yet surely the electorate is influenced by other actors as well. Indeed, some recent work has incorporated the impact of media coverage.[33] What I'm thinking about, however, are the "extra-campaign" groups that act with the intent to influence an election outcome. McClurg and I have unearthed some interesting effects from party spending patterns (Holbrook and McClurg 2005), and party activities undoubtedly are important in other ways as well. The activities of groups—including, for example, political action committees, so-called 527s (see chapter 5 in this volume), religious organizations, labor unions, and the like—certainly need to be explored to a greater extent than has been the case thus far. And this exploration should include attention not just to persuasion and contribution to the outcome, but also to mobilization and voter education effects. A focus on extra-campaign organizations seems especially relevant today, given the explosion in advertising and mobilization efforts in recent election cycles. Looking closely at these sorts of effects should help to broaden our understanding of how campaigns matter.

Conclusion

My goal in this chapter has been to provide a broad overview of the academic literature on the impact of political campaigns. Do campaigns really matter? The answer, I think, is unequivocally yes. Numerous studies indicate that campaign events can produce changes in the distribution of candidate preferences, and others highlight the important civic functions of campaigns— that is, voter education and mobilization. The evidence on campaign effects is in some ways even stronger when our attention shifts from the presidency to congressional, state, and local elections. Campaigns matter, and sometimes they matter quite a lot. Are they *the* determining factor in who wins and who loses? At the presidential level, it is likely that in most cases they are not. Yet even here, campaigns do not have to be the most important factor in an election for them to matter. As I noted earlier, many factors—including the campaign—come together to produce election outcomes, and all of these factors *matter* because each contributes in its own way to shaping those outcomes.

THE POLITICAL PROFESSIONALS RESPOND

Whit Ayres

As a former political science professor and as president of the American Association of Political Consultants, my experience suggests a clear and definitive answer to the question, "Do campaigns really matter?" Of course they matter. They matter a lot. They matter in ways that meet the highest standard in the political science literature: campaigns frequently are not just *a* determinant of election outcomes, but *the* determinant. This is not the case in every campaign, especially those involving entrenched incumbents. But in open-seat races and primary contests, campaigns are often decisive.

From my perspective as a political consultant, the political science literature's argument that campaigns do not matter contains two glaring deficiencies, both mentioned toward the end of Holbrook's chapter. First, these studies focus almost exclusively on *presidential general election campaigns,* one of the tiniest subsets of all American campaigns. Moreover, the literature does not even cover all presidential general election campaigns, but only those that have occurred since data became available to measure changes in voting intentions. So the maximum number of cases available for analysis is the nineteen general election campaigns that have occurred since 1936. Nineteen cases is only slightly larger than the number of participants in one focus group. Those of us who conduct focus groups spend our lives telling clients that focus groups contain far too few cases to support generalized results. It is reasonable to estimate that more than 99.9 percent of American campaigns are *not* presidential general election campaigns that have occurred since

1936. That anyone could plausibly assess the effect of campaigns based on such a unique subset of all campaigns strains credulity.

If the tiny number of cases was not enough to cast doubt on the argument that campaigns do not matter, or matter only at the margins, a second limitation of this research is equally potent. Presidential general election campaigns are the *least* likely kind of campaign to show effects. In these campaigns, voters are bombarded with information from multiple sources. News reports, blogs, third-party campaigns, and countless other communication avenues provide a constant source of information apart from what the presidential campaigns themselves are doing. But how about a primary campaign for governor or U.S. senator? An open-seat contest for a congressional seat? A mayor's race? In those contests the caliber of the candidate, the amount of money raised, and the strategic decisions made by the campaigns are frequently determinative.

None of this undermines the fact that long-term forces have a significant impact on electoral outcomes. Party identification in the electorate, the state of the economy, the popularity of the president, and whether the candidate is an entrenched incumbent clearly have a large influence on who wins elections. Sometimes the best campaigns produce election losses. But acknowledging this in no way undermines the determinative effects of the campaigns themselves. Three examples among numerous possibilities make the point.

2008 Democratic Nomination for President.

During the 2008 Democratic nomination contest for president, most analysts assumed that Hillary Clinton's years of experience, fundraising capabilities, establishment support, and strategic acumen would wash over a neophyte candidate like Barack Obama. While the Obama campaign did numerous things extraordinarily well, nothing it did was more crucial than realizing the potential of convention delegates selected through caucuses rather than presidential primary elections. Early on in the contest, the Obama campaign began organizing in small caucus states that the Clinton campaign was effectively ignoring. On Super Tuesday, Obama won fourteen of the twenty-three contests, including all six caucus states. These wins gave him momentum that allowed him to carry the next ten contests (five of which were caucuses) and seventeen of the twenty-four total contests after Super Tuesday.

Ultimately, among delegates selected in primary elections, Obama won 47 percent and Clinton 53 percent. Among delegates selected in caucus states, Obama won 62 percent, capturing every state except Nevada. Without his advantage among caucus delegates, Obama would have lost the nomination and Hillary Clinton would very likely be the president of the United States. The outcome in this instance had nothing to do with long-term forces and everything to do with the strategic decisions made by the two campaigns. Those strategic decisions determined the outcome of the contest, and changed the person who became president. The two campaigns mattered, a lot.

2002 Alabama Republican Gubernatorial Primary.

During the 2002 campaign for governor of Alabama, the favorite to win the Republican nomination was Steve Windom, the incumbent lieutenant governor. His main challenger, Bob Riley, was a popular congressman but unknown outside his congressional district. In early polling (February 2002), Windom led Riley by 39 to 26 percent among likely Republican primary voters. Then the Windom campaign ran a television ad accusing Riley of using insider information about a defense contract, gleaned from his service on the U.S. House Armed Services Committee, to make a profitable personal investment. Riley took umbrage at the charge, and provided evidence that his assets had been placed in a blind trust before he took office as a congressman.

More consequentially, Riley made the rounds of editorial boards of Alabama newspapers, laying out his case that he had acted appropriately, and that the Windom campaign had crossed the line with its negative ad. Several newspapers wrote editorials strongly critical of the Windom campaign, accusing it of engaging in low blows, dishonest attacks, and gutter politics. The Riley campaign developed a response television ad with those editorials, using the newspapers' third-party credibility to create a devastatingly effective rebuttal.

By June, the Windom campaign had collapsed and polls showed Riley leading Windom by 62 to 20 percent. Riley ultimately won the primary 74 to 18 percent (with the remainder going to another candidate), and went on to become the two-term governor of Alabama. His primary victory had nothing to do with long-term forces. It was the result of strategic decisions made by the two campaigns, and the way they handled the back-and-forth of accusations so often made in the heat of political battle.

2006 Tennessee U.S. Senate General Election.

In the open-seat contest to replace Tennessee senator Bill Frist in 2006, Republican Bob Corker ran against Democrat Harold Ford. For much of the campaign, Corker's fundamental message relied on ideology: he was a conservative and Ford a liberal, and, therefore, Corker was more in tune with the border state's electorate. That message failed to resonate, however, in part because Ford took centrist positions on many issues, and in part because the Ford campaign was very shrewd in sending culturally conservative value messages. One TV ad showed Ford standing in a church saying, "I love Jesus!" Ford also benefitted from the general anti-Republican climate sweeping the country in 2006. By the end of September, the broader climate and Ford's campaign had produced a small but consistent lead of four to five points for the Democrat.

At that point Corker restructured his entire campaign, hired a new team, moved his campaign headquarters from Chattanooga to Nashville, and adopted a very different message: Corker is Tennessee, Ford is D.C. Harold Ford had grown up in Washington, attended elite private schools there, and spent much of his adult life in the nation's capital. On the other hand, Bob Corker had grown up in Chattanooga, built a successful business there, and established an enviable record as mayor of his home town. The contrast was designed to make Ford appear unsubstantial, immature, and an outsider to boot—and it worked. In a state that had become accustomed to electing widely respected senators from both parties (most Tennessee senators during the past three decades have been considered serious candidates for president), Ford did not seem to measure up.

Shortly after TV ads began with the new Corker message, the polling trend lines began to reverse and Corker built a small but sustained lead. (The widely reported *Playboy* ad run against Ford by an outside group froze the Corker advance and almost cost him the election, but his progress resumed after that controversy subsided.[1]) On election day, Corker won by 51 to 48 percent. In the process, he became the only non-incumbent Republican U.S. Senate candidate in the entire country to win in 2006. Once again, this victory had nothing to do with long-term forces. Indeed, all the long-term forces argued for a Ford victory. Corker won because of the kind of campaign he ran over the last five weeks.

Both long-term and short-term forces determine the outcome of elections. Campaigns themselves are one of the most crucial of the short-term forces. Especially for open seats and primary campaigns, they frequently constitute the single most important determinant of the outcome.

---

[1]See http://voices.washingtonpost.com/thefix/senate/racist-or-rough-and-tumble.html.

Notes

1. For example, working-class and Catholic voters generally ended up supporting the Democratic ticket (as they had in the past), whereas most of their middle-class and Protestant counterparts sided with the Republicans.

2. The percentages reported here reflect changes that occurred between May and October; some people in this last group reached a final decision during the closing days of the campaign (Lazarsfeld 1944, 325–326).

3. See Fiorina (1981); Key (1966); Markus and Converse (1979); Nie, Verba, and Petrocik (1976); Page and Jones (1979).

4. See Kiewiet (1983); Kramer (1971); Lewis-Beck (1988); Markus (1988); Tufte (1978).

5. See J. Campbell and Garand (2000); Lewis-Beck and Rice (1992).

6. These two figures differ partly because only 36 percent were undecided in the spring wave of the 1940 panel, compared with 55 percent at approximately the same point in 1984; hence, there were more opportunities for activation in the latter case. Another possible explanation is that Finkel's estimate was based on actual votes, whereas Lazarsfeld and his colleagues looked at October vote intention.

7. The term *counterfactuals* refers to the use of different scenarios to simulate how the results might have changed under each. For example, my analysis showed that if the cumulative effects of the 1988 and 1992 campaigns had been switched, the election outcomes would have changed as well (Holbrook 1996, 148).

8. This happens for a number of reasons, including, for example, the tendency for front-runners to (1) wage relatively "safe" campaigns (trying to protect their lead rather than expand it) and (2) be subjected to closer scrutiny by both voters and media (see J. Campbell 2000, 43–44).

9. For example, in *Do Campaigns Matter?* I listed a series of positive and negative events for each candidate without measuring the actual content of media coverage. Although most of those events probably generated the expected *tone* of coverage, there could have been exceptions, and considerable variation probably occurred in the *amount* of information generated.

10. By *priming* I mean that the increased attention paid to Social Security by the media and the candidates elevated its importance and increased its accessibility in the minds of voters, leading them to assign more weight to Social Security when deciding whom to support. For a more complete discussion of priming effects, see Iyengar and Kinder (1987); Jacobs and Shapiro (1994); Druckman, Jacobs, and Ostermeier (2004); see also chapter 7 in this volume.

11. See Herr (2002); Holbrook (2002a); Hillygus and Jackman (2003); Holbrook and McClurg (2005); Jones (1998); D. R. Shaw (1999a, 1999b, 1999c); Stimson (2004); Wlezien and Erikson (2002).

12. See Holbrook (1994, 1996); D. R. Shaw (1999a, 1999c); Wlezien and Erikson (2002).

13. Knowledge Networks is a private firm that conducts surveys via the Internet, selecting respondents through random digit dialing in such a way that they represent a random probability sample of the entire U.S. population falling within the Microsoft WebTV network. For additional details, see Hillygus and Jackman (2003, 584); Iyengar, Norpoth, and Hahn (2004, 162–163); Clinton and Lapinski (2004, 75); and Knowledge Network's own Web site at www.knowledgenetworks.com.

14. See Herr (2002); Holbrook (2002a); Holbrook and McClurg (2005); Jones (1998).

15. Truman generally campaigned in states that were competitive or had a large number of electoral votes, whereas Dewey's appearances followed a less predictable pattern. Truman also used campaign stops to make localized appeals, whereas Dewey frequently chose to deliver speeches aimed at the national radio audience (Karabell 2000).

16. For reviews of this literature see J. Campbell and Lewis-Beck (2008); Holbrook (2010); Lewis-Beck (2005).

17. See J. Campbell (2000); Hillygus and Jackman (2003); Holbrook (1994, 1996); R. Johnston, Hagen, and Jamieson (2004); Stimson (2004).

18. See Hillygus and Jackman (2003); Holbrook (1994, 1996); Stimson (2004).

19. See Herr (2002); Holbrook (2002a); Holbrook and McClurg (2005); Jones (1998); D. R. Shaw (1999b).

20. See Bishop, Oldendick, and Tuchfarber (1978); Chaffee and Dennis (1979); Holbrook (1999, 2002b); Lemert (1993); A. Miller and MacKuen (1979); Fridkin et al. (2007).

21. Meta-analysis is an approach that uses statistical techniques to combine the results of several different studies in order to provide a quantitative evaluation or summary of the effects of variables common to the studies.

22. See Freedman, Franz, and Goldstein (2004, 726–727) for additional details about the satellite data provided by the Campaign Media Analysis Group. This information was combined with survey respondents' self-reports of their television viewing habits to create a measure of maximum possible exposure (what the authors called an "upper bound on the number of spots" someone might have seen; see Freedman and Goldstein 1999, 1198).

23. Overall, results are mixed as to whether campaigns benefit those who are more or less knowledgeable to begin with; for example, see Alvarez (1997); Holbrook (2002b); Freedman, Franz, and Goldstein (2004); Craig, Kane, and Gainous (2005); Stevens (2005); Arceneaux (2006). The topic of voter learning during campaigns is discussed further in chapter 4 of this volume.

24. See Abramson and Claggett (2001); A. Gerber and Green (2000a, 2000b); Goldstein and Ridout (2002); Huckfeldt and Sprague (1992); Kramer (1970); McClurg (2004); Rosenstone and Hansen (1993); Wielhouwer (1999, 2003); Wielhouwer and Lockerbie (1994); see also chapter 10 in this volume.

25. See Abramson and Claggett (2001); Goldstein and Ridout (2002); Wielhouwer (1999).

26. See Harvard Kennedy School, Joan Shorenstein Center on the Press, Politics and Public Policy, "First-Time Voters Propelled to Polls by Personal Contact," press release, November 11, 2004, available at www.hks.harvard.edu/presspol/research/vanishing_voter/vv_2004_releases.html.

27. See Ansolabehere and Iyengar (1995); Ansolabehere, Iyengar, and Simon (1999); Ansolabehere et al. (1994); Clinton and Lapinski (2004); Djupe and Peterson (2002); Finkel and Geer (1998); Freedman and Goldstein (1999); Kahn and Kenney (1999); Lau et al. (1999); Sigelman and Kugler (2003); Wattenberg and Brians (1999); see also chapter 6 in this volume.

28. One explanation for such inconsistency is that a disconnect exists between how academic researchers define negativity and what voters perceive to be negative (Sigelman and Kugler 2003).

29. Also on this topic, see Geer and Lau (2005); Brooks (2006).

30. See Herrnson (2004); Jacobson (2009).

31. On state legislative elections, see Abbe et al. (2003); J. M. Carey, Niemi, and Powell (2000); Gierzynski and Breaux (1993); Hogan (2004); Van Dunk (1997). On gubernatorial elections, see Carsey (2000); King (2001); Partin (2002); Squire (1992). On local elections, see Gierzynski, Kleppner, and Lewis (1998); Krebs (1998). On initiatives, see Bowler, Donovan, and Happ (1992); Hadwiger (1992).

32. For example, see Hillygus (2005); Hogan (1999); Jackson (1997, 2002); Nicholson (2003); Nickerson (2006, 2007); Nickerson, Friedrichs, and King (2006); Niven (2001, 2004); Partin (2001); S. Patterson and Caldeira (1983).

33. See, especially, R. Johnston, Hagen, and Jamieson (2004); D. R. Shaw (1999c).

2 Campaign Strategy[1]

Michael John Burton, Daniel M. Shea, and William J. Miller

Seventy years ago, a team of scholars from Columbia University tried to measure the effects of presidential campaign activities on the final vote tally. They found that the vast majority of voters in Erie County, Ohio, had chosen their candidate in the 1940 election well before the campaign had begun in earnest (Lazarsfeld, Berelson, and Gaudet 1944). In fact, it seemed that a person's religion, socioeconomic status, and place of residence (urban versus rural) provided the basis for an "index of political predisposition" (16–27) that predicted, in advance and with a reasonably high degree of accuracy, how that person was likely to vote. For example, "[o]f all rich Protestant farmers almost 75 [percent] voted Republican, whereas 90 [percent] of the Catholic laborers living in [the city] voted Democratic" (26). Campaign flyers, political events, and news stories had scant effect on the election outcome. Indeed, in the contest between Republican Wendell Willkie and Democrat Franklin Roosevelt, only 8 percent of those who had backed Roosevelt in 1936 withdrew their support four years later in the midst of the 1940 campaign (102).

Today, the notion that a political campaign caused one in twelve voters to switch sides might be greeted with skepticism, as much of the academic community has come to believe that structural factors inherent in the political environment all but predetermine the outcome of American elections (see chapter 1 in this volume). At the time, however, a finding that seemed to show that the effects of campaigning were limited was somehow satisfying. During the 1930s and 1940s, in a world that feared demagogic dictators, the idea that only a fraction of the population was open to campaign rhetoric reassured people who wanted to believe that American Exceptionalism could secure the home front.[2] Framed in terms of a wartime outlook, the conclusions drawn from Erie County spoke to the virtues of stability induced by a deeply grounded social structure.

We understand the world around us according to the way we frame it: what we believe to be important, what we consider irrelevant, what we understand as the natural state of affairs. If we assume, on the one hand, that voters are eminently persuadable, then a finding of 8 percent volatility reflects the stability of the electorate; if, on the other hand, we assume the electorate is stable, then 8 percent might seem to us a surprisingly high number of conversions. Yet the idea of perceptual framing involves more than just setting a standard; it identifies that which catches our attention and molds our understanding of the world around us. Even simple matters of fact and cause are subject to interpretation. Did the airline crash victims die because the pilot failed to control the plane? Or was the airframe inherently unstable? Or did the wickedness of the world bring down the wrath of God? A grieving spouse, an engineer, and a radical theologian can frame the same event in fundamentally different ways, and each can find support in differing lines of evidence.

At a certain level, we "create" the world we inhabit by constructing storylines we can understand. It is not necessarily a question of who is right and who is wrong, and it is not simply a matter of partial information (for example, the blind scientists who make differing generalizations about elephants because each has examined a different part of the animal). Rather, it is a matter of approaching the subject with dissimilar purposes. We learn about the things we look for, and we all look for different things.

Campaigns and elections are this way. What you are looking for influences what you find. A political scientist who is interested in the big picture of American elections, and whose discipline encourages the examination of large data sets, will tend to find that, in most elections, most of the time, campaigns just do not matter very much. A political journalist, however, looks for "news" (dramatic stories, sensational events) and will therefore seek out hard-driving or controversial campaigns, complete with attention-grabbing characters and tragic ironies that emphasize the volatility of elections. A political practitioner, by contrast, is intimately familiar with the details of campaigns. It is her belief that the quality of a campaign is an important factor in the outcome of elections—in fact, she *must* believe this, because if she didn't then what would prevent her from throwing her hands in the air and waiting for divine intervention? Few consultants have ever picked up a lucrative contract by telling a prospective client that campaign effects are minimal.

In this chapter we explore perspectives on strategy in American elections. Our interest here is in looking at strategic effects from the viewpoints of scholars, journalists, and practitioners. Roughly speaking, we maintain that scholars seek out the role of strategy in the big picture of American politics, journalists assess strategies in the crucible of impassioned politics, and practitioners pursue a ceaseless quest for strategic advantage in the electoral warfare that is their trade. None of these experts is ultimately right or wrong. Rather, each seeks a form of truth that serves a valid professional purpose.

Scholars

Political science developed from the notion that *power* should be sharply distinguished from *knowledge*. Although persuasive rhetoric cannot truly be removed from discussions of public policy—even the most conscientious political scientist has a point of view—we can, if we try, at least spell out some of our biases and offer politicians and the public an alternative view of social problems. Truth, then, should speak to power. Because a well-chosen anecdote can back up any political position, and because opinions can be pressed on all sides, scholars have tried to widen their analyses and identify solid factual grounding. They ask pointed questions: What do we know about the empirical world? What is *generally* true? Even as water-cooler conversations about politics revolve around funny stories and urban legends, academic political scientists try to assemble an understanding of the world that looks not at outlier cases but at typical situations—not passing trends, but enduring regularities.

From the scholars' perspective, the problem with our conventional understanding of politics lies precisely with everyday frames of reference. Ordinary voters watch a campaign performance that appears to be dominated by famous (at least at the highest level) political actors; in fact, it is not a single show at all but rather an assortment of individual campaigns, each connected to the others by only the barest of threads. Lacking a disciplined effort, we can hardly grasp the general nature of elections because we are confronted with an onslaught of discrete elections. To solve this problem, scholars develop structured frameworks to help map the forest without becoming spellbound by the trees.

Empirical analysis of political campaigns is an effort to reproduce within the precepts of social science what other scientists have done for the natural world. Debates over the applicability of scientific methods to the study of human behavior (which often seems utterly unpredictable) have raged for years. But even if political scientists concede that people are more unpredictable than planetary rotation and magnetic fields, there is at least some value in looking for the regularities of political life. To find them, scholars of politics try to work out theories of political action, derive testable hypotheses from these theories, gather evidence that will test the theory, and then compare theoretical expectations with the evidence gathered.

That was the approach taken to analyzing the voters of Erie County in the 1940 presidential campaign. Lazarsfeld, Berelson, and Gaudet surveyed a large number of people over the course of the election to see how many changed sides. They found that most people had made an early choice, and that once made these people stuck with that choice:

> There is a familiar adage in American folklore to the effect that a person is only what he thinks he is, an adage which reflects the typically American notion of unlimited opportunity, the tendency toward self-betterment, etc. Now we find that the reverse of the adage is true: a person thinks, politically, as he is, socially. Social characteristics determine political preference (Lazarsfeld, Berelson, and Gaudet 1944, 27).

The view that elections were largely predetermined by social structure was reinforced by much of the scholarly literature that followed. In their classic study of the 1956 presidential election, A. Campbell, Converse, Miller, and Stokes (1960) introduced a "funnel of causality" that showed how long-term forces, especially one's partisan attachments, create a perceptual lens through which short-term events are interpreted. The typical voter may take issues, character, candidate messages, and other campaign developments into account, but partisanship nevertheless tends to shape the meaning of those factors for most people. A decade and a half later, Nie, Verba, and Petrocik (1976) challenged this view, maintaining that short-term issues had become more important than in the past; at the same time, however, it was clear that many voters were still guided by partisan loyalty.

Contemporary political scientists continue piecing together complex models of electoral behavior. Tufte (1975), for example, was able to explain a great deal of the variance in the two-party distribution of the popular vote in midterm congressional elections by taking into account two factors that are largely outside the control of candidates: national economic conditions and presidential job approval. Lewis-Beck and Rice (1992) showed that a handful of variables can be combined to predict the number of congressional seats that each party will hold after an election: rate of growth (or decline) in personal disposable income, presidential job approval, the number of seats a party has exposed (that is, how many it currently holds), and the length of time the president has been in the White House.

Following recent presidential elections, scholars have attempted to build statistical models that predict electoral outcomes. There are a number of different approaches, but for presidential contests the same two factors identified by Tufte (economic conditions and presidential approval ratings) generally drive the forecasts, which often are very accurate. One assessment of the forecasts offered in 2004 reviewed the calculations of seven teams of scholars, finding that they missed the final vote tally by an average of just 2.6 percentage points. Four of these teams were within two points of perfection—a remarkable feat given that the predictions were made nearly a year in advance. Some models were off the mark by three or four percentage points, an error margin that was attributed to "unexpected developments" such as the war in Iraq, or to measurement error and the failure to consider all significant variables.[3] Overall, though, campaign effects in the 2004 race between George W. Bush and John Kerry seemed to be minimal (American Political Science Association 2005). But in 2008, while some models accurately predicted a win by Barack Obama (Abramowitz 2008; Holbrook 2008; Lewis-Beck and Tien 2008), a forecast by James Campbell that was based in part on economic conditions had the misfortune of predicting a narrow victory for John McCain only days before the stock market collapsed (J. Campbell 2008; 2009).

Election forecasting is motivated, in part, by the desire to develop and test broad theories, many of which stem from fundamental assumptions about human behavior. We may posit, for example, that the typical voter is "rational" in the sense that he or she will try to reach certain goals as efficiently as possible, using resources strategically. One goal might be to vote for candidates who will press for agreeable policies; another might be to spend free time with loved ones. The two goals clash insofar as more time spent researching candidates means less time with family (and vice versa). Some researchers therefore suggest that voters often use "cognitive shortcuts"—that is, simple ideas (or cues) that boil down complicated scenarios—in order to figure out who should get their vote. Such ideas might include the state of the economy, partisanship, peace and war, incumbency, and others.[4]

Looking at the mental processes of individual voters might seem to emphasize the importance of a campaign's message, but the shortcuts identified by political scientists often tie electoral outcomes to structural elements of society rather than to the personal whims of voters. In 1966, V. O. Key suggested that voters are inclined to use past events to guide their behavior on election day; in particular, they are willing to vote against their own party if the party has not performed well in office: "As voters mark their ballots they may have in their minds impressions of the last TV political spectacular of the campaign, but, more important, they have in their minds recollections of their experiences of the past four years" (Key 1966, 9). Fiorina (1981, 106–129) built on Key's argument, maintaining that voters typically compile a "running tally of retrospective evaluations" and that this calculation directly shapes partisan orientation, which, in turn, plays a powerful role in determining future voting decisions. Alternatively, perhaps the strongest voting cue is simple incumbency. Mayhew (1974a, 1974b) suggested that because members of Congress want to be reelected, they spend a great deal of time working toward that end—and that, as public officials, these same incumbents have a disproportionate ability to make their views heard and to claim credit for the good things that government does (including casework on behalf of constituents and programs that provide benefits to the district or state), thereby promoting their standing with voters. Thus, the "electoral connection," as described by Mayhew, emphasizes the power of incumbency over the noise and fanfare of the time-honored American campaign.

A strength of the scholarly perspective lies in its capacity to deflate one of the great myths about elections: that political campaigns are colossal battles between well-armed adversaries. The truth of the matter, when viewed from on high, is that in most elections, most of the time, victory is decided before the race begins. Incumbents usually win. Candidates allied with the president in times of prosperity—they win, too. So do candidates with experience, and those who fit with the demographic, partisan, and basic attitudinal makeup of their constituency. It is a rare campaign strategy that can elect a candidate whose background, ideology, and partisanship are at odds with the people the candidate is seeking to represent. There are half a million elective offices in the United States, and scholars familiar with the literature can predict the outcome of the vast majority of them.

But not all. Some races—not many, but some—are genuine cliff-hangers, or they steadfastly manage in some way to defy conventional wisdom. These elections are the province of political journalists, and they provide the kind of drama that readers and viewers demand.

Journalists

Journalists are, by definition, interested in reporting *news*. News can be defined in terms of "who, what, when, where, why, and how," but there is a relatively well-defined set of people, events, places, and developments that qualify as news. In politics, reporters mostly cover "serious" candidates in "important elections," especially those in which local voters will be casting ballots, and the reporting generally strives to be even-handed toward the competing parties and candidates while maintaining a focus on great "stories." This familiar definition of news, it should be said, is a contemporary notion with roots in a complicated history. To understand what *is*, we should consider what *was*.

In the early days of the Republic, news reporting (if we may call it that) was little more than storytelling, with yarns woven to entertain rather than inform. This "news" was produced by local printers, who saw the publication of broadsheets containing the day's events as a gainful sideline to the production of other printed materials, for example, playing cards, invitations, and the like. On occasion, a printer would obtain government contracts for its wares and, in partial repayment, the news reported in that printer's broadsheet would reflect the views of the party in power. Building a readership often meant inflaming public passion—and with politics a key source of argumentation, printers who wanted to sell papers would align themselves either with the incumbent party or its major opposition (Mott 1962; C. Smith 1977).

With the invention of the telegraph, publishers found economic benefit in combining their reporting efforts. In the middle of the nineteenth century, the New York Associated Press began an effort to coordinate a news-sharing system that would soon enforce new discipline on reporters; specifically, the news they gathered was expected to meet the needs of readers across the country and across party lines (Blondheim 1994). Indeed, with the rising popularity of the so-called penny press earlier in the century, strict party alignment had been on the wane anyway. In the second half of the 1800s, publishers found that the real money was not in hawking papers so much as in selling advertisements. And advertising, it was thought, would be most profitable if newspapers focused on sensational stories dealing with things like crime, death, and political corruption. The resulting spate of "yellow journalism," though frowned upon by intellectuals, was enthusiastically consumed by the public, and it was highly profitable.

The landscape shifted again after the turn of the twentieth century with the rise of the Progressive Movement (McGerr 2003), a middle-class revolt against the corruption and sleaze associated with party machines (White and Shea 2004, 64–69). Openly partisan newspapers found themselves at odds with the prevailing public mood, while many journalists were driven as much by social rage as by career ambition. The "muckrakers," as they were called, wanted to clean up government, and much of their passion was directed against party politics; but they also wanted to make a name for themselves, and perhaps earn a comfortable living wage. Big stories made big reporters. In the 1970s, reporters like Carl Bernstein and Bob Woodward (1974) of the *Washington Post,* who uncovered wrongdoing and a subsequent cover-up in Richard Nixon's 1972 presidential reelection campaign, set a new standard for investigative journalism. After Nixon's resignation, journalists were viewed by some as a powerful engine of social reform that represented, in a sense, a revived progressive movement.

Even in a world where anyone with a computer and an Internet connection has the ability to influence uncounted readers, professional journalism remains the primary gatekeeper of campaign information (which explains why even the most iconoclastic Internet bloggers claim to be "journalists"). Reporters, of course, frequently say they try to avoid bias, but the very notion of simple "objectivity" is flawed. Every perspective begins with a point of view, and even a casual reading of mainstream reportage—including print, radio, and television—reveals a bias toward "fairness" and "good stories," two principles that (along with commercial considerations, as noted earlier) inevitably draw reporters to the most exciting campaigns. They are attracted to hard-fought political games, and this means they generally report on competitive elections.

Reporters devote the bulk of their attention to "horse-race" stories: Who is ahead, who is behind, and by how much? Does the challenger stand a chance? has she peaked too soon? Internal dynamics are also deemed important: Who is working for the candidates? Who has endorsed them? How much money have they raised? The strategic twists and turns of each campaign, the moves that seem to reshape the probability of success, are considered hot news. Media scholar Doris Graber (2010, 211) noted that "although candidates like to talk about broad policy issues . . . newspeople prefer to concentrate on narrower, specific policy positions on which the candidates disagree." For scholars, the important point is the outcome of the election (and the factors that cause people to vote the way they do); for a journalist, however, the real story is the process, the *way* one candidate defeats another. Journalists focus on the details of the game—the ups, downs, twists, and turns of a year-long contest. It is grand sport, a twelve-month Super Bowl, the best reality show on television! Little wonder that an average of roughly 15 percent of television news during election years is about political campaigning (Graber 2010, 207). News is big business, and campaigns are big news.

Strategy has become the preeminent fixation of political journalism in the United States (Fallows 1996; Cappella and Jamieson 1997), with reporters usually zeroing in on each new charge, unflattering revelation, fundraising downturn, lost endorsement, and sagging poll number. Failure, in particular, gives the news media something to talk about. In the waning days of the 2008 presidential election, the discussion of strategy once again took center stage (Journalism.org 2008). While the policy positions of each candidate had been well established prior to this point, each new poll seemed to point to an Obama victory. So what was left to report? The candidates' closing strategy, of course. What is the end-game plan? How could Obama maintain (if not build on) his apparent lead, and how could McCain battle back and make the race competitive? When it was all over, post-election assessments once again underscored the apparent importance of strategy. For Obama, the strategy he and campaign strategists David Axelrod and David Plouffe devised—one that placed blame for all that was wrong with the United States directly on the shoulders of George W. Bush—carried the day. By directly linking issues to Bush, Obama made the case that the answer to our country's problems could be anyone who was *not* Bush. The strategy was most brilliant in that it worked for both the primary and general election. Hillary Clinton and McCain were publicly described as "insider" candidates; they were most easily linked with Bush in comparison to Obama. With McCain spending months attempting to win over the more conservative wing of the Republican Party—and in the process sounding more and more like Bush—and with an eager press corps reporting this, Obama's strategy became easier and easier to implement.

Presidential elections are especially good opportunities for media analysis, as winning the Electoral College necessitates state-by-state battles and a multitude of strategic decisions by each campaign concerning the allocation of time and money. Journalists, kibitzing with each other during a year of campaign travel, are locked in an ongoing competitive search for the next strategic factor, always looking for the next silver bullet that will prove (or appear to prove) decisive in shaping the election outcome. The parallel between electoral analysis and sports analysis on television is uncanny. On one channel Mike Tirico tells us why the Cleveland Browns will lose their next game, while on another George Will waxes philosophical about the limits of American liberalism. Journalists and news editors understand that their focus on "the game" will draw in more listeners or readers; that is, they appreciate the business side of reporting. Yet they also believe in content: decisions by campaign operatives make a difference. They appreciate the long-term structural dimensions that shape a candidate's or party's fortunes, but they also have faith in campaign effects. Moreover, by helping voters understand the complexities of new-style political campaigns (Wattenberg 1998; Semiatin 2004), and by underscoring the most exciting parts of the process, journalists and news editors believe that they will encourage citizens to become engaged. In 2008, traditional journalists even devoted significant time and space to discussing the outreach techniques of new kinds of media, such as Facebook, MySpace, Flickr, and YouTube—media with which they compete.

It should be understood that the mainstream news media are neither left nor right on a consistent basis (D'Alessio and Allen 2000); they are mainly searching for a good story. Because reporters are looking for drama, because they are looking for intriguing personalities, and because they want to be fair, reporters tend to seek out competitive races. And because good storytelling relies on detail, nuance, and a focus on people, reporters approach these campaigns with investigative tools frequently ignored by academics: they talk to voters, they talk to key players (including consultants), and they talk to wise observers (who have seen it all before). They watch campaign events and learn the candidate's stump speech by heart, listening for the smallest shift in emphasis, which may in turn indicate a shift in strategy.

As the 2008 Project for Excellence in Journalism explained, winning politics begets winning coverage, and sound strategy begets winning in politics (Journalism.org 2008). Graber (2010, 211) has pointed out the circular nature of media influence, dubbing this the media echo effect: the press cover what a particular candidate does on any given day, the polls measure the relative impact of that day's behavior, the media analyze whether the campaign is influencing the polls, and this analysis then shapes further candidate behavior. Thus, the choice of what gets covered can directly impact strategic decision making.

The insights gained from personal observation are leveraged by the fact that reporting is actually part of the campaign. Whereas scholars announce their findings long after the election is over, reporters release their stories in real time; this gives them (unlike academic researchers) a certain amount of power, since what they say or write can have an impact on the outcome. To find and write their stories, reporters need information, which they can squeeze from campaigns by methods reminiscent of a district attorney, or perhaps a member of the Soprano crime family: they give campaign operatives an "opportunity" to explain charges leveled against their candidate. They let the candidate know that everyone else is talking, so maybe it is best to go ahead and clear the air right now. Of course, the weakness of news reporting is that it lacks the kind of big-picture viewpoint that scholars enjoy. And while reporters can become thoroughly familiar with the campaigns they cover, they do not know nearly as much about the internal functioning of the campaign organization as do the political professionals who run the show.

Campaign Professionals

The scholar looks at the big picture, and the reporter tries to find a good story. The campaign professional, in contrast, has an entirely different mission: win the election at hand. Few other jobs draw such an absolute distinction between success and failure. If the candidate is not ahead of the pack on election day, it is all over. As a result, campaign professionals often come to believe that elections are like battles—and to prepare for engagement, political professionals throw themselves into "campaign mode" (Burton and Shea 2003).

As electoral strategies are formulated, debated, implemented, and reformulated, an intuitive sense of political strategy takes hold of the professional mind. In Washington and on the campaign trail, one will hear political professionals say, "She understands," or "He gets it," or "She knows how the game is played." A White House official can describe campaign mode as the ability to "think three or four moves ahead" (Burton and Shea 2003, 4). Cold calculations must be made about the strengths and weaknesses of both the candidate and the opposition, the opportunities presented and foreclosed by one's political environment, and the perils that await the candidate once the electoral season begins. Some people "get the joke," while others do not.

Political advice has a long history. Thomas Jefferson, Andrew Jackson, and Abraham Lincoln all had acquaintances who offered campaign wisdom, much of it unsolicited and much of it bad. The rise of campaign consulting as we know it today began with the strategic thinking of William McKinley's longtime advisor Mark Hanna, who devised a systematic approach to the Ohio Republican's 1896 presidential campaign (Reichley 1992, 140–147). Fundraising and voter outreach were mapped along "business principles," meaning that various constituencies would be targeted and solicited according to their relative likelihood of support (Troy 1996). There continued to be plenty of backroom politicking, to be sure, but the fundamental idea of the McKinley campaign was that the electorate needed to be viewed as a whole, then analytically segmented, and then courted according to the needs of individual constituency groups.[5]

As the old political party structure continued to fall away in the 1960s (White and Shea 2004, chap. 3), and as more voters began to assert, "I vote for the candidate, not the party" (Wattenberg 1998),[6] those who sought elective office understood that they needed to find outside assistance. A growing number of campaign professionals were there to help and, of course, make a nice living in the process. In the 1992 presidential campaign, political consultants became media stars. *The War Room*, a popular documentary film about that election, centered less on candidate Bill Clinton than on his principal advisors, George Stephanopoulos and James Carville (both of whom have since become prominent television personalities), as well as on Carville's then-girlfriend (now wife) working on the Republican side, Mary Matalin. More recently, one of the first battles waged among contenders for the 2004 Democratic nomination was for the services of heavyweight political consultant Robert Shrum. This competition was not only a reflection of Shrum's political skills, but also of his reputation. Landing him as an advisor enhanced the credibility of a candidate, especially in the eyes of journalists covering the campaign.

In the twenty-first century, political consulting is a mature industry (see chapter 11 in this volume). Practitioners in Washington and around the country specialize in all aspects of the campaign process, from polling to letter stuffing to grassroots mobilization to video production. In the magazine *Politics* (a monthly publication formerly called *Campaigns and Elections*), political professionals can find advertisements for all sorts of campaign-related products and services. Consultants even have their own professional organization, the American Association of Political Consultants, which gives out "Pollie" awards for distinguished performances in a variety of areas (best television and radio ads, best Web sites, best use of negative or contrast ads, and so on)—an event that political satirist Jon Stewart could not resist lampooning on his *Daily Show* in 2008.

Ultimately, though, consultants are driven not by a desire for recognition but by the need to win elections. Whether motivated by financial and business considerations or by ideological conviction,[7] this imperative compels campaign professionals to view campaigns differently than either academics or journalists. To the political professional in campaign mode, strategy is *everything*. If strategy does not matter, then the strategist has lost all reason for being: Why would any candidate hire someone whose actions had little or no effect on the final outcome? As such, political professionals are to be forgiven if they believe in the power of strategy and tactics even to the point of self-deception. As the race winds down, front-running campaigns often fear the effects of an "October Surprise"[8] even as their ill-fated opponents are telling themselves, "We can do it!" Campaign mode, in this sense, is a state of mind that combines a visceral drive to win elections with a deep-seated habit of strategic thinking. Ideally, strategic thinking in campaign mode is based on an understanding of political terrain that helps a professional choose the course of action most likely to produce victory.

Strategic thinking is as much an art as it is a science. Using election day as an anchor point, a political operative will survey the existing situation and then reverse-engineer campaign victory by designating the week prior to the election for a get-out-the-vote drive, the week prior to that as an opportunity to refine the campaign's voter lists, and so forth, until the plan reaches back to the present moment in time (see C. Shaw 2010, 378). Many campaigns create wall-sized calendars that chart each significant event leading up to the election; everyone in the office can see what needs to be done, and when. With an immovable deadline, there simply is no time to discuss anything that does not relate directly to the task at hand. Backward mapping sets the goal; forward planning shows the way. Sometimes, of course, this process is overtaken by the frenzy of day-to-day events; that is, campaign decision makers establish their strategic plan—but then end up adjusting their approach to fit new developments as they occur.

Strategy is governed by perception. Political professionals of all stripes can understand a state, district, ward, or precinct in much the same way. In campaign mode, electoral victory is the axis around which the world turns. Accordingly, professionals view a voting district as a conglomeration of voters, demographic characteristics, media markets, neighborhoods, partisan and ideological preferences, long-standing political alliances (and disputes), and other politically salient features that must be exploited or overcome in order for their candidate to win at the polls. People in the district are seen as volunteers, staffers, base voters, swing voters, and soft partisans. Segments of the electorate that are unalterably loyal to the opposition simply recede from view. Persuadable voters, in contrast, are "on the radar screen," worth keeping an eye on. Like other electorally significant features of a district, the uncommitted voters (who, as a mass, are capable of turning the election) become prominent features of the political terrain.

Looking back at the 2004 election, Bob Shrum declared, "Everything mattered—everything they did, everything we did, and a series of external events all mattered" (Institute of Politics 2005, 134). To make sense of the chaos, consultants need to know at least a few rules of electoral strategy. Some are drawn as simple imperatives, such as "You have to have a plan" (Grey 2007, 89). Others are statements of political fact that carry obvious strategic or tactical implications. EMILY's List, a political action committee that funds pro-choice Democratic women, named itself after the idea that "Early Money Is Like Yeast—it makes the 'dough' rise." In California, operatives commonly say, "It's not real until it's on television." Redoubtable politician and longtime U.S. House Speaker Tip O'Neill's rule that "all politics is local" is one of the most widely accepted principles of American politics. Thus, putting all the pieces together, a California campaign organization might want to start with a plan, raise early money, get itself on the air, and address local issues whenever possible.

For political professionals, these maxims are not hackneyed clichés, but essential bits of knowledge. While some practitioners might debate the validity, relative priority, or general application of certain presuppositions, much of the conventional wisdom about campaigning consists of some very basic and widely accepted rules. The strength of the professional viewpoint is precisely in its creative thinking, vision, and ability to see not only *what is* but *what could be,* as opposed to the journalist who talks about *what has happened* in a particular campaign, and the scholar who talks about *what usually happens* across the broad spectrum of political elections.

Conclusion

Scholars, journalists, and practitioners—each of these groups can trump the others on its own turf. Scholars understand that most electoral outcomes are utterly predictable, so they marginalize discussions of campaign operations. Journalists, who talk to operatives and to voters on a daily basis, understand the power of structural influence, but focus primarily on the campaigns where strategy matters. Consultants, with a vested interest in the business of campaign strategy, must assume that strategy is everything, or nearly everything, so they are acutely aware of campaign decisions and their potential consequences. Each perspective serves a specific need. Because journalists must engage voters in order to sell papers (or commercials), underscoring the drama of elections becomes critical to their professional livelihood. Because scholars seek to explore and to comprehend general social phenomena, underlying forces are brought to the fore. And because practitioners will not otherwise be successful, they must demonstrate the power of campaign strategy. Thus, consultants are correct in underscoring the weight of strategic moves; journalists are correct in reporting them; and political scientists are correct in reminding everyone that the sum total of all campaign decisions in all elections is, most of the time, something close to a strategic wash.

Of course, there is a degree of crossover. Some journalists are familiar with political science scholarship and know a great deal about the business of campaigning, and many consultants know exactly how reporters think. The presidential campaigns of George W. Bush gained from the strategic advice of Daron Shaw, a prominent elections scholar (see D. R. Shaw 2006). And a growing number of academics are paying attention to ground-level management of campaigns (see Thurber and Nelson 2010). Unlike the early days of campaign scholarship, there are many academics today who understand that campaigns *do* indeed matter. For example, Skaperdas and Grofman (1995) developed a formal model that calculates the likelihood that a given candidate will "go negative" on his or her opponents. Green and Gerber (2008) conducted field experiments with prospective voters to see which voter-contact methods are the most cost effective in getting people to the polls on election day. In a study that brings academic scholarship closer to the thinking of political professionals, Hillygus and Shields (2008) found that even partisan voters can become persuadable if a candidate of the other party talks about the right issue—and if this is the case, then wide swaths of the electorate might be up for grabs.

Each of these efforts assumes, at least implicitly, that campaigns matter. Campaign effects may be small, but they nevertheless do exist. The story of the typical American campaign involves a front-runner who is trying to defend a lead, competing against a dark horse who seeks to defy the odds. There are numerous structural impediments to a challenger's bid to unseat an incumbent, a fact that is well known to scholars, journalists, and practitioners alike, just as other structural factors create inherent advantages and disadvantages on both sides. Yet no single perspective can provide a master framework for understanding electoral phenomena, and there is little use in (and little justification for) trying to persuade political consultants that most campaigning is pointless. Just as practitioners and journalists are wise to track the empirical findings of scholars, political scientists should pay careful attention to the perspectives offered by reporters and consultants. Each has wisdom to offer, and if the purpose of political science scholarship is to understand the big picture, scholars should continue their ongoing reassessment of strategic decision making in American elections.

THE POLITICAL PROFESSIONALS RESPOND

Charlie Black

Campaign strategy wouldn't matter much if campaigns didn't matter much, so let's put this discussion of strategy into the context of *which* campaigns matter. Many academics have presented evidence-based theories that most campaigns don't matter. In contrast, all politicians and political professionals believe that campaigns do matter. There is no need to take sides in this perennial debate because both are right.

The great majority of general elections in the United States—local, state, and federal—are completely predictable based on the partisan makeup of the constituency, demographics, the economic climate, and other factors that are included in academic models. But many elections are closely contested, and predictably so according to those same models. What's more, the results of closely contested elections are apt to produce big changes in local, state, and national policy. In these contests campaigns clearly matter, and campaign strategy can be decisive. Five of the last ten presidential elections in the United States have been close, with models unable to predict the results with any degree of accuracy. In 1972, 1984, 1992, 1996, and 2008, academic models accurately concluded that the election outcome would be determined by Labor Day. There simply were not enough persuadable swing voters for the loser's campaign to change the result. But in 1976, 1980, 1988, 2000, and 2004, the presidential elections were close, the campaigns mattered, the winner's campaign strategy was superior, and academic models were either unable to predict the winner or simply wrong (most famously in 2000).

Now, everyone knows that very different paths in public policy are taken depending on which party wins the presidency. Which party controls the majority of seats in each house of Congress similarly makes a huge difference in the policy direction taken by the government in Washington. We also all know that academic models can predict the winners of about 90 percent of U.S. House races in each election and the winners of 75 to 80 percent of U.S. Senate races in most elections. But the United States has a very competitive two-party system; since 1980, close races have determined majority control of at least one house of Congress in more than half the elections. Majority control of the U.S. House changed, or was in jeopardy, in five of those thirteen elections (1994, 1996, 1998, 2000, and 2006). There are normally only forty to fifty truly competitive congressional general elections (out of 435 seats) each cycle, but campaigns and strategy matter in those and their results can have a huge impact on national policy.

Majority control of the U.S. Senate has been determined by the results of close, competitive races in eight of the last thirteen elections. The majority party ruled by a narrow margin from 1981 through 2008, when Democrats won enough races to reach sixty seats in the one hundred–member Senate. Majority control was at stake and dependent on the outcomes of close elections in 1980, 1982, 1986, 1994, 2000, 2002, 2004, and 2006; a new party took control on six occasions (including 2000, when Jim Jeffords's party switch in 2001 gave the Democrats control by breaking a 50–50 tie). In each of these eight elections, the majority of the thirty-three or thirty-four Senate elections on the ballot were not competitive, so the campaigns didn't matter. But in each year, eight to twelve highly competitive, close races determined which party ran the chamber. That had a huge impact on national policy.

The same pattern holds true in state government elections. Probably half of all gubernatorial elections in the fifty states are competitive and decided by superior candidates, campaigns, and strategies. Majority control of state legislative chambers is closely contested in more than half the states. For example, in the 2010 elections more than forty state legislative chambers are in play, controlled by one party by a margin of fewer than five seats. The competitive state house and senate races will determine majority control and the policy direction of the respective states. Critically important to the nation is the fact that, in most states, new legislatures elected in 2010 will control the process of congressional redistricting. How they draw the lines can affect majority control of Congress for the next decade. In the ten largest states (those with the most congressional seats), thirteen of the twenty state legislative chambers are close in partisan makeup and subject to change of control in 2010. In those ten states alone, as many as twenty congressional seats could be "drawn" into the control of a different party. The outcome of about a hundred close legislative races in 2010 could result in a change of control of Congress and a change of direction in national policy.

Most campaigns don't matter, but those that do *really* matter. So let's talk about campaign strategy and the role of political professionals in those close campaigns that can determine the policy direction of states and the nation. Professors Burton, Shea, and Miller get one thing wrong: they say that "political professionals . . . [believe] in the power of strategy and tactics even to the point of self-deception." In fact, competent political pros spend most of their time working in the close races where campaigns matter. They will be the first to tell you that the quality of the candidates is the most important factor in winning. But strategy and tactics do matter in close races. Many times the better candidate loses a race due to poor strategy or tactical execution. There are many examples of good Democratic members of Congress who lost in 1994 because they ran classic incumbent strategies and did not respond to Republican attacks. The same can be said of several good Republican members of Congress who lost in 2006.

A classic case of strategy deciding the outcome is Republican senator Slade Gorton's loss to Democrat Maria Cantwell in Washington state in 2000. Gorton was one of the finest senators of his generation, highly respected on both sides of the aisle and influential on a variety of policy issues. Cantwell was a junior representative with no particular accomplishments. She beat the superior candidate with superior strategy.[1] Another case is Republican Rick Santorum's defeat of Democratic senator Harris Wofford in Pennsylvania in 1994. Democrats and independent observers considered Wofford an outstanding public servant, having gained his seat initially in a stunning upset of former governor and U.S. Attorney General Dick Thornburgh. Santorum was regarded as an inferior candidate by most observers because they thought he was too conservative for the state's electorate. Yet Santorum won—again, as a result of superior strategy.[2]

Professors Burton, Shea, and Miller provide a good account of the electorate's overall predictability, and their analysis of how journalists cover campaigns is exactly right. The examples cited above demonstrate, however, that even with only about 8 percent of voters persuadable, campaigns often do matter. The fact that campaign strategy must be geared to a relatively small slice of the electorate simply makes it that much more important. Every campaign is different, and there are no reliable formulas for the strategist to take from one campaign to the next. As the professors say, "[s]trategic thinking is as much an art as it is a science."

The strategist cannot overlook the need to unify and galvanize his or her candidate's base in any election, and to make sure that the tactics and mechanics necessary to turn out the base are in place. But the strategist's focus for most of the campaign must be on the swing voters. First, one must conduct and analyze research to determine exactly who they are; their views, values, and motivations must be noted. The strategist must then project what information these voters are likely to receive during the campaign from the opponent and, with this in mind, determine what information and messages they need to receive from the strategist's candidate—and when they need to receive it. This is a high-stakes chess game. Finally, the strategist must be prepared to adjust communication with swing voters on a regular basis, depending on the actions of the opponent, the effectiveness of the strategist's campaign, and developments in the news or from third-party communications.[3] The winner of the swing voters and, thus, the election is usually the campaign that best understands the priorities of these individuals, controls the agenda of the campaign as it relates to them, spends less time on the defensive, and is able to secure the candidate's base without cross-pressuring swing voters on issues.

As long as we have a competitive two-party system in the United States there will be enough close races to ensure that their outcomes greatly affect the future of our country. Every candidate in a close race is in need of a good professional strategist.

---

[1] Even though she was herself a member of Congress, Cantwell ran as a businesswoman and outsider who alleged that Gorton had been in Washington too long and had lost touch with the state. This theme trumped Gorton's message of experience and accomplishment.

[2] While the challenger was certainly more conservative than most swing voters in Pennsylvania, he focused on economic issues, did not talk much about social issues, and promised to be a moderating influence on the Clinton administration. When Wofford tried to portray his opponent as too conservative, Santorum trumped him by tying the incumbent to unpopular Clinton policies.

[3] For most competitive federal races in recent years, between a quarter and a third of the advertising appearing about the candidate is paid for by independent expenditures by third parties (unions, trade associations, single-issue groups, and the like) and not coordinated with the candidate's campaign.

Notes

1. The authors wish to thank Rowman and Littlefield for permission to adapt material for this chapter from Burton and Shea (2003).

2. American Exceptionalism is the idea that the history and development of the United States renders comparison to other nations, including Western European nations, problematic. At its most optimistic (or jingoistic), the notion holds that the United States is immune from the social and political maladies that plague other parts of the world. From a strictly analytic perspective, it holds that, for better or for worse, American beliefs and practices are measurably different from those belonging to citizens elsewhere. For a contemporary treatment of American Exceptionalism, see Lipset (1996).

3. Such variables might, for example, include inflation, crime rates, health care costs, gasoline prices, and a variety of other factors that influence voter sentiments.

4. For example, partisan voters may simply determine the candidates' party affiliations and vote accordingly by reasoning, "I'm a Democrat (Republican) and he's a Democrat (Republican). Chances are we have the same values and agree on most issues. Why should I spend time studying each candidate's positions in detail? I'll simply vote for him."

5. We refer here to the cultivation of support from local party leaders (or "bosses")—individuals who were highly influential during this period, and whose efforts were important in delivering votes for chosen candidates on election day.

6. In fact, some political scientists (for example, Bartels 2000; Hetherington 2001; Green, Palmquist, and Schickler 2002; but see Fiorina 2002) believe that there has been a resurgence of partisanship among voters in recent years.

7. While the popular impression of campaign consultants is that they are hired guns, not beholden to any particular cause, research has shown that most consultants work fairly closely with party operatives (Dulio 2004).

8. The term "October Surprise" entered the political lexicon during the 1980 presidential contest between incumbent Jimmy Carter and challenger Ronald Reagan. Republicans feared that the administration might negotiate a last-minute (in this instance, in October) release of hostages being held by radicals at the U.S. embassy in Tehran, Iran, and thereby give Carter's campaign a big boost. (It didn't happen. The hostages were released on the day Reagan was sworn in as president in January 1981.) Along the same lines, Democrats in 2004 worried that an eleventh-hour capture of terrorist leader Osama bin Laden would ensure the reelection of President George W. Bush. (This also didn't happen, and Bush won anyway.)

3 Swing Voters

William G. Mayer

Imagine that you are the principal strategist for a major-party presidential campaign. The election appears to be close, sufficiently so that both sides have a reasonable chance of winning. Based on polling and recent electoral history, you're pretty confident that your candidate has a solid base of between 40 and 45 percent of the vote. Where can you find the additional votes needed to put him or her over the top?

One answer to this question might be that there is no need to target your message to a particular group of voters; instead, the campaign should concentrate on those issues and themes that seem most attractive to voters as a whole. But this approach ignores a good deal of what we have learned over the years about the nature of presidential voting decisions and the impact of presidential campaigns. Contrary to the impression sometimes fostered in the media, every vote isn't up for grabs in the general election. Voters' partisan loyalties, issue attitudes, and performance judgments have generally been formed months or even years in advance; most voters have already reached a decision by the end of the national conventions; and much of what campaigns do is simply bring out voters' latent attachments and predispositions.[1]

So, if your presidential campaign sends out its messages to all voters as an undifferentiated mass, it will probably be wasting a lot of its effort and energy. Some large percentage of the potential electorate has already firmly decided to vote for your candidate. While you will want to make sure that these voters actually cast a ballot on election day (or vote by absentee ballot), there is no point in trying to persuade them further about the merits of the candidate you represent. The same is true for a large number of your opponent's supporters: while you may be able to get them to adopt a slightly more positive opinion of your candidate, the odds are very slim that you can change their vote intention. If you can target your message (an important issue I will take up at the end of this chapter), you will want to go after that part of the electorate where your efforts might actually make a difference.

It is this insight that explains why "swing voters" have been receiving increased attention from pollsters, campaign strategists, journalists, and, quite belatedly, political scientists.[2] In simple terms, a swing voter is a voter who could go either way—someone who is not so solidly committed to one candidate or the other as to make all efforts at persuasion futile. If some voters know from the beginning which candidate they intend to support and never waver from that intention, swing voters are the opposite: those whose final allegiance is in some doubt all the way up until election day. Rather than seeing one candidate as the embodiment of all virtue and the other as the quintessence of vice, swing voters are pulled (or repulsed) in both directions.

For a campaign seeking to win a plurality of the votes, swing voters thus occupy a position similar to that of battleground states in the hunt for an Electoral College majority. As observers of American politics have long recognized, no presidential campaign spreads its time and money evenly across all fifty states. Presidential campaigns ignore those states where they are so safely and comfortably ahead that their opponent has essentially no chance of catching up; at the same time, they expend little or no effort in those states where their opponent has a prohibitive lead. Instead, almost all recent presidential campaigns have been a struggle over a handful of battleground states—usually no more than ten or twenty in number—that might conceivably be won by either candidate. Any theory of American elections that ignores this point would be hard pressed to explain why in recent campaigns candidates have spent so much time in New Hampshire, Iowa, and Colorado, and so little in California, New York, and Texas. Increasingly, swing voters have come to occupy an analogous position with respect to the search for individual votes.

Identifying Swing Voters

How can we identify swing voters in a survey in order to learn more about their characteristics, attitudes, and perceptions? Most pollsters use a two-question sequence to determine who the swing voters are. They first ask all respondents the standard vote-intention question, which in 2008 generally went something like this:[3]

Suppose that the presidential election were being held today, and it included Barack Obama and Joe Biden as the Democratic candidates and John McCain and Sarah Palin as the Republican candidates. Would you vote for Barack Obama and Joe Biden, the Democrats, or John McCain and Sarah Palin, the Republicans, or someone else?

Respondents who expressed a preference for either Obama or McCain were then asked a follow-up question:

Are you certain now that you will vote for [preferred presidential candidate] for president, or do you think you may change your mind between now and the November election?

Swing voters include (1) those who are undecided, and (2) those who, though they have a current preference, say they might change their mind between the interview and the election.

As many readers of this book will know, academic students of voting and elections rely heavily on the series of surveys conducted every presidential election year since 1952 by the University of Michigan; these are known as the American National Election Studies (ANES). Unfortunately, these surveys have never included a question that tries to assess the firmness of a respondent's vote intention. Hence, in my own research I have used a slightly different method for identifying swing voters, but one that gets at the same underlying idea.

One set of questions that has been included in every ANES preelection survey since 1972 asks respondents to indicate how favorably or unfavorably they view each of the presidential candidates by rating them on a so-called thermometer scale, ranging from 0 to 100 degrees. As a number of scholars have shown, these ratings provide a good summary indicator of how people evaluate a given person or group and are highly correlated with other important political variables such as voting behavior and ideological self-identification (see, especially, Brody and Page 1973; Conover and Feldman 1981; Weisberg and Rusk 1970).

In the case of the two major-party presidential candidates, if we subtract one candidate's rating from the other's we obtain a scale that measures each voter's *comparative* assessment of the candidates. At one end of the scale, marked as –100, are voters who see the Democratic standard bearer as dramatically superior to the Republican nominee. These voters have both a highly positive opinion of the Democratic candidate and a very negative opinion of the Republican candidate. Voters located at +100 have a similarly one-sided view, albeit one favoring the Republican. Those at or near zero, by contrast, have a more even or balanced set of attitudes. They may like both candidates equally or dislike them equally; the important point is that voters in the middle of the scale are not convinced that one candidate is clearly superior to the other. It is this last group, of course, that represents the swing voters.

Table 3.1 Distribution of Respondents and Division of Major-Party Presidential Vote by Difference in Preelection Thermometer Ratings, 1972–2008

Difference in Thermometer Ratings	Percent of All Voters	Percent Voting Democratic	Percent Voting Republican	(N)
−100 to −91	2.2	100	0	(265)
−90 to −81	2.8	99	1	(351)
−80 to −71	0.4	100	0	(50)
−70 to −61	4.1	99	1	(508)
−60 to −51	5.1	98	2	(633)
−50 to −41	5.3	97	3	(654)
−40 to −31	5.2	96	4	(645)
−30 to −21	7.2	94	6	(886)
−20 to −16	4.3	92	8	(535)
−15 to −11	2.4	85	15	(301)
−10 to −6	4.5	84	16	(559)
−5 to −1	0.3	66	34	(35)
0	8.9	52	48	(1,092)
1 to 5	0.3	19	81	(32)
6 to 10	4.6	19	81	(566)
11 to 15	2.2	15	85	(267)
16 to 20	3.9	9	91	(475)
21 to 30	7.1	6	94	(879)
31 to 40	5.7	4	96	(701)
41 to 50	5.4	4	96	(669)
51 to 60	5.6	1	99	(690)
61 to 70	5.2	2	98	(640)
71 to 80	0.5	2	98	(63)
81 to 90	3.8	1	99	(470)
91 to 100	2.9	1	99	(357)
Totals	100.0			(12,323)

Source: American National Election Studies.

Note: These results are based on feeling thermometer scores in the ANES preelection survey.

In Table 3.1 I have added together the thermometer scale scores for all ten ANES presidential-year surveys from 1972 through 2008. As might be expected, the scores are clustered somewhat more densely near the center of the scale, but there are also a surprisingly large number of respondents located at the tails of the distribution. Every four years, about one-third of the electorate places the two major-party candidates more than fifty degrees apart on the feeling thermometer.

Table 3.1 also shows the division of the two-party presidential vote at every point along the scale. Not surprisingly, the score a respondent receives on this scale is highly correlated with his or her eventual vote. What is more noteworthy, however, is what this table shows about the relationship between scale position and "convertability"—that is, the likelihood that a campaign can change a person's vote intention. Since the thermometer ratings in Table 3.1 are taken from the preelection survey, while the voting percentages come from the postelection survey, one interpretation of these results is that they show the probability that a person who holds a given set of attitudes toward the major-party candidates during the preelection campaign will ultimately cast a Democratic (or Republican) ballot. For voters located at either end of the scale, the odds of effecting a change in voting intentions are clearly not very great. Of those who place the candidates more than fifty degrees apart during the preelection campaign, 99 percent ended up voting for their favored candidate. Even among those who see a difference of twenty-five or thirty degrees between the candidates, a mere 5 percent are sufficiently influenced by the campaign to "convert" to the opposition. Only in a rather narrow band near the center of the scale—running from about –15 to +15—does the number of partisan conversions reach 15 percent.

At one level, the data in Table 3.1 reinforce a point made earlier: not many people change their votes during the general election phase of a presidential campaign. But if campaigns cannot create the world anew, they clearly can change *some* votes—and in a close election those changes may spell the difference between victory and defeat. More to the point, if vote changes do occur, they are much more likely to occur among those near the center of the scale— among swing voters—than among those located closer to the end points. If it is difficult to persuade someone who initially rates the Democratic candidate ten degrees higher than the Republican candidate to cast a Republican ballot, it is far more difficult to convert someone who rates the Democratic standard bearer thirty or fifty degrees above the Republican nominee.

One advantage of using a scale of this sort is that it provides a nuanced, graduated measure of a voter's convertability or "swingness." For the analysis that follows, however, it will be helpful to have a simple, dichotomous variable that divides voters into two categories: swing voters and non-swing voters. A close inspection of the data in Table 3.1 suggests that the best way to define such a variable is to classify any voter with a score between –15 and +15 inclusive as a swing voter, with everyone else falling into the non-swing voter category. By this criterion, as shown in Table 3.2, 23 percent of the voters in the typical ANES presidential-year survey qualify as swing voters. Moreover, contrary to a claim often made during the presidency of George W. Bush, there is no evidence in these data to suggest that swing voters have declined as a proportion of the total electorate. While there was a significant fall-off in the

Table 3.2 Percentage of Major-Party Presidential Voters Classified as Swing Voters, 1972–2008

Year	Percentage of Respondents With a Score Between −15 and +15 on the Thermometer Ratings Scale
1972	22
1976	34
1980	28
1984	22
1988	26
1992	22
1996	18
2000	23
2004	13
2008	23
Average	23

Source: American National Election Studies.

number of swing voters in 2004, the number rebounded in 2008 to 23 percent, exactly equal to its average over the thirty-six-year period.

Swing Voters and Election Outcomes

What role do swing voters actually play in determining the outcome of presidential elections? To answer this question, Table 3.3 breaks down the presidential electorate into three major groups: (1) the Democratic base vote, who have thermometer-rating scale scores between −100 and −16; (2) swing voters, who, as defined earlier, are those with scale scores between −15 and +15; and (3) the Republican base vote, who have scale scores between +16 and +100. The table shows the distribution of the electorate across these categories and the division of the major-party presidential vote within each category for each of the last ten presidential elections. For this table, I have followed the lead of James Campbell (2000) and weighted the ANES data so that the survey results are equal to the actual votes cast.

The base vote, as I am using the term here, is the opposite of the swing vote: it includes those voters on whose support a candidate *can* comfortably rely. On average, the twenty major-party candidates shown in Table 3.3 held on to 96 percent of their base vote. The problem for most campaigns is that the base vote falls short of a majority. Hence, the principal goal becomes finding a way to add on to the base vote enough weakly committed, undecided, and even initially antagonistic voters to secure a majority. And that, of course, is where the swing vote becomes important.

Table 3.3 Swing Voters and Presidential Election Outcomes (in percentages)

Year	Voter Type	Percentage of All Major-Party Voters	Percent Voting Democratic	Percent Voting Republican
1972	Democratic base vote	25	96	4
	Swing voters	22	51	49
	Republican base vote	53	6	94
1976	Democratic base vote	32	96	4
	Swing voters	34	54	46
	Republican base vote	34	6	94
1980	Democratic base vote	36	92	8
	Swing voters	27	38	62
	Republican base vote	37	3	97
1984	Democratic base vote	31	97	3
	Swing voters	22	44	56
	Republican base vote	47	2	98
1988	Democratic base vote	32	97	3
	Swing voters	26	55	45
	Republican base vote	42	3	97
1992	Democratic base vote	40	99	1
	Swing voters	22	56	44
	Republican base vote	37	3	97
1996	Democratic base vote	47	96	4
	Swing voters	18	50	50
	Republican base vote	36	2	98
2000	Democratic base vote	39	95	5
	Swing voters	23	52	48
	Republican base vote	38	3	97
2004	Democratic base vote	42	96	4
	Swing voters	13	53	47
	Republican base vote	45	2	98
2008	Democratic base vote	42	99	1
	Swing voters	21	52	48
	Republican base vote	37	4	96

Source: American National Election Studies.

Note: Data have been weighted so that the survey results are equal to the actual results.

The swing vote is most significant, then, in close elections. The basic dynamic can be seen most readily in the elections of 1976, 1980, 1992, 2000, and 2008. In each of these contests, both major-party candidates had a base vote of between 32 and 42 percent of the electorate. When the numbers are in this range, which candidate wins depends on how the swing vote breaks—and in every one of these elections, the candidate who won a majority of the swing vote also won a majority of the popular vote as a whole (though in the case of Al Gore in 2000, this wasn't quite enough to carry him into the White House).

The situation is different when the general election shapes up as a landslide. In 1972, for example, 53 percent of the voters in the ANES preelection survey were already part of the Republican base vote. To win the 1972 election, Democrat George McGovern had to win an overwhelming percentage of the swing voters *and* make some substantial inroads into the GOP base. In fact, as the figures in Table 3.3 indicate, Richard Nixon held on to 94 percent of his base vote, while simultaneously winning a near majority of swing voters. Ronald Reagan in 1984 and Bill Clinton in 1996 similarly began their general election campaigns with a base vote that fell just shy of a majority.

The most one can say about the role of the swing vote in these three elections, then, is that it helped determine the size of the winning candidate's margin of victory. Yet even in an election of this type, both campaigns would probably be well advised to concentrate most of their efforts on swing voters. From the perspective of the leading candidate, the swing vote may provide him or her with the final votes necessary to secure a majority—and can also spell the difference between a comfortable victory and a landslide, a difference that most presidents take very seriously. As for the trailing candidate, though it is most unlikely that he or she can win 80 or 90 percent of the swing vote, there simply is no better alternative. The swing voters are the most likely source of converts. After that, the odds only become even more prohibitive.

The 1988 and 2004 elections are more difficult to categorize. In 1988, the Republican base vote was ten percentage points larger than the Democratic base vote, but the GOP base represented just 42 percent of the major-party electorate, leaving George H.W. Bush well short of a majority. In 2004, as a result of the shrinkage in the number of swing voters, George W. Bush had a base vote of 45 percent, but John Kerry's base vote, at 42 percent, was only slightly smaller. To win the election, each candidate needed to win a substantial share of the swing vote but did not need a majority. In the end, both Bushes carried enough swing votes to win the election, though it was actually their opponents who captured a majority of the swing vote.

The swing vote, in sum, is not the be-all and end-all of American presidential elections. It is much less important in landslide elections—but, then, so are campaigns in general in such circumstances (see chapter 1 in this volume). For a candidate in McGovern's position—trailing an incumbent president by about twenty-five points in most national polls at the start of the fall campaign—there was probably nothing he could have done to avert defeat. Had McGovern run a good campaign, he might have reduced the size of Nixon's victory; but a Democratic win in 1972 was simply never in the cards. In the more typical case, however, where an election is close, the final outcome hinges to a great extent on the decisions reached by swing voters.

One final point should be made about the data in Table 3.3. While the swing voter concept serves a number of useful functions, one purpose for which these data should *not* be used is to claim that whichever candidate won a majority of the swing voters ran the better campaign. To begin with, the ANES preelection interviews generally do not begin until September, by which time many of the best strategic moves and worst campaign blunders have already taken place. In 1988, for example, many analysts believe that George H.W. Bush won the election because of a series of attacks he launched on the gubernatorial record of his Democratic opponent, Michael Dukakis, in mid- to late August and because of Dukakis's failure to respond to those attacks more quickly and effectively. Based on contemporary polling by Gallup and other organizations, it seems likely that Bush's attacks moved many undecided voters to support the vice president and made some Dukakis supporters less comfortable with their choice. Yet any such effects would not have been picked up in the ANES preference data because of the timing of the preelection survey.

In addition, the dynamics of a particular election may produce a swing electorate that is predisposed toward one of the candidates. In 1988, for example, Bush was much more successful than Dukakis in uniting his own partisans around his candidacy during the summer. As a result, of the swing voters identified in the 1988 ANES sample, fully 54 percent were self-identified Democrats; only 35 percent were Republicans. With that kind of initial advantage, it is no surprise that Dukakis ultimately won a small majority of the swing voters—though, of course, this was not enough to defeat Bush.

Who Are the Swing Voters?

Are certain kinds of people more or less likely to be classified as swing voters? Do swing voters, when compared to the rest of the electorate, have distinctive attitudes or demographic traits? These questions go to the heart of the swing voter concept. All of the attention that campaigns lavish on swing voters—and any attempt to argue that they are theoretically important—presumes that swing voters are, in at least some important ways, different from the rest of the electorate. If swing voters are, for all practical purposes, a randomly selected subset of all voters, then a campaign's decision to concentrate on swing voters will not change its strategy. It will talk about the same issues, in the same ways, and make the same kinds of promises that it would if swing voters did not exist and it was targeting its message indiscriminately to the entire electorate. In fact, however, swing voters do have at least some distinctive characteristics.

First, swing voters are substantially less partisan than non-swing voters. As shown in Table 3.4, on average strong partisans accounted for 41 percent of non-swing voters, compared with just 18 percent of swing voters, during the period 1972–2008. This is not to say that swing voters are completely devoid of partisan attachments; only 12 percent are pure independents. Most swing voters (about 70 percent) are either weak partisans or independent "leaners."[4] Nevertheless, the fact remains: swing voters are not likely to respond to highly partisan appeals. While the national conventions are a time to rally the wavering partisans, in the general election a candidate is more likely to win swing voters by promising to govern above partisanship.

Second, swing voters are more moderate than non-swing voters. Those at the more extreme ends of the ideological spectrum tend to have a clearer affinity for one of the major-party candidates: liberals for the Democrat, conservatives for the Republican. Moderates, by contrast, are less certain about which nominee better represents their opinions and interests, and are thus more likely to vacillate. The data behind this conclusion are also shown in Table 3.4. Since

Table 3.4   Partisanship and Ideology of Swing and Non-Swing Voters, 1972–2008 (in percentages)

	Swing Voters	Non-Swing Voters
PARTISANSHIP		
Pure independents	12	6
Independent leaners	29	22
Weak partisans	41	31
Strong partisans	18	41
IDEOLOGY		
Extremely liberal	1	2
Liberal	4	10
Slightly liberal	11	10
Moderate	31	22
Slightly conservative	18	15
Conservative	11	19
Extremely conservative	1	3
Don't know, haven't thought much about it	24	20

Source: American National Election Studies.

Note: Figures represent average percentages for the ten ANES presidential-year surveys from 1972 through 2008. The difference between swing voters and non-swing voters was significant at the .01 level in each of the ten surveys.

1972, the ANES surveys have measured ideology by asking respondents to place themselves on a seven-point scale ranging from extremely liberal to extremely conservative. Averaging across the ten presidential elections between 1972 and 2008, just 17 percent of swing voters located themselves at one of the four outer points on the scale (points 1, 2, 6, and 7), as compared with 34 percent of non-swing voters. At the same time, 31 percent of swing voters placed themselves at the exact center of the scale (point 4), versus 22 percent of non-swing voters.

Third, swing voters are less informed and less interested in politics than non-swing voters.[5] The differences are largest for questions that relate specifically to the current election; for example, 45 percent of non-swing voters, on average, say they are very interested in the current campaign versus just 29 percent of swing voters. The gap is narrower, however, on measures of general political interest. Twenty-six percent of swing voters claim to follow government and public affairs "most of the time," as against 36 percent of non-swing voters. According to ANES interviewers, 42 percent of swing voters appeared to have a very or fairly high level of information about politics; 52 percent of non-swing voters were so rated.

The pattern shown here—that those who need the information most, variously characterized as late deciders, independents, or swing voters, tend to pay less attention to politics and campaign news than those who have already reached a firm decision—is sometimes called the catch-22 of election campaigns. Yet the campaigners' task is not impossible: swing voters are seldom so isolated or apolitical as to make them totally immune to the candidates' appeals. As Dimock, Clark, and Horowitz (2008) have argued, swing voters are best described as a "middle-awareness" group: these voters "do not follow the campaign as closely and do not give as much thought to the election as voters who make up their minds in the early stages of the campaign, but they are not as disengaged as those who are not registered voters" (65).

Finally, swing voters do not appear to be demographically distinctive. Media stories have assigned a remarkable variety of demographic traits to the archetypal swing voter. Among the groups that are often said to be significantly overrepresented within the ranks of swing voters are women, the young, the elderly, Catholics, and Hispanics. In contrast, certain other groups, for example, blacks, are often depicted as firmly attached to one of the parties and thus underrepresented among swing voters. Surprisingly, none of these assertions are strongly or consistently borne out by the data. At least in demographic terms, swing voters are relatively diverse. Of the ten groups I examined—men, women, whites, blacks, Hispanics, white southerners, Protestants, Catholics, the young (aged

18–30), and the elderly (aged 65 and older)—none emerged as significantly over- or underrepresented among swing voters in more than three of the ten elections under consideration. If there is one group that is most often described as a swing constituency in media stories, it is women. Yet not once in these elections do women emerge as significantly more likely than men to be swing voters. To the contrary, in 1996, 2000, and 2004 it was men who were more likely to be swing voters (though the difference never quite achieves statistical significance). Admittedly, I have not tested any of the more exotic combinations periodically floated by commentators or consultants: soccer moms, Nascar dads, national security moms, and so on (most such groups are so ill-defined as to make testing difficult). But the more intricately one defines a target group, the smaller it becomes—and the less gain a candidate gets from winning its votes.

Swing Voters in Nonpresidential Elections and Among Third-Party Sympathizers

To this point I have concentrated on describing and analyzing swing voters in presidential general elections. Indeed, most journalistic discussions of swing voter proclivities and likely behavior are made in the context of presidential elections. Nevertheless, the basic insight surely applies to lower-level elections as well. Congressional, gubernatorial, and state legislative elections, for example, also include voters who are quite certain about their voting intentions and very unlikely to change—and those who are potentially movable. The complication is determining which is which. Unlike presidential general elections, congressional elections[6] often are low-information affairs in which large numbers of voters know virtually nothing about one or both of the major-party candidates. The thermometer-ratings scale described earlier includes only those survey respondents who are able to supply some sort of rating to *both* candidates. In presidential elections, only about 1 percent of voters are unable to meet this standard, but the number would surely be far larger in the typical congressional contest.

The swing voter group in most congressional elections thus includes at least two major groups: (1) those who have at least a minimum amount of information about both major-party candidates and are still either undecided or weakly committed to their current preference, and (2) those who say they intend to vote for the incumbent senator or representative and doubt they will change their minds but who might in fact change if they learned more information about the incumbent and/or the challenger. It is with this second group that identifying swing voters becomes more art than science, for it requires a poll-ster or campaign strategist to speculate about how voters *might* behave based on information they *could* acquire during the course of the campaign. (For a good analysis of how swing voters were actually identified and targeted in cer-tain types of low-information races, see Stonecash 2008.)

Another context where the basic model developed here needs to be expanded comes in elections in which there is a significant third-party or independent candidate. In 1992, for example, in addition to voters who vacillated between George H.W. Bush and Bill Clinton, there were undecided or weakly committed voters who contemplated casting a ballot for Ross Perot. Voting for third-party candidates has, in general, received considerably less attention from scholars than the choice between Democrats and Republicans. We therefore know very little about the proportion of voters who seriously consider voting for such candidates, though in many elections the number is probably substantial.

Some Conclusions and Implications

Swing voters, as I have defined them, play a potentially significant role in the way that political strategists (and political scientists) ought to think about elections. The core insight that animates the swing voter concept is that, in the context of an election campaign, not all voters are equal. Voters receive atten-tion from campaigns according to the expected "payoff" they will yield—that is, the number of votes that can be gained or at least not lost to the other side. Thus, campaigns will generally ignore or take for granted each candidate's most committed supporters and concentrate their persuasive efforts on the unde-cided or weakly committed swing voters.

To make the swing voter concept fully operational, however, campaigns must be able to target their appeals to swing voters. In this context, targeting can occur in one of two ways. One way is for strategists to design issue appeals to the specific needs and concerns of swing voters. As I have already empha-sized, being able to identify swing voters is of little value unless swing voters differ from their non-swing counterparts in significant ways. The data reviewed in this chapter have produced mixed results. Swing voters are less partisan and more moderate than non-swing voters, but they are not very distinctive demo-graphically. Whether swing voters have distinctive positions on specific issues such as abortion, immigration, or health care is not clear.

Alternatively, strategists can concentrate campaign resources (money, organization, candidate appearances) in ways that are designed to increase the likelihood of communicating a campaign's messages to swing voters. Here, the analogy drawn earlier between swing voters and battleground states breaks down. One reason the idea of battleground states is so widely used by both strategists and analysts is that it is very easy to target a campaign's resources on battleground states. Presidential campaigns just need to send the candidate to Ohio and Florida rather than California and Texas; television advertising can be purchased in some media markets and not in others. Swing voters, however, are not as geographically concentrated. Most of what a presidential campaign does in terms of advertising and candidate appearances will disseminate its messages to swing voters and non-swing voters alike. Perhaps as Internet campaigning develops (see chapter 8) it will be possible to send messages directly to swing voters while bypassing the more firmly committed; at present, however, such "micro-targeting" represents only a very small part of most candidates' communication efforts.

In sum, an aspiring political consultant seeking to make his or her mark as a campaign strategist could do worse than to specialize in appealing to swing voters. On the one hand, there is ample reason to think that swing voters are important. At the same time, we still have much to learn about identifying, targeting, and persuading such voters.

THE POLITICAL PROFESSIONALS RESPOND

V. Lance Tarrance Jr.

In the study of politics and government, and in particular of close elections, the search is on for the holy grail of electoral success: understanding the determinative swing voter—a type of voter who, according to Mayer, "could go either way" and "is not so solidly committed to one candidate or the other as to make all efforts at persuasion futile." There are three worldviews concerning swing voters, and these worldviews are often in conflict. Each seeks to identify swing voters and discover the dynamics of how swing voters reach their ultimate decision. The three can be classified as (1) the academic view, (2) the campaign strategist view, and (3) the media entertainment view. Methodologies vary across the three, regional and demographic differences may be identified, and exotic new groups (Internet first-time voters would be a recent example) may occasionally capture the attention of all three perspectives. The fact remains, however, that in today's polarized partisan politics, all political scientists, pollsters, and journalists wish to identify and target swing voters—the media entertainment world for their value in television coverage, the campaign strategist world for the key to political power that they possess, and the academic world for statistical verification and explanatory discourse.

The media entertainment world tends to take shortcuts in identifying swing voters, mostly by necessity given that reporters and news analysts often work in a thirty-second sound bite environment that is incompatible with complex and technical explanations of what actually constitutes a swing voter. As a result, this particular approach usually looks simply at "the middle"—that is, at independent and less committed voters, and what these individuals are saying to pollsters. It relies on public polls, like Gallup, to determine which way the less-certain and independent winds are blowing. Frequent surveys allow journalists to gain insights into pure partisan independence and into the psyches of those voters who "might change their mind" but say they lean toward a Republican or Democratic candidate. Thus, the media entertainment world depends mostly on nonbehavioral (attitudinal) models of election intention; in so doing, it provides only a partial lens through which to view voters.

The academic view helps to clarify issues related to citizens' perceptions of partisanship, particularly in the case of self-described independents. Scholarly surveys have shown that many such individuals (perhaps as many as one half) actually are disguised partisans;[1] to the extent that this is true, it means that party identification questions are not necessarily a good measure of who is likely to be a swing voter. Moreover, as revealed in many previous studies (see, for example, A. Campbell et al. 1960), so-called pure independents are anything but paragons of reason and civic virtue; rather, they are mostly nonideological in their policy views, poorly informed about political matters, generally uninterested in election participation, and so on. This characterization of swing voters did not make sense to political scientist V. O. Key who, in *The Responsible Electorate* (1966), looked at "switchers"— voters who did not support the same party over two consecutive elections—and concluded that they may be the real swing voters. In essence, Key said that we should forget the psychological approach and look at actual behavior when identifying swing voters. Using this approach, he found that the swing or switch voter was anything but apathetic; to the contrary, the switch voter appeared to be "a person who appraises the actions of government, who has policy preferences, and who relates his vote to those appraisals and preferences" (Key 1966, 58–59). In effect, Key rejected the self-identified independent as the prototype of a swing voter and tried to lead the academic world in a more meaningful direction.

Mayer has offered up a new way to identify swing voters; unfortunately, he offers another perceptual approach that suffers the same problem as the party identification model of independents. Mayer uses the feeling thermometer scale ranging from 0 to 100 degrees to measure favorable and unfavorable views of each presidential candidate. To Mayer, it is all about image, not past behavior. The "middle-awareness" group (scoring −15 to +15) is found to be less interested in following campaigns, less informed, and seemingly apathetic about politics generally. This is hardly a breakthrough, and few campaign strategists would employ such a measure to identify swing voters. Even Mayer acknowledges doubt when he notes that "whether swing voters have distinctive positions on specific issues like abortion, immigration, or health care is not clear"—an observation that dooms this approach from any practical application.

The campaign strategist world must work in a much more concrete environment than the two other worlds; attempting to use momentary self-perception, feeling thermometers, and other such "soft" measures ("Do you think you may change your mind between now and the November election?") are of limited value here. Campaign engineers must design minimum winning coalitions of 50-percent-plus-one, and there are no second-place trophies in this competition. To many political engineers, swing voters are split-ticket voters: easy-to-identify voters who already have proven their tendency to move back and forth across current or past ballots by not voting exclusively for candidates of either party. Within their surveys, campaign strategists look for those respondents who have in the past voted, or currently intend to vote, one way for president and the other way for Congress; or one way for governor and the other way for state treasurer; and so on. As David Broder of the *Washington Post* once explained, "this picture of the ticket splitter is closer to the kind of voter I imagine as determining the outcome of close elections" (see DeVries and Tarrance 1972, 14).

In his analysis of switch voting across elections, Key (1966) found a much more involved voter than is suggested by the self-perception models. Some years later, DeVries and Tarrance (1972, 61) also found split-ticket voters to be "slightly younger, somewhat more educated, somewhat more white-collar, and more suburban than the typical middle-class voter." This study offered up a new paradigm by identifying ticket splitters as the swing vote. Today, campaign strategists of both political parties often recalibrate the political universe as Republicans, Ticket Splitters, White Conservative Democrats, White Liberal Democrats, and African Americans or Hispanics, as the case may be. They then apply various statistical probabilities for needed success within each segment. Republican Party strategists typically target a two-to-one positive margin among ticket splitters for their minimum winning coalition, while Democrats usually target break-even percentages for their own winning coalition.

The identification and targeting of swing voters attract enormous attention. Media entertainment, campaign strategy, and academic professionals all expend enormous effort to this end. Even Hollywood has gotten in on the act: during the 2008 presidential election, film producers, in a didactic film about nonvoting called *Swing Vote* and starring Kevin Costner, used the apathetic voter model borrowed from the academic world presumably to embarrass nonvoters into participation. The campaign strategy world, like the media entertainment and academic worlds, has its own institutional biases, proclivities, and needs. However, it is the campaign strategy world that is truly on the line for generating successful election outcomes. And Key, the most visionary of academics, clearly pointed the way to the behavioral approach for the identification of swing voters. By reclassifying some voters as switch voters—later transformed by campaign strategists to ticket splitters—he demonstrated that it was this type of voter analysis that was crucial to understanding election outcomes. In general, past vote behavior is the best predictor of future swing voting. The campaign strategy world has taken note, and it is this world that runs the race.

---

[1] In *The Myth of the Independent Voter* (1992), Bruce Keith and his colleagues observed that most voters who say they are independents will confess to leaning toward one of the parties when asked follow-up questions. This phenomenon has been demonstrated over time in the American National Election Study and Gallup surveys, among others.

Notes

1. See, among others, Lazarsfeld, Berelson, and Gaudet (1944); A. Campbell et al. (1960); J. Campbell (2000); also, see chapters 1 and 2 in this volume.

2. For a summary of previous work on swing voters, from which much of the material in this article is drawn, see Mayer (2008).

3. These particular question wordings are taken from Gallup, but similar wordings and procedures were used by the Pew and Annenberg polls in 2008. For details, see Mayer (2008, chap. 8).

4. These are people who initially claim to be independent but, when asked, say they "lean" toward one party or the other.

5. The following draws on data reported in Mayer (2007, 380–382).

6. I focus here on congressional elections since they have been most intensively studied, but the same principles apply, to a greater or lesser extent, to other types of nonpresidential elections.

4 Voter Competence

Stephen C. Craig and Michael D. Martinez

Democratic theory has never been specific about how much information and knowledge is needed in order for individuals to be able to fulfill the obligations of effective citizenship. Most would agree, however, that at a minimum a basic understanding of the policy differences that exist between candidates for office, and between the parties they represent, is required. Without such an understanding, the public will be unable to cast its ballots wisely and, hence, unable to hold its elected leaders accountable. Unfortunately, more than half a century of empirical research has left the distinct impression that "[v]oters have a limited amount of information about politics, a limited knowledge of how government works, and a limited understanding of how governmental actions are connected to consequences of immediate concern to them" (Popkin 1991, 8).

Academics are not the only ones to have reached this conclusion. A poll sponsored by the McCormick Tribune Freedom Museum in 2006, for example, revealed that whereas just one in four Americans could name more than one of the five freedoms guaranteed by the First Amendment to the U.S. Constitution (freedom of speech, religion, press, assembly, and petition for redress of grievances), and one in one thousand could name all of them, 22 percent were able to name all five members of TV's cartoon family *The Simpsons* (more than half could name at least two) (see Grace 2006). Surveys done by the National Constitution Center show that

> [m]ore than a third [of Americans cannot] list any First Amendment rights; 42 percent think that the Constitution explicitly states that "the first language of the United States is English"; and 25 percent believe that Christianity was established by the Constitution as the official government religion. The young are even more ignorant than their parents and grandparents. About half of adults—but just 41 percent of teenagers—can name the three branches of government.... The vast majority of both adults and teens have no idea of when or by whom the Constitution was written. Among the teenagers, nearly 98 percent cannot name the Chief Justice of the United States (Jacoby 2008, 299–300).

To be sure, failure to identify the five freedoms or name the chief justice does not, in and of itself, signify that a person is incapable of casting a well-informed vote that is consistent with his or her political interests or values. But it does (or should) raise something of a red flag for anyone who believes that a certain "degree of civic and political knowledge is required to be a competent democratic citizen" (Galston 2001, 218)—and that the number of citizens who possess such knowledge is a leading indicator of the quality of democracy that exists in a nation, including our own.

In the following section, we provide a more complete overview of both the level and distribution of political knowledge in the United States; in doing so, we note how the public's informational shortcomings may help to shape the character of public opinion, at least on some issues. Next, in keeping with the central theme of this book, we assess the degree to which campaigns succeed in informing voters about the issues and about candidates' and parties' positions on those issues. Finally, we look at whether voters are able, notwithstanding the limited information that many of them possess, to make "rational" or "correct" choices when they go to the polls on election day. In conclusion, we note that while normative democratic theorists have reason to be alarmed by what the average citizen does *not* know, there is evidence that Americans are perhaps not quite as clueless as some contemporary social critics would have us believe (Jacoby 2008; Shenkman 2008).

Voter Knowledge and the Structure of Public Opinion

"The political ignorance of the American voter," according to Larry Bartels (1996, 194), "is one of the best-documented features of contemporary politics." In fact, this is not a recent development. For more than half a century (Berelson, Lazarsfeld, and McPhee 1954), one study after another has confirmed a basic fact: "popular levels of information about public affairs are, from the point of view of an informed observer, astonishingly low" (Converse 1975, 79). And even though these levels may fluctuate over time in response to changes in the political environment (Neuman, Just, and Crigler 1992; Delli Carpini and Keeter 1996; Popkin 1994; Hillygus and Shields 2008; see also the next section in this chapter), there has been no long-term increase in voter knowledge despite societal developments that should have produced some fairly dramatic changes in that direction.

Russell Dalton, for example, described a process of cognitive mobilization that supposedly "has raised the public's overall level of sophistication" by increasing citizens' "ability to acquire political information and [their] ability to process political information" (Dalton 2008, 19; see also Dalton 1984; Inglehart 1990). Most scholars agree that individual variations in political knowledge are a function of three basic elements: ability, motivation, and opportunity (Luskin 1990). The cognitive mobilization phenomenon addresses all three of these, especially with reference to two important trends: rising educational levels since the end of World War II (which should have made more people capable of learning and increased their motivation to be informed) and the development of television, radio, the Internet, and various other sources of political information (which provided people with more opportunities for learning).[1] Yet despite these changes, there is little to suggest that the American public is significantly better informed about politics and government today than it was fifty or sixty years ago (E. Smith 1989; Delli Carpini and Keeter 1996; S. Bennett 1996; Althaus 2003).[2] One can argue, of course, that information is not the best standard by which to judge the competence of mass electorates. According to Thomas Patterson (2006, 40–41), "[p]olitics is largely about the mobilization of bias, that is, the efforts of people to promote their beliefs and interests. A thoughtful vote is rooted in core values, not bits of information." Philip Converse (2000, 333), however, while conceding that "knowledge of minor facts, such as the length of terms of U.S. senators, cannot address what voters actually need to vote properly," maintained that "differences in knowledge of several such 'minor' facts are diagnostic of more profound differences in the amount and accuracy of contextual information voters bring to their judgments" (see also Neuman 1986; Delli Carpini and Keeter 1996).

A case can certainly be made that estimates of the (very low) levels of information possessed by voters are a reflection, to some degree, of shortcomings in the manner in which political knowledge is typically measured in opinion surveys. Jeffrey Mondak (2000, 2001; but see Sturgis, Allum, and Smith 2008), for example, observed that when respondents are asked factual questions and told that it's acceptable to say they "don't know" if they're unsure about an answer,[3] the result is that some of them will venture a guess, and some of these will guess correctly. Those who choose to guess and guess correctly will *appear* to be more knowledgeable than those who fail to guess (perhaps due to a lack of self-confidence) even though the two groups are, objectively speaking, equally knowledgeable. But when "don't know" responses are discouraged (or eliminated altogether; see M. Miller and Orr 2008), the proportion of respondents who provide correct answers is often at least somewhat higher. In a slightly different vein, Markus Prior and Arthur Lupia (2008) argued that standard measures of political knowledge are flawed because they fail to take into account that (1) some respondents know the answers to questions but lack the motivation to search their memories carefully enough to retrieve the information, and (2) even when it is not readily accessible in memory at the time of the interview, many people will be able to find the correct answer if given the time to do so. The authors' experimental data indicated that, as predicted, a fair number of those who appear to be "know-nothings" based on traditional measures can answer questions correctly when given a small incentive (in this case, $1 for each right answer) or extra time (twenty-four hours versus one minute; see Prior and Lupia 2008, 171) to complete the task.

All of the above is well and good, but, in the end, it does not alter the fact that a large segment of the public has been and remains woefully ignorant about virtually every aspect of American politics. The most thorough overview of this topic was provided by Michael Delli Carpini and Scott Keeter (1996), who examined nearly 3,700 questions in surveys conducted from 1940 to 1994 that tapped respondents' knowledge of the processes, participants, and policies of government in the United States and worldwide. They found that there were some things about which citizens were generally well informed; almost everyone, for example, knew who the president was, and most could identify certain other leading political figures of the day (such as the governor of their state). It also appears that a majority of citizens during this period had at least limited knowledge, if not always a full understanding, of many matters relating to the institutions and processes of American government (length of a president's term, role of the courts in determining constitutionality of laws, the meaning of such terms as "inflation" and "federal deregulation") and to policies and issues both domestic (the minimum wage, energy shortages, existence of a federal budget deficit) and foreign (which countries are/were communist, existence of a U.S. trade deficit with Japan, conflict between Israel and its adversaries in the Middle East). It is not difficult, however, to find huge gaps in the public's awareness of certain facts that are central to the debates and controversies that characterize contemporary political discourse. Less than one-third, for example, knew the substance of the Supreme Court's *Roe v. Wade* decision in 1986, the meaning of "affirmative action" in 1985 (one suspects that the figure for both of these questions would be somewhat higher today), or the nature of Saudi Arabia's government in 1990.[4]

What do things look like now? As any student or professor knows, essay tests and multiple choice tests often yield very different results—and the same is true for measures of political knowledge. Ask someone to name, without prompting, the U.S. vice president or the governor of her state, and there is a reasonably good chance that she will be unable to do so (the figures in a 2007 poll were 69 percent and 66 percent, respectively, which actually represented a decline from a similar survey conducted in 1989[5]). Even when survey respondents are presented with a range of possible answers, and even when the options are reduced to a bare minimum (as with which party holds a majority of seats in the U.S. House; see below), the results are not always impressive—although many people do exhibit a greater *recognition* of political facts than is suggested by questions that employ an open-ended format. With this distinction in mind, a survey conducted in fall 2009 confirmed that there still is much that the public does not know about the contextual details of American politics. Based on a multiple-choice methodology, results indicated that

- 75 percent knew that the Democrats held a majority of seats in the U.S. House;[6]
- 65 percent could identify Sonia Sotomayor as the newest member of the Supreme Court;
- 61 percent knew that health spending was higher in the United States than in most of Europe;
- 53 percent knew that the current unemployment rate was close to 10 percent;
- 40 percent could identify Glenn Beck as a TV/radio host;
- 33 percent could identify Ben Bernanke as chair of the U.S. Federal Reserve;
- 28 percent knew that the current U.S. troop level in Afghanistan was around seventy thousand;
- 23 percent knew that the "cap and trade" proposal dealt with energy and the environment; and
- 18 percent could identify Max Baucus as chair of the Senate Finance Committee.

Although one could reasonably argue that anyone who knew all of these facts was *extremely* well informed, the bad news is that almost no one did. Of twelve total questions asked in the Pew survey (only nine are listed above), just 44 percent of respondents answered six correctly, 25 percent answered eight, 12 percent answered ten, and 2 percent answered all twelve (Pew Research Center for the People and the Press 2009b).

What are the consequences of such low levels of political knowledge among the American public? In the grand scheme of things, does it really matter all that much whether citizens can name their state's governor or know which party controls Congress? According to William Galston (2001, 221–222), there are a number of ways in which "civic knowledge" is important in a democracy. Among these are the following: First, knowledge helps us to "understand the impact of public policies on our interests" and, as a result, to promote those interests more effectively through political action, including voting. Second, "[u]nless citizens possess a basic level of civic knowledge . . . it is difficult for them to understand political events or to integrate new information into an existing framework. (By analogy, imagine trying to make sense of the flow of events in a sports competition for which one does not know the rules of the game.)" Third, knowledge "can alter our views on specific issues," from immigration policy to national security to the death penalty. Fourth and fifth, citizens with higher levels of knowledge tend to be more supportive of democratic values (such as tolerance) and more politically active.

We will return to some of these themes later in the chapter. In the meantime, it should be understood that political knowledge is not evenly distributed throughout the electorate. To the contrary, studies have shown that knowledge levels are significantly higher among those who are politically and/or socially advantaged—that is, among individuals with higher incomes, more formal education, men, whites, and young people. Thus, when the Pew Research Center asked twenty-three political information questions in a 2007 survey, it found that certain types of people were much more likely than others to fall into the "high knowledge" category (fifteen or more correct answers): 63 percent of college graduates (versus 20 percent of those with a high-school diploma or less);[7] 55 percent of respondents with incomes of more than $100,000 (versus 35 percent of those earning between $30–50,000, and 14 percent of those earning less than $20,000); 45 percent of men (versus 25 percent of women); 37 percent of whites (versus 24 percent of blacks); and 43 percent of those aged 65 and older (versus 15 percent of those aged 18–29) (see Pew Research Center for the People and the Press 2007). Further, although there is some variability, it does not appear that such "knowledge gaps" have changed much over time: those who once had high levels of political knowledge still do (relatively speaking), while those who never did have high knowledge haven't gained much ground.[8]

An occasional point of difference among scholars has been the question of whether political knowledge is unidimensional (with those who know more in one area generally knowing more in others as well), or whether it is more domain specific (with citizens paying more attention to, and being better informed about, issues that are personally relevant or about which they care deeply for whatever reason). To the extent that the latter is true, we would expect to find patterns of knowledge that reflect "group differences in experiences, interest, and access to information," and a citizenry that is divided into numerous "issue publics" (Delli Carpini and Keeter 1996, 138; see also Converse 1964; Iyengar 1990; Krosnick 1990; Hutchings 2003) whose members are better informed primarily about the issues central to their concerns (Y. Kim 2009, 225).[9] Indeed, there is some evidence that is consistent with the issue publics model, for example, that blacks are better informed than whites about racial issues, and women are as knowledgeable as men about gender-related issues and issues related to local politics (Delli Carpini and Keeter 1996, 175; see also Hutchings 2003; Price et al. 2006). As a general rule, though, the kinds of people who are either well or poorly informed tend to be well or poorly informed across the board (Neuman 1986; E. Smith 1989; S. Bennett 2003).

At first glance, one factor that does *not* appear to play a large role here is partisanship. When the focus is on knowledge of basic political facts, Democrats often are found to be less informed than Republicans in part because the former are disproportionately drawn from elements of society (lower social status, blacks, women) that possess less information for reasons having little to do with their party preferences; however, observed differences between partisan groups tend to be fairly small. Thus, the 2007 Pew survey placed 69 percent of self-identified Democrats in either the "high" (correct answers to at least fifteen of twenty-three questions) or "medium" (correct answers to ten to fourteen questions) information category, compared with 74 percent of Republicans and 64 percent of independents. Looking at the 2009 Pew knowledge data another way, the mean number of correct answers (out of twelve questions) was 5.7 for both Republicans and independents, versus 5.0 for Democrats (see Pew Research Center for the People and the Press 2007, 2009b).

Against this backdrop, an interesting controversy emerged following the election of Barack Obama in 2008. A survey of 512 Obama voters nationwide, conducted by Zogby International on behalf of former talk radio host, author, and conservative Web site publisher John Ziegler, included twelve multiple-choice questions that tested respondents' "knowledge of statements and scandals associated with the presidential tickets during the campaign." Results indicated that an overwhelming majority (more than 80 percent) correctly named Sarah Palin as "the candidate with a pregnant teenage daughter" and as "the candidate associated with a $150,000 wardrobe purchased by her political party," and correctly identified John McCain as "the candidate who was unable to identify the number of houses he owned"; in contrast, 83 percent "failed to correctly answer that Obama had won his first election by getting all of his opponents removed from the ballot," 56 percent were unaware that "Obama started his political career at the home of two former members of the Weather Underground" (a domestic terrorist group in the 1960s), and 72 percent "did not correctly identify [Joe] Biden as the candidate who had to quit a previous campaign for president because he was found to have plagiarized a speech." On a more neutral note, 57 percent of Obama voters failed to identify the Democrats as having a controlling majority of seats in both houses of Congress during the period leading up to the election. Overall, just 54 percent were able to provide correct answers to at least six of the twelve questions (Zogby International 2008). This story quickly produced a storm of reaction, not only from Obama supporters but from professional pollsters and political analysts who pointed out that many of the questions asked in the survey were biased and misleading (Allen 2008; Bialik 2008; Silver 2008). One other obvious shortcoming of the poll is that, even if the questions were valid, it provided no basis for comparison between those who supported Obama versus those who supported McCain.[10]

In fact, one does not have to look very hard to find examples of limited knowledge on the Republican side. In 2004, for example, a national survey revealed that "Americans who plan to vote for President [George W.] Bush have many incorrect assumptions about his foreign policy positions. [John] Kerry supporters, on the other hand, are largely accurate" in assessing their candidate's positions (Kull 2004). More recently, a poll done in July 2009 showed that 58 percent of Republicans (compared with 7 percent of Democrats) either did not believe that President Obama was born in the United States (28 percent) or weren't sure (30 percent) (Thrush 2009). Earlier in 2009, more than two months into Obama's presidency, only 46 percent of Republicans correctly identified his religious affiliation as Christian (17 percent thought he was Muslim) (Pew Research Center for the People and the Press 2009a).[11] Results such as these bring to mind the distinction between being *uninformed* (not knowing what the facts are) and being *misinformed* (being confidently wrong about those facts) (Kuklinski et al. 2000). Not knowing Barack Obama's religious preferences is one thing, but believing him to be a Muslim in the face of numerous news reports to the contrary is quite another. According to James Kuklinski and colleagues (2000, 794–795), many people overrate the accuracy and reliability of their factual beliefs; when they do, their policy preferences may be very different than would otherwise be the case.

It is likely that being misinformed is, to some extent, a function of one's partisan leanings; that is, some people may accept the accuracy of (false) information that is consistent with their partisanship, while rejecting the accuracy of (true) information that is not. Following the U.S. invasion of Iraq in 2003, a national opinion poll revealed that more than half the public believed that Iraq either was directly involved in carrying out the terrorist attacks in New York City and Arlington, Virginia, on September 11, 2001, or gave substantial support to the al-Qaeda terror network without being directly involved; more than 20 percent thought that weapons of mass destruction (WMD) had been discovered in Iraq after the incumbent regime fell; and one-fourth said the invasion was supported by most people in other countries around the world—all of the above statements are factually incorrect. As we anticipated, a substantially higher proportion of Bush supporters were misinformed (68 percent on Iraq links to al-Qaeda, 31 percent on WMD, and 36 percent on world opinion) on these matters than respondents who planned to vote for a Democrat in 2004 (31 percent, 10 percent, and 11 percent, respectively).[12] Further, Bush supporters who said they followed the news "very closely" (and especially those who watched Fox News) were the most likely to hold incorrect beliefs[13] and, perhaps not incidentally, the most likely to endorse U.S. military action in Iraq (86 percent, compared with between 53 percent and 76 percent of Bush supporters with a lower level of news attentiveness, and less than one-quarter of all Democratic nominee supporters).[14]

We do not intend to single out Republicans since partisans on both sides, as they go about deciding "which information to attend to and how to interpret that information," will tend to "strive for consistency" with their preexisting attitudes and beliefs (Kuklinski et al. 2000, 794); in other words, dissonant information is often ignored or disregarded. This does, however, raise questions about the degree to which ordinary voters are able to acquire information, process that information, and then use it to make decisions about which candidates and policies most closely conform to their political interests and values. Let us consider, then, the "educability" of the American voter within the context of a campaign system that is often criticized for making it harder rather than easier for people to fulfill their role as democratic citizens.

Campaigns and Political Learning

We began this chapter by suggesting that democratic accountability depends, at a minimum, upon citizens having an understanding of the important policy differences[15] that exist between candidates and parties. While conceding that voters may be ill-equipped "to handle every possible situation that comes their way," Patterson (2006, 42) argued that "the critical question is not whether voters are competent but whether election campaigns foster or frustrate their effort to cast a thoughtful vote. Campaigns can be run in ways that make it easier for voters to render a thoughtful judgment about the candidates, or they can be run in ways that make the task considerably more complicated." Political campaigns in the United States are not, according to Patterson, very "voter friendly" due to a number of factors, including (1) "the capacity of interest groups in a money-driven electoral process to pull candidates away from the center . . . where most voters are, and therefore making it harder for them to determine which party better represents their interests" (44–45);[16] (2) a steady drumbeat of negativity as candidates attack each other relentlessly and many citizens are worn down "to the point where they begin to lose interest in the electoral process as a whole" (47); (3) campaign coverage by the news media that focuses on "strategy, tactics, and maneuvering" while diverting attention from "larger issues" of public policy and the candidates' proposals for how to deal with those issues (48–49); and (4) a complex system of election structures and laws (frequent elections, nomination by primaries, separate ballots for executive and legislature) that make it difficult to be fully informed, and a lack of competition for many offices that gives voters "little reason to invest time and energy" in races where the outcome is never in doubt (49–53). In sum, a credible case can be made that campaigns "provide little, if any, information to the electorate—and that whatever information is disseminated by the campaigns is distorted by the mass media and even ignored by voters" (Alvarez 1997, 7). Especially when candidates fail to take clear positions or address the issues of greatest concern to their constituents (Shepsle 1972; Page 1978; Tomz and Van Houweling 2009; but see Franklin 1991; Ansolabehere, Snyder, and Stewart 2001; Spiliotes and Vavreck 2002), it is hardly surprising that there is a high degree of confusion and uncertainty about who stands for what.

Yet even if Patterson's observations are correct (and with one exception, we believe they generally are), there still is evidence indicating that much of the knowledge that citizens do possess regarding candidate and party differences is acquired within the context of spirited electoral competition. Campaigns provide the "single most compelling incentive [for the average person] to think about government" (Riker 1989, 1), and the instability in public opinion polls that often occurs over the course of a presidential election is thought by many scholars to be a direct result of information flow; that is, as additional information about candidates and issues is acquired, voters' preferences may shift as they become better able to identify the choices that are consistent with their preexisting political attitudes, beliefs, and interests (Gelman and King 1993). Indeed, numerous studies reveal that a significant amount of learning occurs during campaigns (Berelson, Lazarsfeld, and McPhee 1954; T. Patterson and McClure 1976; Bartels 1993; Ansolabehere and Iyengar 1995; Alvarez 1997; T. Patterson 2002; Althaus 2003; see also Arceneaux 2006, as well as chapters 1 and 6 in this volume). While such learning is most likely to be observed in high-visibility presidential contests (because the information flow is greater), we also would expect to find evidence of it in some races for lower office (where candidates will initially be less familiar to voters than their counterparts at the top of the ticket).[17]

The basic pattern, then, is clear: at least in high-visibility races, a significant amount of learning occurs during campaigns. The origins of that learning are not yet fully understood, however. Communication scholars agree that, for most people most of the time, the primary source of campaign information is the mass media. Despite their usual preoccupation with the horse race (campaign strategy and poll results) (see Sigelman and Bullock 1991; Just et al. 1996; Cappella and Jamieson 1997), and with scandals and candidate gaffes (Sabato, Stencel, and Lichter 2000), both newspapers and television provide a considerable amount of issue-related information to voters. Not everyone would agree with this assessment, of course. In their landmark study of the 1972 election, Thomas Patterson and Robert McClure (1976, 54) concluded that television news "may be fascinating. It may be highly entertaining. But it is simply not informative." As for newspapers, the absence of local coverage in Pittsburgh due to a strike had no noticeable impact on voter knowledge in the 1992 campaign; the evidence in this case was, according to Mondak (1995b, 99), "shattering for any theory of print superiority." Even less respect is afforded a third channel of campaign communication: paid ads, which often contain more issue content than typically acknowledged (West 2009; Geer 1998) but are regarded by many critics as little more than "self-serving puffery and distortion" (Popkin 1992, 164).

Unfortunately, there is no consensus as to the relative contribution of different communication channels to the learning that takes place during campaigns. Some studies conclude that voters learn more from reading newspapers than from watching television news programs and that, in fact, the latter adds little or nothing to a voter's ability to place candidates on key issues (T. Patterson and McClure 1976; Robinson and Levy 1986); others indicate that TV news may be a significant source of issue awareness after all (Neuman, Just, and Crigler 1992; Bartels 1993; Graber 2001; Weaver and Drew 2001).[18] As for campaign ads, Patterson and McClure (1976, 116–117) reported that "[o]n every single issue emphasized in presidential commercials [in 1972], persons with high exposure to television advertising showed a greater increase in knowledge [about the candidates' positions] than persons with low exposure." Stephen Ansolabehere and Shanto Iyengar (1995), in their experimental study of races for governor and U.S. Senate in California, reached a similar conclusion: "Though political advertisements are generally ridiculed as a serious form of campaign communication, our results demonstrate that they enlighten voters and enable them to take account of issues and policies when choosing between the candidates" (59). Not everyone is ready to jump on the campaign ad bandwagon, however. For every Freedman, Franz, and Goldstein (2004) or Brians and Wattenberg (1996, 185), who argued that "political advertising contributes to a well-informed electorate," there are scholars in the opposite camp whose findings suggest otherwise (Zhao and Bleske 1998; Weaver and Drew 2001; Huber and Arceneaux 2007). Further research is obviously required to determine which of these perspectives is correct.

Another unsettled question has to do with whether campaigns, in general, tend to narrow or widen the information gap that exists between the relatively more and less engaged segments of the electorate. Whereas some studies indicate that people who are more active or knowledgeable to begin with are the ones most likely to acquire information during a campaign (Craig, Kane, and Gainous 2005; Stevens 2005; Nadeau et al. 2008), others conclude that exposure to campaigns primarily benefits those with limited knowledge (Alvarez 1997; Freedman, Franz, and Goldstein 2004; see also Moore 1987; Arceneaux 2006; and Holbrook 2002b, who reports mixed results).[19] Given that knowledge is correlated with one's overall interest in politics (Delli Carpini and Keeter 1996; Converse 2000), and that interest levels tend to rise among marginally involved citizens during campaigns (especially presidential campaigns) (Althaus 2003),[20] it is reasonable to assume that information gains will be concentrated closer to the bottom than to the top of the knowledge chain. The evidence to date suggests, however, that this is not invariably the case.

Finally, if campaigns facilitate learning to some degree, does it matter whether the tone of the campaign is positive or negative? Once again, the answer is a firm maybe. Negative campaigning, and negative advertising in particular, is frequently defended for providing information without which it would be "much more difficult for the voters to make intelligent choices about the people they elect to public office" (Mayer 1996, 450; see also Geer 2006). As for whether voters learn more from positive or negative ads, the jury is out. Some studies show little difference between the two (Ansolabehere and Iyengar 1995), while others suggest that negativity promotes greater learning (Brians and Wattenberg 1996; Kahn and Kenney 2000, 2004). If the latter is true, it could be due to any of several factors, including (1) the higher issue content of negative ads (Geer 2000, 2006; West 2009); (2) the propensity of negative ads to heighten feelings of anxiety, thereby causing voters to seek out more information about candidates' issue stands or other attributes (Marcus and MacKuen 1993); (3) the tendency for people to have greater recall of negative ads (Brians and Wattenberg 1996; but see Geer and Geer 2003); and (4) the tendency for people to give greater weight to negative information than to positive information (Lau 1985; A. Holbrook et al. 2001). Nevertheless, at the risk of repeating ourselves, we must again conclude that further research is needed.[21]

The practical importance of political knowledge (and of all the issues that we have raised in the chapter thus far) is, of course, the belief that having more of it will affect how people vote, specifically, that it will assist them in holding leaders accountable and in casting a ballot that is consistent with their political values, beliefs, and interests. In the next section, we will look at whether this is indeed the case.

Casting an Informed Vote

Despite the accumulated evidence that Americans' overall awareness about politics leaves much to be desired, some scholars still argue, in V. O. Key's (1966, 7) memorable words, that "voters are not fools." According to this view, the lack of specific knowledge about certain political facts or particular office-holders does not necessarily undermine the ability of voters with limited information to make meaningful political choices. In fact, there are three separate theories that allegedly explain how it is the electorate can make choices that generally reflect its political interests: (1) retrospective voting, (2) the miracle of aggregation, and (3) cue-taking. In this section, we will briefly discuss each and explain why each still leaves us with the feeling that our explanatory glass is, at best, only half full.

Retrospective Voting

Baseline political polls now commonly ask voters whether they believe the country (or state) is headed "in the right direction" or is "off on the wrong track." Even voters with minimal awareness of policy debates in Washington or their state capital still have some idea of whether it is getting harder or easier to make ends meet, whether most people seem to be able to find and keep good jobs, whether the streets are getting safer or more dangerous, whether traffic is flowing better or getting more congested, whether America is respected or reviled abroad, and so on. People who use their votes as rewards or punishment don't really need to know how the country got to its current condition; they simply need to have some idea of who was in charge when we started moving in the right direction or veered off on the wrong track. Those who cast their ballots based on "vengeance or rewards" (Key 1942) are known as *retrospective voters*.

Although retrospective voting by definition includes votes cast based on any politically relevant conditions (including the state of foreign affairs and social policy), most research on the topic examines the effects of economic evaluations on voter preference. Investigations of retrospective economic voting have led to a curious puzzle: whereas aggregate analyses show that incumbent parties generally fare better at the polls (winning more elections, receiving a higher percentage of the vote) when economic growth is robust (Kramer 1971), there is only weak and somewhat inconsistent evidence that individual voters who are personally better off are more likely than those who are struggling financially to support incumbent parties and candidates (Grafstein 2009). Instead of thinking just about their own pocketbooks, voters appear mostly to weigh the state of the nation's economy and, to a lesser extent, the fortunes of citizens most like themselves when casting their ballots (Kinder and Kiewiet 1979, 1981; Kinder, Adams, and Gronke 1989; but see Markus 1988, 1992). In short, most retrospective voters seem to evaluate their leaders through a national (or "sociotropic") frame rather than through a personal (or "pocketbook") frame.

In his classic treatise, Morris Fiorina (1981) argued that retrospective voting is common among those with both low *and* high political sophistication. Further research, however, has looked more closely at whether higher levels of political knowledge promote pocketbook or sociotropic voting. One view is that while everyone can make some judgment about whether they are struggling or prospering personally, the natural tendency might be to attribute personal successes more to hard work and to attribute family financial squeezes to idiosyncratic bad luck or life transitions—thereby discounting the effects that national economic policy might have in shaping either personal good fortunes or struggles. According to this view, only the most knowledgeable people who are able to connect the dots between their personal financial conditions and macro fiscal policies are likely to cast pocketbook votes (Gomez and Wilson 2006). Other research suggests that knowledge of national economic conditions, such as inflation and unemployment rates, is more accessible to voters with higher political knowledge, which in turn increases the likelihood of sociotropic voting among those who are more sophisticated (Goren 1997; Godbout and Bélanger 2007). People with higher levels of political knowledge also appear to be more sensitive to structural political conditions in casting retrospective votes, weighing economic outcomes less in open-seat elections than when incumbents seek reelection (Godbout and Bélanger 2007), and attributing responsibility for economic conditions to both the president and Congress (Gomez and Wilson 2003).

Overall, the empirical evidence suggests that political knowledge has an effect on the weight people attach to economic assessments in determining their vote choices. If more voters had high levels of political knowledge, we would expect that governments would be held even more accountable for economic outcomes than they are currently, especially when incumbents seek reelection under conditions of exceptional clarity of responsibility (Powell and Whitten 1993). Conversely, low levels of political knowledge may allow governments to escape responsibility for poor economic outcomes or to receive less of an electoral benefit from good economic outcomes than might otherwise be the case. The irony is that presidents and other incumbents often get more credit and blame than they deserve for their management of the economy, which is much more likely to be affected by global economic cycles and fiscal policies of central bankers than by actions taken by elected leaders. Nevertheless, while retrospective evaluations are relatively easy to come by, political knowledge does appear to enhance voters' ability to use those evaluations when casting their ballots.

The Miracle of Aggregation

Public opinion is the aggregated sum of millions of individual opinions on any given issue, and while low levels of knowledge may distort the beliefs of many people, some argue that voters' errors in judgment will more or less cancel each other out. As a result, the balance of public opinion *as a whole* rests in the hands of those who actually have and can successfully express well-considered issue positions. Converse's seminal essay titled "The Nature of Belief Systems in Mass Publics" (1964) showed that only a few people had reasonably well-thought-out and tightly knit political beliefs, whereas most Americans had unstable and incoherent opinions on most policy issues, characterized by a very low "signal to noise" ratio. Although the image of most people providing responses to survey questions more or less at random is not a flattering one, the notion of "white noise" or random error suggests that those ill-formed opinions might not matter in the aggregate if, for example, roughly half of respondents with no true opinion on an issue said they were "liberal" on that issue and the other half said they were "conservative"; that is, if errors in political judgment basically cancel each other out, then the minority of Americans who *do* hold well-formed, stable, and coherent beliefs on any given issue will determine what public opinion as a whole looks like on that issue. Looking at it another way, imagine a hypothetical ballot measure that is confusing in its wording but, if passed, would make everyone in the state better off. Objectively, everyone should vote for the proposition, but many people have trouble deciphering the ballot language and are unsure what the proposal would actually do. Lupia (2001) observed that under those conditions, even if the probability of any single individual deciding to vote for the proposal barely exceeds the chance of a simple coin flip, it is almost certain that the collective decision represented by millions of individuals' votes put together would result in passage of the universally beneficial proposal. Over time, then, while many people may appear to change their minds randomly from one time to the next, the "miracle of aggregation" produces an impressive stability of opinion for public opinion as a whole.[22]

Aggregate analyses support this view by showing that when public opinion as a whole *does* change, it seems to do so in sensible ways. For example, shifts in opinion generally track commentary by media anchors and experts, who are widely perceived by the public as (relatively speaking) objective sources of information, but not to commentary by interest group representatives who have axes to grind. Further, public preferences seem to respond to pronouncements by popular presidents, but not to those by unpopular presidents (Page, Shapiro, and Dempsey 1987). There also is evidence that the public updates its preferences based on what the government is doing; that is, as government policies move in one direction, either left or right, public opinion will often signal when it's time to tap on the brakes. For example, as government increases spending in a particular policy area, such as defense, public support for even more spending in that area tends to wane. Thus, while most individuals lack concrete information about how much the government actually spends on defense, education, foreign aid, or anything else, the public mood still acts something like a thermostat (Stimson 1999; Wlezien 1995), letting government know if its policies are getting too hot or too cold.

Many scholars, however, are not so sanguine about the assumption that errors among the least informed citizens balance out in the aggregate, and they suggest that overall public opinion might well be different if the public were more fully informed. For one thing, misperceptions of facts are usually one-sided, as illustrated by people's beliefs about the number of minorities (including gays and lesbians) in the population, the proportion of immigrants who are here illegally, and the amount of money spent by the federal government on foreign aid. Those estimates are rarely too low, and are sometimes too high by orders of magnitude. Perceptions (and misperceptions) of facts such as these are interwoven into value orientations, and thus may help shape abstract principles and the ways in which those principles are (or are not) applied in forming particular opinions (Hochschild 2001). In some cases, specific knowledge about a policy proposal is closely related to opinion about the policy, as illustrated by a Gallup (1977) report issued during the ratification debate on the Panama Canal treaties championed by the Carter administration in the 1970s. Gallup's polling data showed that people who had not heard or read about the debate were solidly opposed to ratification (by a margin of 39 percent to 23 percent), but that people who were aware were more closely divided in their opinion (48 percent opposed, 40 percent in favor), and those who were informed about three key facts of the treaties' provisions tilted slightly in support of the treaties (by a narrow margin of 51 percent to 46 percent).[23]

Gallup's findings on the Panama Canal treaties debate are illustrative of the potential for knowledge effects on policy preferences (see also Gilens 2001), but simple contrasts of the opinions of the most and least informed can be misleading if political knowledge depends in part on social class. For example, working class people have both lower levels of political knowledge *and* more isolationist opinions on foreign policy, so it is not clear whether their relative isolationism stems from their low knowledge or their class interests. Careful analyses tackle this problem by estimating the differences in opinion between high-knowledge and low-knowledge people *within* certain social categories; for example, looking at the differences in opinions between Catholics who are more knowledgeable and Catholics who are less knowledgeable. At the same time, these analyses estimate the effects of political knowledge on the opinions of members of other groups, including women, men, blacks, young, middle-aged, old, married, single, union members, occupation groups, income groups, people living in different regions of the country, Republicans, Democrats, independents, and so on. The cumulative contrasts give us an idea of what public opinion on any issue would look like if *everyone* had higher levels of information, but retained their basic demographic and partisan characteristics.[24]

Results of these analyses show that lower knowledge does bias collective opinion on a variety of issues, although the effects of knowledge vary from issue to issue and group to group. If, hypothetically, all members of the public were fully informed, collective public opinion would be more pro-choice on abortion, more supportive of the principle of affirmative action, more supportive of parental leave policies, and less supportive of prayer in schools than public opinion polls have shown it to be. Conservatives, for their part, would find consolation with a more knowledgeable electorate that would be more supportive of free market solutions to health insurance problems, more supportive of decreased spending on welfare, and more hawkish on the federal deficit (Althaus 2003, 128–138; also Delli Carpini and Keeter 1996). Similarly, an "enlightened public" that had the expertise of a Ph.D. in economics would likely be less concerned about the possible negative effects of business profits and executive salaries being too high, technology displacing workers, companies downsizing and outsourcing jobs, and trade agreements between the United States and other countries (Caplan 2007, 50–93).

Thus, the "miracle of aggregation" does not entirely temper our concerns about the implications of low knowledge on the bias in public opinion. It is *not* the case that about half of the less knowledgeable people are more liberal and half are more conservative than one would expect based on their interests, objectively defined. Rather, it appears to us that a more informed electorate would likely be more liberal on some (mostly social) issues and more conservative on other (mostly redistributive) issues. Because a more informed electorate might possess a different set of collective preferences about both kinds of policy, the issue coalitions currently needed to win in general elections may be at least partly a function of the relatively low levels of knowledge present in the American electorate.

Cue-taking

There is some debate about whether cues help people with low levels of political knowledge to reach vote decisions that are similar to the decisions of individuals with higher levels of knowledge. Without knowing a lot of detailed facts about policy, players, or institutions, voters might rely on a variety of heuristics, or cues, to lead them to make reasonable choices in the voting booth. Every day, people make scores of snap judgments based on limited and somewhat biased information, so it seems hardly a stretch to suggest that many people can make a reasonable choice between candidates with only limited information. Analyses of both experimental simulations and survey data from actual elections led Richard Lau and David Redlawsk (1997) to the conclusion that about 70 percent of voters "vote correctly"—that is, they make the same choice they would have if they possessed full information; the estimated proportion is even higher when choices are relatively easier (fewer candidates, clearer issue differences, roughly equal resources for the competing campaigns). But even when choices are slightly more difficult, the fact that a supermajority "gets it right" suggests that a limited amount of information can get most voters a long way.

There is no shortage of cues available to help the average voter try to make sense of a blizzard of potential information; the real question is whether cues are helpful in getting voters to a decision that actually reflects their interests and values. Some cues from the campaign apparently do help, as Lupia (1994) found in his analysis of multiple referenda on insurance reform in California. Though the provisions in those proposals were highly technical, the preferences of those who were knowledgeable about the positions advocated by the insurance industry on various propositions were very similar to those of voters with more "encyclopedic" knowledge of specific provisions in the propositions; in other words, the cues provided by elite groups in the debate served much the same purpose politically as more detailed knowledge about the proposals themselves. If voters have some information about who the protagonists are, they can often get on the "right" side without knowing too much about what all the fuss between the protagonists is about.

Cues are useful substitutes for actual knowledge to the extent that they are relatively accurate, relevant, and available to those who need them the most. Unfortunately, those conditions often fail to hold. When voters look for shortcuts, they are not necessarily seeking the most accurate predictors of information about the candidates that they can find. Rather, they often employ the "drunkard's search" for the information that is most accessible and helps them to paint some picture of the candidate in their heads, accurate or not (Popkin 1991). For example, some people use readily available gender stereotypes to help construct images of relatively unknown female candidates, but those stereotypes often lead people to believe that female candidates are more liberal than they actually are (Koch 2002; King and Matland 2003). Like other heuristics, gender stereotypes have developed over many generations to help humans adapt to unfamiliar situations, but that does not mean that these heuristics are accurate or relevant in electoral settings (Kuklinski and Quirk 2000; Kuklinski and Hurley 1994). Even cues developed within the context of elections, such as partisanship, can overwhelm the role played by candidate policy positions in voter decision making, thereby making the vote choice less a reflection of the voter's preferences than we might expect (Rahn 1993; Arceneaux 2008).[25] Moreover, there is some debate about whether cues help less knowledgeable citizens to reach decisions that approximate choices they would have made with more information. While there is some evidence that endorsements can improve unsophisticated voters' decisions (Boudreau 2009; Arceneaux and Kolodny 2009a), it appears that the use of partisanship as a cue helps to produce "correct" votes more among the *most* politically knowledgeable but produces more "errors" among the *less* politically knowledgeable (Lau, Andersen, and Redlawsk 2008). In effect, then, partisanship may be a more psychologically accessible and useful cue to high-knowledge voters, who need it the least.

The question about whether votes or election results would be different if more voters were better informed is complicated by the fact that political knowledge is concentrated among groups in society (higher education, higher income, men, whites) who are naturally more likely to vote Republican, so simple comparisons of the vote choices between politically knowledgeable and politically naïve voters might simply reflect the class, gender, racial, and other demographic cleavages that exist in contemporary American society. One approach to overcoming this problem is to model vote choice as a function of a "kitchen sink" full of demographic and partisan variables, political knowledge, plus the interactions between knowledge and other variables, thereby producing estimates that can be used to simulate the aggregate vote of a fully informed citizenry that otherwise retains its basic demographic characteristics. The most comprehensive study of this type shows that politically knowledgeable people appear to vote differently than those with less political knowledge but who are otherwise like them; however, the type of bias that is present depends on the electoral context. In particular, low levels of knowledge in the electorate (as compared to a hypothetical fully informed electorate) produce about a 2 percent tilt toward Democratic candidates *and* a 5 percent tilt toward incumbent candidates of both parties in presidential elections (Bartels 1996). Once again, it appears to us that errors among the less knowledgeable voters do not simply "cancel out"; rather, there are real consequences of the low levels of knowledge evident in the American electorate (see also Duch, Palmer, and Anderson 2000).

Conclusion

Reflecting on nearly a half century of research on the political sophistication of the American electorate, Converse (2000, 331) observed that "where political information is concerned, the mean level is very low but the variance is very high." The data and research reviewed in this chapter underscore the first half of Converse's characterization and give us pause about whether most Americans fulfill the basic obligations of democratic citizenship. As we have seen, many people lack information about the leaders, institutions, and policies at the center of American political life, and there is reason to believe that the lack of basic knowledge has very real implications for both the shape of public opinion and the choices that people make in the voting booth.

At the same time, Converse's observation about the diversity in the level of information in the mass public is often underappreciated. While there are a great many "know-nothings" in contemporary American politics, there are also a few "know-it-alls" who recognize most of our leaders and are quite conversant about a lot of what those leaders are doing. Indeed, this group embodies the counterfactual that enabled Scott Althaus (2003) and Larry Bartels (1996) to estimate the significance of the overall low levels of political knowledge in the public as a whole. The presence of some high-knowledge voters, plus a few others who manage to piece together reasonable political choices for themselves from imperfect information, leads us to believe that the glass of voter competence is far from empty. But for many citizens, the lack of motivation to overcome severe limits in their information levels leads to choices that do not truly reflect their own political interests. That diversity in voter competence, thus, leaves us holding a glass that remains only about half full.

Many campaigns implicitly recognize the variation in competence among voters by working through a variety of group opinion leaders. The assumption here is that most such leaders (union officials, prominent businesspeople, influential ministers, and veteran political organizers, among others) are, relatively speaking, politically savvy and both able and willing to assist candidates in (1) connecting their messages to group members' concerns and (2) disseminating the campaign's basic themes to the majority of voters whose relevant political knowledge may be limited, especially for "down ballot" races. Despite a limited base of information, voters (or at least those who make it to the polls on election day) *will* ultimately make a choice. The challenge for candidates is to craft a message that allows their campaigns to fill in some of the blanks in a way that resonates with segments of the electorate whose support is essential to victory.

THE POLITICAL PROFESSIONALS RESPOND

Mark M. Blumenthal

I wish Craig and Martinez's chapter could be required reading for anyone who participates in, writes about, or otherwise pontificates on the subject of American politics. I say that not because I question the competence of the American electorate, but because Craig and Martinez do an exemplary job reviewing the "half century of empirical research" showing the limited information, knowledge, and understanding of politics and government among voters. I restate their theme because we simply cannot repeat it enough. If I had to choose one piece of advice to offer aspiring campaign strategists, it would be this: you can almost never underestimate the level of information about politics and government possessed by the voters who typically decide the outcome of elections.

Consider some anecdotal evidence. Over a span of nearly twenty years as a campaign pollster, I had the chance to conduct or observe hundreds of voter focus groups—informal, unstructured discussions with eight to ten participants that, while not random sample surveys, do typically strive to roughly represent a particular population of interest. In political campaigns, focus groups of "persuadable voters" (those who have not yet formed strong attachments to the candidates) are often the first step in a research process that ultimately proceeds to more rigorous, representative samples of all voters. As such, these early groups are deliberately skewed to exclude the best-informed "know-it-alls" among the electorate. Despite this skew, the paucity of basic information among persuadable voters almost never fails to surprise. Toward the beginning of most groups, a typical practice is to discuss the "most important issues" of the day, with follow-up questions about other pressing issues or controversies—the kinds of issues that would be familiar to anyone who reads a daily newspaper. Yet, more often than not, these issues are unfamiliar to many focus group participants. Voters never have trouble identifying broad areas of concern, such as the economy, taxes, education, crime, or the cost of health care. But what should government do or, alternatively, refrain from doing? What specific responses are being debated in Washington or the state capital? Whenever I asked these questions, I typically got little more than blank stares in response.

So, do these experiences leave me cynical and jaded about the basic competence of the American electorate? No. V. O. Key (1966) had it right, that "voters are not fools." In those same focus groups, I also saw vivid examples of the mechanisms described by Craig and Martinez that allow voters "with limited information to make meaningful choices." Persuadable voters may not know every detail of what happens in Washington or their state capital, but they are able to apply their existing values and preferences when confronted with new candidates and controversies. Sadly, many of my campaign consultant colleagues are likely unfamiliar with the academic literature on retrospective voting and cue-taking, but they share a belief in the underlying concepts. Campaign strategists know, for example, that voters often rely on broad retrospective judgments about an incumbent's performance in office, and are heavily influenced by their perceptions of the condition of the economy when deciding whether to support his or her reelection. They understand that voters apply a wide variety of stereotypes, that is, inferences based on a candidate's party affiliation, age, gender, race, religion, place of residence, profession, or personal appearance—what Popkin described as "information shortcuts and rules of thumb . . . to obtain and evaluate information and to simplify the process of choosing between candidates" (1991, 7).

I will leave to others the debate over whether these sorts of cues and shortcuts translate into "rational" or "correct" voter choices. Instead, I want to focus on the unfortunate consequences of assuming that voters know too much rather than too little.

The "jury box" fallacy.

Too much of modern political commentary suffers from the implicit assumption that all Americans follow politics the way members of a jury follow a trial: as if they are a captive audience sitting at rapt attention, carefully weighing the testimony of each new witness. Our leaders are fond of pontificating about what "the American people" want or believe, but the reality is that relatively few Americans pay close attention to the ongoing debate about policy and politics in Washington, D.C., or in their state or city.

Rather than think about the level of knowledge among voters, consider some statistics on the typical audience for television news. Despite growing use of the Internet, television remains the dominant news source for a majority of the public. A CBS News/*New York Times* survey conducted in January 2009 found that 60 percent of respondents got most of their news "about what's going on in the world" from television, while less than half that number named newspapers (14 percent) or the Internet (13 percent).[1] Yet the actual audience as measured by The Nielsen Company looks considerably smaller than these survey estimates might lead us to believe. Consider the following Nielsen estimates[2] for the 2009–2010 season through mid-February:

- The average combined audience for the three broadcast network evening news programs (*ABC World News Tonight*, *CBS Evening News*, and *NBC Nightly News*) was just over twenty-four million.

- The average combined audience for the three broadcast network morning shows (the *Today Show, Good Morning America,* and the *Early Show*) was a little more than thirteen million.
- The average combined audience for the three major cable news networks (CNN, Fox News, and MSNBC) over the course of their broadcast day was roughly two million.

As of this writing, we are a nation of approximately 304 million persons (of all ages), including 286 million who live in television households. So the combined audience statistics for typical network evening news broadcasts represent about 8 percent of Americans in these households. Even if we assume, implausibly, that the various counts are mutually exclusive—that is, there is no overlap whatsoever among viewers of the three categories of news programming—we would have a combined audience on a typical day of about thirty-nine million. That amounts to roughly 14 percent of television households.

Unfortunately, Nielsen does not publish the number of Americans who watch at least one news broadcast of any type during a typical day or week. Even if we had such a statistic, it would not include those who get their news exclusively from other television or radio programming, or from the Internet or print media. Nonetheless, these admittedly crude statistics still make my point: on any given day, most Americans do not tune in to evening news, morning news, or cable news broadcasts, even though most say they rely on television to get their news. No wonder knowledge of government and politics is limited.

Misinterpreting issue polling.

All too often, the jury box fallacy rears its head in the way we interpret poll questions on public policy issues. We ask questions about unfamiliar concepts that leave the consumers of polling data assuming that Americans are more informed and engaged in political debate than they really are. Consider this example from the fall of 2009: the *Washington Post* and ABC News conducted a national survey in October that included questions on the health care reform debate then raging in Washington. In the survey, virtually all respondents offered an opinion when asked whether they would support (57 percent) or oppose (40 percent) "having the government create a new health insurance plan to compete with private health insurance plans." That result led the poll's front-page coverage in the *Post,* topped by the headline "Public option gains support: clear majority now backs plan" (Balz and Cohen 2009).

Yet just two weeks earlier, the Pew Research Center (2009b) had fielded a survey testing voter knowledge—the same survey cited by Craig and Martinez. Included among their multiple-choice questions was an item showing that only

56 percent of Americans knew that "the public option discussed in Congress" concerned health care. Then, a few weeks later, a poll conducted by CBS News for *60 Minutes* and *Vanity Fair* found that only 26 percent of Americans felt they could "confidently explain what exactly the 'public option' is to someone who didn't know." Clearly, many of those answering the public option question on the *Post*/ABC survey were offering a reaction formed upon hearing the question rather than sharing a preexisting opinion on the "public option" being debated in Congress.[3]

Pollsters should not be surprised that respondents form on-the-spot opinions in reaction to their questions. Decades of experimental research have shown that a third or more of poll respondents will offer an opinion on a fictional issue, such as the nonexistent "Public Affairs Act of 1975" (Bishop 2005). Ironically, that same research shows a process of mental shortcuts at work, in which respondents take cues from the words of the question and draw upon real values and beliefs in forming answers. The problem, then, is one of interpretation: if we assume that all voters are engaged and paying attention, we will likely misread the results.

Misreading the horse race.

The poll question most familiar to political junkies is the one that names the candidates for an office and asks, "If the election were held today, for whom would you vote?" When asked a few days before an election, the so-called horse-race question usually provides an accurate measurement of actual voter intentions. However, when asked months or even years before an election, when voters have not yet engaged in the campaign and may be unfamiliar with the candidates, the question can easily mislead.

Some of the most glaring examples of this come from questions measuring voter preferences in presidential nominating campaigns. The eventual Democratic nominees for president in 1972, 1976, 1980, 1988, 1992, and 2008 trailed badly, sometimes receiving just single-digit support, in early polls conducted prior to those campaigns (Plouffe 2009; Blumenthal 2007). Throughout most of 2007, Barack Obama trailed Hillary Clinton by double-digit margins in national polling on the Democratic nomination contest. Obama's campaign chose, wisely, to ignore the polls and focus instead on winning the precinct caucuses in Iowa, assuming that an early state win would help boost Obama's fortunes nationally when voters elsewhere started paying attention to the campaign in early 2008.

Even though front-running candidates have been upended in many previous contests, the national media and political insiders sometimes continue to treat national horse-race polls as determinative. Consider this bit of reporting in the *Washington Post* from October 2007:

Since he announced his intention to run for the presidency, Obama—and the powerful ebb that surrounded him wherever he woke, spoke, ate and sat—seems to have withered beneath the supernova that is the Clinton campaign. Today, the senator from New York carries with her a fortified sense of inevitability. . . . A recent *Washington Post*–ABC News poll shows Clinton leading Obama by more than 20 percent, with a lead of 13 percent among African-American voters (Pappu 2007).

When voters engaged in the race in earnest a few months later, those early preferences changed rapidly. The mistake was assuming that the early expressions of support were grounded in real engagement or complete knowledge.

Political campaigns see the gaps in voter knowledge explored in the foregoing chapter as opportunity. As Craig and Martinez put it, campaigns craft messages that aim to "fill in some of the blanks in a way that resonates with segments of the electorate whose support is essential to victory." They look for bits and pieces of information that will change the way voters view the candidates or prove persuasive in policy debates. That communication of information is the essence of political campaigning. Whether the process fosters or frustrates voter efforts "to cast a thoughtful vote," as Thomas Patterson puts it (2006, 42), is a question for wiser minds than mine, but it is surely the reality of American politics as we know it.

---

[1] See www.cbsnews.com/htdocs/pdf/SunMo_poll_0209.pdf.

[2] These statistics were provided to the author by The Nielsen Company. I obtained totals for each category of broadcast by adding together Nielsen's estimate of the average audience size during any given minute of the broadcast, a method that likely underestimates the total weekday audience (Prior 2009).

[3] See www.cbsnews.com/stories/2009/11/24/60minutes/main5761182_page5.shtml?tag=cont entMain;contentBody.

Notes

1. To be clear, we recognize that Dalton's argument goes beyond the question of *how much* information a person has and considers how that information is processed and used. Nevertheless, it is difficult to process and use information that one does not possess in the first place.

2. Perhaps it is not education *per se,* but rather some factor(s) related to education—for example, cognitive ability—that drives information levels. If so, this might help to explain why an increase in the proportion of the public attending college has not produced comparable gains in political knowledge; see Highton (2009).

3. Typical wording might go something like this: "Many people don't know the answers to these questions, so if there are some you don't know, just tell me and we'll go on."

4. See Delli Carpini and Keeter (1996, chap. 2) for a more comprehensive discussion of their results.

5. The figures in 1989 were 74 percent for both vice president and governor; see Pew Research Center for the People and the Press (2007).

6. On those occasions when Pew has asked essentially the same question in an open-ended format (without offering response options for Democrats and Republicans), the percentage of respondents who answer correctly drops, for example, to 53 percent in May 2008 (Democrats), 58 percent in October 2006 (Republicans), and a shockingly low 31 percent in June 2001 (Republicans); see http://people-press.org/reports/questionnaires/554.pdf. Similarly, in the 2008 American National Election Study in-person postelection survey (which did not provide the "Democrats or Republicans" response option), only 40 percent of respondents correctly identified the Democrats as the majority party in the House prior to the election, and 34 percent correctly identified the Democrats as the majority party in the Senate; see www.electionstudies.org/studypages/2008prepost/2008prepost.htm. In contrast, data from the 2008 Cooperative Congressional Election Study survey (which provided response options) reveal that 68 percent and 66 percent of respondents correctly identified the majority party in the House and Senate, respectively; see http://web.mit.edu/polisci/portl/cces/material/CCES_Guide_2008_Rough_Draft_v2.pdf.

7. One reason for this disparity may have to do with the differential impact of media—that is, "[d]ifferences in knowledge that have been attributed to education become greater in environments in which information is plentiful" (Jerit, Barabas, and Bolsen 2006, 278). Thus, increased coverage of political news alone is unlikely to reduce the knowledge gap between the better and lesser educated. A more effective approach might be for the media to emphasize contextual information via stories that "provide comparisons with related issues, discuss the consequences of political developments, or supply background information" (Jerit 2009, 449). At the same time, as we noted earlier (see note 2), the impact of education *per se* on knowledge may be less than scholars have generally assumed.

8. See Delli Carpini and Keeter (1996; also Neuman 1986; Althaus 2003), who noted that class and gender differences were the most consistent over the period covered by their research (163). The case of gender is especially puzzling, as it once was assumed that increased opportunities for women in education and the workplace would eventually reduce and perhaps eliminate the knowledge and participation deficits that have long characterized the role of women in American politics. Recent studies suggest, however, that there is more to the story, specifically, that to some degree men (in the aggregate) may simply have a greater "taste" for politics than do women (Dow 2009, 132; see also Verba, Burns, and Schlozman 1997; Mondak and Anderson 2004).

9. One of the main goals of political campaigns today is the identification of such issue publics (although consultants probably won't call them that) and the targeting of communications that address the things they care most strongly about.

10. While defending his organization's work, John Zogby conceded that it was "not our finest hour" and declined Ziegler's offer to sponsor a similar survey of McCain voters; instead, he expressed a willingness to "do a poll of both Obama voters and McCain voters, with questions that I formulated and sponsored either by an objective third party or by someone on the left, in tandem with a John Ziegler on the right—but poll questions that have my signature" (Allen 2008). To our knowledge, no such survey had been done as of the time this chapter was written.

11. Figures for Democrats (55 percent Christian, 7 percent Muslim) and independents (45 percent and 10 percent, respectively) were better, but not by much. Forty-one percent of the sample either didn't know or declined to answer the question.

12. Support for the president was actually more important than party identification *per se*—that is, Democrats and independents who backed Bush's reelection were more likely to hold mistaken beliefs about Iraq than their counterparts who planned to support his Democratic opponent. Nevertheless, to state the obvious, most Bush supporters also happened to be Republicans.

13. The opposite pattern was evident among Democratic supporters, although watching Fox News, in particular, also was associated with high levels of misinformation among this group.

14. These findings are based on nationwide polls conducted from June through September 2003 by the Program on International Policy Attitudes (PIPA) at the University of Maryland and Knowledge Networks, a private firm that conducts surveys over the Internet. See PIPA/Knowledge Networks Poll, "Misperceptions, the Media and the Iraq War," www.pipa.org/OnlineReports/Iraq/IraqMedia_Oct03/IraqMedia_Oct03_rpt.pdf.

15. Trait differences (regarding strength, intelligence, empathy, and so on) also weigh heavily in voters' choices, and there is evidence that different traits matter according to the level of voter sophistication (Funk 1997). It also appears that voters sometimes infer a connection between candidate traits and policy positions (Sullivan et al. 1990; Rapoport, Metcalf, and Hartman 1989).

16. This is at odds with the traditional view that while primaries may force candidates to appeal to their parties' respective core voters (whose views tend toward the ideological extremes), the American two-party system encourages those who are nominated to move toward the center (Downs 1957) or to avoid taking clear positions altogether (Page 1978) during the general election.

17. For example, see Craig, Kane, and Gainous (2005); Partin (2001). Results from the latter study support the information-flow model in that aggregate knowledge levels in 1990 gubernatorial races were higher in states where the races were more hard-fought or "intense" (measured in terms of campaign spending).

18. Some scholars maintain that neither newspapers nor TV news facilitate learning to any appreciable degree (Price and Zaller 1993) or, perhaps most plausibly, that it depends less on the medium *per se* than on the content of the message being delivered (Norris and Sanders 2003). We also should note the potential impact of political comedy programs such as *The Daily Show with Jon Stewart,* which is especially popular among young people (for example, see Cao 2008).

19. Another possibility is that "different types of information have differential impacts on different segments of the population" (Nadeau et al. 2008, 243).

20. According to Dalton (2008, 22), there has been a long-term secular trend toward heightened interest in politics since the 1940s; Gallup surveys reveal an irregular but generally upward trend since 2001 in the extent to which Americans claim to follow news about national politics (Saad 2009). It is not clear, however, that these developments have either reduced the knowledge gap or stimulated a significant increase in overall information levels among citizens.

21. An interesting twist on this topic was provided by Jeffrey Koch (2008), whose analysis of 1998 U.S. House races led him to conclude that an increased volume of negative ads was associated with voters being *more confident* that they knew the targeted candidate's ideological position—and a *greater degree of error* associated with that perception; in

other words, "issue attack ads lead citizens to believe they know more than they actually do" (609).

22. James Kuklinksi and Paul Quirk (2000, 159–160) note the irony that the collectivist view of rational public opinion hinges on Converse's assertion that errors in judgment are mostly random.

23. We refer here to the Neutrality Treaty, in which both Panama and the United States guaranteed the neutrality of the canal operations, and the Panama Canal Treaty, which outlined the gradual ceding of control of the canal from the United States to Panama from 1979 to 1999. President Jimmy Carter (along with foreign policy veterans of previous administrations) argued that the treaties defused the potential for unrest among Panamanian nationalists and possible sabotage of canal operations. Capitalizing on doubts and fears that Ronald Reagan had raised in his unsuccessful bid for the 1976 Republican presidential nomination, conservatives argued that Panamanians might not be willing or able to operate the canal effectively or defend it against communist attacks. Survey respondents who knew that the canal would be turned over to Panama in 1999, that the United States would retain the right to defend the canal against third-party attacks, and that the biggest aircraft carriers and supertankers were unable to use the canal in any case were more supportive of ratification.

24. Technically, position on a public policy issue (such as abortion) is regressed on a measure of knowledge, various other characteristics (such as education, age, gender, religious affiliation, marital status, union membership, and partisanship), and the interactions between knowledge and all the other characteristics in the model. Coefficients on the interaction terms indicate how knowledge affects the opinions of each group of people or, more precisely, the differences in opinions on abortion of high-knowledge people with a particular characteristic (for example, being married) versus low-knowledge people with the same characteristic, controlling for other known characteristics. These results are used to simulate how a hypothetical "fully informed" public opinion would differ from actual opinion, assuming that the public retained the same demographic characteristics (Althaus 2003). Bartels (1996) uses the same approach to model the effects of knowledge on voter choice.

25. In an ingenious experiment, Wendy Rahn (1993) manipulated the presence of partisan cues in issue debates among fictional candidates. Groups that were exposed to strong partisan cues tended to rely more on their partisanship, and less on their actual issue preferences, in deciding which candidate to support. In a similar vein, Arceneaux (2008) found that low-awareness voters did not punish counter-stereotypical candidates (for example, pro-life Democrats or pro-choice Republicans) as much as high-awareness voters, suggesting that partisanship inhibited the former's ability to act on their issue preferences.

5 Money and Elections

Marian L. Currinder and John C. Green

Anyone who has run for elected office knows that money matters. Money pays for candidate travel, advertising, mailings, office space, and for the services of political strategists, pollsters, media specialists, campaign treasurers, and other professional staff. Elections are about attracting enough votes to win, and victory rarely comes cheap. Consider the 2008 congressional elections: winners of U.S. House seats spent an average of $1.4 million, while winners of U.S. Senate seats spent an average of $8.5 million. Defeat does not come cheap, either. Losing candidates for House seats spent an average of $492,928, losing Senate candidates an average of $4.1 million. Spending by all House and Senate candidates combined in 2008 totaled almost $1.4 billion.[1]

Three broad assumptions shape the public's understanding of the role that money plays in elections. First, the more money candidates spend, the more votes they receive; the shorthand expression for this assumption is that money "buys" votes. Second, the candidate who spends the most is most likely to win. And third, money not only helps candidates to win office but also helps them stay in office.[2] Given these assumptions, it is easy to see why Americans hold a mostly negative view of the role that money plays in elections. For example, a 2001 *Time*/CNN poll found that 77 percent of the public surveyed thought campaign fundraising practices were corrupt or unethical (Pew Research Center for the People and the Press 2001); more recent surveys have yielded similar results (Saad 2006).

Since the late 1970s, political scientists have systematically investigated the three assumptions outlined above with the goal of developing a more nuanced understanding of the relationship between campaign spending and campaign success. That money matters in elections is clear. More difficult to explain is *how* it matters and to which kinds of candidates it matters most. Research to date has produced three roughly parallel conclusions about the role of money in elections:

- Money is a dynamic factor in campaigns, with the capacity to change the behavior of voters (and of candidates). All else being equal, money has a market-like impact on the number of votes candidates receive.
- The impact of money varies with the context of the campaign, because all else is rarely equal and other factors influence voting besides money. Money matters more for some kinds of candidates than for others, and its impact varies in accordance with electoral circumstances.
- Money is most valuable in gaining control of elected office and less valuable (but still important) in maintaining control.

In this chapter, we review the academic literature on money and elections, summarizing its findings in a mostly nontechnical fashion. We begin with an illustration of the relationship that appears to exist between campaign spending and winning elections, then look more closely at nonincumbent and incumbent spending. We conclude with a list of research questions that challenge those who study or practice election funding.

Money and Winning Elections: An Illustration

Tables 5.1 and 5.2 provide a simple picture of the relationship between spending and winning elections. Each table covers eleven congressional elections, from 1986 to 2006. Table 5.1 cross-tabulates the levels of spending for Democratic and Republican U.S. House candidates running for open seats. The left-most column categorizes Republican candidates by the level of spending in their campaigns in 2006 constant dollars; the same breakdown occurs across the top row of the table for Democratic candidates. Each entry represents the percentage of time that the Democratic candidate won (the percentage of Republican victories can be calculated by subtracting the entries from 100 percent). For both Democrats and Republicans, the more they spend, the better they do. Democrats do well in the upper-right section of the matrix where they spend more than their Republican challengers, and Republicans do well in the lower-left section of the matrix where they outspend their Democratic challengers (Jacobson 2009, 50–51). The average percentage of Democratic wins rises from just 7.8 percent (among candidates spending less than $200,000) to 61.6 percent (among those spending more than $1 million). When both candidates spent more than $1 million, the results were approximately even (the Democrat won 47.4 percent of the time).

These results appear to confirm the widely held assumption that the more a candidate spends, the more likely he or she is to win. They also are consistent

Table 5.1 Campaign Spending and Democratic Victories in Open House Seats, 1986–2006

Republican Spending ($1,000s)*		Democratic Spending ($1,000s)*					
		<200	200–400	400–600	600–800	800–1,000	>1,000
	Average percent won	**7.8**	**33.3**	**43.1**	**50.6**	**52.9**	**61.6**
<200	**98.7**	75.0	100.0	100.0	100.0	100.0	100.0
200–400	**69.0**	0.0	66.7	83.3	55.7	75.0	83.3
400–600	**44.4**	7.1	16.7	33.3	75.0	50.0	87.5
600–800	**39.7**	0.0	22.2	26.3	21.4	44.4	89.5
800–1,000	**27.3**	0.0	0.0	14.3	30.0	25.0	52.6
>1,000	**29.1**	3.8	0.0	0.0	9.5	21.4	47.4

Source: Adapted from Jacobson (2009, 50).

Note: Table entries are the percentage of Democratic wins in open-seat races. Republican wins can be calculated by subtracting table entries from 100.

*Adjusted for inflation in 2006.

Table 5.2 Campaign Spending and Challenger Victories, 1986–2006

Incumbent Spending (1,000s)*		Challenger Spending ($1,000s)*					
		<200	200–400	400–600	600–800	800–1,000	>1,000
	Average percent won	**0.04**	**3.9**	**3.9**	**13.5**	**17.7**	**26.9**
<200	**0.0**	0.0	0.0	0.0	0.0	0.0	0.0
200–400	**0.0**	0.0	0.0	0.0	0.0	0.0	0.0
400–600	**1.1**	0.0	4.7	11.1	14.3	0.0	25.0
600–800	**1.7**	0.0	2.1	2.2	17.7	42.9	22.2
800–1,000	**3.8**	0.0	5.5	4.4	25.0	15.4	30.8
>1,000	**9.7**	0.3	4.5	3.5	11.2	17.4	27.4

Source: Adapted from Jacobson (2009, 48).

Note: Table entries are the percentage of winning challengers at different combinations of incumbents and challengers. Incumbent wins can be calculated by subtracting table entries from 100.

*Adjusted for inflation in 2006.

with a related assumption—that more money produces more votes. Because incumbents are not included in Table 5.1, however, the observed patterns are not relevant to the question of whether money is critical for maintaining office once a politician is elected. In fact, open-seat House races are rather unusual events, typically accounting for less than one-sixth of all congressional races.

Most congressional races do include an incumbent candidate, and the incumbent usually wins. In 2008, 94 percent of House incumbents were reelected, as were 83 percent of Senate incumbents. Since 1964, the House incumbent reelection rate has dipped below 90 percent just five times; the Senate incumbent reelection rate fluctuates more than that of the House, but nevertheless averages around 85 percent.[3] Table 5.2 depicts campaign spending and challenger victories at different combinations of incumbent and challenger spending. Each entry is the percentage of victories by challengers regardless of their party affiliation. Clearly, the more money challengers spend against incumbent candidates, the more likely they are to win. Table 5.2 reveals that the percentage of challenger victories increases from an average of 0 percent (among candidates spending less that $200,000) to an average of 26.9 percent (among those spending more than $1 million). Even under the best circumstances, high-spending challengers do not win as often as their counterparts in open-seat races. Nevertheless, the results here provide further support for popular assumptions about the importance of money in elections.

Interestingly, a very different pattern emerges for incumbents in Table 5.2. The more money incumbents spend, the more likely they are to lose. None of the incumbents who spent less than $400,000 lost, but almost 10 percent of incumbents who spent more than $1 million lost. At any given level of incumbent spending, challengers do better as they spend more money. But incumbent spending makes little apparent difference in the election outcome (Jacobson 2009, 49). This pattern seems to contradict all three assumptions about the impact of money in electoral politics; it is especially interesting because incumbents typically dominate the finances of congressional elections. In 2008, for example, House incumbents raised a total of $590 million compared to $218 million raised by their challengers.[4] Further, incumbents generally do not have to work as hard to get their names and messages out because they have a number of built-in advantages to start with: staff in Washington, D.C., and in the district, higher name recognition, the opportunity to provide constituent services, the franking privilege, access to the media, and the ability to claim credit for federal legislation.

Yet despite these financial and institutional advantages, incumbents are not always safe. Just ask Rep. Thelma Drake (R-Va.), who lost her seat in 2008 to Democratic challenger Glenn Nye despite spending just over $2 million compared with Nye's $1.3 million. Or Rep. Christopher Shays (R-Conn.), who also lost in 2008 despite spending approximately $3.8 million (roughly the same amount as his Democratic challenger, Jim Himes). In all, twenty-three House incumbents lost their seats in 2008. How, then, do we square our assumptions about the role of money in elections with incumbent spending patterns and rates of electoral success? Tables 5.1 and 5.2 present a very simple picture of a complicated subject. While money is important, it is not the only factor that influences victory or defeat at the polls. Assessing the impact of money on winning elections without taking into account these other factors results in an incomplete (and often inaccurate) view of electoral politics. In the sections that follow, we review the literature on campaign spending with the goal of presenting a more robust picture of why, when, and how money influences elections. Before looking more closely at non-incumbent and incumbent spending, we provide a brief overview of the methodological approaches scholars have used to study the effect of money in elections.

Analyzing the Impact of Campaign Spending

Most of the academic literature on money and elections focuses on campaigns for the U.S. House of Representatives. Research on House elections moved into high gear following passage of the Federal Election Campaign Act (FECA) in 1971 and its amendments in 1974 (Corrado et al. 1997). The FECA created the Federal Election Commission and required that candidates for federal office (presidency, House, Senate) report their campaign finance data to the commission. Once these data became publicly available, research on campaign spending accelerated sharply. Apart from the simple availability of data, however, the focus on House races reflects scholars' long-standing interest in Congress, where the "electoral connection" between voters and their representatives (Mayhew 1974a) is a constant.

From a methodological perspective, U.S. House elections are a good subject for the systematic study of campaign spending because they occur every two years, involve hundreds of candidates, and cover a broad range of political circumstances. Yet the literature tends to emphasize *recent* House elections, which may reduce its relevance to understanding the impact of campaign spending in general. As already noted, House incumbents have won reelection at very high rates since the 1960s, a factor that sets them apart from other elected officials.[5] Studies of spending in U.S. Senate and gubernatorial elections, for example, are far less common. Senators only run for reelection every six years, and Senate races in the aggregate involve far fewer candidates than House races. Gubernatorial elections involve even fewer candidates, there is variation from state to state in the length and number of terms that governors can serve, and these races tend to be more open and competitive than congressional races as a whole. For all of these reasons, academics who study money in elections have relied heavily on U.S. House campaign finance data.[6]

Analysis of campaign spending in congressional races is typically designed to assess the impact of spending on the percentage of votes received by each candidate in the race.[7] This approach allows for consideration of the three, previously described popular assumptions about the role of money in elections because (1) the person receiving the most votes wins, and (2) winners can be either incumbents or non-incumbents. The primary target of interest in such analyses, votes received by the respective candidates, is most often measured as a proportion of the two-party (Republican plus Democratic only) ballots. This figure can be calculated in various ways, but the measure used has had little effect on the results obtained by different scholars.

The central explanatory factor in much of this research is, of course, campaign spending, and it, too, has been measured in various ways. The most common approach is to compare each candidate's spending in thousands of dollars (see, for example, Tables 5.1 and 5.2). In contrast to candidate vote share, different measures of campaign spending have sometimes resulted in modestly different conclusions; for example, measuring spending in thousands of dollars typically shows incumbent spending to have no impact on the vote, whereas measuring it as a percentage of the total shows incumbent spending to have a significant impact.

In addition to campaign spending, numerous other factors have been considered by researchers because they, too, are thought to influence election outcomes. For example, scholars have sought to isolate the impact of campaign spending from the effects of such potentially important influences as candidates' party affiliation, presence or absence of an incumbent in the race, challenger quality, and whether the district/state in question leans Democratic or Republican. The specific factors (or variables) examined by scholars often differ from study to study, however.

A final issue of methodology has to do with the choice of statistics for systematically sorting out the effects of campaign spending on the vote, taking into account the impact of other variables. The most common choice (involving a single linear equation) is to assume that the vote can be accurately predicted by simply adding up the unique contributions of the factors under consideration. Scholars generally prefer this approach because the results of statistical analyses are relatively easy to interpret; the approach does not, however, fully capture the intricacies of the electoral process. As a result, some scholars prefer to use more complex statistical models that they believe do a better job of predicting the various factors that determine who wins and who loses on election day. For ease of presentation, we refer to the most commonly used (simple linear) approach as the "basic model," some of the best examples of which are found in the work of Gary Jacobson.[8] A few researchers have tested variations of the basic model for both House and Senate elections, while others have applied versions of it to nonfederal elections.[9] All of these studies have arrived at roughly similar conclusions.

Finally, we should note that in this section, and throughout most of the chapter, we are describing research done at the aggregate level. Aggregate studies typically combine campaign expenditure data across many races to measure the overall effect that money has on election outcomes. But as Jacobson (1990, 342) has pointed out, "Part of the difficulty [with aggregate models] is that these equations attempt to estimate dynamic processes with cross-sectional data; the endogenous variables, votes and expenditures, are measured after the campaign is over. But the process of raising and spending money and acquiring (or losing) support from voters occurs iteratively and, presumably, interactively over the entire course of the campaign." In other words, aggregate models try to estimate campaign outcomes using data from a number of races without accounting for the differences between those races. Because they rely on spending and voting data collected *after* campaigns end, aggregate studies do not assess how spending *during* campaigns affects election outcomes. Jacobson argues that voter support likely varies in accordance with the timing of campaign expenditures. To address this problem, he created a model that attached aggregate expenditure data to individual survey data in House elections (that is, each survey respondent was coded for the amount of money spent by candidates in his or her own congressional district). Respondents were interviewed twice, once before and once after the election, to gauge how voter support for the candidates changed with respect to spending over the course of a campaign. Although Jacobson's methodology was challenged by other scholars (Green and Krasno 1990; Kenny and McBurnett 1992), his theoretical argument—specifically, that *when* money is spent during the campaign matters a great deal—has resonated.

Building on Jacobson's work, Kenny and McBurnett (1992, 923) created a dynamic model to investigate the cause-and-effect relationship between campaign expenditures and vote choice. Because money matters to both incumbents and challengers, and because expenditures rise and fall over the course of a campaign, Kenny and McBurnett argued that statistical models should account for this fact. Their analysis focused on a single U.S. House election, which allowed them to avoid having to take into account variations in the effects of money between different races. The authors subsequently expanded this line of research to examine the relationship between money and vote choice in order to see which types of individuals are influenced most by candidate spending (Kenny and McBurnett 1994, 699).

The common theme in individual-level studies is that campaign spending is dynamic. It matters *when* money is raised and spent, and it matters *how* money is spent. For the purposes of this chapter, the important question is whether aggregate and individual-level models reach similar or different conclusions regarding the impact of incumbent and non-incumbent campaign spending. Generally speaking, both models conclude that campaign spending is more crucial for non-incumbent than for incumbent candidates. Many individual-level studies, however, do emphasize that incumbent spending matters. By focusing on when money is raised and spent, and how it is spent, individual-level studies present a more comprehensive picture of the effects of spending over the course of a campaign. We will address these findings in the remainder of the chapter, where appropriate.

Non-incumbent Spending

Most tests of the basic model reach a conclusion consistent with the pattern depicted in Table 5.1: in open-seat races, the more candidates spend, the more they increase their own share of the vote, taking into account other explanatory factors.[10] This result is unstable from election to election, however, reflecting in part the relatively small number of races involved—as well as, perhaps, the very high levels of spending by *both* candidates that characterize most open-seat races. When both candidates are extremely well funded, money may have less of an impact than other factors, such as the quality of the candidates' messages.

Studies that use the basic model also confirm that in races involving an incumbent, challenger spending has a strong, positive, and significant impact on the proportion of the vote the challenger ultimately wins, taking into account incumbent spending and various other factors (see Table 5.2). Further, the impact of challenger spending appears at first glance to be much larger than that of incumbent spending. Such results suggest that a challenger's spending is often critical in determining who wins the election. Put another way, challenger spending helps to determine how many votes the incumbent fails to receive on election day.

This point is worth elaborating. Research based on the basic model sometimes concludes that challengers tend to spend money more *efficiently* than do incumbents; that is, the additional return (in votes) for each dollar spent is greater for the former than the latter. This is not really surprising, since challengers have more to gain from their campaign spending: they are typically not well known to voters, and every dollar spent during the campaign can help to overcome this initial weakness. Thus, when a high-quality challenger succeeds at amassing a large enough war chest, he or she can sometimes make the race very close—and once that happens, either candidate has a legitimate chance to win. However, most challengers are not high-quality (politically experienced) candidates and are unable to raise enough money to make the election close, even if they do spend their money more efficiently.

Campaign spending, then, can help open-seat candidates and challengers to overcome some of their electoral disadvantages—most notably, for open-seat candidates, the high level of spending by their opponents and, for challengers, the power of incumbency. In fact, spending appears to be helpful (though not always decisive) in overcoming many kinds of political disadvantages, such as a district predisposed toward the other party or unfavorable national trends that exist in a particular election year (see Jacobson 1985, 1987).

Overall, the findings presented in these studies support the popular claim that money attracts votes for candidates. Yet evidence from the basic model also refines and extends such claims. Not only does the effect of money vary to some degree by candidate status, it also varies with election circumstances. For a non-incumbent, for example, there is a strong *threshold effect*—that is, a candidate needs to spend beyond a certain minimum to have any realistic chance of winning. Many challengers (but few open-seat candidates) fail to exceed the threshold and thus are not competitive. Once past the threshold, non-incumbents spend relatively efficiently, although eventually even they experience diminishing returns. As their standing with the public improves, the net effect of additional spending declines. Few challengers (but many open-seat candidates) reach this point, while incumbent candidates do so regularly. Put another way, until candidates spend adequately, only a small number of voters will receive their message; therefore, that message can, by definition, have only a modest impact on voting decisions. But once candidates obtain an adequate level of spending, additional funds become less important and the content of the message communicated becomes more significant, precisely because many voters have received it.[11]

Incumbent Spending

The basic model of campaign spending also confirms the findings in Table 5.2 for incumbent candidates, but in a somewhat puzzling fashion. As noted earlier, the typical (though not universal) conclusion reached by scholars is that incumbent spending has at best a modest impact on the vote; some estimates even imply that the more an incumbent spends, the worse he or she is likely to do on election day (the pattern observed in Table 5.2). Yet few scholars, including some of the basic model's strongest proponents, would endorse such a counterintuitive conclusion. As Jacobson (1985, 41) pointed out:

> If incumbents really gain nothing by spending in campaigns, ironies abound. Incumbents spend defensively and reactively, but pointlessly: the doubling of their real spending over the past decades has merely compounded the waste. The unpleasant work of fundraising which members of Congress complain about so passionately is not even necessary. Most of whatever influence PACs may enjoy must be based on illusion if incumbents do not really need PAC contributions. It is not easy to believe that irrationality is so pervasive; alternative explanations need to be considered.

In fact, the search for "alternative explanations" of incumbent spending has occupied scholars since the advent of the basic model. It is worth noting two accounts that were initially advanced for the puzzling relationship between incumbent spending and the vote, one substantive and one methodological.

The substantive account follows from the logic of the impact of non-incumbent spending that was outlined earlier: incumbents are relatively well known to voters, partly because they have already won an election and partly because they constantly make efforts to communicate with their constituents between campaigns. Consequently, because incumbents have much less to gain from high spending levels than do challengers, they begin their campaigns at something close to the point of diminishing returns. If faced with a personal scandal, unfavorable political trends, or a well-funded challenger, incumbents generally react by dramatically increasing their spending. But because they are already well known (and already in political trouble), their spending may end up having a modest impact compared to other factors in the race. Although embattled incumbents still win much more often than not, nearly every election features a couple of high-spending incumbents who lose. Virginia Republican Thelma Drake, as previously stated, lost in 2008 despite spending almost twice as much as her challenger. Cases such as these help to create the odd pattern in Table 5.2, where higher spending is associated with a greater likelihood of defeat. At the same time, incumbents who face no adverse circumstances or serious challengers tend to spend relatively little (because there is no need) and cruise to victory by large margins.

While this argument surely contains a large dose of truth, its conclusions have been questioned because of a methodological limitation associated with the simple statistics used to test the basic model. The approach in question assumes that causality flows in just one direction: money is assumed to attract votes, but votes are not assumed to attract money. In fact, both things undoubtedly happen in campaigns. As noted earlier, if the vote is expected to be close, incumbents usually spend more money; but if the vote is expected to be lopsided in their favor, incumbents tend to spend less. Intuitively, this makes sense. After all, the likely outcome of an election will undoubtedly influence the decisions—including whether to run, whether to contribute, whether to work for or endorse—of candidates, political consultants, campaign contributors, and other political elites (Jacobson and Kernell 1983). As a result, the *expected* vote may well attract money even as campaign money is simultaneously attracting actual votes. This "simultaneity problem" can lead analysts to underestimate the impact of incumbent spending and overstate the effect of challenger spending (Jacobson 1985, 29–30). Proponents of the basic model are fully aware of the simultaneity problem, of course, and they have sought to take it into account by using more complex statistics.[12] Their initial tests, however, seemed to confirm the basic model's findings, that incumbent spending has very little impact on the vote.

Four Solutions to the Puzzle of Incumbent Spending

Why, then, do incumbents spend? Scholars have offered four solutions to the puzzle of incumbent spending produced by the basic model. Each provides an alternative account for why incumbents engage in campaign spending that seemingly has little or no effect, and each has contributed to a broader understanding of the role of money in elections. However, none of these solutions changes the basic pattern shown in Table 5.2. Instead, each presents additional circumstances that influence the impact of spending on the vote.

Distortions in Spending

The first solution is to investigate possible distortions in incumbent spending that could cause a modest impact on the vote. One possibility is an *inaccurate measure* of campaign spending. Typically, spending has been defined as the total disbursements by a candidate. Many candidates, however, and especially incumbents, spend money for things other than contacting voters. Indeed, the most extensive investigation of how congressional campaign funds are spent described a "gold-plated politics" wherein some incumbents spend lavishly on activities not directly linked to the campaign at all (Fritz and Morris 1992; also Morris and Gamache 1994).[13] Ansolabehere and Gerber (1994) used the results of that study to reestimate the basic model for the 1990 congressional elections. They found that a more precise measure of campaign spending based on communication with voters (advertising, direct contact, and so on) increased the observed impact of money on the vote, especially for challengers. But, like the basic model, this analysis also indicated that incumbent spending had no significant influence on the vote. Nevertheless, additional refinement in measuring campaign spending may lead to the discovery of an effect for incumbent spending; in fact, Goldstein and Freedman (2000) observed just such an effect when improved measures of exposure to television advertising were used to predict citizens' voting behavior.

Another possible distortion is *strategic spending* by incumbents. For example, some scholars have argued that it is quite rational for incumbents to accumulate and spend money early on in an effort to discourage high-quality challengers from entering the race in the first place. If the basic model is correct, a quality challenger is *the* principal threat to an incumbent's reelection prospects (Bond, Covington, and Fleisher 1985; Jacobson 1989). One way to deter quality challengers may be to build a large "war chest" well in advance of the election, a pattern demonstrated by Box-Steffensmeier (1996). Large war chests also allow incumbents to spend preemptively to undermine the viability of prospective opponents. A few scholars have argued that war chests have purposes other than to discourage potential challengers. For example, Sorauf (1988) and Goodliffe (2001, 2004) have suggested that incumbents build war chests for the purpose of saving money for the next election. It is also possible that some incumbents deliberately spend inefficiently to "run up the score" in their reelection bids as a prelude to seeking higher office (Goldenberg, Traugott, and Baumgartner 1986).

All such distortions help to explain why incumbent spending is rational but relatively inefficient compared with that of non-incumbents. In fact, according to Jacobson (1989, 1990), when a large number of elections are aggregated for analysis, the basic model indicates that incumbent spending has a small, positive, and statistically significant impact on the vote after all. Taken together, these findings provide some support for the popular claim that spending helps incumbents win reelection.

Effectiveness versus Efficiency

The second solution to the puzzle of incumbent spending moves beyond spending efficiency to stress its effectiveness. It may be that despite a low level of efficiency, incumbents win elections because of a high volume of expenditures. Put another way, incumbents may be able to secure the last handful of votes necessary for victory by expending an extraordinary level of money for those voters. This argument is attractive in part because it also helps to explain the close wins registered by well-financed challengers and open-seat candidates. Thus, the marginal effectiveness of funds (that is, the extent to which extra spending produces enough votes for a candidate to win the race, typically 50 percent of the number of ballots cast) may matter as much to winning as their marginal efficiency.

Thomas (1989) estimated a version of the basic model for the 1978 and 1980 U.S. House elections that included an additional variable: share of total spending in the campaign accounted for by the challenger. In this model, incumbent spending measured in thousands of dollars had a positive impact on the vote but challenger spending measured in the same way did not. However, challenger spending measured as a percentage of the total spending by both candidates did have a positive impact on the vote. In other words, it was the *relative size* of the challenger's spending compared to the incumbent's that mattered, and not the actual amount spent (which varied substantially from district to district). This result suggests that well-funded challengers can indeed attract votes at the incumbent's expense—but that incumbent spending is effective at "winning back" such votes. These findings imply that incumbents can win close contests due to the sheer volume of expenditure, even if they spend less efficiently than challengers.

James Campbell took the notion that the overall level of spending is important to winning a step further and investigated the relationship between share of the vote won and share of spending accounted for by the incumbent. His results led him to describe a "stagnation of congressional elections," one important cause of which is the enormous advantage incumbents have over their challengers in terms of total funds spent. He summed up the argument as follows:

> While some claim that money does not buy elections . . . there can be no doubt that at some point it does. . . . The typical election to the House is not one in which the incumbent spends twice or three times what his or her opponent spends. . . . In the typical election to the House in recent times the incumbent spends six to twelve times what the challenger spends (J. Campbell 2003, 151–152).

Many proponents of the basic model tend to agree with the substance of this conclusion, if not the rhetoric, though the pattern may result as much from insufficient challenger funds as from excessive incumbent spending (Abramowitz 1991).

Correcting Incumbent Spending

The third solution to the puzzle of incumbent spending is to develop corrected models of spending. As noted earlier, proponents of the basic model sought to address the simultaneity problem (that money attracts votes, but expectations of probable victory also attract money to a campaign) by conducting more sophisticated statistical analyses, specifically, by "correcting" incumbent spending for expectations about the likely vote. In essence, this procedure attempts to adjust actual spending by taking into account the effects of "expected vote" (which is estimated using such factors as strength of the challenger's party in the district, challenger quality, and number of years the incumbent has been in office). Such a correction is typically applied to the spending of incumbents (but sometimes to challenger spending as well). It yields an estimate of what the incumbent would have spent if expectations about the likely vote had not played a role in the campaign. Although initial results were largely consistent with the basic model, some researchers used different factors to make the necessary corrections and, as a result, obtained evidence of a stronger impact of incumbent spending on the vote.

Green and Krasno (1988), for example, found "salvation for the spendthrift incumbent" in their corrected model of spending and the vote in the 1978 congressional elections (see also Jacobson 1990; Green and Krasno 1990).[14] This model corrected incumbent spending by taking into account the incumbent's funds in the previous election (1976) along with other political factors; it also included a more detailed measure of challenger quality. Results indicated that corrected incumbent spending had a significant and positive impact on the vote. The effect of challenger spending, on the other hand, was somewhat lower than in the basic model and subject to diminishing returns, but it was still larger than for incumbent spending.

In addition, Green and Krasno (1988, 898) found that challenger quality mattered a great deal, changing "the structure of the House vote by increasing the importance of quality and decreasing the role of previous electoral outcome." Indeed, their more accurate measure of challenger quality may be one reason why they found incumbent spending to have a significant impact.[15] Alan Gerber (1998) took a similar approach to investigating spending in Senate elections but used different factors (for example, challenger wealth and the particular offices previously held by challengers) to make the correction for incumbent spending. The results showed that corrected incumbent and challenger spending both mattered in determining the vote, with the former having a greater effect. These studies help to further specify the circumstances under which spending influences the vote.

Elaborate Models of Spending

The fourth and final solution to the puzzle of incumbent spending is to develop more elaborate models of spending that recognize the complexity of political campaigns. The key insight here is that both the vote and campaign spending are products of the same political process and that, to accurately estimate the impact of spending on the vote, all elements of the process must be taken into account simultaneously. Such analyses also correct incumbent spending for the expected vote (discussed earlier) but go a step further by performing similar corrections on challenger spending and other factors such as challenger quality. For example, Goidel and Gross (1994) estimated an elaborate model that systematically corrected spending for both incumbents and challengers, taking into account challenger quality and a variety of other potential influences on the vote.[16] These corrected variables, along with a number of additional ones, were used to predict the vote in congressional elections from 1986 to 1990. Incumbent spending was found to have a positive impact on the incumbent's vote—enough to make a measurable difference in winning an election. However, as in the basic model, challenger spending continued to have a much greater impact than incumbent spending. This research therefore makes a more plausible case for the conclusions of the basic model, fitting even better with popular claims about money and elections.

One of the most comprehensive treatments of spending in congressional elections was undertaken by Erikson and Palfrey (1998). They estimated a complex model that corrected both incumbent and challenger spending for the expected vote in congressional races between 1972 and 1990.[17] Specifically, their model allowed for the effect of money on attracting votes to be estimated separately from the effect of votes on attracting money. They found that corrected incumbent spending had a positive impact on the incumbent's vote. Although the overall impact of incumbent spending was smaller than for challengers, Erikson and Palfrey also concluded that the effect of campaign spending varied over an incumbent's career. The largest impact occurs when a newly elected incumbent seeks reelection for the first time—an election when such candidates are often quite vulnerable. Under these circumstances, incumbent spending appears to be more influential than challenger spending. That influence declines steadily the longer an individual is in office, however, with challenger spending eventually gaining the advantage (see also Goidel and Gross

1994). On the one hand, this result confirms the basic model's finding of diminishing returns for incumbent spending; on the other hand, it suggests that incumbent spending may have a cumulative effect that, in turn, helps to explain the high reelection rate of incumbents.

Erikson and Palfrey (2000) expanded their analysis with an even more elaborate model of what they called "campaign spending games," further illuminating the effect that expectations about an election can have on spending. The authors found that expectations were least consequential in very close elections, in which incumbent and challenger spending had about the same impact once expectations were taken into account. The less competitive an election became, however, the larger the role played by expectations. For veteran incumbents, corrected spending revealed a positive impact of money on their votes but at a level below that for challengers.

Thus, the closer an incumbent-challenger race becomes, the more it resembles an open-seat race where, as we have seen, each candidate's spending has a roughly equivalent effect on the distribution of the vote. The aforementioned race between Rep. Chris Shays (R-Conn.) and Jim Himes is a case in point: both candidates spent roughly $3.8 million; Shays wound up with 48 percent of the vote, and Himes wound up with 51 percent. Despite Shays's loss, this kind of spending still advantages incumbents, who typically "outspend challengers and . . . achieve roughly equal effectiveness per dollar in close races, where it matters most" (Erikson and Palfrey 2000, 606). Consequently, because most races are characterized by a strong incumbent fundraising advantage to start with, the true impact of incumbent spending is often obscured in scholarly analyses. The conclusions reached by these more elaborate models generally confirm, but in a nuanced and sophisticated fashion, the popular claims about the importance of money in maintaining control of elected office.

Raising and Spending Campaign Money: Other Factors to Consider

Our focus thus far has centered on non-incumbent and incumbent patterns of spending. Another important consideration for candidates and election professionals is the question of how campaign money is raised and spent. Does the source of contributions matter? What kinds of contact affect individual vote choice most? How does party versus "outside" money influence campaigns? And how does all of this spending affect the quality of democracy?

Earlier models of campaign spending did not identify whether or how the sources and uses of campaign money affected voters' choices. Recent theoretical work, however, is much more explicit about these links. In his overview of recent research on money in politics, Stratmann (2005) identified models developed by Coate (2004a, 2004b), Ashworth (2006), and Prat (2002) as demonstrating that voters are less responsive to campaign messages when they believe that candidates have secured money from contributors in exchange for policy favors. In fact, voters may actually be less likely to elect a high-quality candidate if they believe that candidate's campaign was financed by special interests (Houser and Stratmann 2008). Likewise, Alexander (2005) argued that some kinds of fundraising are correlated with success, while others are correlated with failure. Examining the effect of out-of-state donations, political action committee (PAC) donations, and self-financing on vote choice, he found that PAC donations are a predictor of candidate success while self-financing is associated with failure. Candidates also may receive a boost from generating a high percentage of their funds in-state. While Alexander was careful to point out that funding source impacts are of a much lower magnitude than other factors (such as the political terrain of the district), they still are relevant, particularly in very competitive races.

Another predictor of candidate success may be volunteer support, though little work has been done on the contributions that volunteers make to campaigns (Stratmann 2005, 151). By calling and contacting voters, volunteers complement funds expended in campaigns and enhance the credibility of a campaign. As a result, campaign spending may become more productive. Barack Obama's 2008 campaign offers a great example of how volunteers can be used to provide campaign services and to raise money. By reaching out to small, first-time donors who could later be tapped for more money and for volunteer recruitment, Obama was able to build a network of 1.5 million donors/volunteers. This tremendous show of financial and grassroots support helped propel him to victory. While Obama also received large amounts of money from wealthy donors, the media focused on his army of small donors, which helped to create the perception that his funding sources were somehow less "tainted" than those of his competitors.

Campaign professionals also need to consider what kind of spending is most effective for promoting their candidate. National survey data suggest that non-incumbent candidates routinely lack name recognition with the public, let alone favorable evaluations (Mann and Wolfinger 1980). Campaign spending can help to remedy such problems (Jacobson 1978, 2001), which is why challenger spending sometimes appears to have a greater impact on individual vote choice than incumbent spending (Jacobson 1990; Kenny and McBurnett 1992;

but see Goldstein and Freedman 2000). Evidence also suggests that the amount of information possessed by voters increases with higher total levels of campaign spending (Coleman and Manna 2000) and that even the much-criticized television advertising that dominates contemporary campaigns may serve, on balance, to improve voters' knowledge and their level of interest in the campaign (Freedman, Franz, and Goldstein 2004). Campaign advertising can reduce voter uncertainty about a candidate's policy positions (Austen-Smith 1987) and inform voters about candidate quality (Coate 2004a). For nonincumbents who have money to spend, television appears to be the way to go (Kenny and McBurnett 1997, 91–92).

By targeting their messages, campaigns presumably can spend money more efficiently. Kenny and McBurnett (1994) found that voting is conditioned by the interaction between spending and individual characteristics such as education and interest in campaigns; those with college degrees were unaffected by campaign spending whereas those with less than a college degree exhibited large and significant effects. Individuals with strongly held partisan attachments were also less likely to be affected by campaign spending.[18] Campaign strategists often quip that half of the money they spend is wasted—they just don't know which half. By targeting their messages to those who are more likely to respond, campaigns may be able to alleviate some of the waste (Kenny and McBurnett 1994, 705).[19]

Campaign spending by political parties (Jacobson 1999) and interest groups (Jacobson 1985) appears to operate in much the same way as spending by nonincumbents—that is, mainly by taking votes away from the incumbent candidate. For example, in the 2008 general election, the Democratic Senatorial Campaign Committee (DSCC) spent a total of $11.7 million opposing North Carolina senator Elizabeth Dole, $3.5 million trying to unseat Kentucky senator Mitch McConnell, and another $5.5 million attacking Georgia senator Saxby Chambliss.[20] These expenditures were reported as "independent," meaning that there was no coordination between the DSCC and candidate campaign committees. The law allows parties to make unlimited independent expenditures in candidate races; in fact, congressional candidates often have no control over how their party committees choose to spend money in their campaigns. Sen. Russ Feingold (D-Wis.), a campaign finance reform proponent, demanded that the DSCC not get involved in his 1998 reelection campaign. The committee, however, was worried that Feingold was going to lose a Democrat-held seat; rather than honor his wishes, it spent hundreds of thousands of dollars attacking his Republican opponent in the last weeks of the campaign.

Relatively little attention has been paid to the new kinds of "outside" spending that are so prominent today. In the 2008 elections, for example, issue advocacy groups spent approximately $350 million. Spending by these groups was concentrated in a few dozen competitive House and Senate races and mostly benefited Democratic candidates. On balance, the available evidence seems to indicate that spending by issue advocacy groups is largely intended to generate votes against incumbents rather than non-incumbents (Magleby and Monson 2004).[21] As a result, many incumbents are compelled to raise even more money for their war chests, as they cannot predict or control how much money these groups will spend opposing them.

A final point to consider: How do all of these forms of campaign fundraising and spending affect the quality of democracy? Although election campaigns are hardly models of civic discourse, higher spending (especially by challengers and open-seat candidates, but perhaps by incumbents as well) may actually contribute to, rather than detract from, the overall quality of democracy in the United States. As total spending by all candidates expands, voter turnout rates tend to increase.[22] In their examination of congressional campaign spending effects, Coleman and Manna (2000, 757) concluded that spending "neither enhances nor erodes trust and efficacy in politics or attention and interest in campaigns .... [To the contrary, it] contributes to key aspects of democracy such as knowledge and affect, while not damaging public trust or involvement."

Conclusion: The Effects of Campaign Spending

Three decades of academic research have yielded considerable support for widely shared assumptions about the role of money in electoral politics, though the findings are not always straightforward. Overall, three conclusions seem warranted:

- Money is a dynamic factor in campaigns, with the capacity to change the behavior of voters (and candidates). All else being equal, the more money candidates spend, the more votes they receive.
- The impact of money varies with the context of the campaign, because all else is rarely equal. Money matters more for some kinds of candidates than for others, and its impact varies in accordance with electoral circumstances.
- Money is most valuable in gaining control of elected office, and less valuable (but still important) in maintaining control.

Scholars do not agree, however, on the implications of this research for the nation's laws governing campaign finance.[23] Proponents of the basic model tend to favor reforms, such as public financing, that would put more money in the hands of challengers. They are skeptical of laws that place overall limits on what candidates can raise and spend on the grounds that it would hurt challengers (who need money the most and tend to spend more efficiently when they have it). In contrast, researchers who find evidence of a positive impact for incumbent spending often advocate spending limits in order to reduce the advantage that well-heeled officeholders typically have over their challengers. The practical and legal complexity of such proposals aside, it may well be that a combination of both approaches would make elections more competitive.[24]

At least three major sets of unanswered questions confront those who wish to study the role of money in campaigns. First, an effort should be made to develop an integrated theory of campaigning and voting. This is critical to enhancing our understanding of what campaign spending does and does not accomplish (Coleman and Manna 2000, 784). Once such a model is in hand, scholars can use it to investigate spending in the full range of campaigns from the courthouse to the White House. It could also be extended to all manner of campaign activities, from outside spending by interest groups to get-out-the-vote efforts.

Second, the practicality of any model might be enhanced if it estimated the number of votes received by a candidate rather than simply the proportion of the two-party vote. After all, real campaigns are dedicated to contacting and persuading actual voters. Such an approach would allow researchers to examine the effects of spending in both large and small constituencies, using the type of office sought as a variable in the analysis. It would be interesting, for example, to know whether campaign spending is more or less important in a presidential or a state legislative campaign. Further, this development would allow for the integration of turnout and vote choice—both of which clearly matter on election day—into the same model.

Finally, having focused largely on total spending, we still do not know a great deal about the effectiveness of different types of campaign expenditures. What, for example, are the relative benefits of spending for television ads versus direct mail? How should campaigns allocate their funds across different areas, and how should those expenditures be distributed over time? What proportion of the budget should be devoted to overhead (in particular, maintaining and staffing a campaign headquarters) versus direct voter contact? Are political consultants worth their fees in terms of helping candidates to win elections? By addressing such questions, scholars can further refine and expand our understanding of the relationship between money and electoral success.

THE POLITICAL PROFESSIONALS RESPOND

Stuart Rothenberg

When candidates for the U.S. House and Senate come to my office to talk about their candidacies and explain how and why they will win election, I ask them dozens of questions. I ask them everything from their dates of birth and their education to what they did after school and what kind of political experience they have had. I also ask them who they have hired to conduct their polling and to produce direct mail and media, and, of course, I ask them what they will talk about during the campaign.

But no set of questions is more important than, "How much money have you raised?" "How much will the race cost?" and "What evidence do you have that you can raise the money you will need?" These questions often determine whether I think a candidate has a chance of winning, or whether he or she is at most a long shot. Money doesn't guarantee victory, but the lack of money almost always guarantees defeat.

I've seen hundreds of candidates over the years who were poised, articulate, thoughtful, sincere, and even knowledgeable about the issues, yet were unable to raise enough money to win. At the same time, I've seen hundreds of less prepared and less appealing candidates who, sometimes because of their own deep pockets, ended up winning because of their financial resources. A blizzard of television ads, particularly during a favorable political environment, can overcome a mountain of candidate liabilities.

All of this explains why the Federal Election Commission's quarterly reports of candidate receipts, expenditures, and cash on hand are dissected by academics, political reporters, and campaign consultants, particularly in the year *before* an election actually takes place. Those figures constitute one of the few reliable quantitative measures of candidate quality, and they usually demonstrate which candidates will have the resources to compete in the crucial post–Labor Day period, and which ones won't.

During the 2007–2008 election cycle, Republican operatives were singing the praises of challenger Steve Greenberg, a businessman who took on incumbent Illinois Democratic representative Melissa Bean. But when Greenberg failed to show much fundraising muscle quarter after quarter (and failed to put in as much personal money as he had led people to believe he would), his stock plummeted and the National Republican Congressional Committee started promoting other candidates who showed greater potential.

In their chapter, Currinder and Green do an excellent job surveying the literature on money and campaigns. They note that money is just one of many factors affecting congressional elections, that money is more important to challengers than to incumbents, and that *when* money is spent is also important. They point out, too, that money both follows strong candidates and creates strong candidates. I wouldn't fundamentally disagree with these conclusions, or with any of the authors' other conclusions about money and campaigns. And yet, Currinder and Green approach campaigns and campaign finance very differently than I do.

Like other nonacademic observers of and participants in the political process, I use rules of thumb to analyze and assess candidates and campaigns. I never concern myself with trying to quantify the impact of one campaign factor; neither do I focus on one factor as if it could be disaggregated from others. And while Currinder and Green look to generalize about campaign spending, I evaluate individual candidates in particular races, always recognizing that each election cycle is different and that campaigns make hundreds or thousands of important decisions that together can mean victory or defeat.

Currinder and Green certainly are correct that money is more important for challengers than incumbents, even though news reports often imply that money is of equal import to both. But after watching thousands of congressional races over decades, I take that as a given, not as a hypothesis needing to be tested. But I also know that, under certain circumstances, an incumbent's money can be crucial.

When I evaluate candidates, I need to know whether they are going to raise "enough" money, not whether they are going to keep pace with the incumbent's fundraising. (Currinder and Green label this the *threshold effect.*) What is "enough money"? It depends. It depends on the candidates (primary and general election); how popular or unpopular the incumbent is; the partisan makeup of the electorate; the size, population, and location of the state or district; the number of media markets and the cost of buying ads; the mood of the electorate; which party controls the White House; how active "outside groups" will be during the campaign; and other factors. In 1994, veteran Illinois Democratic representative Dan Rostenkowski, chairman of the powerful House Ways and Means Committee, was upset by an unknown, underfunded Republican challenger, Michael Flanagan. Flanagan didn't have the money needed to win in ninety-nine of one hundred challenges to Rostenkowski, but 1994 was that rare election when voters were so angry at Democrats that they ousted a long-term incumbent who had not had a serious race since he was first elected in 1958. The cycle was unique, and Flanagan was a fluke. But flukes make politics interesting.

The timing of contributions and spending is also critical. In Minnesota in 2008, Democratic challenger Elwyn Tinklenberg received a flood of contributions after Republican incumbent representative Michele Bachmann made a controversial statement on a cable television program. But his campaign was too weak, and the money came in too late, to allow him to benefit from the financial windfall.

For me and others involved in the day-to-day grind of politics, campaigns are about blood and guts—about real people making daily decisions regarding tactics and strategy. In most academic research, money is about statistical relationships—numbers on a page that, for me, don't come close to telling the whole story about candidates, campaigns, and voters. Yes, money is absolutely crucial to candidates in their efforts to achieve name recognition, to try and define for voters what the election should be about, and to organize telephone banks and direct-mail campaigns. But what did the candidate say on the stump the other day? How effective is the latest television ad likely to be? Is the national political landscape changing in a way that benefits the candidates of one party and severely disadvantages the candidates of the other?

If there is any subject on which Currinder and Green might spend more time it is that of "outside" groups and "outside" money. Spending by outside groups, including the two House campaign committees and the two Senate campaign committees, is large enough to impact the outcome of individual races. Candidate spending still is crucial, of course, but spending by party campaign committees, so-called 527s (a reference to their place in the Internal Revenue Service code), and interest groups increasingly matters, given our current campaign finance laws.

Republican representative John Hostettler of Indiana won reelection after reelection until he was finally defeated in 2006, even though he typically refused to put in the kind of effort or raise the size war chest that most of his vulnerable GOP colleagues did. He kept winning either because his Democratic opponent ran a poor campaign and the political environment strongly benefited the GOP, or because the National Republican Congressional Committee spent heavily on his behalf to pull him across the line. In 2008, the Democratic Congressional Campaign Committee did the same thing for Larry Kissell, who would not have been elected to the U.S. House without the committee's spending on his behalf. More recently, in the November 2009 special election in New York's twenty-third congressional district to fill the seat left vacant by Republican John McHugh, who was appointed Secretary of the Army by President Barack Obama, Conservative Party nominee Doug Hoffman became a factor because of spending by the Club for Growth, an antitax conservative group that spent early and often on Hoffman's behalf. Without the group's involvement, Hoffman might well not have achieved credibility and turned a two-way battle between the major-party nominees into a three-way contest.

Currinder and Green do, of course, mention outside spending. For example, they note the $3 million spent by the Democratic Senatorial Campaign Committee against North Carolina senator Elizabeth Dole (R) in her 2008 bid for reelection. But anyone who watched that race closely knows that it was the *timing* of the spending that was crucial. The committee attacked Dole very early in the cycle, driving up her negatives so that her Democratic challenger, Kay Hagan, looked like a more credible challenger and had time to raise her own funds. Had the committee sat back and waited until late in the campaign to attack Dole, the senator's strong standing in the polls (boosted by early positive television advertising by her own campaign) would likely have prevented Hagan from ever crossing the threshold of credibility. The race, in short, would never have developed.

Political scientists study aspects of politics in minute detail, looking to isolate variables, explain relationships, and quantify the importance of factors. That's what they do. But for those involved in actual races, either as operatives or reporters, the various factors in a race—the candidate, issues, money, media, and organization—are but parts of a whole that change from day to day, and from election cycle to election cycle.

Notes

1. Figures for 2008 are provided by the Center for Responsive Politics, www.opensecrets.org.

2. Interestingly, these claims are stated most clearly in the political science literature; see, for example, Jacobson (1980); Green and Krasno (1988); Erikson and Palfrey (1998).

3. The House incumbent reelection rate was 87 percent in 1964, 88 percent in 1966, 85 percent in 1970, 88 percent in 1974, and 88 percent in 1992; see www.opensecrets.org/bigpicture/reelect.php?cycle=2006 for both House and Senate reelection rates for all years from 1964–2008.

4. These figures are provided by the Center for Responsive Politics, www.opensecrets.org/bigpicture/incumbs.php?cycle=2008&Party=A&Type=A.

5. There are many reasons for the greater importance of incumbency in recent congressional elections, ranging from more precise redistricting to the increased perquisites of office. For a brief summary of these factors, see James Campbell (2003, 144–145).

6. See Abramowitz and Segal (1986), Abramowitz (1988), Alan Gerber (1998), and Goldstein and Freedman (2000) for a few studies that examine campaign spending in U.S. Senate races. Regarding spending in gubernatorial elections, see Bardwell (2005), Partin (2002), Beyle (1986), and Samuel Patterson (1982).

7. The vote measure used is sometimes the challenger's, sometimes the incumbent's, and sometimes the winner's percentage of the two-party total; on other occasions, the winning candidate's margin of victory (winner's minus loser's vote percentage) is the dependent variable.

8. See Jacobson (1978, 1980, 1985, 1987, 1989, 1990). The preferred statistical technique used for testing the basic model is ordinary least squares (OLS) regression analysis; see Jacobson (1985) for a more detailed discussion.

9. See, for example, Glantz, Abramowitz, and Burkart (1976); Abramowitz and Segal (1986); Abramowitz (1988, 1991). For summaries, see Donald Gross and Goidel (2003); Malbin and Gais (1998); Jacobson (1985).

10. The basic model typically shows that party strength in the district, challenger's party, and challenger quality all have a significant impact on the vote. For a good summary, see Jacobson (2001).

11. Although the threshold appears to vary with type of race and year, Jacobson (1985, 43–44) estimated that congressional challengers needed to spend at least $250,000 in 1986 to be minimally competitive; in Table 5.2, that figure would be about $500,000.

12. The technique of choice here is two-stage least squares regression analysis, in which OLS regression is performed on one candidate's spending, typically the incumbent, and the estimated results (called "instrumental variables") are entered into a second-stage OLS regression (Jacobson 1985; see also Abramowitz 1991; Green and Krasno 1988).

13. These might include, for example, such purely personal items as home mortgage payments, country club memberships, and family vacations. On the campaign side, candidates spend money for fundraising, overhead (for campaign headquarters), polling, contributions to other campaigns, and a variety of activities not aimed specifically at communicating with and mobilizing voters.

14. These studies used two-stage least squares regression analysis and instrumental variables; see Green and Krasno (1988) for details.

15. See Green and Krasno (1988, 887–889) for a detailed description of how they capture variations in candidate attractiveness and skill. By separating candidates' personal qualities from their fundraising skills, the authors are able to more accurately assess the characteristics that lead to political (and therefore fundraising) success.

16. The technique employed was three-stage least squares regression analysis; see Goidel and Gross (1994) for details.

17. Erikson and Palfrey used a simultaneous equations technique with a three-equation system and uncorrelated errors solution.

18. Because their analysis was at the individual level, these results are not strictly comparable to those based on aggregate-level data (Kenny and McBurnett 1994, 705).

19. One obvious consideration here is that the people who are most responsive to campaign spending (those with less education) are also the least likely to vote.

20. These represent figures reported to the Federal Election Commission through November 3, 2008. See Campaign Finance Institute (2008).

21. In 2002, Congress passed the Bipartisan Campaign Reform Act, which banned party soft money (funds not subject to federal rules on the size and source of contributions because they are raised and spent to support party-building activities and issue advocacy) and restricted some forms of political advertising. One consequence of the act—usually known as "McCain-Feingold" after Senate sponsors John McCain (R-Ariz.) and Russ Feingold (D-Wis.)—is that some of the banned party soft money was redirected into interest-group committees formed under section 527 of the federal tax code. These "527 committees" are tax-exempt and supposedly exist to express opinions on *issues* rather than candidates; they are therefore not subject to the same contribution

limits as PACs. The line between issue advocacy and candidate advocacy, however, is often blurred. In 2007, the U.S. Supreme Court attempted to clarify some of the ambiguities by exempting from federal law any broadcast advertising paid for by 527 committees that "a reasonable person" would interpret as issue-centered rather than candidate-centered (*Federal Election Commission v. Wisconsin Right to Life*); as a result, there was a marked increase in issue advertising during the 2008 congressional elections, compared to races in 2000 and 2004. In March 2009 and again in September 2009, the Court heard a challenge to the part of the law that prohibited 527 committees from spending money contributed by corporate or union treasuries in federal candidate campaigns within thirty days of a primary, or sixty days of a general election (*Citizens United v. FEC*). In a 5–4 decision that was announced on January 21, 2010, the Court struck down the sixty-year-old federal restriction on corporate expenditures in candidate elections and ruled that the federal government may not ban independent political spending by corporations in candidate elections, although it remains illegal for corporations to contribute directly to federal campaigns from their corporate treasuries. Two other cases currently in the federal court system (*EMILY's List v. FEC* and *Speechnow.org v. FEC*) seek to further loosen federal restrictions on contributions to groups that engage in candidate advocacy. Many campaign finance experts see a broad deregulatory trend in the federal courts, favoring challenges brought forth by opponents of current campaign finance law.

22. See Copeland (1983); Caldeira, Patterson, and Markko (1985); Jackson (1996). Much of the money that candidates spend today is for negative attacks on the opposition. Although some research purports to show that negative advertising reduces turnout (Ansolabehere et al. 1994), the bulk of the evidence seems to suggest otherwise (Clinton and Lapinski 2004; Finkel and Geer 1998; Freedman and Goldstein 1999; Goldstein and Freedman 2002a; Kahn and Kenney 1999; Lau and Pomper 2001).

23. Every major research report cited in this chapter considered campaign finance reform from the perspective of its own findings.

24. For a good summary of the issues involved here, see Goidel, Gross, and Shields (1999).

6 Political Advertising

Michael M. Franz

The 2008 elections were historic in many ways. The race for the White House, for example, featured no incumbent president or vice president for the first time in fifty-six years. An African American topped the Democratic ticket, and a woman was the vice-presidential nominee on the Republican side. Turnout was at its highest level in nearly forty years,[1] and one candidate (Barack Obama) became the first major-party nominee to reject general election public funding since it became available in 1976. In the congressional context, Democrats completed an unprecedented turnaround begun in 2006 by expanding their majority control in the House and approaching a filibuster-proof sixty seats in the Senate. Beyond these qualities, 2008 also featured the most political advertising seen in the modern period of American elections. According to the Wisconsin Advertising Project, which tracks advertising in all 210 media markets in the United States, Obama, John McCain, and their respective party and interest group allies aired 542,199 ads between September 1 and election day; that averages to 8,400 ads per day across the country.[2] It was also 81,000 ads more than the John Kerry and George W. Bush forces mustered in 2004—an 18 percent increase in just four years. The jump in ads was not limited to the presidential contest, however. Between 2004 and 2008, ads for House and Senate races increased more than 33 percent in the top seventy-five media markets.[3]

While the abundance of political advertising may not seem shocking to the casual observer, the stark increase over a four-year period appeared to violate the common presumption that television ads are soon to be replaced by online social networking, a cheaper alternative than broadcast and an innovative way to reach younger voters. In their seminal study of young voters in contemporary American politics, Winograd and Hais (2008, 154) argued that "[Internet politics] present the possibility of an end to the ever-rising cost of thirty-second television campaign commercials, and the time-consuming and potentially corrupting need to raise the money to pay for them." The development of sophisticated online outreach technologies, they added, "will cause television to lose its role as the primary medium for campaigns to get their messages out to voters in the near future" (163).

The trend toward more online electioneering has also been motivated by general declines in viewership of traditional television programs. DVR and TiVo afford viewers the chance to skip commercials altogether, and viewership for national network news has reached an all-time low in recent years.[4] These changes in Americans' consumption of television have compelled some executives to consider altering their programming. In the fall of 2009, for example, NBC briefly abandoned its traditional 10 p.m. hour of drama for the cheaper and (they hoped) DVR-resistant nightly comedy of Jay Leno.

All of this suggests that candidates will likely scale back their engagement of the air war in the future. The advertising totals in 2008, however, belie the point.[5] Obama in particular, a pioneer in the use of online politicking, nevertheless made aggressive use of televised political advertising in the general election. His vigorous fundraising (more than $300 million for the general election alone) precluded the need for the Democratic Party or allied interest groups to raise and spend money for television ads on his behalf. Indeed, Obama sponsored almost 95 percent of all the ads that benefited his campaign, which means that he aired more broadcast ads than any previous candidate since the invention of television. (It should be noted, by the way, that there also were more ads in the Democratic and Republican primary campaigns of 2008 than in any previous primary season; see Ridout 2009.)

The implication is that the study of political television ads is as relevant as ever. With so much money spent on thirty-second ads, the big question is whether television advertising can persuade voters to cast a ballot for the sponsoring candidate. Is the investment that candidates continue to make in television worth the effort? In this chapter I review evidence provided by academic scholarship that addresses this important concern.[6] Assessing the overall impact of TV ads is really only the beginning, however, as candidates and their advisors also want to know what types of advertising are more or less effective at influencing the behavior of voters and what types of voters are more or less likely to be influenced by political ads. In the consideration of these questions, it is important to point out a number of caveats about what academic research can tell us; that is, there are limits to what political science can definitively say about political ads. In addition, I explore an issue that has received relatively little attention from scholars: the sponsorship effects of political advertising. Specifically, are candidate ads more or less effective than party-sponsored ads? What unique effect (if any) do interest group–sponsored ads have? In the concluding section of the chapter, I reflect on the future of political advertising and comment on advertising effects beyond voter persuasion.

The Big Question: Can Political Ads Persuade?

Political scientists have long been skeptical of the ability of media in general to influence voter decision making in significant ways. This skepticism was inspired by some of the earliest research on the impact of campaigns. Lazarsfeld, Berelson, and Gaudet (1944), for example, found weak evidence of campaign effects in their study of the 1940 presidential election. When voters received campaign communications, the researchers discovered, their candidate preferences rarely changed; rather, receipt of these messages either activated individuals, turning undecided voters into supporters of a candidate in line with their existing political beliefs, or reinforced their initial candidate preferences. Klapper (1960) argued further that the media are likely to have little impact overall because of people's selective exposure to media sources they agree with, and their selective perception and retention of messages from those and other sources. (The specifics behind selective exposure and retention are discussed later in this chapter.) In subsequent years, scholars looked for and speculated about effects in different places (for example, in framing the issue debates within a campaign or in the activation of issues that voters use to evaluate candidates[7]), and a consensus eventually emerged: the impacts of campaigns generally, and of the media specifically, *can* be substantial, but only some of the time and with some of the people (Leighley 2004).[8]

Political advertising is one campaign tool that is expected to have some influence on voters. The research in this area often focuses on two dependent variables: vote choice and candidate evaluations. Because voters' affinity toward candidates is a strong predictor of how they will ultimately vote, the ability of campaign ads to influence such assessments is particularly important. As with the research on campaigns more generally, the consensus is that ads can move votes and candidate evaluations, but usually in small doses. Several experimental studies, for example, have analyzed the impact of advertising on voters' candidate preferences and concluded that advertising can indeed benefit the sponsor (for example, Kaid 1997; Kahn and Geer 1994; Pinkleton 1997, 1998; Kaid and Tedesco 1999; Meirick 2002; Tedesco and Kaid 2003; Valentino, Hutchings, and Williams 2004; Clinton and Owen 2006). With these studies, though, scholars are limited to showing participants just one or a handful of ads and recording their perceptions in the immediate aftermath of the treatment. The long-term impact of exposure on ballot-box decisions remains untested and unknown.

Goldstein and Freedman (2000) broadened the scope of research on campaign effects to include survey data, which allowed for asking voters what they actually did at the polls on election day.[9] This particular study examined the impact of advertising in several U.S. Senate races using the 1996 American National Election Studies data set.[10] Combining an extensive database of ads aired in the country's largest media markets with survey-based measures of respondents' television viewing habits, the authors created a relative measure of ad exposure. Their analysis revealed that as exposure to a Senate challenger's advertising increased, the likelihood of voting for that candidate increased as well; the same was true for incumbent advertising. Franz and Ridout (2007) adopted a very similar approach (but with panel data instead of a cross-sectional sample) in their study of how advertising influenced vote choice and candidate favorability in U.S. Senate races in 2004 and in that year's presidential election. They, too, found that advertising had a significant impact.

Johnston, Hagen, and Jamieson (2004) also conducted an individual-level analysis, using ad tracking data at the market level to measure the information environment. Their setting was the 2000 presidential contest, and their key measure of advertising was the difference in the number of ads aired in a particular market between Al Gore and George W. Bush in the previous week. Using the National Annenberg Election Survey, they found that overall ad volumes had an impact on the probability of voting for Bush. The net effect of advertising varied over time, depending on the candidates' relative advertising advantages, ranging from pro-Gore by two percentage points to pro-Bush by four percentage points. This persuasive effect was confirmed by Huber and Arceneaux (2007), who examined the same data as Johnston and colleagues but confined the analysis to non-battleground states, thereby eliminating the correlation between ad buys and candidates' ground efforts in highly contested states.[11]

Other researchers have examined ad effects at the aggregate level through the use of actual vote tallies or poll standings. For example, Daron Shaw (1999b) looked at advertising in the 1988, 1992, and 1996 presidential campaigns, matching the number of ads aired in a state with the percentage of the vote that a candidate earned in that state. In general, statistical models supported the conclusion that advertising had its intended impact, increasing the vote share of the candidate who had an ad advantage. Shaw found, however, that the magnitude of the effect varied from one election to the next, with ads mattering the most in 1996, least in 1992, and in 1988 lying somewhere in between (see also Althaus, Nardulli, and Shaw 2001).

Shaw's approach to the study of ad effects has one important advantage: it allows for the calculation of how many votes the airing of an ad gets a candidate. This is not possible with survey-based research, which in most instances can only estimate the change in probability of an individual's voting for a particular candidate. With only one thousand respondents in a typical survey, for example, there simply are too few cases to aggregate the results up to a predicted campaign outcome. The use of vote tallies or pooled survey data, however, is one method of assessing actual impacts. In Shaw's (1999b) cross-sectional models of state-level vote returns, an increase of 500 gross rating points (GRPs) of advertising in a state boosted a presidential candidate's share of the vote by 2.2 percentage points; this is the equivalent of airing one hundred ads during programs with an average rating of 5 (reflecting moderate popularity). His pooled-time series models using poll data predicted similar impacts of advertising: a 500-gross-rating-points increase in a state for a candidate would result in a 1.6 percentage point increase in support.[12] A follow-up study (D. R. Shaw 2006) discovered a significant impact for advertising in the 2000 and 2004 presidential races, but the size of the impact was smaller. In both elections, a 1,000-gross-rating-points advantage for Bush was estimated to produce a 0.1 percentage point increase in the Republican share of the general election vote.

More recently, Franz and Ridout (2010) used county-level vote returns in the 2008 election to assess the impact of advertising for Barack Obama and John McCain. In line with previous scholarship, they discovered a significant relationship between ad buys and vote returns. Having a one thousand–ad advantage across the entire campaign, for example, resulted in a roughly 0.5 percentage point improvement in a candidate's share of the vote at the county level. The greatest observed difference between candidate advertising in one media market was about five thousand ads, however, meaning that a 2.5 percentage point improvement was a realistic upper limit on the effect of advertising on vote share in a given county.

Caveats

The finding that advertising can influence both individual vote choice and aggregate vote tallies is a comfort to consultants and candidates, who have been buying television ads for more than fifty years. The relatively small overall effect, however, is an important qualifier. One obvious reason for this is the tendency for effective, but competing, messages to cancel each other out (Zaller 1996); that is, someone may be exposed to one hundred John Kerry ads, but also to one hundred George W. Bush ads. In such situations, it is not surprising that little persuasion takes place. Of course, in many races and in many media markets, candidates can score decent-sized ad advantages over their opponent (Goldstein 2004), and these are where effects are usually located.[13] In competitive races, however, both sides (investing considerable sums of money) often have comparable resources and see minimal gains on election day. If one candidate airs no ads while the other airs many, the latter will undoubtedly reap great rewards; but in almost no modern campaign would an otherwise competitive candidate unilaterally disarm in such a manner.

Although one way that candidates can overcome this is to produce *better* ads than their opponent, this is more easily said than done. Geiger and Reeves (1991) tested whether the structure and style of political ads (multiple scenes with quick camera cuts versus a single shot) influence effectiveness, and they found evidence that a dynamic ad does in fact tend to produce more favorable viewer reactions. Political scientists, however, have not produced enough research along these lines to say with any confidence what constitutes an effective ad. If a candidate airs an ad about education or health care, for example, it might be easy (for consultants, candidates, or scholars) to say that it is well produced or compelling in terms of content, but the effect on voters will likely depend on a variety of other factors such as how many times it airs and the nature and timing of ads by the opponent's campaign.

Which Types of Ads Persuade?

The caveat discussed above has led scholars to ask whether certain types of ads, on balance, tend to be more effective than others. This question has generally focused on the tone of political ads, most especially negative versus positive. Negative campaigning is prevalent in American politics. According to the Wisconsin Advertising Project, nearly one in every three ads aired on television is primarily an attack on an opposing candidate.[14] There is also evidence that negativity in campaigns, and on television specifically, is higher in recent elections than in the 1960s, 1970s, and 1980s (Kaid and Johnston 2001; Geer 2006; West 2009).

Attack ads in campaigns are not random, as different candidates operating under different circumstances may have greater or lesser incentive to highlight weaknesses in their opponents. For example, challengers are often more negative than incumbents (Lau and Pomper 2004; Kahn and Kenney 2004) because they need to be, while both candidates in competitive elections are likely to go on the attack (Franz et al. 2008a). The frequency of negative ads also tends to increase as the campaign progresses and voters start paying more attention to the impending election (Kahn and Kenney 2004), and there is some evidence suggesting that negativity in one campaign is driven by (changes in) the level of negativity by the other campaign (Sides n.d.). In addition, the overall negativity of campaign ads sponsored by political parties and outside interest groups appears to be higher than in the case of candidate-sponsored ads (Franz et al. 2008a, 62).

Because negativity is a strategy informed by rational political actors (who presumably would not choose to attack unless experience led them to anticipate a positive result), it is fair to predict that such ads will frequently have the "intended" effect—that is, to lower evaluations of the attacked candidate and generate support for the ad's sponsor. Further, voters' general disapproval of negative campaigning notwithstanding,[15] many political professionals and scholars alike believe that the impact of positive ads is often weaker than that of negative ads. Fridkin and Kenney (2004), for example, found these intended effects in the 1988–1992 U.S. Senate elections, specifically with certain types of negative messages; negative messages deemed legitimate by voters (discussing issues relevant to the campaign) tended to lower evaluations of the targeted candidate. A number of experimental studies, including the work of Pfau et al. (1989) and Kaid (1997; see also Kaid and Boydston 1987), also support the intended effects hypothesis.

However, a second possible effect of negative advertising is a backlash effect (Garramone 1984; Lemert, Wanta, and Lee 1999). In other words, viewers of negative ads might lower their evaluations of the sponsoring candidates if they believe the advertising is untruthful or unfair, and thus they would become less rather than more likely to vote for that candidate. The idea here is that viewers may sometimes punish candidates for going negative, and there is at least suggestive evidence in the literature that such a backlash is not infrequent. Jasperson and Fan (2002), for example, observed an apparent backlash against Republican Party ads aired in Minnesota against Sen. Paul Wellstone in 1996. Lau and Pomper (2004), in addition to some results that were consistent with the intended effects hypothesis, also found backlash effects, particularly among incumbents; a similar finding was noted by Kahn and Kenney (2004) in their own study of U.S. Senate campaigns.

A third consequence of negative advertising is that it might lower evaluations of both candidates, which is called the *double-impairment effect* (Merritt 1984; Basil, Schooler, and Reeves 1991; Shapiro and Rieger 1992; Pinkleton 1997, 1998). Here, the ad has its intended effect, lowering evaluations of the attacked candidate, but also a backlash effect. The net result on persuasion will clearly be small in these circumstances. Fridkin and Kenney (2004) found a double-impairment effect for certain types of negative campaigns, specifically those described as having degenerated into "mudslinging" (attacks on a candidate's character or personal traits).

What remains a puzzle in each of these models linking ad tone and vote choice is the specific mechanism that connects the treatment with the effect, which is generally not well specified. One possible mechanism is provided by a *cognitive account,* in which people presumably learn positive information about the ad sponsor or negative information about the ad's target; that information then leads them to update their evaluations of the candidates. There is a good amount of research, for example, suggesting that negative ads are more memorable (Brians and Wattenberg 1996; Kahn and Kenney 2000, 2004) and contain more information (Geer 2006) than positive ads, a point I will return to later in the chapter. Another possibility is provided by an *affect transfer account* (Marcus and MacKuen 1993; Marcus, Neuman, and MacKuen 2000), where an ad generates positive feelings for the sponsor and a negative ad generates negative affect for the target. Thus, the important mechanism in this alternative model is the emotional or psychological reactions evoked by viewership.

The latter account underlies the work of researchers who examine the specific, discrete emotions elicited by advertising (Chang 2001; Brader 2006). To these scholars, ads that elicit anger, fear, or anxiety, for example, may transfer those negative emotions to the targeted candidate, thereby resulting in lower voter evaluations of that candidate and a diminished likelihood of voting for that candidate. In some sense, then, certain ads might frighten or anger viewers into voting for one candidate over the other. Likewise, emotions such as pride and enthusiasm may be transferred to the ad sponsor, leading to higher evaluations and a greater likelihood of voting for that person. Evidence for the affect transfer model in the realm of political advertising is preliminary. For example, Brader's experimental research (2006) found that exposure to enthusiasm cues embedded in political ads actually lowered affect toward the ad's sponsor (instead of making receivers feel more warmly toward that candidate), although they also reinforced support for the sponsor among his or her initial supporters. Brader also found that fear appeals were effective in moving voters toward the ad's sponsor, particularly among those who initially favored the opposing candidate.

Caveats

In many ways, the evidence is clear that negative ads can work to benefit the sponsor. On the other hand, the risk of a backlash is real, and political consultants and candidates are very sensitive to the possibility. Along with any message that attacks the opposition comes the possibility that viewers will instead reject both the message and the messenger. The problem with the available research is that it does not allow us to predict with confidence which effect is more likely. This is probably the one key area in the study of political advertising where there is the least consensus among academics. Lau, Sigelman, and Rovner (2007) performed a meta-analysis of the large literature on ad tone and persuasion and found very little evidence that negative advertising consistently has its intended impact. Indeed, intended and backlash effects were about as frequent. Lau and colleagues (2007, 1183) concluded that "negative campaigning is no more effective than positive campaigning"—this despite the fact that negative ads tend to be more memorable.

Of course, some scholars speculate that the variation within negativity is of crucial importance. The presence, absence, and type of emotional appeal are sources of variation that have already been noted. Another possible factor relates to the use of contrast ads (Jamieson, Waldman, and Sherr 2000), which compare candidates' issue positions or personal characteristics and may provoke a different response than ads that strictly attack the opposition. Contrast ads contain potentially valued discussions of risks, but are designed not to stray too far from voters' expectations of positive information (Pinkelton 1997). Campaign consultants, in particular, resist characterizing their clients' ads as negative if they contain any comparison of positions or traits. Compared with negative ads, contrast ads are predicted to more frequently have the intended impact.

Another source of variation relates to the difference between negativity and mudslinging mentioned earlier. There is some evidence to suggest, for example, that issue-based attack ads are more likely to have the intended effect than those that attack candidate characteristics or character (Kahn and Geer 1994). Finally, there are a host of other potential intervening variables that might diminish the potential for backlash, including the use of humor (Pfau, Parrott, and Lindquist 1992) or providing content and maintaining a tone that voters consider to be "relevant," "civil," or "fair" (Fridkin and Kenney 2008; Lawton and Freedman 2001). This research is ongoing, and it is certainly possible that intended or backlash effects are more idiosyncratic than scholars might like; in other words, their impact may depend on too many factors to allow for generalized rules of thumb that apply to all races in all circumstances. With this in mind, the message to candidates is clear: negative ads are potentially rewarding but highly risky—tread lightly when going on the attack.

Which Types of Voters Are Persuadable?

Although the characteristics of campaign ads themselves should influence their effectiveness, one should not overlook how the characteristics of those who receive the ads play a role as well. There are at least two receiver characteristics that are important moderators of ad effectiveness: the receiver's level of political awareness and his or her partisanship.

The moderating influence of political awareness on persuasion is expressed most clearly and most succinctly in the existing scholarship through the *dosage-resistance model* (Krosnick and Brannon 1993; Iyengar and Simon 2000). The basics of the model are straightforward. Every voter is aligned at some point on the political awareness scale. At the low end are political novices who know little about politics; when asked, for example, to identify the majority party in Congress or the job that Gordon Brown held, they are unable to do so. They may very well be interested in politics or care about the larger issues, but in practical terms they have no preexisting store of political information. This is in sharp contrast to the political junkies on the high end of the scale who know everything there is to know about politics and keep daily tabs on political events.

These varying levels of political awareness are expected to moderate to a great degree the impact of political information that floods American voters during an election season. The model first predicts that as political awareness rises, the greater the chance voters will "receive" the message in the first place—that is, the greater the chance they will understand and take in political events or news. As an example, imagine a voter watching television who is exposed to a candidate ad about health care. The message is received if the voter understands the point of the ad and is able to discuss the ideas and arguments raised in the message. Zaller (1992) calls the assumed relationship between reception and political awareness his *reception axiom*. In contrast, with rising political awareness comes a decline in a voter's "yielding" potential, referring to the degree to which the person is persuadable. For those who possess little or no political knowledge, new information might easily sway their decision making. But for voters with large stores of political information, new messages have greater difficulty breaking through and are more likely to be counter-argued.

When we combine reception and yielding, we can see that those on the low end of the awareness scale need the information the most (high yielding potential) but are unlikely to attend to or understand it (low reception potential). Those on the high end of the scale are more likely to attend to and understand it (high reception potential) but are less likely to need or respond to it (low yielding potential). The model consequently predicts that those with moderate levels of political information are most likely to "accept" a political message.

Yet one might argue that the nature of the thirty-second spot, expertly designed to convey a simple message and often appeal to emotions, makes it easier for low-information voters to take them in and be influenced by them. This is in contrast to many political messages that are difficult to process and understand, for example, hour-long discussions on the Sunday morning talk shows, candidate interviews or reports on *60 Minutes* and *Nightline,* exposés in *Vanity Fair* and *Newsweek,* detailed policy statements on candidate Web sites or blogs—all of which require a considerable investment by the message receiver, and can often be too complicated for many citizens. Campaign ads, however, are designed to convey a simple, evocative message in short bursts (and with sometimes numbing repetition). Knowing nothing about the issues or the candidates does not preclude someone from reacting to a simple, compelling message about family, morals, the economy, or national security.

From this perspective, the standard dosage-resistance model may be inaccurate for the study of political advertising. For example, some research (Franz et al. 2008a) shows that campaign ads have as much of an impact (and sometimes even a larger impact) on the knowledge and political interest of low-information citizens as on the knowledge and interest of high-information citizens, suggesting that even those without much political awareness are able to receive the message. Such evidence changes expectations about the probable effect of campaign ads. Now, a revised dosage-resistance model predicts that persuasion will be located chiefly among individuals who are low in political awareness. The reasoning here is that, with political advertising, novices have a high chance of reception *and* a high yielding potential.

The few studies of political advertising that look specifically for effects moderated by political awareness appear to confirm this pattern. An experimental study by Valentino, Hutchings, and Williams (2004), for example, showed that persuasion occurred mainly among low-information voters.

Huber and Arceneaux (2007) analyzed the 2000 Annenberg panel survey and found that low to moderately educated voters (though not the least educated) were most influenced by political advertising in the 2000 presidential election. Franz and Ridout (2007) also observed effects for low-information voters who were exposed to presidential and Senate ads during the 2004 campaign. The focus on Senate ads in this last study is worth noting. Some scholars have suggested that political novices are most likely to be influenced by a range of campaign messages in particularly intense campaign environments where the flows of information are so heavy that voters can hardly avoid electioneering efforts. Zaller (1992, 267), in fact, said so explicitly, arguing that when campaigns are extremely intense even the less knowledgeable are able to acquire relevant election information. Presidential races certainly qualify as intense campaign environments, but Senate races tend to be decidedly less intense.

While there is a body of research showing that political messages have the greatest impact on *highly* aware citizens, the bulk of these findings have to do with the impact of news messages and are concerned with priming (the activation of issues that voters use to evaluate candidates), not persuasion (Druckman 2004; Krosnick and Brannon 1993; Miller and Krosnick 2000). On that score, Krosnick and Brannon (1993, 972) argued that high-knowledge individuals "have a greater ability to interpret, encode, store, and retrieve new information." This expectation is most compelling for news reports and other campaign messages because they are sometimes quite difficult to understand, a condition not necessarily true for political ads. The short, intense format of the thirty-second political spot does not preclude low-information voters from processing the message. Consider this point also in the context of our earlier discussion regarding ad characteristics. If the effectiveness of political ads is due largely to a transfer of affect (fear, anger, enthusiasm, anxiety, hope, and so forth), there is no reason to expect that low-information voters will be unable to receive and process such emotional appeals.

The second characteristic of the receiver that should moderate the effectiveness of political advertising is the person's partisanship. One might expect that independents, because they have no basis for resisting the messages of any candidate as being inconsistent with their existing partisan views, are often influenced by exposure to advertising from both sides. In contrast, Democratic advertising should have little impact on Republicans (although it presumably *will* increase support for the sponsor among Democrats), and the opposite should apply for Republican advertising (which should have the greatest effect on independents and Republican identifiers). Thus, in addition to influencing independents, one effect of the campaign may be to bring partisans home, just as Lazarsfeld, Berelson, and Gaudet (1944) noted more than a half century ago.

The literature speaking to this hypothesis has offered a mixed assessment of its validity. Chang (2003) reported that it was partisans who were influenced most by ad exposure, as expected, but not political independents. Likewise, a series of experiments by Ansolabehere and Iyengar (1995) supported the claim that nonpartisan voters are "the least receptive to political advertising" (77). Instead, these authors concluded that the effect of campaign advertising is mainly *reinforcement,* moving voters to cast ballots in line with their existing partisan inclinations (see also Iyengar, Jackman, and Hahn 2008). At the same time, however, a different experimental study (Kaid 1997) found support for the opposite conclusion, that political independents are more influenced by watching political ads than are partisans.

Caveats

There is one major concern associated with political advertising if its primary audience is (or the most receptive viewers are) low-information voters: Are ads manipulating those with less interest or knowledge about politics? Given that the less informed seem disproportionately likely to be persuaded by campaign ads, is it possible that these ads are shifting voters away from a choice that would be more in line with their interests and preferences (see chapter 4 in this volume)? Are less attentive voters being duped into a choice they would not normally make under conditions of full information? This is possible, of course, and if true it would indicate that ads are more harmful to the democratic process than we might want them to be. Yet the evidence discussed above suggests otherwise; the principal effect of ads is more likely to reinforce existing partisan views (not to drive voters away from their predispositions), and their influence on independents is sporadic at best. Indeed, while campaigns in general—and campaign ads specifically—sometimes appear to have little impact (the "minimal effects" model mentioned earlier), their primary role may be as a heuristic (Franz et al. 2008a) that helps people make quick decisions about how to vote and reminds them what they already like and dislike about the candidates or parties (Gelman and King 1993).

Unanswered Questions: What Influence Does Sponsorship Have?

Most existing research on political advertising examines the general impact of campaign ads, the types of ads that work best, and the types of voters that are most strongly affected. Important questions remain largely unexplored, however. One of the most prominent of these concerns the sponsorship effect of political ads; that is, are party, candidate, or interest group ads more effective? The question here is particularly important because party and interest group ads have become more abundant in recent election cycles. In the mid-1990s, for example, these entities exploited a loophole in federal election laws that allowed them to raise and spend unlimited amounts of unregulated campaign cash for the purpose of buying loosely veiled candidate advocacy ads (Franz 2008).[16] The Bipartisan Campaign Reform Act in 2002 (known also as McCain-Feingold) attempted to rein in interest groups and parties by closing the loophole. This had the effect of eliminating unregulated ads from political parties in elections after 2002, but it also compelled interest groups to form so-called Section 527s—a type of outside group (Swift Boat Veterans for Truth, MoveOn.org, and Progress for America are some examples; see La Raja 2008; Weissman and Hassan 2005) that was generally unrestricted by the new law. Consider these numbers for congressional elections from 2000 through 2004: in Senate races for the three election cycles, respectively, interest groups and parties accounted for 27 percent, 40 percent, and 21 percent of all ads in the top seventy-five media markets. In House races, they accounted for 39 percent, 30 percent, and 28 percent, respectively.[17]

Advertising sponsorship raises numerous questions with regard to persuasion effects. For example, is there an impact associated with party or interest group ads that is distinct from the impact of ads aired by candidates? Clearly, if interest group ads are generally less effective, the rising investment by these sponsors in recent years would represent an inefficient use of resources. Might party ads be more effective for challengers who often have trouble raising enough money on their own to compete against entrenched incumbents (Wallison and Gora 2009)? Do party and interest group ads help to shield candidates from the potential backlash produced by negative ads? (Recall, there is a good amount of research showing that such backlash is not uncommon.) That is, does negative advertising by parties and groups allow candidates to deny involvement in attack campaigns (Magleby and Monson 2004)? If so, the increased involvement of outside groups should, in the aggregate, enhance the persuasion effects of political advertising, assuming that candidates shift toward positive ads and outside groups carry the burden of attacks. However, voters may not distinguish well among sponsors. Despite the mandate for candidates to "stand-by-their-ad" (another change mandated by McCain-Feingold in 2002), most ads, regardless of sponsor, do not mention the party of the favored candidate (Holman and McLoughlin 2001); in fact, direct partisan appeals are not common components of television ads at all (Spiliotes and Vavreck 2002). Under the circumstances, it is possible that party, group, and candidate ads will tend to have similar levels of effectiveness.

One exception to the dearth of scholarship on this topic is Magleby (2004), who finds no sponsor-based effects on vote intention in his study of advertising in the 2000 presidential election. Using experimental designs, however, Pfau and colleagues (2001, 2002) found that candidate ads have a greater impact on citizen interest in the campaign and knowledge about the candidates, suggesting that voters pay closer attention to these ads. In contrast, research by Garramone (1985) indicated that a group-sponsored attack ad was more persuasive with voters than a comparable candidate-sponsored ad. Questions such as these are increasingly relevant in a world where outside advertising from groups and parties is expected to grow even more in coming election cycles. More good empirical work is needed in order to provide answers.

Campaign Advertising and Effects Beyond Persuasion

Campaigns spend considerable time and money trying to convince voters to cast ballots in particular ways, but this is not their only goal. Mobilization of the electorate can also be very important to a candidate's prospects for victory. Several studies have examined whether heavy levels of television advertising serve to boost turnout levels. Some scholars believe that they do, although only to a relatively modest degree (Hillygus 2005; Franz et al. 2008a, 2008b); others are skeptical (Clinton and Ashworth 2007; Krasno and Green 2008). Most agree, however, that television ads have a much lower probability of increasing turnout than do traditional forms of voter mobilization, such as direct mail or door-to-door contacts (Gerber and Green 2000b; see also chapter 10 in this volume).

A number of researchers have contextualized the question, asking whether and how negative advertising in particular is related to turnout. Evidence from early studies suggested that negative ads tend to demobilize the electorate (Ansolabehere and Iyengar 1995; Ansolabehere, Iyengar, and Simon 1999), thereby providing support for the argument—shared by many political pundits and voters alike—that attack advertising is damaging to democracy. More recent empirical work confirms more robustly that negative ads potentially have a mobilizing effect on turnout, even if very small (Goldstein and Freedman 2002a; Freedman and Goldstein 1999; Martin 2004; Kahn and Kenney 1999; Djupe and Peterson 2002; Lau and Pomper 2004; Wattenberg and Brians

1999). A few studies, however, indicate that there is no relationship between negativity and turnout, which further undermines the argument that negative ads are harmful to the democratic process (Finkel and Geer 1998; Clinton and Lapinski 2004; Brooks 2006).[18]

Beyond persuasion and mobilization, campaigns use advertising to inform the public about candidates' issue positions and personal traits. There is a good deal of evidence that advertising has consistent effects in this regard (see also chapter 4 in this volume). Most famously, Thomas Patterson and McClure (1976) found campaign ads during the 1972 presidential election rife with issue content, leading them to conclude that "presidential advertising contributes to an informed electorate" (117). Indeed, according to Patterson and McClure, television ads in 1972 led to a greater degree of issue learning among voters than did television news. Similarly, Brians and Wattenberg (1996), in their analysis of the 1992 presidential campaign, reported that self-reported ad exposure (and especially exposure to negative ads) was a stronger predictor of political learning than either newspaper reading or television news viewing.

Zhao and Chaffee (1995) provided additional, albeit partial, support for the learning hypothesis; specifically, examining surveys in six different electoral contests, these researchers found advertising to have a discernible positive impact on learning in only three of those contests.[19] Weaver and Drew (2001) and Huber and Arceneaux (2007), in contrast, were unable to document any knowledge gains from advertising. In fact, after finding that ad exposure had a persuasion effect but not a knowledge effect, Huber and Arceneaux concluded that "by manipulating voters' expressed candidate preferences, the partisan balance of the advertising stream has a direct, important, and underdocumented effect on election outcomes" (976). In other words, because ads can persuade without also educating, it is possible that the candidate with the most resources can win an election that she or he might not otherwise have won. This is certainly possible, but remains speculative. As noted earlier, there is very little evidence in any of the existing scholarship that ads are driving people away from candidates whose policy positions are more in line with their predispositions.

Persuasion, mobilization, and education—these are all important goals of campaigns and of campaign advertising. Some scholars have asked, however, whether ads can have effects beyond the goals of candidates. For example, what is the relationship between ad exposure and democratic attitudes such as political interest and efficacy? Franz and his colleagues (2008a) call these *spillover effects* because candidates and their allies are not explicitly interested in changing such perceptions, except perhaps as a means of mobilizing core supporters.

A host of scholarship has looked for various kinds of spillover effects (Freed-man and Goldstein 1999; Schenck-Hamlin, Procter, and Rumsey 2000; Martin 2004; Franz et al. 2008a), but the findings are mixed. Geer (2006), for example, found there to be little relationship between negativity in presidential elections and assessments of voters' faith in elections and trust in government. Yet in their meta-analysis of the growing literature on negative campaigns, Lau, Sigelman, and Rovner (2007) concluded that the bulk of the evidence suggests a slight harmful influence. Even if this is true, however, it is likely that a host of other factors in contemporary American elections (such as the rise of cable news and the twenty-four-hour news cycle, the skyrocketing costs of campaigns, personal scandals involving candidates) and in society generally (including unpopular policies, an ever-increasing national deficit, scandals involving government, business, and religious leaders) have contributed as much or more to citizens' negative feelings toward the political realm.[20] In other words, campaign ads are almost certainly not the only, nor even the main, culprit.

Final Thoughts

Television is one of the primary weapons of many candidates for office, as evidenced by the intensity of the air war in 2008. New campaign tactics, how-ever, are enhancing the tactical options of many candidates and candidate allies, with clear implications for the future of televised political advertising. For example, what effect are online social networking tools and candidate Web sites likely to have in the near term (see chapter 8 in this volume)? The imme-diate impact, perhaps ironically, is a transformation in how candidates and their allies *fund* the air war. According to journalist Kate Kaye (2009), "many political consultants don't think Internet ads can be used to sway voters. . . . Obama grabbed millions of dollars [in 2008] through online fundraising from countless donors giving relatively small amounts of cash. But, as in every elec-tion in recent history, the bulk of that money was spent on television ads" (14, 19). Thus, Internet fundraising has afforded candidates the ability to raise large sums of campaign cash quickly, and that cash is then typically used to fund traditional forms of campaigning offline. Only in the longer term will online campaigning replace television advertising as a primary means of reaching and persuading voters. This is not to diminish the spread of online technologies in the tool bag of campaign tactics; much has been written (and is being written) about what these tactics can do for youth involvement in politics (Harfoush 2009) and for the mobilization of core supporters. Still, we are in the first act of an unfolding story and should therefore be careful not to overemphasize the effects of the Internet on contemporary American elections.

Another trend in elections involves the aggressive mining of consumer purchasing data (tracked by credit card companies) to identify relationships between retail preferences and political choices (Hillygus and Monson 2008); the information is subsequently used to instruct GOTV (get-out-the-vote) efforts and peer-to-peer contacts. Republicans employed this tactic aggressively beginning in the 2004 elections (Gertner 2004; Sosnik, Dowd, and Fournier 2006). Put simply, campaign consultants want to know if conservatives disproportionately purchase domestic beer and subscribe to hunting magazines; if liberals prefer lattes at Starbucks and give often to charities; and if moderates prefer American-made to foreign-made cars. They are able to get answers to these and similar questions through extensive polling that looks for trends and relationships between consumer habits and political attitudes. Voter files are subsequently linked to data on individuals that is purchased from credit card companies and, because polling has identified which consumer habits are associated with which political attitudes, these data can be used by campaigns to develop a highly tailored message that can be sent (via phone calls or direct mailings) only to certain types of consumers/voters. Targeting along these lines can be so precise that a grandmother in apartment 4B might receive a health care mailing that emphasizes the candidate's efforts to secure the long-term viability of Medicare, while the graduate student in apartment 6C receives the student loan mailing outlining the candidate's commitment to affordable education.

This tactic is intended to reduce inefficiencies that come with the use of blanket communications. For example, most campaign ads air on local television news broadcasts, or on talk shows and game shows (Goldstein and Freedman 2002b). A certain demographic, usually older voters, watches these programs (Rivlin 2008), but the overall exposure is broader; that is, an ad will be seen by your base voters, undecided voters, supporters of the other party, *and a large number of nonvoters.* What you say on television, then, is often wasted on people who will never vote for you, or never vote at all. With microtargeting, however, candidates can avoid wasting valuable campaign dollars by directing messages to likely voters and fence-sitters. Doing so is not cheap, and many campaigns (especially in lower ticket races) have not yet adopted it as a primary method of reaching voters. There also are certain normative challenges, including the question of whether it is possible for a candidate to say or frame an issue one way to one group—but then do so differently (playing both sides of the issue) to another group. This is difficult to accomplish with campaign ads because those ads are public and aired to wide audiences. Another normative concern stems from the purchase and use of credit card data by campaigns, parties, and interest groups; voters might justifiably be uncomfortable with the fact that their personal data is used in ways to influence how they vote in elections.

Like the Internet, micro-targeting probably represents the wave of the future in American elections. Many campaign consultants are powerful advocates of emerging technologies and of efforts to devise new ways of mobilizing, persuading, and educating voters; reflecting this, a growing number of campaigns are investing time and effort in trying to find the best way to maximize the return on their efforts. Television, however, is not a creature of the past. It is likely to remain the primary method of communication for presidential candidates, Senate candidates, and many House candidates (not to mention those running for governor and other statewide and state legislative offices). For political scientists, this means there are still more questions to ask about the effect of political advertising, and many opportunities to look for answers.

THE POLITICAL PROFESSIONALS RESPOND

Mike Murphy

Political advertising is as much alchemy as science, so any purely empirical examination of its effects is daunting. Most successful political consultants hold many of the same overall thoughts about the effectiveness and use of political ads, albeit with many caveats based on the type and size of a campaign, the political environment, and the consultants' own unique experiences and beliefs. Those views can be roughly summarized as follows:

- Political paid advertising, particularly television, is the most powerful communications tool that a campaign has.
- The political communications landscape is very noisy and cluttered, and, as a result, huge volumes of simple and direct advertising are needed to break through to voters.
- Targeting of political TV is possible but often not effective because its mass audience makes TV a shotgun instead of a rifle.
- Radio is more targeted but not usually as powerful as TV.

- Social networking, Web ads, and other new media are interesting and growing in effectiveness, but not as powerful or as effective for communications as paid TV ads since many of the most important voters are older (age 55 and older are the most likely to turn out). That said, it is well understood that the landscape is quickly changing with regard to new media.
- Legal disclaimer rules that require long and cumbersome "paid for by" mechanisms in the actual ads make for less effective ads.
- Negative ads, if properly done, can be more effective than positive ads (it is often said that "bad news travels faster"), although this varies widely based on candidate, issue, and the creative quality of a given communication.

The greatest challenge to academic research on the questions surrounding ad effectiveness and impact is that few campaign consultants think the effect of a given television ad can be simply deconstructed along lines of style and type.

Campaigns are complicated, almost organic, organizations where voter perceptions are affected by a swirling and highly interactive combination of ads, candidate images, press reports, spending levels, political environment, issue terrain, and many other factors. Each of these elements affects and, in turn, is affected by the others. Most important, the greatest impact that an ad can have on a campaign often may come less from the viewing of that ad by voters than from its overall *effect* (if run enough to be seen) on the *entire* campaign. For example: a candidate runs a contrast ad on a small issue not well known to the public, or perhaps airs an attack ad about an unknown but controversial aspect of an opponent's record. Spending for the ad is enough to penetrate the media "noise," and that initially small issue becomes a bigger one—that is, it "becomes famous" thanks to the mass media reach of television and radio. The press, voters, the other candidate, interest groups, and various other players start reacting to this new element of the campaign landscape. The dialogue quickly changes, and every actor within the campaign dynamic is instantly affected.

With the right strategy, such a change can be very helpful in framing the campaign and controlling the public dialogue that can have a huge impact on the outcome. Often, an ad that is less effective *per se* but deals with an issue that people care about will do more to determine the winner than a well-done individual ad on a topic that does not impact the main debate. To be sure, political ads can also vary widely in their creative quality. Some ads are poorly done and therefore mightily ineffective. The skill and experience levels of political ad-makers vary widely and are important factors in determining the "street" effectiveness of any ad—something that is hard to control for in an empirical test. Unlike medicine, incompetent ad-making spin doctors operate in a commercial "wild west" with lax professional standards; moreover, they often stay busy in their professional recklessness for a long time, resulting in large numbers of client casualties along the way.

Nevertheless, what really drives campaigns is the direction in which the loud public debate between candidates is pushed. Voters have a limited attention span, candidates have limited resources, and elections take place in finite time. Thus, bandwidth is limited and controlling the debate is crucial. Advertising is a key strategic tool in achieving that objective by forcing advantageous topics, and doing so with ads that frequently are sensational and negative in tone. The press is a key player here. Since the 1950s, the press has become increasingly focused on the *process* of politics, more so than its substance. Reflecting this, ads often are covered as stories in their own right and even used by campaign staffs to get press attention for their candidate. Issues that are pushed by ads, especially when they are negative, may move to the center of the debate and be amplified in volume both by press attention and, even more so, when the other side decides to run a "response" to the original attack.

It is said in professional consulting circles that a good consultant will do something with his or her campaign early one day that allows him or her to control the important actions of *both* campaigns on that day—or, even better, for the entire week or month or, in a perfect scenario, the entire campaign period. The point, then, is less the ads themselves and the specific viewing experience surrounding them and more the message strategy of the campaign as a whole, of which paid ads are the most important and effective tool. It is true that campaign ad-makers spend a lot of time and effort trying to make their ads effective in a search for the greatest bang for the media buck. Better an effective ad that can do its job for 900 rating points than a less effective ad that requires 1,400 rating points to be noticed. Polling, ad-test focus groups, and other research technologies are used by campaigns to help achieve this goal. But it is understood among top campaign professionals that too much linear interpretation of ad-testing results can mislead and prevent ads that may work better "on the street" than in the focus group from being used. Ad effectiveness "over-think" is widely seen as a potential danger to a strategically well-run campaign.

Finally, it is true that spending levels are important. Volume counts. But often the key distinction is the type of race in which the ads are being run, and the result is not always linear. In a presidential campaign, it is generally believed that press attention is more powerful than advertising. No candidate has the budget to run saturation ads in every state; instead, campaigns must deal with a huge amount of press attention, both negative and positive. Voters receive a lot of information through the media filter that campaigns both fear and need. About a dozen swing states get major buys for paid ads, however, and this can obviously have an impact on voter decision making. Under such circumstances, resource planning becomes critical. Campaigns choose which states to invest in, hoping to catch the opponent in a situation where he or she can be out-resourced in a given situation.

In statewide campaigns for U.S. Senate, governor, or down-ballot offices such as state treasurer or attorney general, paid ads are vitally important. Often they are the largest information source in the campaign—the crucial big megaphone that candidates use to influence voters. In races for local office, ads can be less effective in part because many candidates cannot afford saturation advertising. This is especially true of candidates from districts in suburban or urban areas located near a top-twenty television market. Local cable is possible and can be effective if cable system boundaries dovetail with local political districts, but in these places the (shrinking though still very powerful) big hammer of local broadcast advertising may be out of a candidate's financial reach. Paid phone calling and direct mail is frequently used instead, which can also be effective but is usually not as powerful as television ads run at a heavy level.

Academics face a challenging task in evaluating how political TV ads really work through an ad-by-ad typology. Paid ads are only a part, albeit a hugely powerful part, of the complex and highly interactive dialogue shared by voters, candidates, and the press in the communications whirlwind of the modern political campaign.

THE POLITICAL PROFESSIONALS RESPOND

David B. Hill

Franz, in his overview of political advertising research—and particularly in his take on negative, or attack, ads—is primarily concerned with whether this genre of communications is effective in persuading voters. Consultants know it is effective, even without benefit of the correlational analyses and experimental studies that Franz describes. But the working consultant has to contemplate much more than simple effectiveness. In this essay I offer the reader some insights into the complexity surrounding the use of negative advertising.

Consultants pondering an attack ad have a lot of things to think about, including their own client's feelings about the genre. On several occasions in my career, a candidate has sat down with the consulting team during an early planning session and declared spontaneously that he or she doesn't want to do negative ads at any time during the campaign. In taking this stand, the candidate effectively succumbs to the pleadings of editorial boards and other "good government" advocates. There once were organized and active "clean campaign pledge" initiatives that would attempt early in a campaign cycle to get every contestant to sign a pledge eschewing negative ads, although I haven't seen much of them lately. And in GOP primaries, there's still always someone going on about Ronald Reagan's so-called Eleventh Commandment not to speak ill of other Republicans.

Consultant reactions to candidates wanting to prohibit negative ads invariably involve a lot of eye-rolling and whispered suspicions regarding ulterior motives. There is often the feeling that said candidate must be worried about his own "skeletons in the closet" (perhaps some that even his own consultants are unaware of) that an opponent might bring out during back-and-forth responses to attacks. Occasionally a candidate will challenge an opponent to sign a bilateral pledge not to go negative, hoping to avoid some bloody assault that he knows is coming. A candidate may also allow his more civilized spouse, who worries about the family image at the country club, to influence campaign strategy and tactics. Or the candidate feels that running negative ads will cut into the number of positive image ads that most candidates *really* like—feel-good ads that highlight their accomplishments and show them walking and talking with adoring voters or family members in gauzy commercials shot on the same film used by Hollywood, being transformed in the process into near–matinee idols.

Consultants rarely argue at the outset with candidates who want to ban negative ads, unless they actually threaten to sign a "clean campaign" pledge that would limit the options available for later on in the campaign. No, the consultant just smiles at the conflict-avoider and waits until the negative ad is necessary; the need for persuasion is diminished when a candidate looks over a poll and sees that she is trailing. And if the candidate still wants to avoid negative ads, you agree in principle and then proceed to explain how you'll do comparative ads instead (wink, wink). Everyone is happy. Franz accurately captures the spirit of this sleight of hand in his discussion of comparative versus negative ads.

There is one relatively new development now facing attack campaigns—the federally stipulated regulation that requires the candidate to state on air, "I approve this message." The point of this requirement was ostensibly to leverage a point I just made: that many candidates hate negative ads, or at least say they do, and may not want to appear on camera saying they approve of an attack. In my view, this has not really reduced the number of negative ads, although it has inspired a lot of creative ways and means of diverting the sting of the approval. Some candidates put the disclaimer at the beginning, followed by a second or two of black, or the insertion of something positive before the negative content unrolls—anything to build a firewall between the candidate and the objectionable material.

The optimal production style for negative (or even comparative) ads also is becoming more complicated, requiring greater thought and finesse. The reason for this is that voters are catching on to the method and means behind attack ads and, as a result, these ads are becoming harder to pull off with aplomb. Once upon a time, the negative ad had some or all of the following ingredients: scary, from-the-dungeon music for the soundtrack; grainy black-and-white photos of your opponent, a few of which may have been "enhanced" to make him or her look fatter; and visuals of a few scandal headlines clipped from news sources, perhaps read aloud by someone who sounded like an angry judge at sentencing. And there you were—the perfect recipe for a negative ad of the 1980s and 1990s.

In the new millennium, that stuff doesn't seem to be working the way it once did. Now, when I play a spot of that genre in a focus group, most often people just start laughing out loud, like I am showing them a *Saturday Night Live* or Comedy Channel spoof on politics: "Jane, you miserable slut, get that garbage off my TV."[1] Or else they get mad. One guy in Florida stormed up to me after a dial test of a slyly negative ad, with a hardback copy of *War and Peace* under his arm for reading while he waited for the group to begin, and got in my face, literally inches from my nose, snarling, "I know what you are up to and I don't like it!"

That's a problem. Voters recognize what we're up to these days and it makes producing effective attack ads more challenging than ever. Because of "ad-watch" columns[2] in the newspaper, YouTube parodies and critiques of ads, and an electorate that includes too many people who have successfully completed Psychology 101 and one or two communications courses, the audience is on to our tricks. They hear the ugly music and see the grainy photos for what they are.

Because of the public's increasingly cynical response to disparaging ads, many political ad-makers are turning more often to humor to carry a negative message. This strategy has the advantage of giving a nod and a wink to the viewer who sees attack ads as comedic. And, to boot, an old consultant once told me that if you can ever get voters laughing at your opponent, you've got him or her on the ropes. My friend Mike Murphy once discovered in the opposition research file that a conservative Tennessee congressman had used taxpayer dollars to pay for several car washes for the fancy leased car he was using. Murphy crafted an attack ad against the congressman when he tried to upgrade to a seat in the U.S. Senate in a GOP primary. The ad featured a deadpan car wash operator shouting, "Another super-deluxe for the congressman!" as the car started trundling through the tunnel. Then the announcer lampooned the use of tax dollars paying for a car wash. Murphy's client was a moderate, but the fiscal conservative he smacked ended up getting hosed. People were guffawing at the hypocrisy of his misfeasance.

In addition to the credibility of a negative message, campaigns must also worry about the endless cycle of attack and counterattack that frequently ensues. Every consultant worth his or her salt knows that you must respond to an attack. And, generally, the best response is to make a counter-charge. You say that your opponent voted to raise taxes. He responds that you let a little old lady die by not getting her her Social Security check on time. You respond that his divorce file has innuendos of spousal abuse. He brings up that public records show that your child has multiple arrests for marijuana use. And so it goes. It's a vicious and wild ride. And in this day and age of campaign finance restrictions, the more money you spend on rebutting attacks, the less time you have for building name identification and cultivating a positive image.

In some ways, the "all negative, all the time" campaign favors an incumbent or well-known personality who already has an identity and doesn't need to spend as much time and money establishing her persona and bona fides. A newcomer who gets pulled into the grips of a response and counter-response campaign is distracted from the business of establishing her identity. As a result, attack campaigns may ultimately be more advantageous to incumbents, especially where levels of ad spending are limited.

Negative ads also depend on good opposition research. The best research comes from independent sources like the media because you can say, "According to the *Daily Gazette*, Representative Doe has the worst attendance record of any member of Congress." Knowing the raw data that he has the worst record is not as good as saying that independent sources confirm he is often absent; with the latter, you get third-party credibility. The problem with trying to use this approach today is that media outlets are slashing budgets for investigative reporting, so it's harder to get the media to provide the basic grist for negative messaging. Now, campaigns can do the research that newspapers once performed and put the results on a dedicated attack Web site like "TheTruthAboutSenatorDoe.com," perhaps accompanied by some crude Web ads of two minutes or less. The media may then look at these attacks and comment on them in blogs, and eventually the essence of the attack ends up in a "real" news story that a campaign can exploit in an ad that's good enough for broadcast TV. But that ad and the content on which it is based might never have been developed without the investment made in the attack Web site and the research it contained. The moral is that it sometimes takes months to develop the factual and substantive content of a negative ad. It's not something that just happens by walking into a studio with a desire to do damage. Proper attacks require serious preparation to be effective and persuasive.

---

[1]For those too young to remember, this was Dan Ackroyd's typical response to an editorial point (usually from the liberal side of the spectrum) made by Jane Curtin in the show's "Weekend Update" segment during the 1970s.

²See Bennett (1997); Tedesco, Kaid, and McKinnon (2000); Frantzich (2002); Richardson (2008); and West (2009) for overviews of media efforts to monitor ads for accuracy and fairness. Academic research to date reports a mix of effects and noneffects on voters from ad-watch efforts by the media; for example, see Cappella and Jamieson (1994); Ansolabehere and Iyengar (1996).

Notes

1. According to the United States Election Project, 61.7 percent of eligible voters cast a ballot in 2008. The last presidential election with that level of turnout or higher was 1968. See http://elections.gmu.edu/voter_turnout.htm.

2. Information on the Wisconsin Advertising Project can be accessed at http://wiscadproject.wisc.edu.

3. The Wisconsin Advertising Project tracked only the top 75 markets in 2004 for congressional races, compared with the top 210 markets in 2008. For ease of comparison, I looked only at the top 75 markets in each year.

4. In 2006, roughly 26 million people reported watching the network evening news on a daily basis—down from 34.5 million in 1997. These figures were accessed from the Pew Research Center's Project for Excellence in Journalism at www.journalism.org/node/1363.

5. Alternatively, one might argue that candidates will be forced to increase their ad buys in a fragmented media environment because more ads are needed to break through to viewers. This assumes, of course, that candidates will continue to view television as a worthwhile investment, important enough to spend even more money seeking out a tougher-to-reach and dwindling audience.

6. Readers should note that I look almost exclusively at televised political advertising. For some research (of which there is comparatively very little), on the effects of radio ads, see Geer and Geer (2003); Overby and Barth (2006).

7. This latter effect is called "priming." See Druckman, Jacobs, and Ostermeier 2004; also chapter 7 in this volume.

8. This is often called the "minimal effects" model; that is, the effect of a campaign is believed to be small and likely to matter only when the election is close (Holbrook 1996; J. Campbell 2000). Moreover, a close election is seen as mainly the consequence of factors outside the campaign, such as an open seat when an incumbent retires, national (especially economic) conditions, and exogenous events such as a scandal. See chapter 1 in this volume for further discussion.

9. Goldstein and Freedman were not the first to use survey data to investigate such questions (see, e.g., Atkin and Heald 1976). A major limitation of this earlier survey-based scholarship, however, is that exposure was operationalized using respondents' recollection of the advertising they had seen or heard—an approach that makes causal relationships difficult to disentangle. For example, does advertising recall lead to higher turnout, or are those more likely to vote paying greater attention to campaign ads in the first place (Franz et al. 2008a, 32–33)?

10. See www.electionstudies.org.

11. Because advertising and voter canvassing efforts both tend to be heaviest in the most competitive states, it is possible that what appears to be an effect of ads is actually

a campaign effect more generally. By looking at noncompetitive states with limited exposure to battleground media markets (for example, voters in New Jersey who live in the Philadelphia market) but few contacts (because the campaign doesn't want to waste resources in a state that it has no chance to win), that potential problem can be eliminated.

12. Shaw combined weekly tracking polls in the states to get a measure of a candidate's change in support at various points during the campaign.

13. Franz and Ridout (2010) noted, for example, the unprecedented advertising advantage of Obama over McCain in 2008. No previous presidential candidate in modern elections had such a resource advantage over his opponent.

14. This number is from the author's review of advertising data in 1998, 2000, 2002, 2004, and 2008, when the project tracked ads in the top media markets for House, Senate, and presidential elections. Of the nearly 5 million ad airings in these five election cycles, more than 1.5 million were attack ads.

15. In 2006, for example, 63 percent of respondents in a *Newsweek* poll (see www .orspub.com) reported that Republican candidates' ads were "too negative," while 61 percent said the same about ads for Democratic candidates. Nearly 70 percent indicated that neither Democratic nor Republican ads "provided useful information."

16. The loophole was known as the *magic word distinction*. If parties and groups avoided the use of certain action words (such as "vote for" or "vote against") in their communications, the ads were considered issue advocacy and not candidate advocacy. This simple distinction resulted in a proliferation of ads that urged viewers to contact or write elected officials and urge them to take a particular stand on an issue. While the content of the ads was generally perceived as involving candidate advocacy, the lack of a specific exhortation on how to vote classified them as being outside the scope of federal election laws. The same distinction does not apply to candidate ads, since federal election laws consider any and all expenditures by candidates' campaigns as designed to affect election outcomes.

17. These data are from the Wisconsin Advertising Project.

18. See also Geer (2006, 141–143), who demonstrated that across presidential elections turnout rates fell at about the same time that negativity was going up. He offered this only as a two-way plot, however, not as proof of the demobilization hypothesis. See also Lau, Sigelman, and Rovner (2007) for a review of the literature on the relationship between attack advertising and turnout.

19. For more evidence that citizens learn from campaign ads, see Atkin and Heald (1976); Faber and Storey (1984); Zukin and Snyder (1984); Hitchon and Chang (1995); Kahn and Kenney (2000); Valentino, Hutchings, and Williams (2004). See Lau, Sigelman, and Rovner (2007) for a review of the literature on the specific effect of negative advertising on learning.

20. For example, see Hibbing and Theiss-Morse (1995, 2001); Hetherington (2005).

7 Campaigns and the News Media

Thomas A. Hollihan

Democratic governance demands an informed, engaged, and empowered citizenry. And citizens need access to news if they are to understand the world around them, evaluate the choices before them, and wisely determine how they should cast their votes. They need opportunities to engage in conversations and even arguments with peers about their political choices. These interactions challenge them to formulate their own opinions and enable them to compare and contrast their views with those held by others. It is through argument that citizens test the quality of their judgments and display the strengths or expose the weaknesses in competing worldviews. Democratic societies are sustained when citizens can generate and recognize good reasons for their beliefs and actions. The formation of these good reasons, and the shared deliberation that occurs when citizens find that their own good reasons are competing with those offered by others, enables them to recognize and act in their individual interests while also understanding the interests and concerns of others. It is in the give and take of deliberative political arguments that a notion of the common good begins to emerge and the bonds of connection that draw people together form. When people come to recognize their shared sense of purpose, they can begin to act collectively to meet their goals and resolve their problems.

In a democracy politics is fundamentally about communication. Candidates and elected officials must communicate their visions, plans, and policy proposals to public audiences as they seek to sell themselves and their ideas. Effective communication enables political leaders and the citizens they serve to establish and maintain their connections to each other. Political communication occurs in many different forms. Candidates and elected officials give speeches, issue press releases, engage in direct mailings to constituents, maintain Web sites, and purchase advertisements, all in an attempt to get their messages out to voters. In addition, politicians hold town hall meetings and, more recently, sponsor Internet chat rooms to enable them to hear from their constituents. These communications begin during the earliest stages of a campaign for office and continue after an elected official is sworn into office. Today, in fact, it seems that campaigns continue in seamless fashion even as elections are won and terms of office begin. For example, President Barack Obama's approach to managing such issues as the debate over health care reform remains largely unchanged from the approach he employed as a candidate. In this chapter I will summarize research findings on the current media marketplace for political messages and discuss the changing dynamics in the relationship between politicians, the media, and citizens. I focus especially on what is known as "free" or "earned" media rather than on paid political advertising.

In recent years it has become clear that many citizens in the United States are withdrawing from the political sphere; as a result, many rarely if ever seek political information or pay attention to news coverage about political issues (Cappella and Jamieson 1997; T. Patterson 2002). Some of these citizens may still vote in most elections, perhaps out of habit, but it is more likely that they vote in some elections but not others, or never bother to cast their ballots at all. To reach these citizens in an attempt to convince them either to turn out and vote or to discourage them from voting for the opposing candidate, campaigns raise huge sums of money to produce political advertisements. These advertisements are useful because campaigns have control over the content of the message and because, if enough advertisements can be purchased, it is difficult for voters to avoid exposure to them. Campaigns and elected officials also understand, however, that to get their messages out to the public they must develop strategies to take advantage of the free media coverage available in the form of news stories produced by political reporters. It is also important that the campaigns develop strategies to manage these stories to encourage mostly favorable coverage.

The media are more than mere conduits of information. The news media must transform raw information and make it useful to citizens so that it can be understood, contextualized, and developed as a resource for belief and action. They also contribute to a common sense of identity and a structuring of ordinary life by helping citizens become a community of shared social purpose (Carey 2002). Healthy news media are vital to a healthy democracy because the media shape public perceptions that will subsequently be pieced together to form the social reality that motivates political action. The distinguished American philosopher John Dewey (1927) argued that a free press is vital to democracy not simply because it pursues those issues and stories that influence the public's understanding of ongoing events, but also because it helps create and sustain a broad social conversation of deliberating citizens. The media therefore play an important role in shaping the masses into an articulate and organized populace that is capable of self-government and aware of the connections among its citizens (Hollihan 2009). A similar view was articulated by Graber (1993, 292), who claimed that "[m]edia do more than depict the political environment; they *are* the political environment. Because direct contact with political actors and situations is limited, media images define people and situations for nearly all participants in the political process."

Theories of Media and Communication

Media usage is utilitarian. People seek out certain forms of media either because they need or are interested in the information available to them in those sources or because the information amuses or entertains them. A constellation of studies offering support for this claim have come to be known as the *uses and gratification approach* (see Blumler and Katz 1974). This approach theorizes that people will pay the greatest attention to the news coverage of those public events that impact them directly. Those citizens who are keenly interested in the "game" of politics are more likely to seek out political news and may follow that news with the same interest and devotion that an avid sports fan follows the news of his or her home team. These citizens may also be more likely to read newspapers, watch network and cable TV news programs, and look for political information online. The explosion in the number of TV channels and Internet Web sites has dramatically increased the possible sources of political information for these news junkies. At the same time, the increased access to alternative programs and sources of information and amusement both on TV and on the Internet means that people who are not interested in political news coverage find it much easier to avoid even incidental exposure to political news. When there were only three or four broadcast television channels in a community, all of them delivered a daily diet of news. Now, however, TV viewers can watch all sports, all movies, all cooking programs, all home improvement channels, and so on. The result is a dramatic widening of the rich-poor information gap. Most damaging, a lack of political information or knowledge, even when self-inflicted, decreases an individual's sense of political efficacy and perceived influence.

Those who are exposed to news, whether they actively seek it out or not, will generally pay closer attention to those news stories that they see as having the greatest impact on their lives and livelihoods. The parents of young children will pay attention to stories about violence in schools or about sexual predators who threaten children. Elderly people will attend to stories about the escalating costs of prescription drugs or proposed changes in Medicare. Even stories that touch upon the interests of most citizens may be perceived and understood very differently by different people. For example, the very deep economic downturn that began in 2008 impacted almost everyone in the United States and even around the world; accordingly, millions of people looked to the media for information that would enable them to better understand the financial markets and relieve their anxieties. Yet these people may have been drawn to starkly different stories, and their reactions to these stories may have varied considerably. Stories about the decline in real estate prices may have sparked panic in homeowners who were seeing the value of their property fall and who, possibly, faced foreclosure unless they could refinance their mortgages. Middle-aged and older citizens nearing retirement or living off their investments fretted about their "golden years" as they saw the value of their investments plummet. In contrast, many young couples, eager to purchase a first home, may have seen the falling prices and low interest rates as encouraging, and those investors who still had liquid assets began shopping for bargains. Thus, the information that people seek, and their reactions to it, are shaped by their own situations, interests, and motivations.

The media play an important role in shaping people's attention and awareness of what issues merit their concern. This has been called the *agenda-setting function* of the press (McCombs and Shaw 1972). There have probably been more studies conducted on agenda-setting than on any other topic in the field of communication studies (Rogers, Dearing, and Bregman 1993). The theory of agenda-setting holds that persistent media attention on an issue or controversy suggests to audiences that the issue must be important and deserves their attention. Even if the public seems not to care about a particular topic, studies suggest that over time, and after repeated exposure to messages on that topic, people will come to believe that it is one about which they should care. Diana Mutz (1994) noted that

> [i]t is through media coverage that the unemployed worker learns she is one of many thousands nationwide, and the crime victim learns that his robbery was not an isolated incident, but rather part of a pattern of increasing drug-related crime. . . . Media coverage legitimizes a problem as something for which national leadership can be fairly held accountable (692).

The decisions about which stories will be covered are informed by the news judgment of journalists and editors, and of course these judgments reflect their notions of readers' needs and interests. Although strong professional norms help to define what is "important" or "significant" and therefore a worthy news story, there are business considerations influencing these decisions as well. Competition for the public's attention has become increasingly stiff in recent years. Today newspapers, magazines, radio stations, TV stations (and with cable and satellite systems in place viewers may now have hundreds of channels to choose from), Internet Web sites, and videogames all compete for attention. It is therefore unsurprising that news and entertainment have become ever more closely intertwined. This in turn has made it more difficult for the media to provide sustained attention on the reporting of complex issues such as the environment, the financial crisis, or proposed health care reform.

Research suggests that one of the most important aspects of the agenda-setting role of the media is its part in "priming," that is, in bringing an issue to the public's attention and in so doing signaling its significance. Perloff (1998) argued that when people see a story receive a substantial amount of press attention they will be more likely to take it into consideration when making their decisions about how to cast their ballots. During the 2008 campaign, for example, one of the dominant topics of news coverage was Barack Obama's relationship with his pastor, the Rev. Jeremiah Wright. The issue emerged when newspaper and magazine stories and video clips surfaced of an angry Reverend Wright condemning racism in America and thundering that instead of "God Bless America it should be God Damn America" (Weiss 2008). From the pulpit of the Chicago church where Obama had worshipped for twenty years, Wright also accused the federal government of conspiring against blacks. The videos of these sermons dominated cable television for weeks (Associated Press 2008). Although Wright's sermons may have seemed outrageous and provocative, it is nonetheless noteworthy that they received so much attention and became one of the dominant issues in the election campaign at a time when the nation was involved in two wars, in the midst of a financial meltdown, and facing an environmental catastrophe. Obama tried at first to ignore the issue, but it would not go away. Ultimately, he was compelled to give a speech on the topic of race in which he carefully attempted to distance himself from his pastor's comments without repudiating the pastor himself.[1] Wright, for his part, refused to quietly leave the public eye; instead, he stoked the controversy by making new incendiary remarks. In the end, Obama had no choice but to sever his ties with his spiritual leader (Associated Press 2008).

One of the reasons that the Reverend Wright story persisted, of course, was that it offered the type of "made-for-TV" material that plays out well in the contemporary era. It is an excellent example of the power of the media to frame stories in such a way as to give them a particular meaning. Entman (1993) defined "framing" as the ability to select some aspects of a perceived reality and make them seem more significant than others in news accounts. In this particular case, the Wright sermon was framed as an opportunity to gain insight into Senator Obama's beliefs and character. If Obama sat in the pews of the church where such sermons were given, and if in past statements and indeed in his autobiography (Obama 1995) he specifically mentioned how important Pastor Wright was to the development of his faith, are Wright's remarks not then somehow important as a means to help voters understand Obama's beliefs? Media framing promotes a particular understanding of an issue or a particular definition of a problem. At the same time, it offers an interpretation of likely causation, suggests a moral evaluation, and often recommends a certain policy or at least a policy approach for responding to that problem. The way the media frame the issues in campaigns has an impact on what issues citizens will see as most important, who is given praise or blame for current conditions, and which candidates are seen as credible and able to address those conditions (Devitt 1997; Golan and Wanta 2001; Graber 1987; Iyengar 1996).

The Changing Media Environment

Historically, newspapers have been Americans' primary source for political information. Peer and Nesbitt (2004) reported that 24.4 percent of weekday and 21.8 percent of Sunday news coverage focused on politics. The same study also found that approximately 45 percent of front-page news concerned political campaigns or issue coverage, that these stories tended to be substantive (averaging almost 87 square inches in length), and that 86 percent included a jump to an inside page.

As recently as the 1950s, most large cities boasted more than one newspaper, and many readers read more than one newspaper each day. A State of the News Media study (Journalism.org 2004) reported that "[i]n 1950, 123 percent of households bought a newspaper (in other words there were 1.23 papers sold per household). By 1990, only 67 percent of households bought a newspaper. By 2000, it was 53 percent." The decline in newspaper circulation began to hasten in 2003 and has further worsened in every year since. From 2001 to 2008, print circulation declined approximately 13.5 percent daily and 17.3 percent on Sunday. In 2008, one study found that only 34 percent of Americans reported that they had read a newspaper the day before, compared to 40 percent in 2006

(Journalism.org 2009). Moreover, those who do buy and read a daily paper are spending less time with it; the average reader now spends less than fifteen hours a month reading a paper. The future looks particularly bleak for print newspapers: although readership is declining among all age and demographic groups, it is declining fastest among young people. "Only nineteen per cent of Americans between the ages of eighteen and thirty-four claim even to look at a daily newspaper. The average age of the American newspaper reader is fifty-five and rising" (Alterman 2008).

Newspaper publishers have responded to circulation declines with an unending spiral of budget cuts. Hundreds of reporters and editors have been laid off, bureaus have been closed (especially expensive overseas bureaus), and whole sections of newspapers have disappeared (the publishers of the *Los Angeles Times*, for example, have whittled away at the paper by eliminating the Sunday magazine, the book review section, the real estate section, and, finally, even the separate "California" section that focused on state and local news). Since 1990, more than a quarter of all newspaper jobs have disappeared (Alterman 2008). In such circumstances it is not unreasonable to question whether any business can successfully respond to a declining audience by shrinking the scope and quality of its product. Inevitably such cuts diminish the newspaper to the point where even its most loyal readers no longer find coverage of the news they are most interested in reading.

So far, at least, it is clear that the tide of red ink has not been stemmed; indeed, declining print newspaper readership and newsroom budget cuts have had devastating implications for the industry. Several large daily newspapers have ceased operations altogether, including such well-known and long-established papers as the *Rocky Mountain News* and the *Seattle Post-Intelligencer*. The Tribune Company, which publishes the *Chicago Tribune, Los Angeles Times, Baltimore Sun*, and *Long Island Daily News*, is currently in bankruptcy. The value of newspaper stocks has plummeted. The McClatchy Company, which owns the Knight Ridder chain, has lost more than 80 percent of its stock value in recent years. Even the *New York Times*, America's most prestigious newspaper—the paper known as the "newspaper of record"—has seen its stock decline by more than 50 percent over the last five years (Alterman 2008). Detroit, one of the largest cities in the United States, boasted two dynamic and independent newspapers as recently as the late 1980s. Then, in response to circulation declines, the *News* and its rival *Free Press* reached a joint-operating agreement.[2] In March 2008, however, faced with further circulation declines, the papers decided to end home delivery of both papers, except on Thursdays and Fridays, and of the *Free Press* on Sundays. On other days of the week, "compact" editions of both papers are sold at newsstands, and readers are forced to turn to the Internet to access electronic versions (Wilkinson and Hurst 2008).

There is significant support for the claim that many of those who used to get their news from the print editions of newspapers are now seeking that information from online editions of newspapers. According to Mullins (2009), "Websites that American newspapers operate attracted more than 73.3 million unique users a month in the first three months of this year [2009]. That same study found that online newspaper readers average more than 3.5 billion page views per month so far this year . . . an increase of 13 percent over the same period last year." There are, of course, several complicating factors in this shift to accessing news online. First, most online users have proven unwilling to subscribe and thus pay for the content that they access. Second, advertisers have been skeptical about paying the same rates for their online advertisements as they do for print ads, perhaps because they can now track precisely how many (or in most cases how few) readers actually see and "click on" their ads (Mullins 2009). As a result, newspapers have found that online news operations are unable to generate the revenue streams necessary to support budgets for effective, yet costly, investigative journalism.

Perhaps an even more significant consequence of online news is that readers do not attend to Web news as closely or as conscientiously as they do printed news. A study undertaken by the Nielsen organization that tracked media usage in 2008 reported that "[t]he average Internet user spends around 56 minutes a month on 'News' sites (12.6 minutes a week)," in contrast with "the average Newspaper reader [who] spends 12.4 hours a month reading a Newspaper (2.8 hours a week)" (cited in Shepherd 2009). Another problem with online news readers is their wanton promiscuity. The audiences for traditional print newspapers have tended to be quite loyal. Newspaper brands had value, and readers would usually renew their subscriptions when they expired or buy the same brands at the newsstand so that they could follow their preferred columnists and find comfort in the structure and display of the content. Internet readers are very different, however. Approximately half of those who seek their news online use general search engines (such as Google and Yahoo) to find content, but only 20 percent use search tools built into a newspaper or magazine site. This essentially means that most who visit online versions of newspapers do not come through the front door but instead through a linking service or a news aggregator (Gartner Newsroom 2009). One obvious consequence of this path to accessing online news is that readers are increasingly active in exercising their own news judgment regarding those stories that interest or engage them. In a traditional news environment an editor is actively exercising news judgment regarding what stories deserve to dominate the public agenda, and what information an informed citizen needs in order to function in a democratic society. In an online environment, however, citizens are increasingly turning to news sources that may not share the same set of values or a systematic and objective approach to reporting the news.

One must remember that Internet news sources largely require consumers to go to the Web and "pull" the information they are interested in; this is in contrast to traditional media, which instead "push" the information out. The front page of a daily newspaper features the stories that an editor has deemed most important, and the brand of the newspaper becomes an indicator of the credibility of the information contained. A Web site, however, may contain only a myriad of links to news stories from a wide array of sources of varying degrees of quality. Because space is not a scarce commodity in the digital world, editors do not have to make rigorous choices about what links to include. Consumers, on the other hand, more than likely do have a limited amount of time and so will choose those stories that they find most useful or most gratifying (read amusing or entertaining). What we know about these usage habits is that readers will be more inclined to read stories that confirm what they already believe to be true, rather than challenge their worldview by exposing themselves to information that might create tension within their belief framework. Popkin (1991) described such behavior as the work of *cognitive misers,* arguing that voters will tend to look for information that confirms their existing beliefs and habits, thus taking shortcuts that reduce the mental effort required to perform a task. Popkin (1994) also referred to this as *low information rationality.*

The pursuit of news that confirms preexisting convictions leads those who are most interested in politics, and most likely to cast ballots, to seek a growing proportion of their political information from openly partisan news sources. Thus, liberals increasingly turn to Web sites such as the *Huffington Post* or *Daily Kos,* while conservatives turn to the *Drudge Report* or *Little Green Footballs* (Hollihan 2009).

Cable television news channels have also become an increasingly important and increasingly partisan source for political news. The segment of cable news programming that has grown most quickly in recent years has been the personality-driven talk shows. On the left, the *Rachel Maddow Show* on MSNBC quickly gained popularity, and the audience for Keith Olbermann's show also has grown. On the right, Bill O'Reilly's show on Fox News became the highest-rated program on cable news (Journalism.org 2009). Further evidence of the partisan fragmentation of the cable news audience is that during the Democratic convention in 2008, CNN easily beat out all the broadcast networks when eight million viewers tuned in for Barack Obama's acceptance speech. A few weeks later, Fox News won the highest ratings during the Republican convention (Journalism.org 2009). According to one survey, two Fox News programs (O'Reilly's and a program hosted by Sean Hannity) drew the most sharply partisan viewers. Fully 66 percent of O'Reilly's viewers self-identified as politically conservative versus 3 percent liberal, while 68 percent of Hannity's audience called themselves conservative versus 7 percent liberal (Journalism.org 2009).

The consequences of repeated exposure to highly partisan sources of news have arguably been significant and have contributed to a public that is deeply polarized. One popular conservative cable TV personality, Glenn Beck on Fox News, made headlines when he declared that President Obama was a racist with a "deep-seated hatred for white people or the white culture." The comment prompted many advertisers to abandon his program for fear that their association with him might drive some customers away (Siemaszko 2009)— and yet even as advertisers withdrew from the program, Beck's audience expanded (attracting almost three million viewers, perhaps in part due to a conservative backlash against the boycott; see *Los Angeles Times* 2009a). The growing audience served only to inspire Beck toward even more strongly worded attacks. For example, stating that the Obama administration was infiltrated by radicals who would undermine the Constitution, he claimed credit for demonstrating "that these radicals are not only instrumental in shaping legislation that is being jammed through at light speed, they are also by invitation personally advising the president of the United States." He also declared that they were "radical wolves that are about to devour our republic" (*Los Angeles Times* 2009a). One of Beck's targets was Van Jones, a San Francisco political activist and a special advisor on environmental policy. In rhetoric that was starkly reminiscent of the McCarthy era Beck asked, "Should you have a communist, self-avowed revolutionary who named his 4-year-old son after a Marxist guerrilla leader, should that person be advising the president of the United States?" (*Los Angeles Times* 2009a). Jones ultimately resigned his post with the Obama administration after a videotape surfaced in which he referred to Republicans as "assholes" (Fox News 2009).

Highly partisan commentators such as Beck may also have had a significant impact on public deliberations over health care reform. On one program, for example, Beck argued that "Obama's health reform is just one tactic designed to 'collapse the system,' all part of a plan by the president to implement '1960s radical ideology'" (Rainey 2009). Such extreme rhetoric no doubt helped contribute to the frenzied public reactions to the prospect of reform. A series of town hall meetings held during the summer of 2009 became increasingly confrontational as protesters likened Obama to Adolf Hitler because he allegedly sought to undermine the American medical care system, impose a government bureaucracy to ration health care, and deny care to very sick individuals. Former GOP vice-presidential candidate Sarah Palin fed public anxieties regarding health care reform when she wrote on her Facebook page that government "death panels" would decide the fate of the very ill and elderly (Shaer 2009). When questioned about her claim, Palin referred to language in one of the proposals that "would require Medicare to pay for some end-of-life counseling sessions with a healthcare practitioner" (Shaer 2009). The claim that this bill would lead to the creation of death panels was refuted by the independent, nonpartisan, and nonprofit group Factcheck.org, which declared that the section of the bill in question "requires Medicare to cover counseling sessions for seniors who want to consider their end-of-life choices—including whether they want to refuse or, conversely, require certain types of care. The claim that the bill would 'push suicide' is a falsehood" (cited by Shaer 2009). Nonetheless, a poll conducted by Pew Research found that 86 percent of respondents had heard of the death panel controversy, and that 30 percent said it was true (Shaer 2009).

The impact of citizens' exposure to increasingly partisan sources of media was also in evidence during the dust-up that occurred when U.S. representative Joe Wilson (R-S.C.) interrupted President Obama during a speech delivered before a joint session of Congress on the topic of health care reform. When the president stated that those who believed the proposed plan would provide coverage for illegal immigrants were wrong, Wilson loudly interjected the declaration, "You lie!" The comment brought significant criticism from Wilson's colleagues in both political parties. For example, Arizona senator John McCain (R) said the outburst was "totally disrespectful" and demanded that Wilson apologize to the president. The pressure on Wilson to make amends for his interjection was sufficiently strong that he apologized shortly afterward. Wilson wrote a letter to the president and also issued the following public statement: "This evening I let my emotions get the best of me when listening to the president's remarks regarding the coverage of illegal immigrants in the healthcare bill. While I disagree with the president's statement, my comments were inappropriate and regrettable. I extend sincere apologies to the president for this lack of civility" (*Los Angeles Times* 2009b).

The apology emphatically did not end the public attention focused on the episode, however, for in the days that followed it became the dominant topic on talk radio, cable news outlets, and Web-based political discussions. Conservative radio host Rush Limbaugh, for example, declared on his program that Wilson should not have apologized to the president for articulating "what millions of Americans are saying." Limbaugh went on to say that he too was convinced that President Obama was not being truthful when he declared that illegal aliens would not be covered under the Democrats' proposed health care reforms (Calderone 2009).

Both Wilson and his Democratic opponents used the issue to drive fundraising and to motivate their respective bases of supporters. Within just a few days following the remark both Wilson and Rob Miller, his Democratic challenger, had raised more than a million dollars from donors across the country; in contrast, when Miller ran against Wilson in 2008 he managed to raise and spend a total of just $625,000 (Elliot 2009). In the immediate aftermath of the incident, Speaker of the House Nancy Pelosi (D-Calif.) resisted efforts to sanction Wilson and indicated that his apology to the president should be considered sufficient and the matter should be allowed to die (Soraghan and Allen 2009). Soon, however, Democrats recognized that their interests might be better served by keeping the issue alive. The party's House leadership then demanded that Wilson apologize again, this time before the entire body, and announced that if he did not do so a resolution would be introduced admonishing him for his breach of rules governing civil conduct. Wilson declared that he would not apologize to the House, saying, "I've apologized one time. The apology was accepted by the president, by the vice president, who I know. I am not apologizing again" (Elliot 2009). The House then debated and passed the resolution disapproving of Wilson's conduct. Even though Wilson's interjection had been condemned by members of both parties, the resolution was passed by a margin of 240–179 and closely followed party lines, with almost all Democrats voting in favor of it and almost all Republicans voting against it (New York Times 2009). In this highly partisan era, even the norms of politeness are ferociously contested.

Passage of the House resolution did not end the controversy, of course. Former president Jimmy Carter further stirred the pot when he speculated during an interview that Wilson's comment and much of the animosity directed toward President Obama was based on racism. Carter told an NBC news interviewer, "I live in the South, and I've seen the South come a long way and I've seen the rest of the country that shared the South's attitude toward minority groups at that time . . . and I think it's bubbled up to the surface because of a belief among many white people, not just in the South but around the country, that African Americans are not qualified to lead this great country" (Orr 2009). Naturally, the Republicans strongly denied that they were racist. Former House Speaker Newt Gingrich (R-Ga.), for example, told Fox News that "it's very destructive for America to suggest that we can't criticize a president without it being a racial act" (Orr 2009). The national chairman of the Republican Party, Michael Steele, who is himself African American, issued a statement declaring:

> President Carter is flat out wrong. This isn't about race. It is about policy. This is a pathetic distraction by Democrats to shift attention away from the president's wildly unpopular government-run health care plan that the American people simply oppose. Injecting race into the debate over critical issues facing American families doesn't create jobs, reform our health care system or reduce the growing deficit. It only divides Americans rather than uniting us to find solutions to challenges facing our nation. Characterizing Americans' disapproval of President Obama's policies as being based on race is an outrage and a troubling sign about the lengths Democrats will go to disparage all who disagree with them. Playing the race card shows that Democrats are willing to deal from the bottom of the deck (Murray 2009).

As discussed earlier, however, the voices of talk radio have not been subtle in interjecting race into their political conversations. The declaration by Fox's Beck that "Obama hates white people" has already been discussed. Limbaugh, who earlier defended Wilson's interjection, argued that attacks on the president made by conservative opponents were not racist by offering the following, somewhat curious diatribe about violence between black and white children on a school bus in Bellville, Illinois:

> It's Obama's America, is it not? Obama's America, white kids getting beat up on school buses now. You put your kids on a school bus, you expect safety but in Obama's America the white kids now get beat up with the black kids cheering, "Yay, right on, right on, right on, right on," and, of course, everybody says the white kid deserved it, he was born a racist, he's white. *Newsweek* magazine told us this. We know that white students are destroying civility on buses, white students destroying civility in classrooms all over America, white congressmen destroying civility in the House of Representatives (Limbaugh 2009).

Highly partisan media coverage has clearly impacted political opinion in the nation. For example, a new social protest known as the "Tea Party Movement" has emerged, motivated by a desire to combat the "takeover" of American government by "liberal elites." The Web site for the Tea Bag Party declared that it was protesting the fact that "[s]uccessful and hard working Americans are being forced to pay through the nose for the mistakes of others and for a massive new social agenda that is antithetical to America's work ethic. The party in power is no longer representing the interests of the individuals and small businesses who make this country successful."[3]

In sum, it is evident that many citizens are essentially "unnewsed" and uninformed about politics, while others who do seek news do so by turning to highly partisan sources. A third development that merits attention is that many Americans see politics primarily as a source of amusement. These are the people who often get much of their political news from TV comedy shows. Programs such as *The Daily Show with Jon Stewart* and *The Colbert Report,* for example, draw relatively large audiences of faithful viewers. Indeed, in September 2008, during the closing days of the presidential campaign, Jon Stewart's TV comedy news program was drawing almost two million viewers per night, with Stephen Colbert's show not far behind (Star 2008). These programs have become so important to candidates and elected officials alike that they are now essential stops on the campaign tour. During the 2008 campaign, virtually all of the presidential candidates made appearances in an attempt to reach potential voters who might not otherwise be paying attention to political news, and in order to demonstrate (one presumes) that they were at least somewhat "hip," could take a joke, and had a good sense of humor. On election night in November, Stewart and Colbert hosted their own TV special offering viewers a place to turn for election results.

Likewise, the long-running comedy show *Saturday Night Live* offers satirical accounts of current political news stories and parodies of both candidates and elected officials. Some observers believe that the show may even have impacted the outcome of the presidential race in 2008. *SNL*'s Tina Fey, in particular, was so effective in her parody of GOP vice-presidential candidate and governor of Alaska Sarah Palin that her performance became a topic of conversation in the mainstream media and excerpts were played across the news spectrum. Again, some candidates feel that there is more to be gained by going onto such programs and joining in the shenanigans than by protesting that the depictions are somehow unfair. In fact, Palin did just that, later appearing on *SNL* to poke her own fun at the process. In addition to Stewart, Colbert, and *SNL,* the various late-night TV comics also use politicians as the butt of their jokes. Jay Leno, Conan O'Brien, and David Letterman, for example, routinely skewer politicians in their monologues (when not welcoming them as guests). Only Letterman has at times seemed to go too far. He offended Palin, and no doubt many others, when he dragged the governor's daughters into the public eye by offering tasteless and—as even Letterman later acknowledged—inappropriate jokes at their expense.

These programs exemplify the creative blurring of news and entertainment, and they have led academics to study their importance as sources of information and as venues that serve to enhance citizens' sense of political efficacy (Xenos and Becker 2009). However, while it is reasonable to claim that *any* exposure to politics is better than none, and that these comedy shows are therefore beneficial, at least one study suggests that there may be a down side. Specifically, Baumgartner and Morris (2006) found that those who were exposed to jokes about candidates George W. Bush and John Kerry on Stewart's *The Daily Show* during the 2004 campaign were more likely to rate both candidates more negatively than those who weren't, even when the study controlled for partisanship and other demographic variables. These scholars also found that viewers were more cynical about politics than nonviewers. Perhaps most troublesome, however, is the possibility that people who watch TV comedy news programs may think that they are getting real news. Respondents in the Baumgartner and Morris study who watched *The Daily Show* reported having greater confidence in their understanding of politics than other TV viewers. This feeling of confidence may come from the fact that the program plays upon an underlying narrative that assumes viewers are sufficiently sophisticated to see through the media manipulation of messages. *The Daily Show,* in particular, routinely excerpts clips from other newscasts, re-edits them, and uses them to trivialize messages and underscore the superficiality and repetitiveness of political news coverage. Stewart has especially focused on Fox News and has had something of an ongoing food-fight with Fox personalities Bill O'Reilly, Sean Hannity, and Glenn Beck. While these interactions are no doubt entertaining, and some would argue informative and accurate, they also characterize politics as a performance, more closely akin to a circus than a substantive conversation about the important issues and choices facing our society.

Managing the Free Media

Today's political candidates and elected officials find themselves enmeshed in a communication environment that is substantially changed from that which existed only a few decades ago. The electorate seems increasingly disengaged and cynical, and its attitude toward government and elected officials has been trending strongly negative (Cappella and Jamieson 1997; T. Patterson 2002; Hollihan 2009). Making matters worse, the reporters who cover campaigns and the pundits who dominate TV news programs are also increasingly negative. Anyone who has watched Lou Dobbs on CNN or listened to Rush Limbaugh on the radio has heard these personalities offer brutal attacks against those in power. Even mainstream reporters have become far more likely to frame their messages in such a way as to emphasize the negative characteristics, traits, and ambitions of our political figures (David Shaw 1996; Hollihan 2009). Given this environment, it should come as no surprise that politicians have learned to be increasingly guarded with the press.

Perhaps no administration took this further than that of George W. Bush, who conducted far fewer press conferences than any other recent president (Silva 2008). President Bush was not only reluctant to talk to the press, his administration went to extraordinary lengths to manipulate these encounters when they did occur. The story of Jeff Gannon is a case in point. Gannon was awarded media credentials at the White House despite the fact that he had no journalistic background. Instead, Gannon wrote for a Web site called Talon-News.com, which was operated by a Texas Republican activist and touted itself as committed to "bringing the conservative message to America." Gannon's role was to ask the president "softball" questions. When called on at one press conference, he attacked the Senate's leading Democrats, referring to them as "divorced from reality." Gannon's question was so transparently favorable to Bush that it prompted criticism from a media watchdog group, which claimed that Gannon was not a journalist at all, but rather a stooge intended to soften the media's coverage of Bush (Savage and Wirzbicki 2005). The story blew up a few days later when it was discovered that in addition to his work as a reporter, Gannon also worked as a gay escort providing sexual services to paying clients. Nude photographs of him provided the kind of indisputable evidence that is often missing in even the best scandals in the nation's capital (Kurtz 2005).

Although the Gannon story was perhaps the most dramatic, this was not the only instance where the Bush administration was caught trying to manipulate press coverage and manage the news. In addition, there were disclosures that the Department of Education secretly paid newspaper columnist Armstrong Williams to write columns that promoted the administration's education policies, and the Bush White House occasionally sent out video press releases promoting its policies that purported to be "news stories" written by journalists (Savage and Wirzbicki 2005).

Compared to the Bush administration, the Obama administration was, at least early on, far more accessible to the media. After six months in office, Obama had held twenty-three press conferences; Bush at the same point had held only ten (Kiely 2009). Yet even though President Obama may feel comfortable and confident when answering questions from the fourth estate, and though the kinds of flagrant efforts to manage the news that were common during the Bush presidency have not been in evidence, the new administration has clearly sought to influence the press coverage that it receives. Indeed, some argue that it has tried to intimidate reporters into providing favorable coverage. The clearest example of this was the Obama team's declaration that Fox News is part of the political opposition. As Anita Dunn, the White House communications director, told the *New York Times*, "We're going to treat them the way we would treat an opponent. . . . As they are undertaking a war against Barack Obama and the White House, we don't need to pretend that this is the way that legitimate news organizations behave" (Stelter 2009). White House attacks, if anything, seemed to please the Fox leadership. Bill Shine, a vice president for programming at the network, declared of the White House criticism, "Every time they do it, our ratings go up." Another Fox executive said that "the jabs by the White House could solidify the network's audience base" (Stelter 2009). The same *New York Times* article also reported that the number of people watching Fox News programs was at an all-time high, up approximately 20 percent during the first year of the Obama presidency, and now averaging 1.2 million per night (Stelter 2009).

The Obama administration also sought to limit the number of appearances by members of the administration on Fox programs. For example, on a Sunday morning in October President Obama appeared on the morning talk shows on several networks—but refused to appear on Fox News, calling it an "ideological outlet" (Stelter 2009). This stinging criticism prompted the host of *Fox News Sunday,* anchor Chris Wallace, to label the administration "the biggest bunch of crybabies I have dealt with in my 30 years in Washington" (Stelter 2009).

Historically, there has been a strong and mutually beneficial relationship between elected officials and the reporters who cover them. Politicians need the press to get their stories told, and reporters need access to candidates and elected officials lest they be scooped by their competitors. It will be very interesting to observe whether this co-dependent relationship continues into the future, or whether the current adversarial and partisan political climate will become so deeply entrenched that politicians and media outlets are better served by out-and-out conflict with one another and by playing only to their partisan base of supporters.

The political and media climate has changed significantly. A smaller percentage of the American citizenry seems to be actively seeking political information; the fragmentation of media has led to the creation of market-focused and highly segmented and partisan news reporting; media coverage increasingly blurs the line between politics and entertainment; and politicians have become more wary of the press as they seek to manipulate and control the news environment. The consequence of these changes is that the opportunities for meaningful public deliberation over complex policy questions have been significantly diminished. Although it would be a mistake to become too nostalgic for a "golden era" of political news coverage that never really existed, it would also be a mistake for our citizens to become complacent in the face of recent changes and to simply accept current media and political practices as the best we can achieve. It is in the country's best interests for current and future generations of citizens to expand their media literacy and demand a higher standard for news and for civic discussion about politics.

THE POLITICAL PROFESSIONALS RESPOND

Adam Smith

A political writer increasingly lives in a minute-by-minute news cycle, where the drive to be a must-read source for political insiders—get it fast, get it first, get a lot—can easily overwhelm the ability to produce stories with any depth and context. Typical morning: while helping to get three kids off to school, I skim through news aggregators to (1) make sure I have not been beaten on any significant story, and (2) know what's happening. I cull through thirty to forty e-mails delivered between midnight and 6 a.m., including news releases, Google alerts, junk mail, and the occasional tip or complaint about an anonymous comment posted on our politics blog that needs deleting.

If there's a political news nugget too trivial even to post on our blog specializing in political minutiae, I'll probably tweet something about it. If the blog hasn't had anything new added since about 9 p.m., I'll also post another item. It doesn't even have to be especially compelling. I just want to make sure we have some fresh content up by the time Florida's political junkies start their day. I also tweet a link to that item to help drive traffic. By the time I arrive at the office, I will have received several e-mails, text messages, and phone calls passing on political gossip and spin or asking me to blog something. I try to take thirty to forty minutes to actually read some of the day's journalism across the country and plan the day or days ahead, but I'll be interrupted several times with e-mails or phone calls that usually compel me to blog another couple items. I tweet links as well.

You get the point: the role of a political writer has changed. We've changed our rhythm to serve a seemingly insatiable demand for political news. The bright side is that we're attracting a lot of traffic to our political blogs. The downside is that there often is little time to pause and reflect on the bigger forces shaping national, state, and local politics. We're so busy tweeting that there isn't enough time for thinking.

Thomas Hollihan is right to be concerned about the changing media climate— not only the effects of new technology, but also the dated financial model that perhaps no longer can sustain decent journalism. I work in America's biggest battleground state, which has long been blessed with an array of strong papers (at least ten with circulations topping one hundred thousand) that cared about and competed fiercely over government and political coverage. Only a few election cycles ago, five Florida newspapers would routinely send reporters to cover presidential campaigns in places like Iowa and New Hampshire. In 2008, only two did.

At least wire services can fill the gap there. Far more ominous for accountability and informed citizenry is the quality of state capital reporting across the country, an area where the bottom has fallen out on the business of journalism. In Florida, the Tallahassee press corps has shrunk by one-third in just eighteen months. I hear similar things from reporters in other states. Wire services don't fill in the gaps with state and local government, which has greater impact on the day-to-day lives of people.

Here's the thing, though: despite the depressing hand-wringing about journalism and democracy today from Hollihan and so many of my beleaguered colleagues, I'm really not especially glum or pessimistic. Talk all you want about citizens withdrawing from the political process, but we recently concluded a presidential election that produced the strongest voter turnout in four decades—partly due to the sheer drama and epic personalities involved, but also because it was an election that sent cable news ratings and Web traffic soaring. Sure, modern media are so diverse and fractured that countless citizens skip public affairs coverage and turn instead to the Food Network, ESPN, or TMZ. But in this lousy business climate, I'd sure rather specialize in politics than most other beats I can think of.

Why? Because I get clicks, and clicks matter more than ever in my business. Our politics blog consistently draws heavier traffic than any other we have. Likewise, political articles consistently draw heavy readership. The Web has changed the marketplace for consumption of political news. Suddenly there is a demand for "small ball"—incremental stories that wouldn't find a home on newsprint. We're giving readers what they want and, in the process, broadening our reach. Granted, much of what I produce caters to hard-core political junkies rather than average citizens. In today's political media climate, campaigns, especially at the start of a cycle, work feverishly for coverage even on an insider blog, knowing that it can shape the early views of key opinion leaders and donors.

Perhaps Hollihan is correct that the broad electorate is not following political news as it once did. But the interest in and demand for political coverage appears to have spiked dramatically in recent years. The problem, of course, is that we haven't yet figured out a financially feasible way to meet that demand. Our overall readership is steadily climbing between the paper edition and online products, but almost nobody has figured out how to make enough money online to support the journalism.

Meanwhile, I don't share Hollihan's anxiety that many Americans see politics "primarily as a source of amusement" and get their political information from Jon Stewart or Stephen Colbert. Those fake news shows present a fair amount of relevant factual information, even if they do consistently lean Democratic. The author cited a study that found that people exposed to jokes about John Kerry and George W. Bush were more likely to rate both candidates negatively. Well, maybe that's because they learned something accurate about them in those jokes. I suspect that Richard Nixon, Jack Abramoff, and Rielle Hunter have done far more to promote cynicism about our politicians than any late-night comic.

It's not only the kind of hard-edged, partisan coverage Hollihan notes from sources like Fox News and CNBC that are attracting audiences lately. My newspaper in the 2008 election cycle launched an ambitious product, www.PolitiFact.com, to fact check statements made by politicians, interest groups, and media figures. Traffic at PolitiFact was enormous during the campaign and continues to be robust. Amid all the he-said/she-said political coverage, voters are hungry for objective, accurate reporting and analysis of political claims, whether these involve Obama's transparency, his birth certificate, or his alleged "death panels."[1]

It's easy to belittle new forms of journalism as we rely on such methods as tweeting to inform our readers. But the fact is that thanks to the many ways we publish, voters today have more opportunities than ever to learn about their elected officials and the current state of politics. If they don't read our blog or follow me on Twitter, I still produce lots of valuable news the old-fashioned way: on newsprint.

I think that I detected Hollihan tut-tutting the press for devoting so much attention to the Rev. Jeremiah Wright "God Damn America!" controversy "at a time when the nation was involved in two wars, in the midst of a financial meltdown, and facing an environmental catastrophe." Those explosive sermons from Obama's longtime pastor raised enormous and valid questions about the candidate's character and values. The uproar also showed a lot about how Obama responds to a crisis—very well, it turned out. Voters don't make up their minds based on blank paper. They want to know what the candidate is like, and how he or she behaves and responds under pressure. When a focus group of undecided Tampa Bay voters was convened during the final months of the presidential election, we learned that John McCain's erratic reaction to the financial meltdown hurt his standing, while Obama's response helped him. Group participants, by the way, were overwhelmingly turned off by the rancor and overtly partisan brand of politics so often on display on certain cable outlets and talk radio shows (and when we reconvened the group in January 2010, the turbulent town hall meetings held during the previous summer could be added to the list).

Elections in America's largest battleground state are still decided by those in the middle—swing voters and independents who are hungry for credible and reliable news sources. As long as that's the case, and I'm doing my job by helping them to better understand their world, I feel very upbeat about my business. Before I get to that, however, I'd better find something new to blog.

---

[1] See www.factcheck.org/2009/08/palin-vs-obama-death-panels.

Notes

1. For a discussion of the speech and Obama's strategy in responding to the public controversy, see Hollihan (2010).

2. This agreement, reached in 1989, allowed the *News* and *Free Press* to merge their printing, advertising, and circulation operations while maintaining the independence of their newsgathering and editorial staffs. The circulation declines at both newspapers continued, however, and in 1998, the *Free Press* staff moved into the same building with the staff of the *News* (Vaughn 2008). The joint-operating agreement changed further when Gannett, which had owned the *News,* acquired the *Free Press* from Knight Ridder in 2005. The *News* agreed to join the *Free Press* in putting out a morning edition, and the two papers, which had been publishing joint editions on the weekend, decided that there would be two separate papers on Saturday but that only the *Free Press* would publish on Sunday.

3. See http://teabagparty.org.

8 Campaigning in the Internet Age

Michael T. Heaney, Matthew E. Newman, and Dari E. Sylvester[1]

The 2008 presidential campaign of Barack Obama set a new high-water mark for use of the Internet in election campaigns. Obama astonished most observers by raising approximately half a billion dollars online, much of it through small donations (Balz and Johnson 2009, 366). This achievement enabled Obama to forgo public financing for the campaign and the spending limits that would have come with it (Luo 2009). Obama's Facebook page registered more supporters than any other candidate—approximately 3.2 million by November 2008—thereby giving the campaign access to an expansive online social network (Vargas 2008). Viral videos[2] championing Obama's candidacy, such as the "Yes We Can" collage organized by performing artist will.i.am, were downloaded millions of times, providing the campaign with valuable, free advertising (Wallsten 2009). These and other factors led some observers to agree with the journalist Arianna Huffington (2008), who proclaimed that "were it not for the Internet, Barack Obama would not be president." Indeed, the 2008 election helped to do for the Internet what the 1960 election did for television: legitimize its role and demonstrate its potential.

Since the embryonic efforts of the Clinton-Gore campaign to use the Internet in 1992, campaign professionals and their candidates have sought to harness the power of the Web to win elections (Chadwick 2006, 131). Candidates started creating Web pages in the mid-1990s, though the Internet did not begin to show its significant fundraising potential until John McCain's campaign utilized it in McCain's bid for the 2000 Republican presidential nomination (Bimber and Davis 2003). Democrat Howard Dean was perhaps the first candidate to integrate the Internet extensively with the logistics of a campaign, but his loss in the 2004 Iowa caucuses and subsequent withdrawal from the presidential contest that year cast a shadow on this achievement (Hindman 2005). However, Obama's decisive victory in 2008, as well as the tremendously visible role that the Internet played overall in the election that year, left potential candidates clamoring for ways to make the Internet work better for them.

In light of recent expansions in the use of the Internet in the electoral process, it is important to ask how the development and diffusion of online technologies have affected the practices and outcomes of campaigns. The past few years have witnessed the proliferation of handheld wireless devices, the growth of online social networks, and the intertwining of the Internet with everyday life. These developments collectively have been dubbed "Web 2.0," which refers to Internet applications that facilitate interactivity and collaboration (Chadwick 2009). It is tempting to assume that these changes have transformed every aspect of modern campaigning; after all, the 2008 presidential election was won by the candidate with the strongest Internet presence. Yet that candidate also was challenging the party of an outgoing president with low approval ratings, was opposed to an unpopular war, and was running during a period of economic hardship. Such conditions historically have prompted rhetoric calling for change and the replacement of an incumbent party (Abramowitz 2008). Thus, while campaigns are increasingly using the Internet, they may do so in ways that simply extend established formats, leaving campaigns working today much as they have for the past fifty years. To understand how the Internet has affected campaigning, it is necessary to differentiate between where it has altered the organizational practices of campaigns and where it has been compatible with traditional practices.

In this chapter we assess how the Internet has and has not influenced the practices and outcomes of campaigns. We do so by focusing on four interrelated aspects of the Internet: (1) low marginal costs of communication, (2) decentralization, (3) digital social networks, and (4) rapid technological change. In some ways these four factors have the ability to alter campaigns noticeably, but in other ways they exert little or no effect. We discuss how these aspects matter for campaign organizations, the media, and the electorate. We then look forward to the 2010 and 2012 elections to consider how the Internet might make a difference in coming years.

Low Marginal Costs of Communication

Communicating through the Internet brings the marginal cost of sending information close to zero. Once a single copy of a document, graphic, or video is produced, it can be distributed widely at little cost since printing and postage is not required. The only marginal costs incurred come from responding to feedback from recipients and from server capacity to handle the requested downloads of the material. Costs are low both for candidates, who wish to distribute information about their campaigns, and for their potential supporters, who can communicate with the campaign instantly at any time of the day or night without leaving the house or even using a stamp. What are the implications of this cost structure for campaigns?

The low costs of Internet communication only matter for campaigns if the Internet actually allows them to reach potential supporters. Consistent with this need, recent surveys show that the Internet's audience is expanding. According to a 2009 survey conducted by the Pew Research Center,[3] nearly three-quarters of Internet users in the United States (representing 55 percent of the adult population) went online to get information about or to discuss the 2008 election (A. Smith 2009, 3).[4] Although traditional media outlets are still the dominant sources of political news, an increasing proportion of voters are learning about politics through the Internet (A. Smith 2009, 6). Indeed, the audience is there—but can campaigns connect with it?

One problem with reaching audiences through the Internet is that viewership is self-selective. In one study of media use, Stroud (2008) found that individuals choose the political content of the material they view on the Web partly based on their own ideology and partisanship (see also Baum and Groeling 2008). This finding suggests that when candidates reach out through the Internet, they more often connect with likely supporters than with genuinely undecided voters. Thus, the Internet has more potential as a tool for organizing and mobilizing than it has as a tool for persuading (but see Davis et al. 2008). However, ideological self-selection only accounts for a portion of people's viewing behavior on the Internet; other viewing choices may be made based on other factors, or through "surfing," which has the potential to expose nonsupporters to campaign materials. Further, Stroud's (2008) findings show that choices about other media (such as newspapers, talk radio, and cable news) are similarly selected partly on the basis of ideology. If campaigns confront a self-selected audience on the Web, the same is true for almost any other media outlet in which they might choose to advertise or otherwise communicate with voters.

Regardless of whether campaigns are reaching out to their core supporters or to potentially undecided voters, however, the low marginal cost of Internet communication has three principal implications for campaigns. First, campaigns have incentives to post as much content online about their candidate as possible. Second, campaigns can expect greater efficiency in fundraising through the Internet than through traditional means. Third, the low cost of communication over the Internet brings with it a broader, more diverse audience that is able to participate actively in campaigns.

Expanded information about candidates is a first implication of the low marginal cost of publishing information on the Web. Virtually all candidates in congressional campaigns publish material to a Web page, regardless of whether or not they are engaged in a competitive election (Druckman, Kifer, and Parkin 2009a). In contrast, many campaigns never use television or radio advertising if the competitiveness of the race does not call for it. Beyond posting "brochureware" materials on their Web pages, candidates often make their pages interactive through blogging and by accommodating user comments (Chadwick 2006). Political advertising is increasingly moving to the Web, as "the Internet is an extremely cost-effective medium when compared with its traditional counterparts" (Institute for Politics, Democracy, and the Internet 2008, 1). Campaigns can take made-for-television commercials and distribute them for free on YouTube (Gueorguieva 2008; Gulati and Williams 2009). Or they may benefit when Web advertising earns attention from major media outlets (Lipinski and Neddenriep 2004). The fact that Internet advertising is cost-effective, though, does not imply that it necessarily is inexpensive. Campaigns are well advised to match their online expenditures to what they have become accustomed to spending offline, and to develop an online media strategy in conjunction with an offline strategy (Institute for Politics, Democracy, and the Internet 2008).

As candidates publish more material online, some scholars have speculated that the new medium may affect the content of what they post. One hypothesis is that a shift to low-cost online advertising will exacerbate trends toward negativity in political advertising (Klotz 2003; Schweitzer 2009). Counter to this view, Druckman and colleagues (2009b) provided evidence that candidates go negative on the Web with about the same likelihood that they go negative in traditional media. Thus, the degree of negativity is one area where campaigns do *not* appear to have been affected by the rise of the Internet. Nonetheless, the nature of the information that candidates espouse about their issue positions may change in an online environment. Sulkin, Moriarty, and Hefner (2007) reported that competing candidates' issue positions in online discourse are less likely to converge to similar positions than they are in offline discourse; in other words, candidates appear to make less of an effort to appeal to the median voter online. This result is consistent with the view that Internet communication promotes more issue-driven campaign politics (Bimber 1998).

A second implication of the low marginal cost of Internet communication is that it is vital to making the Internet a bountiful fundraising tool. Traditional fundraising methods are expensive for both candidates and contributors. If a candidate stages a fundraising event, then a certain percentage of the funds raised must pay for the cost of the event. Contributors must make a minimum contribution and plan to attend the event. Direct mail must be sent to a large number of noncontributors to reach those who *will* give, and it requires that people who want to contribute receive the solicitation and have it in hand at the time that they want to donate. In contrast, receiving contributions via the Internet requires few overhead costs for the campaign. Mailings are not sent to people who will never give, and contributors need only have an Internet connection and their credit card handy. Thus, by greatly reducing the transaction cost of fundraising, the Internet expands the base of contributors to include people who are unable or unwilling to pay those transaction costs, namely small donors. Techniques for raising money in this way have proved effective not only at the national level, but also among candidates in state-level races (Rackaway 2007).

The shift to small donors may have a "profound impact on who contributes, and how they become involved in politics" (Wilcox 2008, 1). The Internet helps to "engage people who in the past would not have participated, due to time constraints, geographical and transportation issues, and personal inclination" (Vaccari 2008, 658). Many of these new participants are younger and less affluent (Wilcox 2008). This shift gives an advantage to outsider candidates, such as Rep. Ron Paul (R-Texas), who raised millions of dollars through the Internet during his 2008 campaign for president at a time when he was showing less than 1 percent support among Republicans nationwide (Wilcox 2008, 1).

While Internet fundraising did not win the Republican presidential nomination for Ron Paul, it did allow Barack Obama to gain leverage vis-à-vis Hillary Clinton in the Democratic primaries. Senator Clinton's long association with Democratic Party elites gave her extensive access to large donors that Obama did not have. However, by raising money on the Internet, Obama was able to compete with Clinton throughout 2007, leaving him in a strong position when the Democratic primaries and caucuses got under way in 2008. These examples support the view that Internet fundraising has the potential to alter which candidates are competitive at the nomination phase.

A third implication of the low cost of communication over the Internet is that it is now easier to organize supporters and thereby engage a more diverse range of people to participate actively in campaigns (K. Schlozman, Verba, and Brady 2009). The Internet is especially effective as an organizing tool because it "integrates different modalities of communication" that include "reciprocal interaction, broadcasting, individual reference-searching, group discussion, [and] person/machine interaction" (DiMaggio et al. 2001, 308). Internet

communication makes it possible for campaigns to interact with their supporters in a more cost-effective way than in the past.

Campaigns started using the Internet to organize their supporters on a large
scale during the 2004 election campaign. Howard Dean sought increased visibility
by using Meetup.com, a Web site that facilitated meetings of about seventy-five
thousand Dean supporters in 612 cities (Hindman 2005, 125). Other candidates
noticed and imitated this approach. John Kerry followed Dean in relying on
Meetup,[5] while the George W. Bush campaign adapted Meetup's organizational
form by encouraging supporters to throw "house parties" for the president. Campaigns may even try to recruit canvassers directly through the Internet, eliminating
the intermediate step of the house party/meetup (Fisher 2006). These communication methods bring supporters together and put them to work on various tasks
without the expense of paying field organizers to make the arrangements, in the
process allowing campaigns to expand their reach at a relatively low cost.

Campaigns may gain an edge if they are able to use the Internet to communicate more effectively than their competitors. Fisher (2009) examined the manner in which the two major-party presidential campaigns used their campaign
Web sites to mobilize the ground war in 2008. She compared my.barackobama.
com (also known as MyBO) with www.mccainnation.com (McCain Nation).
Fisher and her students used the Web sites in an effort to attend campaign
events in New York City. They found that the technology used by the MyBO
Web site allowed users to pinpoint effectively the locations of campaign events
and to interact directly with event organizers; McCain Nation lacked these features. Fisher may have obtained different results if she had repeated the same
study in a swing state, or in a Republican-dominated area, but the deeper point
of her research is that potential differences in organizing technology may give
advantages to one candidate over another. The Obama campaign claimed that,
by the end of 2008, more than thirteen million people had been recruited
through the MyBO Web site (Fisher 2009). While the exact number is unverifi-
able because the data have not been made available to scholars, the sheer magnitude of the claim suggests that the Obama campaign raised the possibilities
for computer-mediated grassroots organizing to a whole new plane. It seems to
have discovered a formula for turning *supporters* into *activists* (Vaccari 2008).

While the lower costs of Internet communication facilitate genuine grassroots organizing, such as Bush's house parties, they may also spawn less authen-
tic forms of participation. Campaigns sometimes enlist the Internet to lay
"astroturf" rather than to plant grassroots—for example, encouraging supporters to submit letters to the editor that are actually written by the campaign.

This approach saves letter writers the time and effort of writing the letter themselves, while giving the campaign a greater chance of having its talking points appear on editorial pages around the country. Klotz (2007) described these submissions as "plagiarized" participation. Although newspaper editors may be able to spot plagiarized submissions and choose not to run them, many such submissions are published nevertheless. A Republican National Committee letter praising President Bush's economic leadership was printed in more than one hundred newspapers under different names (Klotz 2007, 5). Through plagiarized participation, the Internet opens new pathways for campaigns to reach the traditional media.

While major parties and their candidates benefit from being able to organize supporters at low costs, interest groups and minor parties may benefit from this aspect of the Internet too. Howard Dean's early front-runner status in 2004 owed much to his win in an "online primary" sponsored by MoveOn .org in June 2003 (Hindman 2005, 123). By holding this "primary," MoveOn upended the Democratic Party establishment and significantly raised the prospects for outsider candidates. Even though the primary had no legal standing, it generated the media attention that Dean needed to stand out from his rivals. Because of these tactics, major parties may face greater complications in controlling their nomination processes in the future.

Whereas MoveOn sought to circumvent the process specifically within the Democratic Party, Unity08 attempted to buck the two-party system as a whole four years later. Unity08 was crafted by Doug Bailey, Gerald Rafshoon, and Hamilton Jordan (former advisors to Presidents Gerald Ford and Jimmy Carter), who sought to counter the polarization of the two major parties with a centrist, bipartisan approach to the presidential election (Rapoport et al. 2009, 1). Their plan was to host an online convention in the summer of 2008 that would nominate a high-profile candidate, such as New York City mayor Michael Bloomberg or former U.S. senator Chuck Hagel (R-Neb.). Ultimately, the effort attracted 124,000 members and raised $1.5 million (Rapoport et al. 2009, 2). The campaign was scuttled, however, by (what it perceived as) obstruction from the Federal Election Commission, inability to secure ballot access in the fifty states, and difficulties in attracting a high-profile candidate.[6] It disbanded without nominating a standard bearer. The Unity08 effort suggests that it is now at least imaginable that a third-party candidate with broad appeal might be nominated solely using an Internet infrastructure. Yet it also brought into focus the limits of Internet-based organizing. While the Internet certainly aids party-based organizing, it seems unlikely that an Internet presence alone is ready to replace the grassroots infrastructure of a major party, which plays a critical role in recruiting candidates, raising money, and gaining ballot access.

In sum, the low marginal cost of communicating via the Internet offers several advantages for campaigns. Candidates are able to make more information about themselves available on the Internet than in printed materials, and to employ a wide array of Web 2.0 technologies in doing so. The option of advertising online does not promote greater negativity in campaign advertisements, but it does widen the range of issue positions between competing candidates. The Internet has been a boon for fundraising, especially for nonestablishment candidates, and has drawn a new cadre of citizens into the electoral process. Finally, the Internet enhances the organizing capacity of campaigns, although this ability may be as much a threat as a benefit since interest groups and minor parties are also able to exploit these tools in ways that disrupt the plans of major candidates and parties. At the same time, it is difficult for alternative actors to replace the role of major parties, which have evolved to perform innumerable functions for candidates (Aldrich 1995). In the following section, we consider the implications not only of the Internet's low marginal cost, but of its proclivity to decentralize communication.

Decentralization

The Internet is a highly decentralized forum for the exchange of information, especially in comparison with other forms of mass media (Bimber 1998). In the traditional media model, information is collected by a small number of centralized news bureaus, filtered by an editorial staff, and then passed on to the general public with limited opportunities for feedback. In the Internet model, information is collected by a much larger number of people—some professional and some amateur—and then posted both filtered and unfiltered, allowing comment from the general public. In theory, virtually anyone can gain an international audience on the World Wide Web. We argue that the decentralization of communication through the Internet has two principal implications for campaigns. First, decentralization removes some control of information from the hands of campaigns, exposing them to new risks and benefits. Second, decentralization empowers new actors, especially bloggers, who are able to influence campaign dynamics.

A first implication of the decentralized information dynamics of the Internet is that it undermines the ability of campaigns to control the flow of information about their candidates (Gueorguieva 2008). Nonaffiliated actors now have a greater capacity than they once did to disseminate both damaging and beneficial information during a campaign. In a traditional media environment, campaigns may be able to impose some limits on which credentialed reporters have access to their candidates; persons without bona fide credentials can be denied access altogether. In an Internet media environment, virtually anyone could be a "reporter," so candidates worry that anything that they say or do could be caught on video and used to their detriment (see Newsom 2008). Of course, campaigns have never been able to exert outright control over news about their candidates in the face of a free press corps. Media have long exploited candidates' gaffes—for example, when the national press corps caught President Gerald Ford eating a tamale improperly in Texas during the 1976 Republican primary campaign (Popkin 1991, 1). Yet by dispersing the power of the press more widely, the Internet loosens to an even greater degree candidates' abilities to shape and contain stories about them.

The risks to candidates from Internet decentralization are well illustrated by former senator George Allen's (R-Va.) so-called Macaca moment in 2006.[7] Allen's reelection was being contested by Democratic nominee Jim Webb, whose campaign asked a University of Virginia student, S. R. Sidarth, to follow the senator with a handheld video camera. At one of Allen's rallies, he introduced Sidarth (who is of Indian-American descent) to the crowd by referring to him as "Macaca," which is considered a racial slur. The video of this comment was played more than four hundred thousand times on YouTube over the course of a few weeks, and was the subject of extensive discussion in the blogosphere. Ultimately, it contributed to Webb's narrow victory of about nine thousand votes (or only 0.4 percent) to claim the Senate seat. These events gave the appearance that a U.S. senator was brought down almost single-handedly by a college student with a handheld camera, suggesting the potential power of viral videos in shaping campaign outcomes.

Recounting Allen's Macaca moment as a David-and-Goliath story, however, may be more hyperbole than truth. Karpf (2009) has argued that the political impact of the story came not only from its dissemination on YouTube, but from other factors as well. Allen's presidential aspirations and the expected closeness of the national contest for control of the Senate, for example, made him a relatively high-profile target. And the clip not only played widely on YouTube, but was the basis for an article appearing in the *Washington Post*. Further, the Webb campaign had worked closely since its inception with liberal bloggers, especially DailyKos, and these allies amplified the Macaca story within the national media. Thus, the senator was brought down not simply by a lone posting on YouTube but rather through coordination among the opposing campaign, a team of bloggers, and traditional media, all of them working to leverage the YouTube framework. Decentralization mattered, but it was not the entire story of Webb's victory.

Like the risks of Internet decentralization, the potential benefits of decentralization also may depend on the involvement of campaigns. For example, will.i.am's "Yes We Can" video set to music Obama's concession speech after the New Hampshire primary and included appearances by Kareem Abdul-Jabbar, Scarlett Johansson, and various other celebrities calling for change (see the image on the following page). It spread virally through the Internet and amounted to considerable free advertising for the Obama campaign. Wallsten (2009, 41) used statistical analysis to demonstrate that "bloggers and members of the Obama campaign played crucial roles in convincing people to watch the video [twenty million times] and in attracting media coverage." He showed that postings about the video on the Obama campaign's blog, and on other noncampaign-affiliated blogs, made a crucial difference to the viewership of the video.

If any person with a handheld video camera has the potential to post a video that is viewed worldwide, then candidates clearly are subject to a higher level of scrutiny than they have been in the past. It is harder, for example, for them to claim that they were misquoted or misunderstood when video of the statement is replayed thousands of times on the Internet. Lightning may not strike twice, however. George Allen's Macaca incident raised awareness of the potential consequences of unscripted remarks on the campaign trail, such that "it is not surprising that the 2008 Senate campaign did not produce any influential tracker footage despite a concerted effort to find it" (Klotz 2009). The 2008 presidential race, however, did feature a minor fracas when Obama's comments to Samuel Joseph Wurzelbacher (otherwise known as "Joe the Plumber") were caught on video. Although Obama's interaction with Wurzelbacher did not include a flub comparable to Allen's, the candidate's suggestion that tax policy should be used to "spread the wealth around" became a focal point for the McCain campaign's cries of socialism in its final month (Rother and Robbins 2008).

The accountability function of the Internet is about more than amateur videographers catching candidates making egregious statements. In fact, the most popular political YouTube videos are professionally produced spots posted by the campaigns themselves (Klotz 2009, 149). But the archiving of videos on YouTube forces a candidate to remain accountable after an ad has aired on television, as videos that are pulled from the air may remain archived online indefinitely. The 2008 race in North Carolina between incumbent senator Elizabeth Dole (R) and challenger Kay Hagan (D) is an example of online accountability

Home   Videos   Channels   Shows

Search

Yes We Can - Barack Obama Music Video

II   0:48 / 4:30

★★★★☆ 77,532 ratings   19,878,650 views

in action. When Dole's campaign ran a television ad implying that Hagan was an atheist, the online record of that ad enabled the blogosphere and the Hagan campaign to respond that Dole had taken a cheap shot (Klotz 2009). While the final vote tally ultimately was not close, the enhanced ability to respond might have mattered in a more tightly contested race.

A second implication of the decentralization of the Internet is that it empowers new actors who can have an important impact on campaigns. Blogs (or weblogs) and those who write them are perhaps the most visible of this new species of political animal. Established political institutions have resisted blogs because they are published without editorial supervision, are generally written by people without journalistic credentials, and effectively challenge the roles of traditional media (Heaney 2008). Nonetheless, Farrell and Drezner (2008) explained that blogs play an important filtering function for the news media by quickly proposing a set of interpretive frames for events. Although there are thousands of blogs, only a small number of them develop reputations for being especially reliable sources of political commentary. Social networks are vital to building these reputations, as most leading blogs are connected in some way (if informally) to traditional media outlets. Thus, while blogging is a quintessentially decentralized activity (as anyone can write a blog and post it online instantaneously), hierarchy determines which blogs are able to influence the flow of political information.

While most bloggers are content to influence the rhythms of the news cycles, others become more directly involved in politics. According to Pirch (2008), bloggers were instrumental to Ned Lamont's defeat of Joseph Lieberman in the 2006 Democratic Senate primary in Connecticut. Lieberman had grown in disfavor with some Democratic Party activists because of his support for the war in Iraq and for much of President Bush's foreign policy agenda. In response, several political blogs (especially DailyKos.com, MyDD.com, MyLeftNutmeg .org, and ConnecticutLocalPolitics.net) became forums for anti-Lieberman sentiment (Pirch 2008, 279). Not only did the bloggers discuss Lieberman, but they tried to persuade Lamont and other prospective candidates to oppose him and provided financial and logistical support once Lamont did enter the race. Bloggers thus acted as a kind of "virtual political party" as they sorted among candidates and helped to solidify a plan to remove Lieberman from office (Pirch 2008). The blogosphere's initial victory was undone in the general election, however, as the incumbent was reelected as an "Independent Democrat" with the support of the Connecticut Republican Party and moderate Democrats. As of this writing, Lieberman remains a favorite target of liberal online activists.[8]

While it is tempting to conclude that decentralization has reversed the power dynamics of campaigns, only a partial power shift has taken place. Decentralization has had important consequences in some races, including the 2008 Allen-Webb contest in Virginia, but the involvement of campaigns in interpreting, disseminating, and amplifying information remains critical. Nevertheless, candidates are now increasingly accountable for how they behave in public, with bloggers and other Internet users functioning as a new estate within the media. The extent to which bloggers and other online actors will become an autonomous political force is uncertain, but it is clear they that are already becoming part of expanding party networks (Koger, Masket, and Noel 2009, 2010). In the next section, we explain how online social networks create navigable structures, both to the advantage and to the detriment of campaigns.

Digital Social Networks

Social networks are at the heart of how people think about politics. We learn about politics from our family, friends, and coworkers; we talk with them about political events and what they mean. Social networks matter for deciding when and how to become involved in campaigns and elections, or not (Huckfeldt and Sprague 1995). The Internet greatly enhances citizens' abilities to build and use social networks. Since the early to mid-2000s, Web sites dedicated to social networking (such as MySpace, Facebook, and Twitter) have proliferated online. These networks are of limited value if they are entirely online, as network studies have shown that face-to-face communication is a key ingredient in building trust in relationships (Nohria and Eccles 2000). However, when online social networks are combined with offline ties, they have the potential to strengthen communities and build social capital (Putnam 2000, 180). The key challenge for campaigns, then, is to find ways either to use the Internet to create and sustain offline interaction or to tap into already existing offline relationships through social networking sites.

Two types of online social networks are relevant in campaigns. One type is created for general uses that are not necessarily political. LinkedIn, Friendster, MySpace, Facebook, and Twitter are prominent examples. All these sites allow users to build social networks and include such functions as e-mail; instant messaging; sharing photos, videos, and music; status updates; and games. Since these sites are not built for exclusively political purposes, users develop connections with a diversity of uses in mind. Of course, they also can use these platforms politically by "friending" a candidate, creating or participating in a political group (such as Student Veterans of McCain-Palin 2008), or simply by exchanging opinions about politics. Many campaigns have concluded that these sites can work to their benefit. According to Williams and Gulati (2009, 23), more than two-thirds of all congressional candidates had an updated Facebook page in 2008, up from only 16 percent in 2006.

Presidential candidates and potential candidates have turned to social networks as well. As of this writing, Barack Obama has 7,063,365 supporters on Facebook, more than any other politician in the world; 2008 GOP vice-presidential nominee Sarah Palin (see the image on the following page) is a distant second with 1,141,614 supporters. These networks are valuable not only because they contain lists of supporters but also because they provide campaigns with access to information about friends of their supporters. As a result, contact is made with people who might not otherwise have thought of themselves as supporters of the candidate in question. Further, such sites enlighten supporters about their own social networks. For example, someone who visits Palin's Facebook page will see which of her or his friends support Palin. Upon receiving this information, the person may think differently about these social ties, perhaps taking the initiative to engage one or more of the friends in conversations about politics.

A second type of online social network is created specifically for political purposes. Both John McCain and Barack Obama added social networking features to their Web sites in 2008. These sites often allow users to create a personal profile, search for other supporters in their geographic neighborhood, join issue-based groups (for example, concerning the environment or border security), volunteer, and donate money. Unlike general social networking sites that put the candidates in touch with many people, some of whom may not be strong supporters, candidates' social networks allow campaigns to interact with their core supporters and enable those supporters to network with one another. If such tools are used actively by campaigns and supporters alike, then they have the potential to transform the social structure of campaigns from a heavily top-down, leader-to-follower model to one that is more horizontal or peer-to-peer.

We believe that there are two principal implications of online social networks for campaigns. First, digital social networks (sometimes in combination with other media) enable campaigns to refine and target their appeals more effectively than do traditional approaches. Max Harper (2009), who worked with the Obama campaign's online video division, explained how in 2008 the campaign would determine the width of the audience that it wanted to reach with a video and then decide which media should be used to transmit it. A video could be posted on the Web site only, blogged, or added to Facebook, with the campaign monitoring diffusion of the video on the Web. Harper noted that videos that were added to Facebook had the widest reach, since they were viewed not only by Obama's registered supporters but also by friends of those supporters, and perhaps even friends of the friends of those supporters.

Alternatively, networking tools can be used to identify narrow demographic segments of the population and produce content that is micro-targeted directly to individuals in those groups. For example, Obama's sister, Maya Soetoro-Ng, recorded messages on his behalf in twelve Asian languages (including Hmong) in order to transmit targeted appeals based on information available through Facebook. Critically, this approach allowed the campaign to be more effectively multivocal—that is, to speak in different voices at the same time. While campaigns have been micro-targeting for years, the ability to parse a message such that each subdemographic receives its own targeted appeal might be better described as "nanotargeting." According to Josh Koster (2009, 23), "It's based on the idea that the Internet audience is extremely fractured. So, instead of identifying the most universally persuasive messages and broadcasting them to a wide audience . . . you take the most persuasive messages and nanotarget each one to the right niche." This approach leverages the diversity of interests on the Internet by using scattered, but narrowly targeted, messages to attract support.

Targeted appeals to supporters may be employed not only during the campaign proper, but also during the messy aftermath that sometimes occurs following close elections. For example, the 2008 race for the U.S. Senate seat from Minnesota required a recount after an especially tight contest between incumbent Norm Coleman (R), Al Franken (D), and Dean Barkley (I). To identify monitors for the recount, Franken's campaign used online social networks to pull together lists of supporters who were lawyers or paralegals who could help with a mobilization that eventually involved approximately one thousand volunteers on the Democratic challenger's team (The Big E 2009). This example underscores the versatility of online social networks, showing that they can be mobilized quickly and for reasons only tangentially related to why they were originally created. Franken did not build an online network with the idea of networking with lawyers and paralegals in particular but, when the need arose, information embedded within the online social networks made forging these connections possible.

Some scholars have hypothesized that social networking may be a way to target appeals to younger voters, who are more likely to use these sites than are their elders. Candidates who use social networking and respond (or have their staffs respond) to comments may be perceived as more "in touch," especially by the young (Utz 2009). However, studies of the 2008 election suggest that younger users of online social networking sites were no more likely to participate in politics than nonusers (Baumgartner and Morris 2010; Zhang et al. 2010). Thus, if there are benefits to candidates in reaching out to youth in this way, those benefits must be something other than boosting participation. The Internet seems unlikely to cure the problem of youth nonparticipation.

A second implication of social online networks is that they can empower a candidate's supporters in ways that are beyond the control of (and not always in the best interests of) the campaign. Allowing "supporters" to post comments on a Facebook page, for example, gives them a forum for rendering criticisms of the candidate as well. This problem can be addressed by having a member of the campaign staff monitor the page and delete critical comments. But such issues grow more complex as the sophistication of online communities increases. Consider that one of the strengths of Obama's MyBO Web site—its capacity to allow supporters to form user-generated discussion groups—is also a point of vulnerability. MyBO groups, for the most part, worked to the benefit of the campaign, as participants mostly focused on how to win the election. However, shortly after Obama secured the Democratic presidential nomination in the summer of 2008, some of his supporters formed a MyBO group called "Get FISA Right" that, with fifteen thousand members, became the most popular group on the site (Kreiss 2009c). Obama had earlier voted for reauthorization of FISA (Foreign Intelligence Surveillance Act) in the Senate, which many civil libertarians complained would undermine judicial oversight of government surveillance within the United States (American Civil Liberties Union 2008). This group sought to pressure the Democratic nominee into changing his position on the reauthorization.

The FISA protest left Obama in a difficult position, as "Get FISA Right" was not created by Republican provocateurs seeking to disrupt the campaign but by genuine supporters. Simply deleting the group from MyBO might have led to a backlash and negative media attention with consequences worse than the protest itself. Allowing the protest to continue exposed Obama's problems in unifying the liberal wing of the Democratic Party as he attempted to move to the center of the political spectrum during the general election campaign. The irony of the situation was that the Obama campaign had put into place the social structure that was now opposing Obama's decision. The fact that Obama neither changed his position on FISA nor stopped the protest did not prevent him from winning the general election. Yet these kinds of feedback effects are sufficiently troublesome that campaigns must consider whether the benefits of actively building online networks are worth the costs. Consistent with this worry, one study found that candidates in highly competitive races are less likely than candidates in less competitive races to use "advanced interactive innovations because these . . . options interfere with the candidate's message" (Druckman, Kifer, and Parkin 2007, 425). Interactivity is indeed both a blessing and a curse for campaigns.

Online social networks are the latest aspect of the Internet to be incorporated into campaigns. Candidates only began to exploit these tools in a sophisticated manner during the 2008 presidential election, so their full implications are only beginning to become apparent. The real test of their value will be in the extent to which campaigns use these networks to reach people who might not otherwise have received the campaign's messages. The more that campaigns target their supporters' friends, the more likely they are to synergize online and offline social networks to expand social capital and build "thick" communities (Bimber 1998). At the same time, campaigns must do this in such a way that the communities they create do not bite back at their creators. In the next section, we consider how campaigns manage not only changes in online networks but also the rapid technological changes brought about by the Internet in general.

Rapid Technological Change

More significant than any specific technology available online is the fact that the overall environment of the Internet is one of rapid technological change. Meetup.com was a key part of the story of the 2004 presidential election, yet it was scarcely mentioned four years later. Facebook, which became a major media outlet for presidential politics in 2008, had been a little-known social networking site on Ivy League campuses in 2004. Understanding what it means to campaign in the Internet age is not about any one Web site or method of communication. Twitter, Facebook, or YouTube may be obsolete or bankrupt by the time the 2012 elections roll around. Instead, the key to understanding communication in modern campaigns rests in why some campaigns respond effectively to technological change online and others do not.

Rapid technological change poses a challenge to campaigns because learning how to implement new technologies within dynamic campaign environments takes time. While it may be a simple task for any one person to learn to use an online technology, it is a complex task for an organization to channel these individual uses toward a collective goal. Consider what a campaign needs to learn to make Facebook an effective campaign tool. First, it has to know how to build a broad network of supporters. The campaign must not only attract supporters directly, but then also attract the friends of its supporters, and the friends of the friends of its supporters. This process requires the campaign to navigate the network structure effectively so that a small core group grows into a broad community. Second, it has to know how to target messages within that community and to the people who are linked to members of that community. If a presidential campaign has one million supporters, and each one of these supporters has an average of five hundred friends, then the resulting network is very large (though the exact size is indeterminate because of redundancies in the network—that is, person A is friends with many of the same people as person B). Knowing where to broadcast information within this network is a strategic challenge, since reaching the entire network is not feasible. Third, the campaign must be able to monitor and react to feedback from members of the network, including managing any disputes or protests in a way that will not tarnish the campaign's overall image. Given a network of one million supporters, this task is highly sensitive and enormously labor intensive. What's more, it may take an election cycle or two to learn how to do the job effectively. The problem here is that a campaign may find that a social site such as Facebook, once mastered, has become outmoded. By 2012, a new technology may be at the cutting edge of campaigns. Campaigns that learn how to harness these new technologies before their opponents have even thought to do so are the ones that may have the real advantage.

Which campaigns come out on top of the technological change game is partly a matter of serendipity. Howard Dean's campaign mastered Meetup.com before opponents had even heard of this tool, but that did not prevent the demise of his campaign in the 2004 Iowa caucuses. Prior to the 2008 election, a panel of prominent bloggers rated the use of online technologies by Democratic and Republican presidential campaigns (Perlmutter 2008). The panel concluded that Sen. Christopher Dodd (D-Conn.) had the "best blog," former senator John Edwards (D-N.C.) had the "best videos," and Barack Obama had the "best Facebook." Christopher Dodd did not fare well in his quest for the Democratic presidential nomination; if he had, perhaps we would be devoting more space in this chapter to writing a good blog instead of building an effective Facebook network.

Adapting to rapid technological change, however, is more about organization than it is about luck. Daniel Kreiss examined the use of technology by Howard Dean in 2004 and concluded that the nature of the campaign's formal organizational structure was critical to its technological effectiveness.[9] First, the campaign displayed the willingness to take risks by relying on new technology. William Finkel, the outreach manager of Meetup.com, contacted all of the Democratic primary candidates in 2003, but the Dean campaign was the only one that showed any interest in this new technology. Dean's receptivity and risk-taking was encouraged by campaign manager Joe Trippi, whose professional career arc had spanned both political campaigns and Internet start-up companies. Second, the campaign adopted a "postbureaucratic" structure that emphasized flexibility of internal roles, sensitivity to the external environment, and integration of the campaign with an online social network. A Director of Online Organizing was hired to command an Internet Division, which had the largest staff of any unit within the campaign; members played boundary-spanning roles and often worked closely with other divisions. Third, the campaign created a set of novel practices, such as the Blog for America, which was the first time a major presidential campaign had written a blog. Collectively, these factors yielded an organization that, like MoveOn.org, hybridized the structures of interest groups, grassroots social movements, and political parties (Chadwick 2007; Goss and Heaney 2010). Essentially, the Dean campaign succeeded at incorporating new technologies into its own organization by networking with elements in the environment that used these technologies.

The Obama campaign's adaptation to rapid technological change, like Dean's before it, was born out of a combination of strategically cultivated networks and wise choices regarding organizational structure. Kreiss has shown that, despite Dean's loss in 2004, members of his campaign staff (Kreiss called them "venture progressives") were in great demand by the Democratic Party establishment in the years that followed.[10] Dean alumni went to work for the Democratic National Committee, Barack Obama, Gov. Bill Richardson (D-N.M.), John Edwards, 21st Century Democrats, America Votes, WesPAC, and former senator Mike Gravel (D-Alaska), to name a few. The most prominent business firm to emerge from this group was Blue State Digital.

The Obama campaign's decision to contract with Blue State Digital to work on its behalf made all the difference for the campaign's online strategy. Blue State Digital developed "Party Builder" software that became the basis of the MyBO Web site and allowed the campaign to use Facebook Connect to synchronize data between MyBO, Facebook, and other online sites. This move "allowed the campaign to directly leverage these external networks. For example, Facebook Connect users could see a list of their friends in battleground states and easily contact them with voting reminders" (Kreiss 2009b, 20). Thus, the Obama campaign did not figure out online campaigning on its own; rather, it drew heavily on technical and campaign expertise that existed within a newly emerging organizational field in Democratic Party circles. It then integrated these new technologies into its organizational structure in a way that bore greater resemblance to a social movement than to the marketing approach traditionally used in campaigns (Ganz 2009).

The next stage of adapting to rapid technological change will be to find ways to create greater continuity between campaigning and governing. After the 2008 election, the question arose as to what campaigns planned to do with the e-mail lists and online social networks they had created. To this end, President-elect Obama took his campaign organization (Obama for America), renamed it Organizing for America (OFA), and brought it within the organizational structure of the Democratic National Committee (Trish 2009). This reconstituted organization was intended to help the president pass health care reform and other items on his agenda while in office, while keeping his supporters engaged during the intervening years between elections. Indeed, Dean campaign manager Joe Trippi had envisioned something similar several years earlier:

> [Imagine that] the president of the United States shows up in Washington with the e-mail addresses of six million of his closest supporters. [Imagine that] the president vows to govern the way he'd won—by tapping into the will of the American people. [Imagine that] he drops them all a note that says, "Hey, if you're really interested in health care, I need your help. Go to your computer right now and e-mail your congressman and tell him that you don't want him listening to the pharmaceutical lobby, that you don't want him listing to the HMO's. Tell him that you want him listening to *you* . . ." (Trippi 2004, 224, emphasis in original).

Despite the fact that OFA followed Trippi's script to the letter, it was not successful in transporting the organizational energy of the Obama campaign to the Obama presidency. Part of OFA's failure may have stemmed from the decision to merge it with the formal organization of the Democratic Party rather than allow it to remain an independent organization (Trish 2009). During the debate over national health insurance in 2009, for example, OFA was not effective in rallying the grassroots to support a public option insurance plan, one of President Obama's signature provisions, partly because it did not have access to the same level of resources that Obama for America had in the presidential campaign and because of activist burnout (Zeleny 2009a). Instead, conservative activists who were mobilized through the "Tea Party" movement proved more agile in summoning the Internet to promote the view that the Democrats were overreaching in their health care reform effort (Zeleny 2009b).

Adapting to rapid technological change is about more than just recognizing technological developments and attempting to use them. It is about creating organizational structures that are capable of channeling these technologies in pursuit of collective goals. The campaigns of Howard Dean and Barack Obama formed hybrid organizational structures that enabled them to blend with their environments, making them more like social movements than like traditional campaigns. As of this writing, OFA has yet to assist substantially in the governing process in the way Joe Trippi and others anticipated. Perhaps solidifying this campaign-governing connection will be the next important step forward. In the next section, we look to these potential changes as we consider how the Internet is likely to matter in future campaign cycles.

Looking to 2010, 2012, and Beyond

As we look into our crystal ball, we expect to be surprised by how the Internet factors into the 2010 and 2012 elections. The surest bet we can make about the Internet's place in elections is that it will keep changing. The campaigns that are able to integrate new technologies within their organizational structures are likely to benefit with enhanced performances at the polls.

For the past several election cycles, Democrats have held the upper hand in using the Internet. They have seized upon new technologies and used them more effectively than have Republicans. Concomitant with this advantage has been the development of a network of experts who advise Democratic campaigns in implementing Web 2.0 technologies—resources that allowed Democrats to dominate grassroots organizing from 2004 to 2008 much as Republicans had from 1994 to 2002. Looking ahead, it is reasonable to expect the pendulum to swing back in the Republican direction. With the 2010 midterm congressional election campaigns gaining steam as of this writing, Republicans are anticipating that political momentum will be on their side as Democrats face some degree of public dissatisfaction with Obama's handling of the economic crisis, health care reform, Afghanistan, terrorism, and other issues (Thrush and Kady 2009). Republicans will likely also benefit from the fact that midterm elections traditionally tend to favor the party that does not hold the presidency (Born 1990). With the perception of momentum on their side, Republican candidates may be especially motivated to close the technology gap with the Democrats.

Analysis of early technology use by candidates for the 2010 elections suggests that Republicans may be accelerating their use of online technology vis-à-vis Democrats. We examined Facebook and Twitter use by all declared candidates for congressional seats in 2010 as of the first week of July 2009. Our data yield only a snapshot of a dynamic process, but they are nonetheless informative of current trends. To determine if there was a difference between Democrats and Republicans, we gathered data on (1) the candidate's number of Facebook fans, (2) the number of posts to the candidate's Facebook page, (3) whether or not the candidate uses Twitter, and (4) the candidate's number of Twitter followers. Results are reported in Table 8.1.

Our analyses support the expectation that Republican candidates gained some ground relative to Democratic candidates in early preparation for the 2010 congressional elections. First, no significant difference existed between the two groups in the number of Facebook friends, both averaging about 700. Republicans, however, held a statistically significant advantage on the other indicators: Republican candidates averaged more items posted to Facebook (21, compared with 6 for Democrats); more than half (53 percent) had a Twitter account, compared with just one-quarter (25 percent) of Democrats; and among candidates with Twitter accounts, Republicans averaged 1,701 followers, compared with 812 for Democrats. We also checked to see whether these results held up when factors other than party affiliation were taken into

Table 8.1 Average Use of Social Networking Sites by 2010 Congressional Candidates

	Democrats	Republicans	T-score	Significance	Sample Size
Number of Facebook fans	765	693	−0.48	No	574
Number of posts to candidate's Facebook page	6	21	5.31	$p < 0.01$	574
Candidate uses Twitter	25%	53%	7.18	$p < 0.01$	574
Number of Twitter followers*	812	1,701	5.04	$p < 0.01$	215

Sources: www.facebook.com; www.twitter.com. Data were compiled the first week of July 2009.

Note: Current or former presidential candidates are excluded from these computations.

*Number of Twitter followers is only computed for candidates having a Twitter account.

account. Multivariate regression models were estimated, including variables on characteristics of the candidate, the race, and the district. Multivariate analysis allows the analyst to assess the impact of a focal variable—such as a candidate's party—while holding constant the effects that may be due to other factors. Results indicate that taking the impact of multiple variables into account does *not* explain away the basic difference between Democrats and Republicans. The latter appear to be taking the lead in using online social networks.[11]

Such findings are noteworthy because they stand in direct contrast to Williams and Gulati's (2009) analysis of the 2008 election, which revealed a clear advantage for Democrats on Facebook. This outcome is the product of a concerted Republican strategy to improve its online presence (Bellantoni 2009). Of course, having a Facebook or Twitter account is not the same as using it effectively in a campaign context. Still, the fact that Republicans are moving forward in this area is a harbinger that the balance of power online may be about to change.

In keeping with our statistical results, many of the interesting dynamics in 2010 and 2012 may be on the Republican side of the political spectrum. We should look for whether Republicans employ online technologies differently than do Democrats, as the organizational structures and networks in the two parties differ considerably (Freeman 1986; Masket et al. 2009). With Barack Obama as the incumbent, there is not likely to be a serious contest for the Democratic presidential nomination in 2012. Thus, innovations in Internet technology will probably not emerge during the Democratic primaries. With the Republican nomination up for grabs, however, the leading candidates may be distinguished by their uses of the Internet. As Internet technologies penetrate more exhaustively within campaigns, greater variations in style of use will likely emerge. In the not-too-distant future, it may not make sense to talk distinctively about "campaigning on the Internet," as the Internet may be practically inseparable from any other aspect of campaigning.

Conclusion

The development and diffusion of new online technologies is truly astonishing. From BlackBerries and iPhones to new applications on Facebook and Google, the world is becoming linked electronically at a rapid pace. Just because new technologies appear, however, does not mean that they will become relevant to campaigning. Candidates and their advisors must not only learn how to use the technologies in question, but also how to incorporate them into the organizational structures of campaigns. The more that campaigns facilitate the creation of political networks online, the more resources they will have to devote to monitoring these forums, commenting on the discussions that take place there, and coordinating the work of volunteers. Such a shift will draw staff away from working in the field, leaving more field operations to volunteers working in tandem with central office personnel online. While campaigns have recently chosen to hire distinct directors of online campaigning, in the future they may lean more in the direction of merging online campaigning with all divisions within the organization. Such a move would place the Internet firmly at the center of the action.

The benefits of campaigning in the Internet age are numerous. Candidates are now able to communicate with their supporters and potential supporters at radically reduced marginal costs; they can leverage decentralized communication structures to build their organizations. Online social networks promise access to vast expanses of information about voters that never existed in the past. Those campaigns that are able to manage the rapid pace of innovation will be more likely to win their electoral contests. A wider audience of diverse peoples will become activists in campaigns, which will bear a closer resemblance to social movements. Yet these factors may not change some fundamental aspects of campaigning. Even in the Internet age difficulty in reaching young voters continues to be a problem, and decisions about the valence of advertisements (positive or negative) may not be significantly affected. Long-standing traditions such as week-long party conventions and network television debates appear secure for now. The major parties will not be replaced by online skeletons that nominate candidates without ever meeting in person.

The excitement of introducing new technologies into the political world comes with ill-understood risks. Candidates may create online social structures that begin to operate counter to candidates' own strategic objectives. If candidates are not sufficiently responsive to user comments posted on their Web sites, supporters may become more alienated than if they had never interacted with the campaign online at all. Blogs and amateur videos transform the press corps from an elite circle of trained journalists to an ocean of episodic participants seeking to advance their personal political agendas. While the result is something short of a genuine "democratization" of campaigns, the political world today is more open and less controlled than ever before. The Internet is defining the reality of communication in the early twenty-first century; accordingly, the future of the United States rests with those who learn to use it to speak to "We the people."

THE POLITICAL PROFESSIONALS RESPOND

Chris Casey

What do you want? A Web site like Obama's. What should it look like? You have total creative license, so long as it's red, white, and blue. When do you need it? Yesterday.

So begins a typical conversation between a political consultant who specializes in online campaigns and a candidate or first staffer who is looking to bring a fledgling campaign online. Weeks of effort follow—designs, revisions, development, content, testing—all leading up to a Web site launch, which is inevitably followed within a day by a question from the campaign: "How come my site isn't #1 in Google's search results?"

Online campaigns have come a long way in almost twenty years of practice, but we still have far to go. Every presidential election since 1992 has brought renewed attention to the art of campaigning on the Internet. Each cycle sees new innovations that others will want to replicate—and discovers missteps to avoid. And at the end of each cycle, a search begins for the candidate who would not have won were it not for the Internet. In 1998, it was Jesse Ventura's third-party victory to become governor of Minnesota that was hailed as the first major election in which the Internet made a difference; in the dozen years since, scores of campaigns may have turned out differently if not for their use of the Internet. And maybe Barack Obama would indeed not be president today were it not for the Internet. Regardless, while it's a fun discussion to analyze and ponder whether the Internet provided a critical push, tipping a particular candidate to victory, it can safely be said that no serious candidate for elective office today can afford to ignore it. Candidates do so at their own peril.

Presidential elections are relatively few and far between, a quadrennial Super Bowl of campaigning in which only a few candidates will ever compete. Things are different in the thousands upon thousands of races that take place every year for lower offices. Can candidates for a state or local office really expect their shoestring budgets to deliver "a Web site like Obama's" multimillion-dollar effort? And even if they're able to, can they really expect their campaign to generate similar levels of interest and support? Not bloody likely! But that doesn't mean they can't employ and benefit from techniques developed and refined at a higher level. With realistic expectations, scaled to their appropriate size and nature, even the smallest campaigns can benefit from the advantages of campaigning online and innovations developed at the top of the ticket. And guess what? There is plenty of innovation coming from down the ballot as well.

Establishing an online presence, especially getting critical list building and contribution functionality in place quickly, has rapidly climbed the list of high-priority "to-dos" for all candidates, particularly challengers. Content and interactivity can come later (naturally, the sooner the better), but what's needed immediately is a pair of buttons on a Web page labeled *Sign Up* and *Contribute*. Building an e-mail list of supporters has become THE critical first step for campaigns, as they have come to understand (usually) that with proper care and management, said list can grow into one of their most powerful campaign assets—one that they will use to share news, deliver calls to action, and, of course, appeal for contributions (again and again).

The self-selective nature of the online audience is probably the most fundamental characteristic that distinguishes it from traditional means of campaign communication such as television, radio, direct mail, or phone banks. In each of those instances, the campaign selects an audience and attempts to communicate with it. Only on the Internet does the audience truly self-select. Users decide they want to learn more about a candidate, or find a way to help him or her, and they go online to do so. They may not yet even know the person they are looking for. But campaign Web masters see the proof in their referrer logs and understand the importance of Google and other search engines for delivering such visitors. Online advertising offers powerful opportunities to bait a hook in search of specifically targeted audiences, but they still must self-select in choosing to take that bait and follow an ad to a specific Web site. Self-selection is not a problem for using the Internet to campaign for office; in fact, it is an advantage of online campaigning over traditional means of campaign communication.

The growth of online social networks was to the 2008 campaign what blogs and Meetups were in 2004. Emerging Internet technologies spread quickly across campaigns at all levels, offering easy-to-use audience benefits such as Flickr for photos and YouTube for video without burdening campaigns with the task of hosting infrastructure. Internet technologies potentially increase the audience for candidates' content by making it available to users of those sites, rather than just to those who find it on a campaign's own Web page. On Facebook and Twitter, candidates need to work to engage these networks in the same way as their users do: with a genuine personal voice. Campaigns shouldn't be looking to control their growing and dispersed online supporters; on the contrary, they need to engage, enable, and energize them.

Online fundraising is clearly an area where innovations at the presidential level have been successfully adopted for down-ballot races. Innovations introduced by the campaign of Howard Dean in 2004 stand out as excellent examples. Dean's campaign stole a page from the telethons of Jerry Lewis, with their baseball bat thermometer and fixed fundraising goal with a fixed deadline. These successful tactics have been repeated in recent elections with countless variations by campaigns at all levels. Another of Dean's innovations involved sending an e-mail appeal to the candidate's own mailing list, but seeking support on behalf of someone else. Dean asked his enthusiastic supporters for contributions to Iowa's representative Leonard Boswell, whose support Dean sought in the presidential race and who reaped the financial boost as Dean's backers obliged. Tools that allow supporters the ability to create their own fundraising goals, solicit their friends and family, and raise money have also now come within the reach of smaller campaigns, though they may remain impractical for those below the state level that lack potential for broad-based support.

How much money will you raise online? That question has an easy answer: none, some, or a lot—it depends. It is actually becoming harder to raise "none." Online contribution services such as ActBlue permit supporters to contribute to campaigns that haven't yet bothered to implement a contribution system of their own. "Some" is a relative term that can mean vastly differing amounts to campaigns of different levels, budgets, and interest. But few campaigns today would be satisfied with the modest goal typical of the late 1990s—specifically, that an online campaign just raise enough money to pay for itself (the goal then being one of promotion). "A lot," of course, is what every campaign wishes for, and it can strike when you least expect it—for example, when the congressman you are challenging yells "You lie!" at the president on national television. It's at times like these when the decision to go with bargain-priced Web hosting at twenty dollars a month proves not to be the good idea it initially seemed. Campaigns can't know how much money they will raise online, but they must prepare for such unexpected opportunities or be left to wonder how much they might have raised if their Web site hadn't buckled under the load when lightning struck and people who an hour earlier had never heard of them suddenly wanted to give them money. A meaningful investment in infrastructure, people, and technology is necessary in order to reap the maximum benefit of online campaigning.

Online innovations can come from down the ballot as well. In 2009, Bill de Blasio, a candidate for the office of New York City Public Advocate, sought to bring attention to the issue of poor housing conditions and negligent landlords. His staff worked with NGP Software to develop a Google map mashup dubbed the "Slumlord Watch List" that allowed visitors to submit their buildings for consideration for inclusion on the map. While this particular feature may not be the sort that lends itself to widespread use among other campaigns, it certainly served a useful purpose in generating earned media attention for de Blasio's winning effort. And that is but one example among many—some of which may take hold and see widespread use, and others that will pass by unnoticed. As online campaigning approaches twenty years of practice, it remains an area of political campaigning still ripe for innovation.

It is no surprise that innovation is more likely to come from a challenger with nothing to lose than from an incumbent who is often campaigning defensively and hoping to avoid fatal mistakes. Likewise, a minority party might be quicker to embrace new technologies: as Heaney, Newman, and Sylvester point out, Republicans are forging ahead with Twitter. The GOP does, after all, have more time on its hands while the Democratic majority in Congress and the president work at governing. My own partisan stripes will show, however, in my disagreement with the notion that the current Democratic advantage in national politics necessarily foretells a technological pendulum swing toward the Republicans. Instead, I believe that both parties will continue to innovate online. Sometimes those efforts will fail, as with the recent problem-filled re-launch of the GOP.com Web site; others will join a growing number of proven techniques for online campaigning that future campaigns will replicate. But don't expect Democrats to rest on their online laurels in cycles to come.

As online campaigning has matured over the last decade, expectations for what it can deliver have increased tremendously. Campaigns can't fake it. They must dedicate genuine effort, staff, and resources to the development and management of their online activities to meet these expectations. And yet, despite the growth of a professional class of online political consultants, online campaigning is still likely to be tasked to the inexperienced.

The fictional sports agent Jerry McGuire asked his football star client to "help me help you." A candidate for office turns that around, seeking to use the Internet to "help you help me"—to win, and to win using information, tools, and resources that allow you to make meaningful contributions. Campaigns that best utilize the proven strategies of the past while pursuing innovative Internet technologies will gain an online advantage, and that just might be all it takes to deliver an electoral one.

Notes

1. The authors are grateful to Fabio Rojas and Edward Walker for helpful suggestions. Our research was funded in part by a grant from the University Scholars Program at the University of Florida.

2. As described by Wallsten (2009, 1), viral videos are "online video clips that gain widespread popularity when they are passed from person to person via email, instant messages and media sharing websites."

3. See www.pewinternet.org/Shared-Content/Data-Sets/2009/April-2009-Economy.aspx.

4. Lack of access to the Internet among certain groups (the so-called digital divide) remains a serious problem. A recent study by the Pew Internet and American Life Project found that online political engagement is dominated by people with higher levels of income and education (A. Smith et al. 2009). As a result, we make no claim that everyone has access to the Internet or that access is evenly distributed throughout the electorate; instead, we simply note that a growing share of the polity is online.

5. See http://johnkerry.meetup.com.

6. See the open letter to group members at www.unity08.com.

7. The facts about the Macaca incident in this paragraph and the next are taken from Karpf (2009).

8. For example, see www.youtube.com/watch?v=8vS6kIbJu64&feature=player_embedded.

9. All of the facts about the Dean campaign reported in this paragraph are taken from Kreiss (2009a).

10. Unless otherwise noted, all of the facts about the Dean and Obama campaigns reported in this paragraph and the next are taken from Kreiss (2009b).

11. Models were estimated for the number of Facebook fans, Facebook posts, and Twitter followers using Tobit Regression, since these dependent variables were left censored at zero for candidates without Facebook or Twitter use. We estimated the model for whether a candidate had a Twitter account using Probit Regression, since our dichotomous dependent variable evaluated whether or not a candidate uses Twitter. Complete results are available from the authors upon request. For information on how to use these methods, see Greene (2008).

9 Direct Democracy and Candidate Elections

Daniel A. Smith

When casting ballots in voting booths or filling out absentee ballots at home, citizens are asked to choose from an array of candidates running for federal, state, and local offices. More often than not, voters also are asked to weigh in on a spate of policy questions placed on the ballot for their consideration either by citizens, interest groups, or state and local lawmakers. These ballot measures may alter state constitutions; create new state laws; or amend local, municipal, or county charters. From statewide ballot initiatives, to legislative referrals, to down-ballot local referendums and advisory questions, citizens are increasingly being asked to serve as election-day lawmakers (see Mendelsohn and Parkin 2001; Tolbert, Lowenstein, and Donovan 1998; Waters 2003). Though the process of direct democracy entails binary (yes-no) choices on sometimes complex policy questions with long-term consequences (Chambers 2001), political scientists have found that voters are generally able to use limited information to make competent choices on ballot measures (Lupia 1994, 2001).

Political consultants working on candidate elections are increasingly cognizant of the potential impact that ballot measures can have on their own races. "A candidate [who] ignores an initiative on a ballot that shares his or her name," cautioned Kellyanne Conway, the president of a Washington, D.C.–based consulting and market-research firm, "does so to their own peril" (Fulk 2004). Campaign consultants working on candidate elections tend not to welcome ballot measures, however. "Candidates hate ballot initiatives," longtime GOP consultant David Hill noted, "because they skew voter turnout and create competition for money, interests and votes" (Fulk 2004).

Unfortunately, most campaigning textbooks neglect the topic of how ballot measures might condition candidate races (Bailey et al. 2000; Burton and Shea 2003; DiClerico 2000; Herrnson 2001; Salmore and Salmore 1989; Semiatin 2004; Shea and Burton 2001; Thurber and Nelson 2000, 2004; Watson and Campbell 2003). This is surprising, as there is a growing body of scholarly literature that reveals how ballot measure campaigns can influence candidate campaigns and electoral outcomes. In particular, scholars have begun to systematically assess the procedural byproducts of ballot measures on candidate races, what are known as the *educative effects* (D. Smith and Tolbert 2004) and *spillover effects* (Nicholson 2005) of direct democracy. Since the Progressive Era (D. Smith and Fridkin 2008), observers of the three mechanisms of direct democracy—the initiative, popular referendum, and recall—have noted that these processes have a series of indirect, attendant effects that can alter the attitudes and behaviors of citizens and political organizations at the state and local levels. The importance of ballot measures is not, however, limited to state and local politics; statewide ballot propositions can also affect the course of candidate races in national elections.

In this chapter I examine the impact of ballot measures on candidate races. Following a brief discussion of the growing use of the mechanisms of direct democracy (and paying close attention to statewide initiatives), I provide an overview of recent scholarly literature on the instrumental as well as the indirect effects of citizen lawmaking—that is, respectively, how the plebiscitary mechanism provides citizens with an institutional check on the system of representative governance and how the byproducts of that process affect the attitudes and behaviors of citizens and political organizations. I then discuss several ways that ballot measures can affect candidate campaigns, specifically, looking at how (1) certain propositions on the ballot may underscore campaign themes and set the agenda in candidate elections, (2) ballot measures can alter the campaign financing parameters of candidate elections, and (3) ballot measures affect the composition of the electorate by mobilizing certain voters to the polls. The potential impacts of ballot measures on candidate races in these three realms, which are not necessarily mutually exclusive, are attendant byproducts of the process of direct democracy. I conclude the chapter by arguing that candidates and campaign consultants need to be ever more attentive to the presence of ballot propositions, not simply for their intrinsic merit or policy substance, but for their electoral effects on candidate races.

The Growing Use of (and Scholarship on) Direct Democracy

Over the course of the twentieth century, the use of direct democracy was cyclical; the propensity for citizens and groups to place measures on the ballot in the American states ebbed and flowed over the decades (Magleby 1984; Tolbert 2003; Waters 2003). Between 1911 and 1920, a period during which many states initially adopted the mechanisms of direct democracy, citizens considered 293 initiatives on statewide ballots; yet by the 1960s, the number of initiatives qualifying for statewide ballots had fallen below 100. The downward trend reversed, however, following the passage in 1978 of Proposition 13, California's property tax–slashing proposal; the landslide adoption of this measure created an explosion in ballot initiative use throughout the American states (Schrag 1998; Sears and Citrin 1982; D. Smith 1998; Tolbert 2003). Between 1981 and 1990, citizens across the nation considered 271 statewide initiatives; in the next decade, they voted on 389 initiatives, including 93 statewide initiatives in 1996 alone.[1]

Although the number of initiatives on statewide ballots has tapered off slightly since the 1996 high-water mark, many states continue to exhibit initiative fever. Nationwide in 2008 there was a total of 153 statewide measures on the ballots of thirty-one states, including fifty-nine citizen initiatives in seventeen states.[2] Voters in the fifty states also considered hundreds more local referendums and initiatives.[3] Substantively, ballot measures cover a remarkable range of issues. Some of these are complex; others are relatively straightforward. Some ballot propositions make national headlines, but others remain obscure in terms of public or media attention. In many of the two dozen states that permit statewide ballot initiatives, voters have cast ballots dealing with issues as diverse as punishing negligent doctors, prohibiting the confinement of pregnant pigs, limiting the taxing and spending powers of state governments, funding stem cell research, and ending affirmative action programs and social welfare benefits to illegal aliens. On the November 2004 ballot alone, six states offered initiatives banning same-sex marriage, and another five featured legislative referrals on the same topic. In 2008, the issue was on the general election ballot of three more states (Arizona, California, and Florida). Virtually no subject is off limits. Fickle as they may sometimes be, citizens generally embrace the plebiscitary power of the initiative (Bowler and Donovan 2002; Matsusaka 2004; Waters 2003).

Critics of direct democracy argue that the process has spun out of control, with ordinary citizens and special interests, rather than elected officials, having too much power to shape legislation and tinker with state constitutions (Broder 2000; Ellis 2002; Schrag 1998; D. Smith 1998). Writing in the late 1990s, journalist David Broder (1997) observed that "ballot measures are as copious in California as convertibles. They pop up in primaries and in general elections like Shasta daisies." A few years later, the *Los Angeles Times* (2003), a longtime and persistent critic of the initiative process, editorialized (once again) that "direct democracy is running amok." Critics in other states agreed, including the late president of the Florida Senate, Jim King, who warned of the potential "Californication" of Florida resulting from the rash of initiatives on the state-wide ballot (Ulferts 2003).

With increased use of direct democracy, and the accompanying prominence and criticism of controversial ballot measures, scholarly literature on the topic has burgeoned (D. Smith and Tolbert 2007; Lupia and Matsusaka 2004). Most studies have focused on the instrumental use of the initiative to achieve policy outcomes. In their endeavor to examine the policy outcomes ballot initiatives, researchers have examined the role of money and special interests in determining ballot outcomes, the competence of voters in casting votes on ballot measures, the impact of direct democracy on the rights of minorities, whether or not initiative outcomes reflect public opinion and state policies, and whether ballot measures are implemented effectively.[4]

Unfortunately, these academic works on the instrumental outcomes of direct democracy have little relevance to campaign consultants working on candidate races, as the research is largely divorced from the broader electoral environment. Recently, though, political scientists have begun to address how ballot measures can affect candidate races by taking a page from early twentieth-century writings. During the Progressive Era, a handful of scholars theorized—and reformers fantasized—about how direct democracy might have a transformative "educative value" (D. Smith and Tolbert 2004; Bowler and Donovan 2002). In addition to any substantive changes to public policy it produced, the process of voting on ballot measures could transform the electorate. Harvard political scientist William Munro (1912, 20–21), for example, highlighted the "educative value of direct legislation," arguing that "a spirit of legislative enterprise is promoted among the voters; men are encouraged to formulate political ideas of their own and to press these upon public attention with the assurance that they shall have a fair hearing." Similarly, scholar and diplomat Paul Reinsch (1912, 158) argued that the processes of direct democracy would "assist the people, the body of the electorate, in the development of its political consciousness," making it "more familiar with legislative programs and more interested." Thus, irrespective of the policy consequences of direct democracy, these and other Progressives emphasized the educative aspects of citizen lawmaking, suggesting that the process itself could not only bolster turnout but also stimulate civic engagement, increase citizens' trust in government, and even minimize the political power of interest groups and party bosses (see Boehmke 2002, 2005; D. Smith and Tolbert 2001, 2004; M. Smith 2001, 2002; Tolbert, Grummel, and Smith 2001; Tolbert, McNeal, and Smith 2003; Tolbert and Smith 2005).[5] Many Progressives, then, understood full well how voting on ballot propositions could shape the political attitudes and political behavior of the broader electorate, which indirectly could affect candidate elections.

How Ballot Measures Can Set the Agenda in Candidate Races

One of the most obvious ways in which ballot measures can shape candidate races is by bringing into sharp relief the issues on which politicians running for office may agree or disagree. As with the anti-gay-marriage initiatives in 2004, ballot measures are sometimes used strategically in an effort to control the agenda; that is, by sponsoring or speaking out on a proposal, candidates attempt to gain instant name recognition and political credibility. Then, during the campaign, the candidates tie their messages directly to an issue they are backing (or opposing), or perhaps have backed (or opposed) in a previous election. In this way, ballot measures can have a synergistic effect by connecting tangible, substantive policies to what otherwise might be vacuous or vague policy commitments floated by the various contestants. In short, by tethering themselves to ballot measures, candidates attempt to use issues to set the agenda and energize their own campaigns.

A growing body of evidence suggests that ballot measures do help to set the agenda in candidate contests. Nicholson (2005), for example, found this to be the case and concluded that, as a result, ballot measures are yet another issue source that can provide useful information to voters at relatively low cost. While voters may not necessarily link issues on the ballot directly to specific candidates, Nicholson maintained that those issues nevertheless can have "spillover effects" that "indiscriminately" affect citizens' judgments in candidate races (128). In other words, the "indiscriminate priming effect[s]" of ballot measures may help to reinforce (rightly or wrongly) voters' partisan stereotypes of the issue positions held by candidates (71).[6] Building on research that shows candidate choice to be influenced by issue preferences, especially when information about an issue is readily accessible to voters (Nie, Verba, and Petrocik 1976; Popkin 1991), Nicholson argued that the effect of ballot measures is likely to be most pronounced in election contexts where information is relatively scarce (in particular, below the presidential level).

Putting his theory to an empirical test, Nicholson demonstrated that ballot measures—from tax-limitation, to environmental regulation, to illegal immigration, to affirmative action, to the freezing of nuclear weapons production— can indeed influence the agenda in candidate races. For example, he found that the nuclear-freeze issue in 1982,[7] irrespective of whether it was openly discussed by candidates, was one of the most important considerations to voters in candidate races in the ten states that had such a measure on their ballots but was largely irrelevant in states that did not. According to Nicholson, the various freeze measures helped to set the agenda for candidates not only in U.S. Senate elections but also in low-information U.S. House races and even in some gubernatorial contests. Nicholson (2005, 111, 124) also showed how the indiscriminate priming effects of California's Proposition 187 (in 1994, concerning social services to illegal immigrants) and Proposition 209 (in 1996, concerning affirmative action) shaped the agenda not only in high-profile statewide races (president, governor, U.S. Senate) but also in some down-ballot contests as well.

Using ballot initiatives to advance a candidate's profile has become a refined art in California, which ranks second behind Oregon as the leading initiative-use state in the country (D. Smith 2009). Peter Schrag, an astute and longtime observer of politics in the Golden State, described in his scathing book on direct democracy, *Paradise Lost*, how the initiative process encourages the "embracing and demagoguing [of] hot-button issues" by candidates who hope to "showcase" their credentials (Schrag 1998, 226). The use of ballot propositions in California to help candidates define and differentiate themselves from the pack dates back at least to Democrat Jerry Brown's run for governor in 1974. To boost his primary campaign, Brown brought together Common Cause and a group called the People's Lobby to place Proposition 9, the California Political Reform Act, on the June ballot (Allswang 2000). The measure (which dealt with campaign finance regulations) passed easily, and Brown became his party's nominee; he continued to exploit the issue in the months that followed, while sailing through to a comfortable win in the general election (Schrag 1998).

Perhaps pushing the effort to campaign on initiatives too far, in the 1990 Democratic gubernatorial primary, Attorney General John Van De Kamp co-sponsored no less than three ballot measures: Proposition 128 (dealing with the environment), Proposition 129 (a proposal to increase spending on prisons, jails, and drug education and treatment), and Proposition 131 (a measure to create legislative term limits and some public financing of campaigns) (see Schrag 1998). In fact, the candidate contributed $277,000 out of his own campaign fund to the political committee sponsoring Proposition 133[8] and another $560,000 to the committee behind Proposition 131 (Allswang 2000). Unfortunately for Van De Kamp, he fared as poorly at the polls as did his three measures, all of which went down to defeat in the June primary (Schrag 1998). On the Republican side of the 1990 California gubernatorial primary, moderate Pete Wilson latched onto Proposition 115, a tough-on-crime initiative, in a successful effort to "beat off a group of conservative opponents" in the election (Schrag 1998, 227). In 1994, Wilson again turned to the initiative process, this time to invigorate his flailing bid for reelection. The governor actively campaigned that year on two ballot measures that had broad levels of popular support: Proposition 184 (a severe "three-strikes" measure for repeat criminal offenders) and Proposition 187 (a proposal to deny social services to illegal immigrants and their children). Serving as Proposition 187's spokesperson, Wilson was able to bolster his image of being tough on illegal immigrants and even contributed roughly $2 million from his own reelection campaign coffers to pay for campaign ads touting the measure (Chávez 1998; Schrag 1998; D. Smith and Tolbert 2004).

As governor of California, Republican Arnold Schwarzenegger took campaigning via ballot initiatives to further heights. More than a year before deciding to toss his hat into the October 2003 recall election that led to the replacement of Democratic incumbent Gray Davis,[9] Schwarzenegger sponsored a measure that was placed on the 2002 general election ballot. His successful initiative, Proposition 49, required the state to direct surplus general revenue funds to pay for after-school programs in public schools. For those who are inclined to be more cynical, this policy proposal was seen as part of a broader calculus designed by Schwarzenegger's political advisors to prepare him for a gubernatorial bid in 2006 (Hasen 2005). The measure presumably would help to soften the film star's often violent and callous on-screen persona, promoting instead a portrayal of a strong supporter for educational programs to benefit the state's children; rather than voters thinking of the former bodybuilder as "Conan the Barbarian" or "the Terminator," Proposition 49 would frame him as a more congenial and children-friendly "Kindergarten Cop." When the 2003 recall election became a reality, the foundation had already been laid and Schwarzenegger was able to accelerate his time frame for capturing the governorship.

As governor, Schwarzenegger attempted to use the ballot process to advance his policy agenda and political clout. He officially endorsed or opposed nine of sixteen measures on the November 2004 ballot and had the state GOP mail a slick multipage brochure—titled "Governor Arnold Schwarzenegger's Ballot Proposition Voter Guide"—to millions of registered voters (Donovan, Mooney, and Smith 2009). In office for little more than a year, Schwarzenegger subsequently threatened to use direct democracy to circumvent the recalcitrant Democratic-controlled legislature in Sacramento if it did not place referendums on the ballot in support of his fiscal agenda; in addition, he sought to funnel unlimited campaign contributions from special interests to a host of ballot-measure committees that he controlled (E. Garrett 2004; Hasen 2005). Then, in 2005, he once again attempted to govern by using direct democracy, making good on his promise to take policy questions directly to the people by calling for a special election that would ask citizens to vote on several measures (none of which passed, however).[10]

Other instances of how ballot measures are used by political operatives to set the agenda and frame candidate elections abound, with some tactics less seemly than others. In 1998, for example, Democratic and Republican Party operatives in Colorado each tried to link statewide candidates from the opposing party to what they viewed as unpopular measures that were on the statewide ballot that year. Howard Gelt, a former state Democratic Party chair, formed a political committee to raise money for campaign ads linking Republican gubernatorial candidate Bill Owens, who was trying to distance himself from the social conservatives in his party, to three conservative initiatives on the ballot (including two antiabortion measures and a third dealing with school vouchers). Responding in kind, Don Bain, a former chair of the Colorado Republican Party, founded a political committee to air negative television ads depicting Democratic candidates running for statewide office as supporters of liberal ballot measures, most notably Referendum B, a statutory referral placed on the ballot by the legislature that would have allowed the state to retain excess tax revenues to pay for education and transportation projects rather than refunding those revenues to taxpayers as required by the state constitution (see D. Smith and Tolbert 2001; E. Garrett and Smith 2005).[11]

More recently, in Florida, where there were eight measures overall (six initiatives) on the 2004 general election ballot, the rival U.S. Senate candidates attempted to craft their campaign themes accordingly. Republican nominee Mel Martinez mentioned several ballot issues in his standard stump speech and at the candidate debates. Martinez endorsed Amendment 2, a measure placed on the ballot by the GOP-controlled state legislature that required parental notification before a minor is able to obtain an abortion, but spoke out (quietly) against Amendment 3, a tort reform measure placed on the ballot by the Florida Medical Association and favored by Florida governor Jeb Bush and President George W. Bush. At the same time, Martinez, a former president of the Academy of Florida Trial Lawyers, attempted to distance himself from his barrister past by actively criticizing Amendments 7 and 8, two initiatives backed by trial lawyers that protected patients' rights and penalized wayward doctors. Martinez also strongly criticized Amendment 5, an initiative that sought to raise the minimum wage by $1 and index future increases to the rate of inflation.

While Martinez's Democratic opponent, Betty Castor, also opposed Amendment 3, she routinely spoke of her support for Amendment 5 and tried (in vain) to make it a wedge issue in the campaign (S. Erickson 2003). As Martinez consultant David Hill said during the campaign, "There has always been a belief that when you put a measure like raising the minimum wage or anything that would help blue-collar workers on a ballot it would bring more Democrats to the polls and actually hurt Republicans" (Fulk 2004). Trying to seize on the moment, Castor's communications director endeavored to make Amendment 5 a polarizing issue, emphasizing that "Betty Castor supports raising [the] minimum wage, Mel Martinez does not" (Fulk 2004). But while there was considerable excitement among Democrats that the minimum-wage measure would help both Castor and presidential nominee John Kerry in Florida, the direct impact of Amendment 5 on the candidate races was overstated: Castor and Kerry lost to their Republican opponents, even as the minimum-wage proposal passed with more than 70 percent of the vote.

Finally, initiatives placed on the ballot can be used by political operatives to divert the attention of the media and the public from a candidate's record. Dave Noble, executive director of Stonewall Democrats, a gay and lesbian group, claimed that the anti-gay-marriage measures on eleven statewide ballots in the 2004 general election were "being used as one way to distract voters from what we think should be the real issues." In particular, "[e]very time something goes wrong in Iraq," according to Noble, Republicans would try to "scare voters" by bringing up the subject of gay marriage (Lowy 2004). Although the GOP did not sponsor any of these ballot measures, and publicly downplayed the effect they might have on the presidential vote, party leaders were privately excited by their presence on the ballot in several key swing states, including Michigan, Oregon, and Ohio. As the chair of the Ohio Republican Party said after the election, "I'd be naïve if I didn't say it helped," especially "in what we refer to as the Bible Belt area of southeastern and southwestern Ohio, where we had the largest percentage increase in support for the president" (Dao 2004; D. Smith, DeSantis, and Kassel 2006).

How Ballot Measures Can Alter the Financing of Candidate Races

Ballot measures can have a profound, if indirect, effect on the financing of candidate elections, although scholarly research on this topic is fairly thin. In contrast to all federal and most state and local races for political office, where ceilings have been placed on the amount of money that can be given to a candidate, there are no limits on the size of contributions (or expenditures) in ballot campaigns. As a result, the equivalent of a "soft-money" loophole exists when it comes to ballot measures, making the sky the limit for these contests.[12] Also unlike federal and many state candidate races, corporate and labor union treasuries are permissible sources for contributions to ballot campaigns (E. Garrett and Smith 2005; D. Smith 2009). In 1998, for example, nearly $400 million was spent by ballot-issue committees nationwide to support or oppose sixty-one initiatives and dozens more referendums in forty-four states (D. Smith 2001b). The national Republican and Democratic Parties, by way of comparison, raised *only* a total of $285 million in soft money during the 1997–1998 election cycle (D. Smith 2001a).

While the amount of money being channeled into ballot campaigns is noteworthy in and of itself, the indirect (strategic) use of the initiative process by crafty practitioners is a development that candidates and their campaign staffers should be concerned about. In the early 1990s, Grover Norquist, the well-connected head of Americans for Tax Reform (ATR), a conservative nonprofit organization with a primary goal of curtailing taxes and government spending, provided a detailed blueprint of how conservatives could use the initiative process to promote their agenda in the states (D. Smith and Tolbert 2004, 177). Writing in 1993, Norquist correctly anticipated how ballot initiatives limiting legislative terms and cutting both taxes and government spending, as well as anticrime, victims' rights, and parental rights ballot measures, could potentially bring fiscal and "social conservative Republican voters to the polls" in 1994 and 1996, while at the same time draining the resources of Democratic allies, most notably organized labor (Norquist 1993).

In October 1996, the Republican National Committee (RNC) transferred $4.6 million in soft money to Norquist's ATR to run issue ads. The details of this transfer were not publicly disclosed until formal hearings were held by the U.S. Senate in 1997 (E. Garrett and Smith 2005; D. Smith 2004). ATR subsequently transferred a substantial amount of RNC money to groups in California, Colorado, and Oregon that sponsored conservative ballot proposals in 1996 and 1998, including several antitax, right-to-work, and so-called paycheck-protection measures.[13] In the 1996 general election, ATR contributed $509,500 to the tax-slashing Oregon Taxpayers United, which amounted to nearly 60 percent of the total amount raised by the group that year (D. Smith 2004). Then, during the 1998 June primary in California, ATR funneled $441,000 to Campaign Reform Initiative, the group backing Proposition 226 on paycheck protection. Although Proposition 226 went down to defeat at the polls, Norquist is on record as saying that "[e]ven when you lose, you force the other team to drain resources for no apparent reason" (D. Smith and Tolbert 2004, 108).

Norquist's innovative approach of using the initiative process for ulterior motives—that is, seeking to divert resources from the opposition's candidate campaigns—appears to be gaining acceptance. "Activists in both parties are also taking advantage of election laws that permit unlimited contributions to campaigns for and against ballot measures as a way to pump money into key presidential campaign states," said Kristina Wilfore, former executive director of the Ballot Initiative Strategy Center, a nonprofit organization promoting progressive ballot measures (Lowy 2004). Recently, labor unions in California and Oregon have had to spend more than $40 million to defeat various ballot initiatives. "That's $40 million that didn't go into races and didn't go into other issues," Wilfore argued. According to Wilfore, more than $75 million was spent in the 1990s to defeat conservative ballot measures that were intended not first and foremost for their policy outcomes but rather to drain the resources of key Democratic support groups (Lowy 2004).

Although the precise amount of money that various interests have diverted over the years into ballot campaigns is impossible to verify, the claim still resonates with a certain level of credibility. The "initiative industrial complex," as some commentators (Schrag 1998, 189) have called the process of direct democracy, is clearly fueled by money from special interests (Broder 2000; Ellis 2002; D. Smith 2001c; but see also E. Gerber 1999). Indeed, the process has long been influenced by the role of money, with paid signature gatherers, professional consultants, and lawyers employed to write the text of the ballot language becoming a regular occurrence in ballot campaigns by the early 1900s (McCuan et al. 1998; D. Smith and Lubinski 2002). Facilitated by recent campaign finance regulations banning soft money in candidate races,[14] however, it seems likely that contributions once invested in those races are now increasingly finding their way into ballot campaigns (E. Garrett and Smith 2005). Campaign and elections scholars are only beginning to investigate the financial nexus that exists between ballot measures and candidate races.

How Ballot Measures Can Alter the Composition of the Electorate

Perhaps the most exciting academic literature concerning the indirect effects of direct democracy on candidate races has to do with how the former can help to alter the composition of the electorate and affect candidate elections. Public opinion data indicate that citizens have some degree of interest not only in the candidates who are seeking office, but also in the policy proposals that happen to be on the ballot in the same year (Cronin 1989; Waters 2003). Since, as we have seen, these proposals can be used to set the agendas of candidate races (Donovan, Tolbert, and Smith 2008; Nicholson 2005; D. Smith 2008; D. Smith, DeSantis, and Kassel 2006), adroit consultants who run such campaigns are increasingly looking to use them strategically in ways that tweak the electorate to their clients' advantage.

With regard to the impact that ballot measures have on voter turnout, researchers have discovered that the plebiscitary process does, in fact, alter the electoral landscape. At the aggregate level, states that use the initiative process frequently are more likely to have citizens turn out to vote not only in midterm elections when presidential candidates do not compete with ballot measures for media attention, but also (though to a slightly lesser degree) in presidential elections (Tolbert, Grummel, and Smith 2001; Tolbert and Smith 2005). In municipal races, parallel evidence indicates that the use of direct democracy boosts voter turnout locally (Hajnal and Lewis 2003). Using more sophisticated methodological tools, these findings serve as a corrective to earlier state-level research showing minimal effects of the initiative on voter turnout (Everson 1981; Magleby 1984).[15]

At the individual level, research using survey data has shown that salient ballot measures tend to generate higher turnout in midterm elections. Arguing that not all ballot measures are the same, studies have found that the presence of salient initiatives and legislative referenda (defined as those with a greater amount of front-page newspaper coverage devoted to them on the day following the election) increase the probability of voters turning out in midterm, but not presidential, elections by roughly three percentage points (M. Smith 2001; Lacey 2005). Researchers have also shown that citizens living in states that allow the initiative tend to be more knowledgeable and engaged in civic affairs (Mendelsohn and Cutler 2000; M. Smith 2002; Tolbert, McNeal, and Smith 2003; D. Smith and Tolbert 2004; but see also D. Schlozman and Yohai 2008) and more trusting of government (Bowler and Donovan 2002; Hero and Tolbert 2004; D. Smith and Tolbert 2004; but see also Dyck 2009; Dyck and Lascher 2009) than those who do not. Scholars also have found that different types of voters are motivated to participate because of ballot measures. Recent studies indicate that initiatives and referendums tend to have a greater mobilizing effect on those who vote regularly as opposed to more episodic (including younger) voters. Partisanship appears to play a role as well, with self-identified Republicans and Democrats being more likely than independents to say they are aware of and interested in ballot measures, and to report that their decision to participate in an election was influenced by the presence of such measures on the ballot (Donovan, Tolbert, and Smith 2009).[16]

Cognizant of the potential mobilizing effects of ballot measures, parties and candidates have tried (with varying degrees of success) to use them to mobilize their base supporters as well as episodic voters. Though this happens rarely, in a few instances more votes have been cast on a ballot measure than in the candidate races being held simultaneously. Proposition 13, for example, the tax-cutting measure in California, garnered more votes than all the gubernatorial candidates who were listed on the state's 1978 primary ballot. More recently, in Missouri's 2004 primary, turnout exceeded 40 percent of the eligible electorate for the first time in more than a quarter-century. Most observers agreed that many voters were attracted to the polls in this election not to cast their ballots in the contested Republican and Democratic races for governor and U.S. Senate, but rather to vote on a legislative referendum banning gay marriage. Roughly 137,000 and 39,000 more citizens cast ballots on the anti-gay-marriage amendment than participated in the Senate and gubernatorial contests, respectively (Donovan, Tolbert, and Smith 2009).

Clearly, proponents of the gay-marriage bans in several swing states, most notably Ohio, had ulterior motives for placing these measures on the ballot; that is, they wanted to encourage Protestant evangelicals and ideological conservatives to turn out at the polls in support of a ban—and, at the same time, to cast a vote for George W. Bush in the presidential race. The degree to which this mobilization strategy succeeded is open to interpretation. Turnout in Ohio, for example, was up ten points statewide in 2004, yet counties with greater numbers of evangelicals did *not*, all else being equal, experience a disproportionate jump in turnout relative to the 2000 election (D. Smith 2008). Indeed, across the country, turnout rates in 2004 were lower, on average, in the eleven states that had gay-marriage proposals on their general-election ballot than in the thirty-nine states that did not (Abramowitz 2004; Burden 2004). Nevertheless, as pollster Brad Bannon predicted prior to the November election, the presidential race "is going to be so close in these battleground states where there are ballot measures" that the impact of initiatives on turnout "may very well decide" the outcome (Lowy 2004). In the end, the gay-marriage proposals may have helped to tip the election in Bush's favor, especially in the battleground state of Ohio, by mobilizing some conservatives who had actively championed the issue to turn out and support the president.[17] Further, as I noted earlier, beyond merely setting the agenda in candidate races, ballot measures can prime vote choice in those races (Nicholson 2005); in other words, issues that are on the ballot sometimes become highly salient and, as a result, are given greater weight when voters decide which candidate to support. As Donovan, Tolbert, and Smith (2008) documented using survey data, the anti-gay-marriage proposals had strong partisan priming effects on 2004 presidential vote choice in three battleground states (Arkansas, Michigan, Ohio), with supporters of the gay-marriage bans, all else being equal, more likely to vote for President Bush than for Senator Kerry.

In addition to generating turnout, candidates (and parties) have tried to use ballot measures as cross-cutting wedge issues with the intent of splintering their opposition's base constituencies (Donovan, Tolbert, and Smith 2009; Hasen 2000; D. Smith, DeSantis, and Kassel 2006; D. Smith and Tolbert 2001). Perhaps the best example of a ballot proposal serving as a wedge issue was Proposition 209, the 1996 California initiative that successfully banned the use of affirmative action guidelines by public agencies. Republicans, led by Gov. Pete Wilson and U.S. House Speaker Newt Gingrich, hoped that the measure would garner support from white ethnic voters, prying them away from the Democratic Party (Chávez 1998; D. Smith and Tolbert 2004). In a teleconference call with Gingrich, Wilson crowed that Proposition 209 was "a partisan issue ... that works strongly to our advantage [and] has every bit the potential to make a critical difference" in helping to defeat then-president Bill Clinton (Schrag 1998, 226). Although Clinton won reelection handily, the measure produced some internal tensions within the Democratic Party's base coalition.

Voter preferences are generally understood to be less stable in ballot campaigns relative to candidate races, with people tending to make up their minds much later in the former (Bowler and Donovan 1994, 1998; Magleby 1984, 1989). Even so, partisanship is increasingly important in structuring vote choice on ballot measures (D. Smith and Tolbert 2001; Branton 2003; Tolbert, Smith, and Green 2009). The framing of ballot questions, of course, remains crucial to their success (Karp 1998; D. Smith and Tolbert 2001, 2004; Hasen 2000, 2005), but several studies indicate that parties, candidates, and other political elites have increasingly taken positions on them (Karp 1998; D. Smith and Tolbert 2001, 2004; Hasen 2000, 2005) and that citizens rely heavily on partisan cues to inform their voting decisions (Bowler and Donovan 1998; Branton 2003; Donovan, Tolbert, and Smith 2008, 2009; Lupia 1994).

Finally, political context undoubtedly matters with respect to the magnitude of any effect that ballot measures might have on a local, statewide, or even national election. Not all such measures affect turnout to the same degree, with their mobilizing potential depending partly on how they are used to target certain voters. For example, in six states with competitive gubernatorial, U.S. House, and U.S. Senate races in the 2006 election, progressive activists, with the blessing of the Democratic National Committee, introduced initiatives to raise the minimum wage in an effort to attract low-income voters to the polls. Based on focus groups and preelection surveys that pretested the language of a variety of different proposals, Democrats anticipated that the ballot measures would help to mobilize low-income workers who would then support Democratic candidates. All six of the minimum-wage measures passed, with turnout higher in those states than the national average. According to Smith and Tolbert (2010), the information environment was altered by the minimum-wage initiatives on the ballot; the measures created "state-specific issue publics," elevating the importance of the economy in the minds of many voters, which in turn affected candidate choice. They found that direct exposure to a minimum-wage ballot measure campaign in 2006 primed support for Democratic gubernatorial and U.S. House candidates. As mentioned previously, this was true too in 2004 for Republicans when the eleven gay-marriage proposals on statewide ballots boosted the saliency of moral issues among Republican voters, priming support for President Bush (Donovan, Tolbert, and Smith 2008).

Conclusion

Political consultants running candidate races have become more attuned to the indirect impact that ballot measures can have. First, recognizing the strong partisan voting patterns exhibited in most elections, consultants are beginning to understand how these measures can be useful in helping their clients to set the agenda and frame the issues that will be raised in their campaigns. Accordingly, there is an increasing willingness to coordinate candidate messages with issues appearing on the ballot and a growing awareness that ballot measures can often be used to attack the policy positions of their clients' opponents. Second, because of recent regulatory changes in campaign finance law at both the federal and state levels, consultants are looking for ways to use direct democracy to circumvent contribution and expenditure limits in candidate races; using ballot measures to channel otherwise prohibited soft money into candidate races may help to synergistically advantage or disadvantage those running for office. Finally, savvy consultants understand that ballot measures may have a positive effect on electoral turnout, mobilizing certain voters to come to the polls on election day. In turn, the priming effects of ballot measures may help to shape voting patterns in candidate elections. Although using ballot measures to tweak an electorate to achieve electoral gains—by bringing out the candidate's partisan base or dividing the opponent's supporters over a cleaving issue—is far from an exact science, candidate campaign consultants will likely continue to try to "take the initiative."[18]

In his book *Democracy Derailed*, David Broder (2000, 1) contended that direct democracy "threatens to challenge or even subvert the American system of government in the next few decades." Whether or not one agrees with the dire assessments and predictions of Broder and other critics of the process, the practice of direct democracy remains robust. The sooner more campaign consultants (and the political scientists studying campaigns and elections) realize the potential synergistic effects of ballot measures on candidate races, the better off candidates (and the scholarly literature) will be. It is time for scholars of direct democracy and, more important, those studying candidate campaigns and elections to catch up to political reality: ballot measures impact candidate-based electoral contests.

THE POLITICAL PROFESSIONALS RESPOND

Celinda Lake and Daniel Gotoff

As campaign consultants, we see firsthand the wide-ranging impact that ballot measures have on elections. Strategically placed and properly exploited, ballot measures not only have the ability to set the issue agenda and reframe the broader context of an election, they also can mobilize key segments of the electorate to show up to vote, including in low-turnout elections. These factors, combined with the increased frequency of ballot referenda, add layers of complexity to the political landscape and present both opportunities and risks to candidates running for office on the same ticket. This is the reality of election dynamics today—and for the foreseeable future. Campaigns that ignore this reality do so at their own peril.

As public opinion researchers, we use a variety of metrics to analyze the potential synergistic effects of ballot measures on candidate races. At the most basic level, we assess support for, and opposition to, a given ballot measure; the intensity behind those positions; and the percentage of the electorate that is either undecided or can be persuaded to shift its opinions. We also look at the overall salience of the issue at hand within the broader political landscape; the issue's ability (particularly in an engaged communications environment) to generate enthusiasm and interest in voting; and the interaction of the measure with perceptions of, and support for, both our candidate(s) and our opponent(s). In addition, we design sample frames that allow us to understand the potential turnout impact on frequent and infrequent voters.

Perhaps the most prominent example of a ballot measure's ability to influence the issue agenda in an election is the spate of anti-gay-marriage initiatives in 2004. That year, the GOP placed these measures on the ballot in eleven states,[1] using them not only to effect policy, but also to excite the Republican base and reframe the issue debate in what was shaping up to be a challenging year. As a result, the gay-marriage issue drew an inordinate amount of attention—and not only in those states where voters would have to decide the fate of the measure, but in national coverage of the presidential race as well, even inserting itself into the second presidential debate. When pressed on the issue by moderator Jim Lehrer, President George W. Bush took the opportunity to defend his support for a constitutional amendment banning the practice of gay marriage and attack John Kerry for his opposition to such a ban. On election day, the anti-gay ballot measures passed in all eleven states and exerted influence that reached beyond the unfortunate (in our view) policy implications. Specifically, that an issue that polled in the low single digits in terms of salience could rise to such outsized prominence in a national election, while drawing attention away from growing public unrest over the national economy and the war in Iraq, underscores the extensive impact ballot measures can have on elections.

While the right has traditionally been more active in exploiting direct democracy to achieve multiple ends, in recent years progressives have started to catch up. In 2004, we analyzed message strategies for Amendment 5 in Florida, a ballot measure proposing an increase in the state's minimum wage. We found that the strongest argument in favor of raising the minimum wage revolved around the dramatic disparity between CEOs' and workers' earnings: "In the last ten years, CEO salaries have skyrocketed even as the economy struggled, but average and low-income workers' wages have barely budged. In 1990, the average CEO made 85 times more than the average American worker. Today, the average CEO makes 531 times more. If passed, this would be the first increase in the Florida minimum wage in 18 years." The power of this message allowed progressives to expand the debate beyond a single policy reform and frame the question in broader populist economic terms. We found that this line of reasoning was not only persuasive to Democrats and independents, it also served as a mobilization tool that increased the likelihood of voting among GOTV (get-out-the-vote) targets for the Democratic candidates for president and U.S. Senate. (Unfortunately, as Smith points out, neither John Kerry nor Betty Castor took advantage of the issue. Castor, for her part, acknowledged as much in statements after the campaign had ended.) Initiatives can also help to energize voters at precisely the time when hard-fought negative campaigns may be turning voters off. In Florida, we found that some younger minority voters who had become disenchanted with the tone of both campaigns responded to the idea of "voting themselves a raise" and taking direct action.

While the agenda-setting potential of ballot measures is more widely acknowledged, less recognized is the ability of ballot measures to shape the composition of an electorate. As campaign consultants, we spend considerable time assessing changes in the electorate and noting which groups of voters are energized and which are not. It is worth noting that in political campaigns, few goals are more desirable and yet more difficult to achieve than affecting targeted surges in voter turnout. To provide some context, in 2008 the Obama campaign, employing the most expensive grassroots campaign in American history, managed to increase the percentage of the electorate that was African American by two percentage points (from 11 percent in 2004 to 13 percent in 2008); it also generated a small increase in turnout among voters under the age of thirty, another key target for the campaign (from 17 percent of the electorate in 2004 to 18 percent in 2008). These seemingly modest increases in turnout translated into millions of additional votes for Obama and are widely, and justifiably, considered monumental achievements by campaign professionals on both sides of the aisle. A ballot measure that has a comparable impact on the composition of an electorate at the state level can mean the difference between victory and defeat not only for the measure itself, but for races up and down the ballot.

Achieving this objective is easier said than done, however. It bears mention that while Republicans successfully used gay-marriage initiatives to influence the issue debate in 2004, they met with decidedly mixed results in their other goal of increasing turnout among the GOP base of white, born-again Christians. While President Bush improved his vote among this group by ten points between 2000 and 2004, the overall share of the electorate that was white, born-again Christian actually did *not* increase between the two elections (23 percent in both cases). In 2006, progressives were determined not to be outdone in the strategic use of direct democracy and diligently applied lessons drawn from the Florida minimum-wage battle during the previous cycle. In those midterm races, minimum-wage measures were placed on the ballot in six swing states,[2] and broad-based, populist economic message campaigns were waged that built on the Florida model. The measures passed in every state, often by wide margins and with the strong support of a broad mix of Democrats, independents, and even many Republicans.

Our firm worked with the Ballot Initiative Strategy Center to assess the unfolding dynamic in four of the six states where minimum wage was on the ballot (Arizona, Colorado, Missouri, and Ohio). In each case, the initiative generated higher levels of reported interest in the election *and* higher levels of reported motivation to vote among supporters of the initiative, who tended disproportionately (but not exclusively) to be Democratic base voters. At the same time, opponents of the minimum-wage initiatives reported less interest and less motivation as a result of their position on the issue. Exit polls in Ohio and Missouri, in particular, substantiated these findings, as minority voters comprised larger portions of the electorate in both states than they had in past midterms, or even in the 2004 presidential election. In Ohio, the percentage of the vote that was African American grew from 8 percent in 2004 to 12 percent in 2006. In Missouri, the difference in the composition of the electorate (from 8 percent African American in 2004 to 13 percent in 2006) was key for Democratic Senate candidate Claire McCaskill, who eked out an exceedingly narrow win after having lost a bid for statewide office just two years earlier. In addition, our own research showed that the initiatives were particularly motivating for unmarried women—a group of voters who have become a GOTV target for Democrats in recent elections, but who also tend to vote less consistently in nonpresidential election years. The minimum-wage ballot measures are not the only explanation for these increases in turnout, but empirical evidence suggests they were a significant factor.

Minimum-wage measures provide a solid example of an issue that is broadly popular, and for which intensity and increased likelihood to vote fall largely on one side. Measures that generate equal excitement among opponents and supporters are volatile and can backfire. For example, in 2006 a Missouri ballot measure to protect stem cell research in the state narrowly passed, but our research showed that it generated as much enthusiasm to turn out among opponents as it did among supporters, and tended to mobilize more conservative voters. Analysis of ballot initiatives in states like Michigan has also shown that initiatives can help get people to vote not just the top of the ticket but the entire ballot, including lower-level races.

As we look to 2010, an election that promises to be especially challenging for Democrats, the need to re-engage and mobilize not just typical drop-off progressives but Obama surge voters as well will be critical. Ballot initiative strategy will be central to understanding the measures that mobilize the Democratic base without simultaneously generating turnout increases from the opposition. For campaign consultants, the research that Smith and other academics provide on these matters is invaluable.

---

[1]Arkansas, Georgia, Kentucky, Michigan, Mississippi, Montana, North Dakota, Ohio, Oklahoma, Oregon, and Utah.

[2]Arizona, Colorado, Missouri, Montana, Nevada, and Ohio.

Notes

1. Twenty-four states currently permit citizen initiatives, and twenty-seven allow for popular referendums. The legislatures in all fifty states have the authority to place issues on the ballot for voter approval. See Waters (2003).

2. These figures are from the National Conference of State Legislatures ballot measures database; see www.ncsl.org/default.aspx?tabid=1658.

3. Use of the initiative process (whereby citizens gather signatures petitioning to place either statutes or constitutional amendments on the statewide ballot) is not evenly distributed across the twenty-four states where it is permitted. Since first adopting the initiative process, Oregon (1902) and California (1911) have led the pack in initiative use, averaging 6.5 and 6.6 initiatives, respectively, per general election (D. Smith 2009). Other western states, most notably Colorado, North Dakota, Arizona, and Washington, have also been relatively heavy users of the initiative process since the Progressive Era. Indeed, roughly 60 percent of all initiative activity since the beginning of the twentieth century has taken place in these six states. At the opposite end of the spectrum, Utah, Wyoming, Illinois, and Mississippi have seen limited use of the initiative. The popular referendum, which allows citizens in roughly half the states to challenge laws passed through the legislative process, is seldom used by any state.

4. On the role of money and special interests, see E. Gerber (1999); Lowenstein (1982); Magleby (1984); D. Smith (2001a, 2001b). On the competence of voters, see Bowler and Donovan (1998); Lupia (1994). On the impact on the rights of minorities, see Bowler and Donovan (2002); Cronin (1989); Gamble (1997); Hajnal, Gerber, and Louch (2002); Matsusaka (2004); Tolbert and Hero (1996); Wenzel, Donovan, and Bowler (1998). On the reflection of public opinion and state policies, see Camobreco (1998); Craig, Kreppel, and Kane (2001); E. Gerber (1996); E. Gerber and Lupia (1995); Hero and Tolbert (2004); Lascher, Hagen, and Rochlin (1996); D. Smith (2001c). And on implementation, see E. Gerber et al. (2001).

5. For an alternative perspective, see Daniel Schlozman and Yohai (2008); Dyck (2009); Dyck and Lascher (2009).

6. "Priming" occurs when ballot measures capture the attention of voters and cause them to give greater weight to certain issues than they otherwise would; these issues may then be used as a basis for evaluating candidates. Even if a candidate does not take an official stance on the ballot measure (such as ending affirmative action programs in his or her state), the issue may nonetheless prime voters to think about the candidate in terms of stereotypical positions held by his or her party (in this instance, Democrats generally supporting affirmative action programs and Republicans generally opposing them).

7. The production and deployment of nuclear weapons is, of course, a matter of national rather than state policy; as such, nuclear-freeze ballot measures were of symbolic value only—that is, election results were not binding on elected officials in Washington or anywhere else.

8. A competing measure to Proposition 129, Proposition 133 was sponsored by Leo McCarthy, the Democratic lieutenant governor who was seeking reelection in 1990 (Allswang 2000).

9. Davis's opponents were able to gather more than 1.3 million valid signatures (far more than the 897,158 they needed) to force a special vote on whether to recall the California governor. On October 7, 2003, a majority of voters elected to remove Davis from office and replace him with Schwarzenegger.

10. During the 2003 recall campaign, Schwarzenegger controlled a ballot-issue committee called "Total Recall" (after one of his earlier films); this committee, which was not subject to contribution limits (state law at the time restricted gifts to candidate committees from individuals and political action committees to $21,100 per election cycle), raised more than $4.5 million in support of the recall. After taking office, Schwarzenegger created "Governor Schwarzenegger's California Recovery Team," yet another ballot-issue committee with no caps on contributions. Recovery Team raised approximately $18.7 million in just a few months to support Proposition 57 (a bond measure) and Proposition 58 (a balanced budget measure), two successful referendums placed on the March 2004 primary ballot by the legislature that the governor said would help dig California out of debt. Prior to the November 2004 election, Schwarzenegger created several new ballot-issue committees, soliciting large contributions from individuals and corporations to help finance campaigns for or against specific initiatives on which he took positions (see E. Garrett 2004; Hasen 2005).

11. Whether revenues are considered "excess" is determined by a formula that takes into account both population growth and the rate of inflation in Colorado; this policy was itself set by a citizen initiative adopted in 1992.

12. Until the 2004 election cycle, national parties were permitted to raise unlimited contributions from individuals, corporations, and labor unions for "party-building" activities. Much of this unregulated soft money, however, was spent on issue ads, which by and large supported or attacked candidates running for office but did not explicitly urge viewers to vote for or against any of the candidates.

13. By forcing union members to regularly check off whether they wanted a portion of their dues to go to explicitly political causes (as opposed to the current practice of allowing union leaders to make those decisions), this measure would have sharply curtailed the political voice of organized labor.

14. In 2002, Congress passed and President Bush signed into law the Bipartisan Campaign Reform Act (BCRA), also known as McCain-Feingold, which, among other provisions, banned the national parties from collecting or spending unregulated soft money. See Malbin (2003).

15. Magleby (1984, 197), for example, concluded that "turnout is not increased by direct legislation, and alienated nonparticipants are not moved to the polls by the initiative and referendum." Occasionally, he conceded, highly salient measures such as California's Proposition 13 in 1978 (see above) "might encourage" higher turnout; even so, Magleby maintained that "only the educated will be able to master the complicated ballot whenever the election is held."

16. In addition, research shows that partisanship is a strong predictor of the *direction* of vote choice in ballot measure elections (Branton 2003; Citrin, Reingold, and Walters 1990; Donovan and Snipp 1994; D. Smith and Tolbert 2001; Donovan, Tolbert, and Smith 2008).

17. The salience of the gay-marriage issue is, however, evident from the fact that in two Ohio counties, more votes were cast for and against the ballot measure than for all the presidential candidates combined (D. Smith 2008).

18. The long-term effects on the parties of tying candidates to ballot measures are not clear, however. By tacitly backing gay-marriage ballot measures, for example, Republicans run the risk of alienating younger voters, many of whom (including those who support the GOP) oppose the measure or see it as a nonissue.

10 Grassroots Mobilization

Peter W. Wielhouwer

The second political lesson I learned from my first campaign came from Mrs. O'Brien, our elocution-and-drama teacher in high school, who lived across the street. The night before the election, she said to me, "Tom, I'm going to vote for you tomorrow even though you didn't ask me to."

I was shocked. "Why Mrs. O'Brien," I said, "I've lived across from you for eighteen years. I cut your grass in the summer. I shovel your walk in the winter. I didn't think I had to ask for your vote."

"Tom," she replied, "let me tell you something: people like to be asked."

—Tip O'Neill (1987)

After unprecedented grassroots political activism during the 2004 presidential campaign, the 2008 election reflected rapidly maturing modern grassroots mobilization techniques. While Republican John McCain in 2000 and Democrat Howard Dean in 2004 were innovative in their use of the Internet and emergent social networking technologies, both candidates ultimately failed to capture their respective parties' nominations for president. The 2008 campaign, however, marked a new era. Barack Obama was unmatched in his application of virtual media networks to build grassroots support, and his efforts met with great success: first in his surprising defeat of Hillary Clinton, the Democratic Party establishment's favorite, for the Democratic nomination, and then in ultimately defeating Republican nominee McCain for the presidency. These grassroots mobilization techniques were later applied to generate support for President Obama's political agenda and, by the summer of 2009, had been adopted by conservative political activists to mobilize opponents of the Democrats' health care reform proposals at congressional "town hall" meetings and at hundreds of anti-tax "Tea Parties" nationwide.[1]

After a couple of decades in which mass media campaign advertising nearly supplanted the importance of individualized campaign politics, grassroots politics seems to be healthy and vibrant in American politics today. It would appear that everything candidates and parties need to know about grassroots campaigning is well in hand, wouldn't it? Answering that question is the point of this chapter. What exactly do we *know* about grassroots campaigns? How is what we know different from what we *don't know?* Is there a knowledge gap between the extraordinary claims made by the parties and by professional political consultants and the conclusions reached by academic scholars who study campaigns and elections? To answer these questions, and others, we need to understand how what we *do* know was ascertained. Once we have a handle on how grassroots politics has typically been studied, we will be better situated to assess the state of our knowledge on the subject.

First things first. The term *grassroots* refers to mass-based political activity; that is, political activity that involves large numbers of "real" people, as opposed to activity that involves mainly political elites. Thus, when I refer to a grassroots campaign, or grassroots campaigning, I mean campaigns related to the electoral process that involve many people. A grassroots campaign would include efforts to distribute political information to large numbers of people using what appear to be very personal methods. For example, a group of campaign volunteers going from house to house in various neighborhoods would be considered a grassroots campaign, whereas phone calls made by a candidate to a relatively small number of people for the purpose of generating cash donations would not.

There are certain aspects of grassroots campaigns that will not be reviewed here. For example, an interest group that encourages its members to phone or e-mail their representatives in Congress is engaging in a grassroots lobbying effort that falls beyond the scope of the present discussion. I also will not consider the merits of an election campaign that has been labeled (either by itself or by the media) a "grassroots" campaign. There is a positive connotation to such a label, one that implies that a candidate enjoys wide-ranging popular support and is relying upon the involvement and contributions of large numbers of citizens to get elected. This would be in contrast to a candidate who is perceived as out of touch with the public, or who is seen as the favorite of political elites (such as a party machine or some other self-serving and unrepresentative group of political actors).

In this chapter I will discuss various aspects of grassroots politics. I will start by examining the role of grassroots politics in the 2008 election. From there

I will offer a review of what social scientists have learned about grassroots politics. Central to our knowledge of grassroots campaign effects is both early and more recent research on political party organizations, the role of individuals in the American polity, and intermediate mobilizing organizations. I will then compare the scholarly literature with the insights and observations of today's political and campaign professionals. I will conclude with a summary of both answered and unanswered questions facing students of election campaigns.

Grassroots and the 2008 Presidential Campaigns

Grassroots campaigning has long been part of the American political scene. Formalized procedures for conducting such campaigns were articulated as early as 1840, when a Whig committee that included Abraham Lincoln distributed instructions to state party chairs. The committee's strategy, sometimes referred to as the "Lincoln Four-Step," lays out fundamental principles for segmenting, targeting, and mobilizing voters:

> Our intention is to organize the whole state, so that every Whig can be brought to the polls in the coming presidential contest. We cannot do this, however, without your co-operation; and as we do our duty, so we shall expect you to do yours. . . . 1st. To divide [each] county into small districts, and to appoint in each a sub-committee, whose duty it shall be to make a perfect list of all the voters in their respective districts, and to ascertain with certainty for whom they will vote. . . . 2nd. It will be the duty of said sub-committee to keep a constant watch on the doubtful voters, and from time to time have them talked to by those in whom they have the most confidence, and also to place in their hands such documents as will enlighten and influence them. 3d. It will also be their duty . . . on election days [to] see that every Whig is brought to the polls.[2]

These instructions summarize the steps for effective grassroots campaigning: divide states (or counties, cities, and so on) into districts of manageable size; make a list of all the voters in each district and determine their underlying political preferences (now called voter identification); distribute campaign information, especially to swing or uncommitted voters; and make sure that partisans show up to vote on election day. Interestingly, in a Republican analysis of their own get-out-the-vote (GOTV) shortcomings in the 1990s, four of the top five identified weaknesses (including inadequate person-to-person campaigning, insufficient GOP base turnout, and the recruitment of too few new Republican voters) were directly related to failed implementation of the Whig strategy, especially compared with Democratic efforts in the same time period.[3]

The technologies for implementing these processes have obviously advanced in recent years for national, state, and local elections (Wielhouwer 2003; Strachan 2003). Lists aren't kept by pen and paper anymore; they're maintained on large voter databases. Voter identification is still accomplished by door-to-door canvassing, but records in many campaigns are updated via handheld personal data assistants that synchronize with voter lists via satellite. Campaign materials are distributed by hand, mail, television, e-mail, portable DVD players, streaming video, YouTube, and texting. In 2008, the Obama campaign's application of online and mobile technology to the problems of information distribution, voter identification, and mobilization was innovative, even revolutionary, in its scope and success.

Though grassroots mobilization has long been central to elections, Obama's campaign was remarkable in its innovation in engaging Americans in multiple aspects of the campaign effort. David Plouffe, Obama's campaign manager, described it this way:

> We would strive to be a grassroots campaign. That meant volunteers. . . . Over time the volunteers became the pillars that held the whole enterprise aloft, but at the outset, we thought the grassroots could play three pivotal roles for our campaign. One, we hoped our volunteers could help fund our campaign with small contributions to a greater degree than any previous candidate had succeeded in doing; two, we wanted them to organize their local communities for the campaign—the best way to get people to caucuses and polls was to have a family member, friend, or neighbor ask them to go; and three, we needed them to help deliver our message, person to person, which was critical—trust in and attention paid to traditional media sources seemed to be dwindling rapidly (Plouffe 2009, 20–21).

In terms of the first goal, grassroots fundraising, the campaign's efforts were an unqualified success. Reports showed that "nearly four million people contributed money to the Obama campaign—more than twice as many as had donated to any candidate in the past" (Center for the Study of Elections and Democracy 2009a, 1). While both candidates raised substantial amounts from "big contributors" (those who give at or near the maximum allowable by law, which was $4,600 in 2007–2008), Obama's "small contributors" (in amounts less than $200) were responsible for nearly one-fourth of his total; McCain's "small contributors" accounted for only about 7 percent of his overall fundraising (Center for the Study of Elections and Democracy 2009b, 1). Plouffe emphasized the importance of the small and online contributors to the campaign's early credibility during the nomination phase: "[By summer 2007,] our overall donor base had swelled to more than 255,000, with over 95 percent of them not yet giving the maximum amount . . . meaning they could give again and again if they were so inclined. The Clinton campaign had a much higher percentage of their donors giving the maximum, but we had built a larger donor base" (Plouffe 2009, 77–78). Relative to those who gave to the McCain campaign, Obama's contributors were more diverse, representing a broader cross-section of the electorate in terms of age, sex, and income (Center for the Study of Elections and Democracy 2009b).

The Obama campaign's second and third grassroots goals were successful as well, helping to generate not only high turnout on election day but also large rallies that regularly attracted tens of thousands of the candidate's supporters. Equally central to Obama's grassroots efforts were the ways in which technology was applied to regular campaign activities. The campaign Web site, barackobama.com, included a fully integrated social networking capability (including my.BarackObama.com) so that users could find local supporters, engage in discussions, organize meetups, buy campaign paraphernalia, and, of course, make campaign contributions that could be tracked online. While it is tempting to believe that many of the techniques and technologies used in 2008 were innovated *for* Obama, this expertise resided in a cohort of Democratic and liberal/progressive technology experts who honed their skills in the ten years leading up to Obama's candidacy (Kreiss 2009b). The purpose of the technology was to empower grassroots volunteers. Discussing the campaign's new-media methods of increasing its donor base and contact lists, Plouffe wrote, "Central to this effort to grow was our supporters' continued use of social networking sites like MyBO.com and Facebook to build the campaign and organize themselves. We wanted to make it easy for these self-starters to connect with our huge staff in the battleground states, most often our young, talented, and fearless field organizers" (2009, 255–256).

John McCain's campaign also employed a social networking component, but one analyst noted that using it was less effective, because

the McCain site was much less usable and not as transparent for users who wanted to get involved. For example, if you wanted to participate in an Obama-related event, you could pull up all events taking place within five miles of your location, get information about the organizer, and register to participate in the event. Then, you received an automatic e-mail confirmation that you had signed up and soon thereafter, the organizer usually got in touch.

Getting involved in a McCain-related event was harder: participants could only pull up events within a wider radius, and when they tried to RSVP for an event, the request was sent out into the ether of cyberspace. Only rarely did organizers respond to requests from supporters to participate in events. There is no question that the differences between these sites had an effect on the ways individuals got involved in each campaign, as well as the degree to which they participated (Fisher 2008).

Making grassroots supporters feel like part of the broader Obama team was an important aspect of this process as well, so people could sign up for e-mail and text message updates during the campaign. In one notable moment, the campaign announced the selection of Joe Biden as Obama's running mate by texting supporters on August 23. According to one analysis, campaign organizers sought to thoroughly exploit the "riotous wonderland" of the Web, while merging it with the Obama team's internal discipline. Their strategy effectively corralled supporters into "sites and groups in which their energy could be harnessed most productively. They courted the new liberal online media—websites such as the Huffington Post or Daily Kos—but [supporters] organised by themselves: the social networking component of BarackObama.com, set up by a co-founder of Facebook, had more than a million and a half members. Obama's secret, then, was to fuse a movement and a database into a machine" (Colvile 2008). In doing so, the campaign effectively matched classic grassroots techniques with modern technology. While 2010's college students may see nothing remarkable in this, the campaign truly broke new ground in its grassroots organization and mobilization.

Early Research on Grassroots Campaigning

Three major themes are found in what might be considered the early grassroots mobilization literature that grew out of research on the distribution of political information and getting out the vote by party workers in studies of urban political machines. These activities continued even as the power of most of those machines degraded during the first half of the twentieth century. The first theme that emerged from the early research had to do with the activities of *local party organizations.* A second theme emerged from experimental research on political propaganda that examined the impact of different vehicles of *campaign information delivery* on registration and voter turnout rates. It is impossible to completely separate these two activities, because the party machine's principal tactics for influencing votes revolved around the distribution of party propaganda (Key 1942).

A third theme emerged as the use of social science opinion surveys took root during the 1940s; in particular, researchers from Columbia University began to study the development of *individuals' political attitudes and behaviors.* As heirs of the original two themes, these scholars examined information distribution in the electorate and the organizational activities of parties using a combination of case study and survey research. The American National Election Study surveys also were developed around this time.

Party Organizational Activities

Historically, one of the sources of power for local party organizations was their ability to generate electoral support as a byproduct of their traditional social-service activities. In the 1930s Chicago Democratic machine, for example, precinct captains' service role included such tasks as providing food and coal and acting as a broker between residents and the local governments and courts. Their political activities, on the other hand, involved canvassing for votes, the central purpose of which was to distribute candidate and party information, solidify voter registration lists, and deliver votes for machine candidates. Electioneering was, of course, directly related to party workers' social-service duties. According to early researcher Harold Gosnell (1968 [1938], 81), "Precinct captains who have put themselves out in many ways to serve their constituents do not have many difficulties in trying to get a hearing when they canvass their districts for votes."

The power of the local machines degraded with the incorporation of political reforms and the assumption by both national and state governments of the kinds of social services that had traditionally been converted by the machines into political power. These changes, combined with an expansion of the American electorate between the 1860s and 1950s and the advent of radio (and, later, television), brought about important alterations in the electoral role of the machine and in the responsibilities of political parties generally. V. O. Key observed in the early 1940s that it still fell to local party organizations to get out the vote on election day on the theory that proximity to voters made personal and machine-based appeals more practical, as compared with the far-removed context of the national party organizations. However, knowledge about the relative effectiveness of party workers compared with the mass media was, at that time, slender. What had emerged regarding the art of campaigning was a set of "common-sense" rules that Key characterized as "superstition" and "folklore of the trade" (Key 1942, 582–583).

Experiments on Campaign Information Distribution

Central to the parties' campaigning techniques was propaganda, "the management of collective attitudes by the manipulation of significant symbols" (Lasswell 1927, 627), that bypassed "deliberative" processes of opinion manipulation in favor of simple competition among culturally defined political symbols. Propaganda distribution efforts were concentrated where they seemed likely to do the most good, usually in closely contested and marginal areas. Messages were conveyed through both mass and partisan media; political rallies and campaign tours; and a variety of leaflets, pamphlets, and circulars. Consistent with Key's observations, however, local party organizations continued to provide the structure through which campaign information was distributed and votes were delivered. In fact, research through to the current day traces candidate performance at the polls to the organizational activities of party and campaign operatives, even as the personal party attachments of individuals in the American electorate have weakened.[4]

Beginning in the 1920s, experimental research on campaign propaganda distribution emerged to assess effects on the political behavior of prospective voters. Harold Gosnell, for example, conducted a field experiment to assess the effect of a nonpartisan mail canvass on voter registration and turnout in Chicago (Gosnell 1926, 1927). After obtaining a list of residents who were not registered to vote, he mailed three sets of nonpartisan materials to half of this group. The first mailing contained a factual notice of the registration requirement for voting. The second, sent to those who had not promptly registered following the initial contact, took one of two forms: one notice simply reiterated the original message while the other included with that message a cartoon depicting the nonvoter as a "slacker." The registration rates of individuals who received either of the reminder cards were substantially higher than those of citizens who did not receive them (the cartoon didn't seem to make much difference). A second experiment involved sending postcards to registered voters containing "a cartoon notice picturing the honest but apathetic citizen as the friend of the corrupt politician" (Gosnell 1926, 870). This time, voter turnout (as opposed to registration) rates were higher among citizens who received mailers. As might be expected in those golden days of the Chicago machine, context was important. Where local party organizations were strongest, the mailer had less of an effect (because turnout was already relatively high in those areas). In areas where party organization was weaker, larger effects were noted. Twenty years later, Gosnell (1948) still believed that voters were influenced by the campaign information they received and that this information informed their vote choices—not simply the decision to register and vote. In spite of widespread evidence of specious campaign messages, he remained optimistic about voters' powers of discrimination and good judgment when making their vote decisions.

In the 1950s, Samuel Eldersveld and his colleagues conducted experiments using their political science classes to assess various campaign influences.[5] In a municipal election (revising a city charter), Ann Arbor residents indifferent or hostile to the proposed changes were selected for either personal contact by college students arguing in favor of the revision or for mailed "propaganda" also in support. The results suggested that opinions and voter turnout were positively influenced by both types of communication. A second experiment assessed the ability of different personal contact techniques and mailers to affect the turnout of citizens who had never voted in municipal elections. Mobilization effects of the experiment were rather large, though residents recalled personal contacts at a much greater rate than the mailed propaganda. In short, personal contacts and, to a lesser extent, mail appeals yielded increases in voter registration rates, voter turnout, and support for the ballot propositions.[6]

Individuals and Survey Research

By the 1950s, the experimental approach gave way to a new technique for studying political behavior and public opinion, the individuals and survey research approach—an approach that in the years since has dominated academic work on this topic. This technique allowed researchers to collect information about, and assess the attitudes and behavior of, large and representative numbers of citizens. In so doing, it vastly improved our knowledge about, for example, the mechanisms of political mobilization, the effects of campaigns on individuals and groups, and the orientations of people to their social and political contexts. In particular, two sets of researchers, one based at Columbia University and the other at the University of Michigan, were instrumental in these developments.

In a groundbreaking analysis of voting decisions in Erie County, Ohio, during the 1940 presidential election, Columbia researchers found three important sets of campaign effects. First, party-based campaign information *reinforced* previously held partisan preferences; second, it *activated* people's interest in the campaign beyond their latent political predispositions; and third, in some instances it *converted* people to new political positions. Central to these findings was the role of informal personal contacts and channels of influence that existed among friends. While outlining the advantages of these influences,[7] the authors nonetheless emphasized their unstructured, informal nature and their distinct lack of connection to formal campaigning (Lazarsfeld, Berelson, and Gaudet 1944).

However, in a subsequent analysis by Berelson, Lazarsfeld, and McPhee (1954) of voting in the 1948 election, the political party reemerged as a significant object for research in the formation of individual opinions and behaviors. This study examined personal-contact campaigning, focusing on the patterns of information distribution by party workers who served as a link between the local party organization on the one hand and local activists and ordinary voters on the other. While the local organization was largely ineffective at connecting "real" people with national party leaders, it did act as a cog in the administrative machinery of the national party to make the process work. Specifically, local party leadership sought to mobilize not only voters of like political stripe, but also "problem voters" who needed extra stimulation to get out to the polls on election day. The latter group included aged citizens who needed rides to polling places, absentee and new voters, wives "who must be brought to the polls by husbands who take the family responsibility in such things," and "the 'vote-if-induced' people, who in some districts have come to expect a little extra compensation (in the way of a few dollars or a drink) to exercise their franchise" (Berelson, Lazarsfeld, and McPhee 1954, 172). Changes in candidate preference that occurred were small in number and could often be related to the personal relationships that some voters had with activists in the opposing party.

During this same time period, the American National Election Studies (NES) were being developed and implemented through the Center for Political Studies at the University of Michigan. These national-level surveys asked a broad range of questions relating to political opinions and behavior, and, in the process, revolutionized research on public opinion and political participation. Having inherited the body of knowledge we are discussing, the NES in 1956 began asking respondents whether they had been contacted during the election campaign. The question was, "Did anybody from either one of the parties call you up or come around and talk to you during the campaign?" Early analysis of this item uncovered variation in contacting by political context, with competitive areas having relatively greater incidences of canvassing than party strongholds (including the one-party South). While nonvoting was prevalent among citizens who had not been contacted by the parties, and mobilization was inferred among voters who were contacted, the effects of the canvass on presidential vote choice was weak (Janowitz and Marvick 1964 [1956]).

Modern Grassroots Campaign Research

Modern research on grassroots campaigning has continued to study party organization, propaganda, and the behavior of individual voters, yielding a body of knowledge that musicians might call variations on a theme. It is clear, for example, that the central role of party organizations has diminished somewhat, undermined by changes in election and campaign finance laws;[8] those laws, in turn, produced what some have described as a "candidate-centered" process (Wattenberg 1991) in which candidates and their advisors are the driving force behind campaign organization and funding. Accordingly, expertise in campaign conduct is no longer limited to party operatives but increasingly resides with professional consultants, and each new election cycle sees a wide range of interest groups undertake massive voter education and mobilization drives, some of them nonpartisan and others in support of specific candidates. Nevertheless, the parties-as-organizations have not withered away altogether; they continue to serve as clearinghouses for expertise, strategy, innovation, and, importantly, the coordination of mass-level campaign activities. Recent research shows that the relationship between consultants and the parties is largely collaborative, though there is some consensus among party officials and consultants that parties continue to be very important for field work and getting out the vote (labor-intensive work involving high levels of personal contact with voters), while consultants are most influential in the campaign areas of media production and opinion polling (Dulio and Nelson 2005; Bohne, Prevost, and Thurber 2009).

On the academic front, the number of survey-based studies that look at national-level mobilization efforts has mushroomed, while direct evidence concerning the effects of campaign communications such as campaign advertising, direct mail, and literature drops is growing as well. Analyses of media information flows (including campaign information provided through network and cable television, radio, and the Internet) are ubiquitous, though this research is only indirectly related to grassroots campaigning. Finally, experimental research on the impact of GOTV efforts has witnessed a resurgence since 1998, with important implications for our understanding of the efficacy of various methods of grassroots campaigning.

Survey Research

Our principal source of knowledge about national-level grassroots campaign activities over an extended period of time is the American National Election Studies series, which allows us to track long-term trends in mobilization efforts. After a period of low levels of personal contact campaigning in the early 1990s, recent elections have witnessed much higher levels. Since 2000, more than 35 percent of NES respondents have reported personal contact from a political party worker on behalf of a candidate, and in 2004 the rate reached 43.5 percent, with Democrats contacting about 33 percent and Republicans about 26 percent (Wielhouwer 2006). In 2008, personal contact campaigning by the parties was down slightly, with 43.2 percent of Americans reporting contact by a major party, 32.6 percent by the Democrats, 24.6 percent by the Republicans, and 15.3 percent by both parties. These numbers should be interpreted with a bit of caution, as respondents may be recalling one of several types of campaign contact as coming from "party" sources. At a minimum, we can assume that they were spoken to by a campaign worker on behalf of a candidate. This almost certainly understates the full rate of campaign-related contacts in 2008, however, because of the Obama campaign's emphasis on individuals' mobilizing their own social networks. For example, if your college roommate became an Obama supporter after getting information from my.BarackObama.com, and he or she then encouraged you to vote for Obama, you may or may not report this conversation as a "party" contact in the manner that academic surveys would hope, but it is an informal campaign-related contact in the tradition noted by the Columbia University researchers in the 1940s and 1950s.

Research shows that the parties' grassroots contacting efforts are not random, but rather are strategically targeted toward specific segments of the population. The rationale for this is straightforward: the likelihood of victory hinges on *who* shows up to vote, not on whether *more* people show up. Campaigns therefore work to shape the electorate in ways that give them a higher likelihood of winning. Taking into account a host of individual and contextual factors, the people most likely to be contacted are those who already are predisposed to participate (that is, they have high socioeconomic status, are registered to vote, and are socially connected to their communities) and to vote for a particular party's candidates (that is, Democrats mainly contact Democrats, Republicans mainly contact Republicans).[9]

Whom did the campaigns contact in 2008? Table 10.1 presents a demographic overview of respondents who reported that they were contacted on behalf of a major-party candidate during the 2008 campaign season. Each subgroup can be compared with the total contacts at the top of each column as a way of determining whether the differences in contacting any particular

Table 10.1 Rates of Personal Contacting by the Political Parties, 2008 (percent)

Contacts		Democrats	Republicans	Both Parties
Total Contacts		**32.6**	**24.6**	**15.3**
Age	18–29	20.1	7.5	3.8
	30–39	28.6	19.5	15.0
	40–49	29.3	21.9	13.2
	50–59	37.4	29.8	16.6
	60–69	41.9	33.4	20.9
	70 and higher	49.2	47.7	32.0
Household income	$0–$29,999	32.9	16.2	9.3
	$30,000–$49,999	30.8	22.6	15.0
	$50,000–$89,999	38.6	28.4	19.5
	$90,000 and higher	30.1	32.2	16.7
Education	Less than 12 years	24.5	11.2	9.9
	HS diploma/equivalent	31.0	22.6	14.2
	Some college	30.9	24.7	14.5
	Bachelor's degree	39.2	34.1	19.0
	Advanced/professional degree	41.8	30.9	23.3
Sex	Male	32.3	26.0	16.5
	Female	33.0	23.5	14.3
Ethnicity	Black	33.9	8.9	6.2
	White	33.3	29.0	17.9
	Hispanic	26.6	15.6	10.5
Party identification	Strong Democrat	49.0	18.5	15.6
	Weak Democrat	38.5	21.2	16.2
	Independent Democrat	33.3	20.0	12.9
	Independent-Independent	19.5	12.2	7.6
	Independent Republican	30.4	32.2	21.0
	Weak Republican	25.1	32.8	17.7
	Strong Republican	24.0	39.8	16.5
Church attendance	Almost/every week	33.4	32.0	18.0
	Once or twice a month	32.8	18.5	11.5
	Few times a year/never	31.9	21.4	14.6
Voted in 2004?	Yes	39.3	32.2	19.8
	No	19.1	9.1	6.5

Source: 2008 American National Election Studies.

subgroup are politically relevant. Comparing differences in contacting by age, for example, we can see that while eighteen-to-twenty-nine-year-olds were much less likely than average to be contacted, Democrats contacted them much more (20.1 percent) than did Republicans (7.5 percent). Each of the parties was much more likely to contact people who were older than fifty. Nearly half of people age seventy and older were personally contacted; in fact, close to one-third of this group were contacted by both parties. In comparison, less than 4 percent of young Americans (eighteen to twenty-nine) were contacted by both parties.

Poorer households were much less likely to be contacted by the Republicans; instead, the GOP sought out upper-middle and upper-income individuals. Both groups were competing actively for votes in households with incomes between $50,000 and $90,000. Americans with less than a high-school education were much less likely to be contacted, while the well educated were much more likely to be contacted, on average. Among those holding bachelor's degrees, nearly 40 percent reported contact by the Democrats and about 34 percent reported contact from the Republicans. Democrats were most likely to contact people with advanced degrees (like college professors), with more than 41 percent reporting personal contacts; roughly 10 percent fewer were contacted by the GOP. Men and women were equally likely to be contacted by the parties. The three major ethnicities received comparable levels of contacts from the Democrats, with Hispanics falling somewhat lower than the others. There were large differences in GOP contacts by ethnicity, however. Less than 9 percent of African Americans and about 16 percent of Hispanics reported a Republican contact, compared with 29 percent of whites.

Turning to party identification, strong partisans are much more frequently contacted by their own party than by the opposition. Nearly half of strong Democrats were contacted by the Democrats, compared with only 24 percent of strong Republicans; similarly, nearly 40 percent of strong Republicans were contacted by the GOP, but only 18.5 percent of strong Democrats were. More than 30 percent of independents who leaned Republican were contacted by the Democrats, and 21 percent were contacted by both parties. These figures reflect the Obama campaign's efforts to reach out to this group and the GOP's efforts to retain them. So-called "pure" independents were the least likely to be contacted by either party (19.5 percent by the Democrats and 12 percent by the Republicans).

Finally, in looking at contacting patterns by church attendance and prior voting, we see that there were no differences in Democrats' contacts based on people's frequency of church attendance. This was not the case with Republican contacts, however. The data show that those who attended church every week or almost every week were heavily contacted by the GOP, reflecting the importance of churchgoers in the Republican electoral coalition and the role played by churches as venues for political mobilization (see Guth et al. 2002, 2007; Wielhouwer 2009). Campaigns also attempt to target people who are reliable voters, identify likely future voters, reinforce previous supporters' voting patterns, and get out the vote as election day nears. In 2008, the Obama campaign sought out people who had never voted, especially young people (most of whom had no voting history), in constructing its electoral coalition. In Table 10.1 we see that 19 percent of people who didn't vote in 2004 were contacted by the Democrats, whereas only 9 percent were contacted by the GOP.

The effects of contacting are well documented. People who are personally contacted by campaigns are significantly more likely to become politically active, even taking into account their predisposition to participate. They are more likely to vote, to work for campaigns, to display campaign paraphernalia (such as buttons, bumper stickers, and yard signs), and to contribute financially to campaigns (Wielhouwer and Lockerbie 1994; Rosenstone and Hansen 1993). Moreover, a national survey (the Citizen Participation Study, or CPS) conducted in 1989–1990 showed that (1) of those who were asked to work for a campaign, about half said yes, and (2) of those who were asked to contribute financially, about one-quarter said yes (Verba, Schlozman, and Brady 1995, 137). The success of requests for political participation frequently hinges upon who does the asking, with personal acquaintance continuing to play a key role. As with voters in the Columbia studies in the 1940s and 1950s, CPS respondents reported that more than half of requests to work on a campaign came from someone known personally to them; another 28 percent came from people just one relationship removed from the respondent. Recent research also suggests that single contacts may have negligible or modest effects, while multiple contacts can have large effects. This appears to be the case especially for citizens who are generally considered the least likely to vote (Parry et al. 2008).

Research dating back to the early Columbia studies has demonstrated that the social context within which people live also influences their political preferences and behaviors. It appears, for example, that the educational level of an individual's neighborhood can affect the likelihood of that individual's engaging in activities such as voting and registering people to vote; moreover, political activity (such as party canvassing and yard signs) in a neighborhood helps to shape both the candidate preferences and participatory choices of people living there. In this way, the effects of an action (here, the original canvass) can have what are called "cascading consequences"—that is, consequences that spill over to other people, whether in a household, neighborhood, or social organization (Huckfeldt 1986; Huckfeldt and Sprague 1992). And to the extent that our political attitudes and behaviors are indeed influenced by the people with whom we have close personal relations, and with whom we discuss matters of importance to us (our "discussion network"), academic studies of voter mobilization efforts may tend to underestimate their overall impact.[10]

Experimental Studies

Recently, political scientists Donald Green and Alan Gerber have spearheaded a resurgence of experimental approaches to analyzing the impact of nonpartisan and campaign mobilization efforts. Their numerous studies examining door-to-door canvassing and literature distribution, direct mail, phone calls, and e-mail have provided new levels of specificity regarding the effects and costs of grassroots campaigning. Asserting the superiority of their methods over survey research, and in contrast to the "war stories" often told by campaign professionals, Green and Gerber (2008, chap. 1–2) highlight the strengths of social experimentation's well-defined control groups and parsimonious models.[11] The historical record highlights the importance of face-to-face contacts for campaign information distribution and getting out the vote—recall the Lincoln Four-Step and the anecdote from Tip O'Neill that began this chapter.

Before turning to academic experimental studies of grassroots campaign tactics, we note that the political parties have also experimented in this area. For example, the Republican National Committee in 2001 sponsored a series of pseudo-experiments in state and local elections.[12] It found that by making modest organizational changes and undertaking certain GOTV efforts (such as placing full-time staff in political districts, "flushing" known Republicans, using volunteer-based rather than paid GOTV phone calls, and implementing well-organized programs for mobilizing social and religious conservatives), the party's performance in these elections improved enough to justify future application of the methods. These and other results also were used by the GOP to form "72-Hour Task Forces" (teams armed with detailed strategic plans to be implemented in the three days prior to election day) across the nation in the 2002 and 2004 elections.

Academic experimental studies have addressed several questions relating to grassroots and personal contact campaigning. First, the research strongly suggests that face-to-face canvassing is effective at generating more voters—that is, at increasing voter turnout (A. Gerber and Green 2000b; D. Green, Gerber, and Nickerson 2003; Nickerson 2006, 2007, 2008). In addition to the individuals who are contacted personally, there also appears to be a mobilizing effect for members of their households, though that effect appears to be stronger for people who vote at traditional polling places rather than by mail (Arceneaux, Kousser, and Mullin 2009). Finally, face-to-face contacts appear to be effective at mobilizing people who are not regular voters (Niven 2004), but are more effective in high-profile elections than in elections of lesser salience (Arceneaux and Nickerson 2009).

Second, the method of campaign message delivery matters. Experiments have examined the effects of campaign mail and leaflets delivered to people's homes, finding that this staple of grassroots campaign tactics does generate additional votes. Some research suggests that mail and leaflets are only slightly less effective than face-to-face contacts (Nickerson 2005), while other research shows more substantial differences. Niven (2006), for example, found that repeated negative campaign mailings increased voter turnout by as much as 6 percent, compared with a single negative piece of mail, which had no effect at all. There is substantial evidence accumulating about campaign phone calls as well. The most effective phone-based method of generating votes is that which uses a script delivered in a slow, casual, and conversational manner; volunteers do this best, though professional phone banking callers can be trained to do the same thing to good effect (Nickerson 2006, 2007). Pre-recorded phone calls delivering taped messages from candidates or their surrogates (known as "robocalls") have been found to be ineffective (A. Gerber and Green 2000b; A. Gerber and Green 2005). The timing of calls appears to have an impact: they seem to be more effective during the final week of a campaign than earlier (Nickerson 2007; D. Green and Gerber 2008; also see Alvarez, Hopkins, and Sinclair 2010), though multiple phone calls do not appear to increase the impact of a single, well-timed call on turnout (see also A. Gerber and Green 2005; Nickerson 2005; Cardy 2005; McNulty 2005). The more casual and conversational kinds of phone calls tend to increase turnout by 2 to 5 percent, while simple get-out-the-vote messages increase turnout by about 1 percent (Ha and Karlan 2009).

Finally, turning to the effects of grassroots campaigning on people's opinions about candidates and issues, evidence suggests that contacts do exert an influence. Some research finds that campaign contacts increase awareness of candidates and concern about election outcomes and successfully promote identification of candidates with particular political positions (Arceneaux 2007; Niven 2006); other experiments show modest or negligible effects of messages on preferences (Arceneaux and Nickerson 2010). In an analysis of the 2006 election, Arceneaux and Kolodny (2009b) concluded that campaign contacts produced no changes in attitudes on the high-salience issue of abortion, but recipients of those contacts were able to connect abortion with less well-known birth control issues and were more likely to view abortion as an important campaign issue; in this experiment, face-to-face campaign contacts were more influential than those made by phone.

More Than Just the Parties

Historically, party organizations at the national, state, and local levels were the principal source of expertise for running campaigns (Key 1942). That is no longer true. Political consultants (including professional campaign managers and, in the modern era, pollsters, media advisors, fundraisers, opposition researchers, grassroots organizers, and others) have been present in American politics for many years, but since the 1960s both the number of people for whom campaigning is a profession and the degree of specialization in the services offered have greatly increased. Further, the campaign professionalization that we normally associate with presidential, gubernatorial, and U.S. Senate campaigns has now trickled down to state legislative and even local elections (Medvic 2000; Strachan 2003; Johnson 2007).

Although some scholars once suggested that consultants and political parties stood in opposition to one another (Sabato 1981), recent research reveals widespread collaboration and coordination between party organizations and independent campaign professionals (Bohne, Prevost, and Thurber 2009; Kolodny 2000; Dulio and Thurber 2003; Dulio 2004; see also chapter 11 in this volume). The national and state parties today work closely with consultants, retaining some directly while simultaneously maintaining lists of preferred consultants to whom they refer candidates. There are some areas where party leaders believe (correctly or not) that they do a better job than consultants, including the areas of fundraising, getting out the vote, candidate research—and grassroots organization (Kolodny 2000). Whatever the truth may be, parties and consultants now work together to coordinate campaign activities designed to maximize their candidates' chances of winning on election day.

As for grassroots mobilization, many intermediary organizations undertake this activity as well. Labor unions, for example, have long been a critical component of the Democratic Party's ground war, though as the number of union members in the United States has declined, so too has the mobilization capacity of this segment of the coalition. Other interest groups provide important resources, human as well as fiscal, for candidates of both parties. The success of religious conservative organizations in mobilizing their members since the 1970s is well documented, though these effects are not always uniform at the national, state, and local levels. Nevertheless, groups such as the Christian Coalition of America are effective fundraisers and a resource for conducting the ground war, especially on behalf of conservative GOP candidates (J. Green, Rozell, and Wilcox 2003). In 2004, significant resources were spent by organized interests, and especially by Democratic-leaning groups, on grassroots mobilization efforts. In 2008, the extremely large amounts of money pouring into the Obama campaign dwarfed these expenditures. Moreover, both major-party candidates discouraged contributions to interest groups dedicated to electioneering (known as 527 organizations); even so, organized labor reportedly spent as much as $250 million during the 2008 campaign (Boatright 2009).

Summary: What We Know and Don't Know

As things currently stand, what do we know about grassroots campaigning and its effects in U.S. elections? Most conventional forms of mobilization are at least somewhat effective at encouraging people to participate in politics who might not otherwise do so. People personally contacted by campaigns (or whose family, friends, and other discussion partners are contacted) will vote, take part in campaign activities, and make a financial contribution at significantly higher rates than those who are not contacted. If this were not the case, then the energy of millions of volunteers and hundreds of millions of dollars spent over the last few election cycles would have been wasted. What Key (1942) once characterized as "common-sense," "superstition," and "folklore of the trade" is largely confirmed in modern times. Although doubts have been raised about the efficacy of phone banks in delivering votes, volunteer phone calling—and sometimes even professional calling—does seem to be somewhat successful at getting people to the polls (D. Green and Gerber 2008; Nickerson 2007). In this instance, it appears to be the quality of the contacts made that is important, with impersonal robocalls less effective than high-quality mailers and personal contacts. Future study needs to be directed at a better understanding of the varying effects of *partisan* messages, since most experimental research to date has assessed nonpartisan GOTV efforts (Levine and Lopez 2005; but see Nickerson, Friedrichs, and King 2006; A. Gerber, Green, and Green 2003).

African-American mobilization has received substantial attention from scholars, largely in case studies of municipal elections or as a function of the organizing capacity of predominantly black churches.[13] Blacks have long been integrated into the Democratic Party's mobilization efforts, while at the same time largely excluded from GOP contacting efforts. Since 1996, however, the Republican Party has increased its outreach at the grassroots level appreciably. African Americans tend to respond to mobilization efforts with higher rates of participation, even taking into account existing predispositions to vote and varying political contexts (Leighley 2001; Wielhouwer 2000). In contrast, Donald Green (2004) found little mobilization among blacks in response to interest-group advocacy phone calls or personal contacts; direct mail had modest effects.

Evidence on the impact of mobilization efforts among other minority groups comes from a small but growing literature. Leighley (2001), for example, concluded that Latinos were mobilized into political activities predominantly by friends and acquaintances; that being recruited was largely a function of an individual's education, income, and sociopolitical context; and that political participation was affected by interactions between context and mobilization efforts. The messenger also matters—that is, knowing the mobilizer personally or having an ethnic "match" (with a Latino being recruited by another Latino) influences whether mobilization is likely to be successful. Overall, the effect of mobilization on Latino turnout can be quite large (see also Michelson 2003, 2005; Michelson and Villa 2003). Similar results obtain for Asian-American voters (Wong 2005).

One area where our knowledge remains limited has to do with the effects of particular kinds of messages on the people who receive them. Some experimental evidence suggests that simply reminding people about election day, encouraging them to perform their civic duty, and not being too negative will help get voters to the polls (D. Green and Gerber 2008). In fundraising, appeals to emotions such as fear and anger apparently motivate people to contribute money (Godwin 1988), and it is therefore assumed—without much supporting evidence—that a similar approach works in mobilizing people to become involved in other campaign activities as well. We also know relatively little about the role of message repetition. Campaign professionals assume that repetition is good, and that free repetition (with coverage by the media, especially television) is even better than the original ad buy. Do multiple messages from the same group have a cumulative impact on voters? What are the consequences of conflicting messages? Do partisan and nonpartisan messages have similar effects? Further research on the full range of campaign communications (and its impact on vote choices and participation) is needed.

At the individual level, scholars lack a well-formed body of knowledge about the nature of people's responses when they are contacted. For example, when someone receives a piece of political literature amidst other mail, what does he or she do with it? When someone comes home from work and there is campaign literature on the door, what happens to it? Is it read and consciously considered, or simply thrown out? Phone calls appear to have modest effects, but what happens after the call? We assume that the message prompts some level of conscious thought and perhaps conversation, producing cascading consequences—but what mechanisms actually set this process into play? Additionally, we don't know much about the effects of different campaign messages on different recipients. What, for example, are the consequences of GOP campaign contacts on strong Democrats, weak Democrats, and independents? We know that campaigns are generally advised to avoid the opposition, and that demobilization efforts (much accused but little used) are difficult to make work, but there isn't much empirical evidence to tell us what actually happens when opposition contact is made. These effects, if extensive enough, could have significant implications for coalition building and expansion, as opposed to mere coalition maintenance and getting the base out.

There is a high level of uncertainty in any GOTV effort directed toward groups perceived as traditionally part of the opposition. Much was made of Republican efforts in 2004 to expand the GOP coalition by courting Latino and African-American votes. But whereas George W. Bush earned as much as 44 percent of Latino votes, exit polls also revealed that his showing among blacks was about the same as other Republican presidential candidates since the 1970s (roughly 11 percent). John McCain performed even worse, garnering only 4 percent of the black vote and only 31 percent of Latino votes.[14] In talking with GOP consultants and officials, I find that they are mostly receptive to including (as opposed to excluding) blacks in their mobilization strategies, but are perplexed about how to do so. Some complain about blunders committed by "the old guard" (an example would be Senate Majority Leader Trent Lott's praise of Strom Thurmond's 1948 presidential campaign, which was founded on opposition to racial desegregation; see Mercurio 2002), while others feel locked out of black social networks and don't know how to get in. Parallel concerns can be assumed about the Democrats and conservative Christians. In the latter case, an effort to resolve this impasse involved bringing in liberal Christians like Pastor Jim Wallis of the Sojourners organization to provide advice to the Democratic Party on how to use religious language to frame its policy messages (see Milbank and Balz 2005).[15] This aided moderate and religious Democrats in the 2006 congressional elections, though Obama in 2008 did not seem to need such tutorials. Still, with Democrats and Republicans alike having (relatively) limited resources and time, campaigns are most likely to revert to well-known and default campaign mobilization targets.

Conclusion

The involvement of large numbers of people in the American political process may be seen as a measure of the nation's democratic health. Grassroots campaigns have been essential to elections at least since the development of the mass parties in the 1820s, and broader participation lends greater legitimacy to electoral outcomes. Political parties have historically been the major vehicles for mobilizing voters, and they transitioned into being service providers as elections became more candidate-centered. Now, working in concert with political consultants and a broad range of organized interests, the parties continue to be clearinghouses of expertise, fundraising, and data for the candidates running under their labels. The 2004 cycle, in particular, saw major changes in the ways in which campaigns generated grassroots activism. Howard Dean's campaign for the Democratic presidential nomination, for example, applied innovative techniques such as text messaging to generate "spontaneous" meetups and Internet-based appeals to aid in fundraising. Dean's subsequent election as chair of the Democratic National Committee positioned the party for a more technologically progressive approach to networking the grassroots, though significant advances had already been made in database management and exploitation even before Dean came aboard. Barack Obama's campaign directly benefitted from Dean's innovations, and 2008 witnessed extensive and imaginative methods of engaging in grassroots mobilization.

Decades of research involving case studies, surveys, and social experiments have given us a substantial body of knowledge about what works and what doesn't. Nevertheless, our grasp of the processes through which individuals respond to grassroots mobilization efforts is not as well developed as it could be. Further empirical observation will undoubtedly increase our knowledge. So, too, will simple questioning—because, as Mrs. O'Brien knew, people like to be asked.

THE POLITICAL PROFESSIONALS RESPOND

Jack St. Martin

Let me start by saying that my definition of grassroots is a bit different than Wielhouwer's. I see grassroots not as "free" programs (nothing is really free in this world) but as volunteer-based efforts with a local emphasis. In other words, paid voter contact programs, such as direct mail and robocalls, that have virtually no volunteer involvement do not constitute grassroots activities in my opinion. With that in mind, my comments here are limited to the portion of grassroots mobilization that deals with volunteer-based activities.

It is true that, as Wielhouwer points out, mass media campaigning all but supplanted meaningful grassroots activities in campaigns during the 1980s and 1990s. It is true too that grassroots campaign tactics have, since the turn of the century, become increasingly popular and received greater attention than ever before. To understand why grassroots mobilization is important in any campaign, it is instructive to understand some of the causes of its reemergence. It is also important to understand its initial decline as a campaign tactic.

A campaign can be compared to an equation—a very long, very complex mathematical equation. In fact, each campaign is so complex and so complicated that the equation is never fully understood. That is why the best political operatives are able to make wise decisions based on hunches and gut feelings. Seemingly endless lists of factors contribute to the equation for any given campaign. For example, a candidate's personal appearance can be a great benefit or detriment, but so can the weather on election day. Thousands of factors, from the economic and political to the sociological and religious, can determine the outcome of an election—not to mention the thousands of personal attributes a candidate brings to the mix, or the hundreds of positions that he or she must take on public policy issues. Of course, the opponent's positions and personal attributes complicate the equation even further.

Campaigns for public office are an exercise in resource allocation. Campaign professionals, including campaign managers and consultants, and often the candidates themselves, spend a great deal of time determining the best allocation of resources to maximize their campaign's effectiveness, and to best change the equation in their favor. More often than not, resources are severely limited. Between campaign contribution restrictions and limits on expenditures imposed by some states, and by the Federal Election Committee on national-state campaign coordinated expenditures, most campaigns have surprisingly small budgets. It is in this context that we can begin to better understand why grassroots efforts were largely paid lip service for a period of time only to reemerge with force in recent years.

In the 1980s and 1990s, decisions about resource allocation increasingly became skewed toward paid media efforts. The value of organizing local volunteers and activists was not just deemphasized, it sometimes was openly derided. Campaign operatives and consultants reasoned that a thousand gross rating points of broadcast TV were a much better allocation of resources (and of their attention) than a door-to-door program that produced few measurable results. And who really wanted to deal with those crazy volunteers when you could just stick with a few professionals? Additionally, grassroots and volunteer activities were perceived quite often as "free"; since volunteers, by definition, should not cost anything, the reasoning was that it would be foolish to invest in organizing them. Like a self-fulfilling prophecy, field efforts typically received less emphasis, were underfunded (if funded at all), and understaffed. The inevitable result was that these efforts were rarely judged to be a success, which meant that even fewer resources were allocated to the field in the next election, and the downward spiral continued one cycle to the next.

Another factor that contributed to the demise of grassroots campaigning was the historic reliance on party structure as the principal vehicle for grassroots programs. Campaigns would routinely shift most of their volunteer efforts to the party after capturing the nomination, with the party then proceeding to implement a multi-candidate effort on behalf of the entire ticket. With the party's built-in hierarchy of national, state, and local committee officials and staff, those efforts would theoretically reach down to the precinct level—so why bother to reinvent the wheel? Why not just let the party folks deal with the messy organizing of volunteers?

But there was a problem with this approach. Political parties had suffered the same dramatic decline in civic participation that had characterized other local organizations in recent decades (see Putnam 2000). In a social trend that began sometime prior to the 1980s, Americans became increasingly "busy" and factors such as two-income households, a longer work week, children's extracurricular activities, and expanding entertainment options (including television), just to name a few, contributed to less civic involvement. Where only a generation ago citizens were active in organizations such as the Jaycees, Knights of Columbus, and Junior

League, today we are less likely to participate in *any* kind of local organization, including the political party. As a result, candidates who had always been able to depend on their local, state, and national parties for volunteer support saw less and less real impact from volunteer efforts. And the cycle of skepticism over grassroots efficacy spun on.

Finally, in the Republican Party at least, there has existed a strong aversion among political professionals to expenditures on overhead. In Republican ranks, this reluctance is a reflection of the strong influence of the business community. Businesspeople running for office generally place the same emphasis on the bottom line and containing costs that they would in the workplace. Grassroots and volunteer efforts are labor intensive, however, and to be executed properly a real commitment to overhead is required. It is easy to see that campaign mail, phones, and television require little to no staff (just well-compensated consultants), but organizing and equipping thousands of volunteers at any given time requires huge commitment to both staff and office space.

This, then, was the landscape for quite some time. And while most campaigns were careful to pay lip service to the idea of grassroots and volunteer-based efforts, they in fact utilized very little in the way of grassroots involvement. There were notable exceptions, of course, including Linda Smith's write-in primary campaign in Washington's third congressional district in 1994 and Paul Wellstone's dramatic grassroots victory over incumbent Rudy Boschwitz for the U.S. Senate in 1990. But these races were the exceptions. What changed, then? What event brought grassroots activity back to the fore? In fact, the presidential recount in 2000 seems to have marked a sea change in campaigns' attitudes toward grassroots mobilization. With a five-hundred-vote margin determining the outcome of a presidential election, suddenly volunteer phone calls and door-to-door canvassing took on a whole new feel. Very few operatives were heard to say, "If we had just run one more ad in primetime," as they slogged through county courthouses during those six weeks in Florida. Instead, there was clear recognition that volunteer efforts and just a few more field staff in Florida that year could have made the difference for either campaign. What followed four years later on the GOP side, under the direction of Karl Rove and Ken Mehlman, was an unprecedented emphasis on grassroots activism through programs like the Republican National Committee's 72-Hour Task Force and Team Leader.[1] Democrats followed suit in 2008 with Barack Obama's Organizing for America grassroots organization. Today, both parties are competing to perfect their get-out-the-vote efforts.[2]

This campaign epiphany was accompanied by other developments that not only contributed to a recognition of and newfound respect for the importance of grassroots and volunteer activities, but also reestablished those efforts at the center of national campaigns. The first development was the advent of the Internet. Technology has enabled national and state parties to "flatten" the organizational structures of their volunteer efforts. Traditionally, three or four levels of hierarchy were needed to organize effectively at the local level: national to state, state to congressional district, congressional district to county, county to precinct. In fact, in the past it would have been virtually impossible to organize in a precinct for a national campaign without three or four intervening levels of staff or volunteer hierarchy. But with the growth of the Internet and Internet-based volunteer tools, and now smart-phone volunteer tools as well, the need for hierarchy is rapidly disappearing. All of these programs can be easily supervised from the national headquarters of any campaign or party with a minimum amount of staff. Volunteers are empowered to work at their own pace, from the comfort of their own homes. As a result, get-out-the-vote, voter identification, and voter contact programs have taken on a whole new look. They can now be executed at a fraction of the labor costs and accommodate busy volunteers with easily digestible and accessible tasks.

The second contributing factor is counterintuitive. Just as a societal shift away from civic participation at the local level led to the demise of the party structure, so too has it contributed to the reemergence of grassroots volunteer activities as a "desirable" means to electoral success. An argument can be made that as we lose touch with our local communities as an integral part of our identity, the impact of direct contact grows accordingly. In other words, if I don't have occasion to interact with my friends and neighbors on a regular basis at the local Rotary gathering, as I might have a generation ago, the interactions I do have become more meaningful. In fact, this interaction has greater impact precisely because it is less common. My family member, friend, or neighbor can get my attention the way a TV commercial simply cannot. A great deal of emphasis has been placed on peer-to-peer marketing precisely for this reason, and the lesson has not been lost on the national parties. Entire voter programs were built around this central concept at the Republican National Committee as part of the 72-Hour Task Force and Team Leader efforts in 2004.

The final factor contributing to the reemergence of grassroots and volunteer activities has been the explosion of money in presidential campaigns. With the record-breaking fundraising of the George W. Bush and Barack Obama campaigns came dramatic increases in the amounts of money available to invest in field staff, technology, and offices. By emphasizing these activities, their benefits became more apparent, and other campaigns began to embrace them as an important, valuable, and, perhaps most significantly, cost-effective way to win an election.

The truth is there is no single factor that guarantees a win or a loss on election day. For each campaign there exist multiple pieces of an equation that will determine the outcome. While history teaches us that ignoring or relying exclusively on any one factor is foolish, it is nevertheless apparent that grassroots volunteers are here to stay as one meaningful factor in the complicated equation of a well-run campaign.

---

[1] See www.72hour.org/72Hour.pdf. Team Leader was an online program aimed at creating a social network for Republican voters; see www.cbsnews.com/stories/2003/10/20/politics/main578935.shtml.

[2] See http://politicsmagazine.com/magazine-issues/october-2009/72-hours-is-so-5-years-ago. Grassroots efforts can also work in primary elections; see www.texasobserver.org/contrarian/the-untold-story-of-perrys-win.

Notes

1. See, for example, the articles on the Tea Party Movement archived at the *New York Times* Web site; go to www.nytimes.com and search for "Tea Party."
2. This document is from *The Collected Works of Abraham Lincoln,* available at http://quod.lib.umich.edu/l/lincoln.
3. These shortcomings were identified in a 2002 PowerPoint presentation ("72-Hour Task Force") prepared by the Republican National Committee (personal copy).
4. For some research on party organizations and their capabilities for mobilization, see McClurg (2004); Gershtenson (2003); Wielhouwer (1999); Wielhouwer and Lockerbie (1994). On the erosion of mass partisanship, see Wattenberg (1998); Fiorina (2002); but see also Bartels (2000); Hetherington (2001); Brewer (2005).
5. In particular, see Eldersveld (1956); Eldersveld and Dodge (1954).
6. In an interesting twist, Eldersveld eventually parlayed his understanding of campaign dynamics into getting elected mayor of Ann Arbor.
7. For example, the ability of personal relationships to convey information informally and casually made that information more credible and influential; informal networks also facilitated information flow from political elites to undecided voters via trusted and intimate relationships (see Lazarsfeld, Berelson, and Gaudet 1948, chap. 16).
8. These would include, among others, introduction of the Australian ballot (designed to reduce election fraud perpetrated by local party machines) at the turn of the twentieth century, expansion of primary elections to determine nominees for a wide range of offices (making it more difficult for party bosses to control the process), and campaign finance reforms passed by Congress in the 1970s that forced candidates for national office to raise money with appeals that were geographically diverse rather than predominantly local. See Ladd with Hadley (1978); Reichley (1992); Hershey (2008).
9. See Panagopoulous and Wielhouwer (2008); Wielhouwer (1999); Rosenstone and Hansen (1993); Verba, Schlozman, and Brady (1995); Huckfeldt and Sprague (1992). The basic approach involves "attempts to elevate gross turnout within certain definable groups where the candidate has overwhelming strength . . . [and] to identify

and selectively increase participation among voter subgroups where strength exists but is not dominant" (Tyson 1999, 133). From paper-and-pencil targeting plans to high-performance computer applications, the goal is to segment the electorate and avoid the opposition (Shea and Burton 2001; Kim 2004).

10. Organizations, especially churches, have been used quite effectively as mobilizing institutions throughout American history (Ahlstrom 1972). The remarkable mobilizing strength of African-American churches (Frazier 1963; Harris 1999) has been matched in recent years by that of socially conservative evangelical churches (J. Green et al. 1996; J. Green, Rozell, and Wilcox 2003). More generally, churches of all stripes are contexts where political discussions can be influential because the people with whom those discussions take place may be more important to us than other, casual acquaintances (Kenny 1992; Huckfeldt and Sprague 1991; Huckfeldt, Plutzer, and Sprague 1993).

11. See also A. Gerber and Green (2000a, 2000b, 2001); A. Gerber, Green, and Green (2003). The discussion here draws heavily on D. Green and Gerber (2008).

12. See the "72-Hour Task Force" presentation cited in note 3. By *pseudo-experiments*, I refer to efforts to assess the effects of various GOTV and organizational methods without employing the rigorous controls and measurements required by true experimentation.

13. For example, see Pinderhughes (1992); Preston, Henderson, and Puryear (1982); Browning, Marshall, and Tabb (1997); Walton (1994); Brown and Wolford (1994); Calhoun-Brown (1996); Dawson, Brown, and Allen (1990); Harris (1999).

14. See www.msnbc.msn.com/id/5297138 and www.msnbc.msn.com/id/26843704 for results in 2004 and 2008, respectively.

15. For a critical view of this relationship, see www.traditionalvalues.org/pdf_files/jim_wallis.pdf.

11 The Impact of Political Consultants

David A. Dulio

On the heels of his historic victory on November 4, 2008, Barack Obama took to the stage and recited the customary litany of postelection acknowledgments. However, after thanking his running mate, Joe Biden, his wife, Michelle, daughters Sasha and Malia, and other relatives, Obama also recognized two men who were instrumental in helping to craft his electoral win: campaign manager David Plouffe and chief strategist David Axelrod. He called Plouffe "the unsung hero of this campaign who built the best political campaign . . . in the history of the United States of America" and noted that Axelrod had been "a partner every step of the way" (Fitzgerald 2008). The importance of these two individuals to Obama's victory was captured in a headline that appeared shortly after the election: "Two Davids behind Obama's Goliath of a Campaign" (Fitzgerald 2008). Such lauding of one's advisors is nothing new to presidential victory speeches; in 2004 President George W. Bush famously described his chief political advisor, Karl Rove, as "the architect" of his successful reelection campaign (*New York Times* 2004).

The 2008 presidential race clearly illustrates the central role and impact that political consultants can have in modern American elections. Chief strategist Axelrod is a longtime Chicago-based political consultant who founded AKP&D Message and Media (formerly Axelrod and Associates) with three partners, including Plouffe. In 2008, Axelrod was "involved in virtually every aspect of [Obama's] campaign, integrating message with policy and speechwriting" (Sweet 2008). He also is credited with working closely with Obama in shaping the campaign's overall theme of change. Campaign manager Plouffe, on the other hand, made sure that all trains ran on time within the large organization. More important, it was Plouffe who devised the strategy that helped secure the Democratic nomination over Hillary Clinton, thereby paving the way for Obama to face Republican John McCain in the general election. Specifically, during 2007, when Obama was behind both in the polls and in fundraising, Plouffe mapped out a path to victory that focused on the currency of presidential nominations: delegates to the national convention where the party's candidate would be chosen. He was credited with the decision to place heavy emphasis on Iowa's caucuses, "the first event of the campaign, and [then] focusing on winning delegates wherever possible, even in states that Hillary Clinton would carry" (Shepard 2008) or that Clinton ignored, many of which were smaller caucus states. This strategy helped the Obama campaign to overcome Clinton's initial advantages and eventually yielded the candidate enough delegates to wrestle the nomination away from his opponent.

Eric Holder, who co-chaired Obama's search for a vice-presidential running mate and later became U.S. Attorney General, said about the two top advisors: "In terms of substance, the inspiration, Barack supplied that, but when it came to execution, what Axelrod and Plouffe did will be studied for a couple of generations. They have created essentially a template for what a presidential campaign is going to look like in the 21st century" (Goldman and Tackett 2008). Even Rove praised "the two Davids" for having "carefully built an army of persuasion" aimed at registering new voters (and turning them out on election day) and picking off previously Republican votes that helped win states like Florida, New Mexico, and Iowa (Rove 2008). The Obama victory was a team effort, however, that included numerous advisors and consultants. In fact, Obama's general election band of consultants may be the largest ever assembled. According to one account, the campaign assembled six "teams" to handle polling, electronic media, and direct mail, splitting the country into different regions to be overseen by a group of consultants with specialties in a given area (Cillizza 2008).

The Obama campaign was not the only one to hire professionals in 2008, of course, nor was 2008 the first election cycle in which candidates for public office hired consultants to assist them in achieving their electoral ambitions. In her primary battle with Obama, Hillary Clinton employed Democratic bigwigs such as chief strategist and pollster Mark Penn (who had done polling for Bill Clinton), campaign manager Patti Solis Doyle, and other holdovers from the earlier Clinton campaigns (including Paul Begala, Mandy Grunwald, Howard Wolfson, and Harold Ickes). In the general election, Sen. John McCain had numerous professionals as part of his team, including campaign manager Rick Davis, pollster Bill McInturff, senior advisor Charlie Black, and a coterie of other consultants. Moreover, scores of candidates at all levels of campaigns hire consultants during each election cycle. In campaigns today, no serious contender for a seat in the U.S. House of Representatives, the U.S. Senate, or a governor's mansion goes into battle without help from political profession-als—a trend that is rapidly extending into state legislative races and local contests for mayor, county commissioner, and even school board (Herrnson 2004; Johnson 2001; Medvic 2001). Moreover, consultants have played an active part in elections for quite some time, dating back at least to 1933.[1]

In this chapter I provide an overview of research that has been done to assess the impact of political consultants in modern American elections. Before turning to the literature on the impact of consultants in elections, I review the limited theoretical work that has been done to date on political consultants generally. I then proceed to examine the effects consultants have in modern campaigns. Central to my discussion is the question of impact: What are the effects of consultants in candidates' campaigns on election day? Specifically, by hiring consultants do candidates tend to receive more votes than they otherwise would? Do candidates, who often pay consultants a great deal of money, get a fair return on their investment? Another, related question is, can consultants help candidates with their fundraising efforts (an important consideration given the influence that money can have in shaping election outcomes; see chapter 5)? Further, the impact of political consultants in today's elections may extend beyond their clients' campaigns. For example, after consultants came onto the electioneering scene in the United States some critics voiced concern over the negative consequences they allegedly were having on political parties, voters, and the electoral process as a whole. Are such criticisms valid? In this chapter I also review the literature that examines consultants' effects in these less tangible areas.[2]

Political Consulting as a Profession

More than a decade ago, James A. Thurber (1998) noted that the academic study of consultants was "a subfield in search of theory." Not much has changed since Thurber wrote this, though there has been some progress. For example, efforts have been made to define important aspects of the industry and to expand our understanding of what it means to be a political consultant. For several reasons, this is easier said than done. First, many different individuals work in campaigns, from the candidate's spouse and family to the "kitchen cabinet" of close advisors, from volunteers who walk neighborhoods and stuff envelopes to pollsters and media consultants who make their living by providing electioneering services. Only members of this last group are truly professionals. Further, "[u]nlike those that apply to other professionals such as attorneys, physicians, or even cosmetologists, there are no barriers to entry, no certification procedures, and no training requirements to become a political consultant" (Dulio 2004, 43). Because of this, anyone who wants to be a political consultant need only hang out a shingle and find a client. This makes it difficult to differentiate between the professional who offers advice to candidates for a living and the college professor who conducts a poll for a friend who is running for state legislature.

In their research, scholars have offered a number of definitions of a political consultant. This variety of operational definitions has led to an inconsistency that is troubling because, as Medvic (2003, 119) noted, "conceptual clarity is a prerequisite to systematic empirical investigation in any field." The earliest studies were mostly silent, and only after consultants were associated with the public relations field for many years did Sabato (1981, 8) offer the first real definition. Sabato defined the political consultant as "a campaign professional who is engaged primarily in the provision of advice and services (such as polling, media creation and production, and direct-mail fundraising) to candidates, their campaigns, and other political committees." While this helped to clarify matters somewhat, the definition was still too vague. As Sabato (1981, 8) himself noted, his definition can apply to "almost any paid staffer on even the most minor of campaigns." In addition, some individuals in campaigns provide services that are strategic in nature, while others provide services that are more technical. This distinction is similar to the one made by Johnson (2000, 2001) between "strategists" and "vendors."

It would seem reasonable to assume that true consultants are those who provide strategic advice and services that are central to the execution of a campaign. Yet a review of the scholarly research on the topic offers little consistency. Herrnson (1992), for example, used results from a survey in which candidates were asked to identify the services that consultants (as opposed to party workers, staff, or volunteers) were hired to perform for their respective campaigns. Medvic (1998, 2000, 2001; Medvic and Lenart 1997) relied heavily on a standard first offered by *Campaigns & Elections* (now *Politics*) magazine, which said that to appear in their "Consultant Scorecard" list of winners and losers in each election cycle, a practitioner must have "worked" on at least two (increasing to three in 1992) statewide or congressional campaigns. Medvic went beyond the two-race threshold, however, by including those who had grossed the most revenue in their field during a particular cycle (Medvic 2001, 66). Many of the studies to which I refer below used surveys of consultants for their data. To identify the individuals to survey, several scholars turned to the various lists of consultants that are publicly available. Kolodny and Logan (1998) used a list of general consultants available from *Campaigns & Elections*. My own work (Dulio 2004; Thurber, Nelson, and Dulio 2000a; Dulio and Nelson 2005) also relied, in part, on surveys that drew names of respondents from *Campaigns & Elections* as well as the *Political Resources Directory*.

In my studies, I defined a consultant as "an individual or firm that provides campaign services on a fee-for-service basis during an election cycle for more than one candidate, political party, organized interest group, or initiative and referendum campaign for more than one election cycle" (Dulio 2004, 44). This definition is designed to differentiate true consultants—the people who are responsible for strategic decision making in campaigns, such as pollsters, media consultants, and direct mail specialists—from vendors who supply campaigns with voter lists or firms that make phone calls for pollsters. Let me be clear: none of the definitions discussed here are wrong. They simply are different, which makes comparing results from different studies difficult at times. In an effort to bring scholars together, Medvic (2003, 124) suggested that a professional political consultant be defined as someone "who is paid, or whose firm is paid, to provide services for one presidential/national or more than one non-presidential/sub-national campaign (whether candidate or issue) per election cycle for more than one such cycle, not including those whose salary is paid exclusively by a party committee or interest group." Whether scholars use this definition, or any other, as they go forward with their research remains to be seen.

Conventional wisdom holds that the United States is home to the most professionalized campaigns found anywhere in the world (Scammell 1998; Plasser 2000). Indeed, even the earliest works on political consultants typically considered the people who provide electioneering services to be professionals, and this has continued through many contemporary studies.[3] There are some good reasons for this, starting with the fact that political consulting not only constitutes a multibillion-dollar-a-year business worldwide but, in the United States, also maintains a professional organization (the American Association of Political Consultants, or AAPC).[4] Moreover, while the practice of consulting has elements that make it more art than science,[5] there is general agreement among practitioners on how to wage a successful campaign. Nevertheless, some skeptics continue to question whether political consultants fit the definition of a true professional. Scammell (1998, 269), for example, concluded that "[p]olitical consultancy is a prospering business, but it falls short of the mark of professionalism in two crucial respects: a self-policing ethical code and the professionalization of campaigning knowledge."[6] However, a code of ethics has in fact been produced (though almost never enforced) by the AAPC and, as I note below, a small but growing number of university courses and degree programs are helping to train the next generation of consultants.

Grossmann (2009, 86) adopted a standard established by the sociological literature to judge professionalism, specifically, Freidson's notion of ideal-typical professionalism: "According to Freidson (2001), ideal-typical professionalism arises as a form of social organization with five primary features: (1) an occupational division of labor, (2) occupation-controlled career lines, (3) a specialized training program, (4) a body of applied knowledge, and (5) an ideology that transcends economic interest to support established practices." Grossmann concluded that consultants meet some of these standards but not others. On the plus side, consultants define themselves as professionals, they "have outlined a model of campaign strategy by using applied knowledge," and they "adhere to an ideology of service to help clients win elections." In the end, however, consultants rise only to a "middle stage of professionalization," failing to meet the ideal-typical definition set forth by Freidson because the occupation does not control the division of labor or career paths, because there is resistance to government regulation within the industry, and because a wide network of formal training or education is lacking (Grossmann 2009, 101).

There are some inherent and structural impediments to political consultants meeting such standards. With respect to the occupation's failure to control the division of labor or career paths (through AAPC), this is difficult in politics for two reasons. First, the partisan nature of the business leads to a divided network of consultants—one on the Republican side and one on the Democratic side.[7] Second, the occupation cannot control the division of labor because more actors engage in the campaign business than just consultants and candidates; parties and organized interests are involved as well. On another front, although it is true that consultants resist government regulation, it is true as well that regulation of the business of campaigning would be problematic given the language of the First Amendment to the Constitution, which protects political speech and, in so doing, has helped to create the often rough-and-tumble world of politics.[8] Finally, no formal training or certification procedure for consultants exists, though several colleges and universities now offer courses or degree programs that help introduce individuals to the business.[9] Given these considerations as well as Grossmann's conclusions, I would argue that political consultants are professionals who work in an industry that practices both art and science.

The study of consultants in the academic literature is in its infancy compared to more traditional areas of inquiry in the field of campaigns and elections. Many of the first works devoted to the study of consultants were focused on describing the phenomenon and providing basic information about what consultants do. My purpose in the remainder of this chapter, however, is not to review the growth of the consulting industry in the United States, nor to describe the job of a consultant in great detail. Rather, it is to understand what consultants bring to our elections. I begin by considering the impact of consultants on political parties and the general public because, in many ways, this can help us to better understand their more clear-cut and distinguishable campaign effects in the form of fundraising and vote totals, which are the next topics considered. Finally, I briefly examine future possibilities for the study of political consultants.[10]

Consultants' Effects on Political Parties

Initial assessments of the impact of political consultants on the parties were consistently negative. This view was summed up nicely in Sabato's *The Rise of Political Consultants* (1981, 286):

> The "personality cult" campaign and the general deterioration of the party system are perfectly acceptable to most political consultants. In fact, they themselves, along with their electoral wares, have played a moderate part in personalizing and glamorizing American politics and in the continuing decline of party organization. While certainly not initiating the party's decline, they have nonetheless aided and abetted the slide, sometimes with malice aforethought. . . . The services provided by consultants, their new campaign technologies, have undoubtedly supplanted party activities and influence.

An interwoven set of criticisms relating to consultants' negative effects on parties is contained in Sabato's statement, including that consultants have (1) contributed to the parties' decline, (2) willingly and knowingly aided this decline, and (3) commandeered areas of electioneering once dominated by parties. Also embedded in this argument is the notion that consultants and the parties are locked in a competition for modern candidates' loyalties.

Consultants supposedly have contributed to the parties' decline by becoming the main service providers to candidates; this, in turn, leads to candidates severing ties with their party and, ultimately, to parties no longer playing a meaningful role in elections. According to Sabato (1981, 286), "Party leaders used to be the ones thought to have the keys to success, *the* secrets to winning elections. Now political consultants . . . are the new experts, and their advice and support are considered to be more valuable publicly and privately than almost any party leader's" (emphasis in original). Much of this transformation occurred during a time of great technological innovation that included the development of radio and then television as channels of communication with voters, and the shift was noticed by scholars and journalists alike. Farrell (1996) described this as a transition from campaigns that were labor intensive to ones that were capital intensive. Not long after the preeminence of television became evident, Broder (1971, 239) argued that consultants were usurping the parties' dominance in communicating campaign messages and that television was making "one of the party's old functions irrelevant—that of serving as a bridge between the candidate or officeholder and the public." Nimmo (2001, 9) concurred, suggesting that because consultants came in and took over the provision of campaign services from the parties, they were responsible for "displacing the full-time [pols] of party machines."

According to Sabato (1981, 289), "A natural consequence of the consultant's antagonism toward the party is his willingness to run his candidates apart from, or even against, their party label." Nimmo (2001, 10) agreed and claimed that the growth of the consulting industry had brought forth "the means for candidates to secure office regardless of the wishes of the party leaders, indeed over the heads of those leaders; what was replaced was party control of candidate recruitment, selection, and election." As one of the most severe critics of consultants and their impact on political parties, Sabato (1988, 21; see also Crotty and Jacobson 1980) argued that consultants had become "the main institutional rivals of the parties, luring candidates away from their party moorings and using the campaign technologies to supplant parties as the intermediaries between candidates and the voters."

Making matters worse, in this view, was that consultants generally did not have the same degree of ideological or broad programmatic commitment as did the parties. Broder (1971, 237), for example, complained that "the professional campaign managers tend to be as anti-party as they are nonideological," and recounted that by 1971, "all of the major states—California, New York, Illinois, Pennsylvania, Ohio, Florida—[had] seen wealthy or well-financed men, with little background in party activity, little support among the party cadre, and little allegiance to the party or its programs, come in and beat the formally or informally designated organization favorite with expensive campaigns managed by outside political consultants" (238). Thus, allegedly lacking ideological principles themselves, consultants were accused of encouraging candidates to wage campaigns outside the traditional party structure and (in the process) to take positions that sometimes were inconsistent with basic party principles.

The most damaging critique of consultants in this regard is that they pushed parties to the side of electioneering on purpose and as a power grab. Such characterizations of the relationship between consultants and parties have been challenged by more recent work, however, which takes the position that rather than displacing parties knowingly, consultants came in to fill a void created by changes in the electoral environment (Dulio 2004). Among these changes are reforms instituted during the Progressive Movement of the early 1900s (including the direct primary, initiatives and referendums, and the Australian ballot) and, more recently, the great technological advancements that ushered in the era of campaigns conducting scientific public opinion research, communicating with voters over the airwaves through television, and carefully targeting citizens to receive direct-mail pieces (Dulio 2004; Farrell 1996). As campaigning moved from a system based mainly on candidates canvassing and shaking hands to one dominated by television and the mass media, parties found that they could no longer either help their entire slate of candidates or campaign the way they once had. Moreover, candidates started to behave like any consumers would as they increasingly demanded services that were part of the technological revolution. In short, many contemporary inquiries have concluded that consultants were not a reason for the decline of parties, but rather that they were a reaction to what had already happened and that they came in to fill a void left by that decline (Dulio 2004; Dulio and Nelson 2005).

One last point about the effects that consultants have had on parties is that the early work examining the relationship viewed it as a competitive one. O'Shaughnessy (1990, 136), for example, argued that "party and consultants are in competition and see each other as rivals: to some extent they duplicate each other's functions." Today, it is recognized that this is not always the case. Kolodny and Logan (1998) were among the first to systematically examine the question of whether consultants and political parties are adversaries or allies. "According to the adversarial view," they wrote, "consultants do not complement parties and act as little more than advertising agencies"; campaign professionals tend to see parties and candidates as clients whose main purpose is to increase their revenues (155). Under the allied view, however, consultants "value party goals" and, more important, "do for candidates what political parties simply cannot: they offer targeted technical assistance and personal advice to the candidate who hires them" (155).

Kolodny and Logan (1998), in a study that examined consultants' attitudes toward parties, found evidence for the allied view. Specifically, rather than pushing parties into decline or being a detriment to their cause, these scholars learned that consultants see themselves as assisting parties in achieving the goal of electing candidates to public office. Other recent work also has been consistent with the allied view of the consultant-party relationship. In particular, studies that survey campaign professionals and party elites generally find agreement among both groups that consultants have replaced parties in providing some services to candidates, and that there are some things consultants can do that parties simply cannot (Dulio and Thurber 2003; Dulio and Nelson 2005). However, this is not a negative consequence because, according to consultants and party leaders alike, the parties continue to play a meaningful role in campaigns. If anything, a fairly clear division of labor has emerged between the two groups that allows each to focus on its own areas of efficiency and expertise (Dulio 2004); that is, a cooperative and symbiotic relationship has developed in which consultants are the main providers of campaign services that center on message creation and delivery (for example, strategic advice and management, survey research, television advertising) while parties are looked to for services that require large amounts of staff and time (for example, opposition research, fundraising, get-out-the-vote efforts), which the parties have in greater supply than do individual consulting firms.

Additional evidence of this alliance or partnership is provided by the fact that parties frequently looked to consultants for assistance during the parties' so-called resurgence or revitalization in the 1980s and 1990s.[11] According to Kolodny (2000, 112), "As some were predicting the death of political parties, the parties instead found that forming alliances with consultants was a rational solution to the upheavals of modern campaigning." In other words, parties began to hire consultants to help with their fundraising efforts and to provide some of the other services demanded by candidates and utilized directly by the parties themselves[12]—a trend that continues today, as both Republican and Democratic Party organizations pay a great deal of money directly to outside consultants and recommend consultants that candidates might choose to hire on their own.[13] The overall picture is one of cooperation more than of conflict or competition.

In sum, whereas it was once believed that consultants had a decidedly negative effect on political parties, the truth may be just the opposite; that is, by working for individual candidates as well as the party apparatus itself, consultants have helped the parties to become more efficient in seeking their primary goal: to elect more of their candidates to public office. In the process, the parties have learned "that today's skilled professional consultants are essential to modern electioneering, and moreover, that the campaign techniques they provide have not destroyed the parties but have strengthened them" (Luntz 1988, 144).

Consultants' Effects on Citizens

Research dealing with the effects of political consultants on the individuals who are on the receiving end of their work is nearly as divided as that exploring the consultant-party relationship. Once again, we can see a division between more dated work (which generally portrays the consequences as harmful) and recent studies (some of which come to a rather different conclusion). Even contemporary scholars, however, are not agreed as to whether the impact of consultants on ordinary citizens is positive or negative.

The notion that the presence of consultants in campaigns is likely to have some effect on citizens is based on three considerations. First, as already noted, members of the electorate are the targets of what most modern political campaigns produce—that is, messages designed to yield votes on election day.[14] According to pollster Mark Mellman, these messages can have different purposes, from activating latent partisanship to attitude change (Medvic 2006, 22).[15] Second, they are delivered principally through television and radio ads, or direct-mail pieces, which then become a candidate's public face and have the potential to shape how people think about the campaign. Third, a number of academic studies make clear that campaign communications can and do have an impact on viewers and readers. For example, the literature leaves little doubt that citizens' evaluations of candidates are subject to influence from effects such as agenda-setting, priming, and framing that result from strategic messages delivered either directly (by candidates) or indirectly (through earned, or free, media).[16]

In the eyes of some critics, consultants are dastardly and devious. As O'Shaughnessy (1990, 135) wrote, "Consultants have been regarded by some as the agents of corruption, the mercenary pimps and whores of the political waterfront." This corruption allegedly comes in a variety of forms, including through the use of campaign ads that distort the records of candidates, selective reporting of results from an opinion survey, and the fostering of ambiguity and symbolism in campaign rhetoric.[17] Because of their actions, consultants are accused of engaging in "manipulation" (Johnson-Cartee and Copeland 1997b; O'Shaughnessy 1990), saturation of "the mass electorate with partisan and image propaganda" (Nimmo 2001, 222; see also Kelley 1956; Sabato 1981), and the use of "mercantilist metaphors" (Johnson-Cartee and Copeland 1997a). In short, a crucial impact that consultants supposedly have is to deceive and manipulate the public through their use of sophisticated campaign techniques such as polling and television ads. In a related vein, consultants are frequently criticized for relying too heavily on so-called negative advertising that is believed by some to undermine campaign learning, turn people off to the electoral process, and even drive down voter turnout (Lau and Pomper 2004; Lau and Sigelman 2000; Lau, Sigelman, and Rovner 2007).

The argument here deserves closer scrutiny. First, there certainly are cases throughout the history of American elections in which campaigns have distorted the truth. One might argue, however, that such incidents do not reflect a problem with advertising *per se,* but rather with the unethical nature of a specific message or communication. Yet for some people there is no difference, and all advertising is suspect. According to Johnson-Cartee and Copeland (1997b, xxii), "Political advertising as a science and an art is a manipulative business" and, therefore, due to the ads that pollsters and media consultants create, "millions of voters are manipulated each campaign season." This assessment is not new. As far back as Kelley's (1956, 214) writing about "the public relations man," it was noted that the consultant (who represented an outgrowth of the public relations field) "strives to determine a vote by controlling attitudes." Petracca (1989, 13) described this type of manipulation using the words of one of the first modern political professionals, Joe Napolitan, who advised, "Decide what you want the voter to feel or how you want him to react. Decide what you must do to make him react the way you want. Do it."

Petracca's contention was that consultants do not always strive to create clear distinctions between candidates. Nimmo (2001, 221), writing originally in the 1960s, agreed, claiming that in situations in which consultants have a strong presence, "[e]lections are approached neither as conflicts between parties nor as confrontations of principle. They are viewed instead as contests of personalities and, even more basically, they offer a choice between the sophisticated engineers working on behalf of those personalities." And while politicians may argue that they would never fall victim to the perils of using a consultant, "the fact remains that these technicians can make a candidate appear to be what he is not" (221). Reflecting this, political professionals have been called "image merchants" (Hiebert et al. 1971) and are said to be in the business of "impression management" (Johnson-Cartee and Copeland 1997b) and "product management" (O'Shaughnessy 1990)—labels that clearly come with a negative connotation attached. Beyond the shaping of candidate images, there is the fact that consultants are able to place new issues on the agenda. This is supposedly a cause for concern because first, issues are chosen based on what is wrong with the opponent rather than on whether the issues are genuinely important to voters (O'Shaughnessy 1990; Peele 1982), and second, being able to set the agenda gives unelected consultants more power than they should have in democratic politics (O'Shaughnessy 1990).

To some critics, then, the work of political consultants amounts to nothing more than selling candidates as more traditional marketers would sell laundry detergent. Sabato (1981, 321) argued, for example, that "the ad man's selling instinct among political consultants is the most degrading and repulsive aspect of their profession." Accordingly, Sabato endorsed Adlai Stevenson's observation that the merchandising of "candidates for high office like breakfast cereal is the ultimate indignity to the democratic process."[18] Nimmo (2001, 219) expressed concern that the consequences of consultant activity may extend beyond a simple vote choice on election day; such activity, he said, hits at the heart of the democratic nature of elections and "introduces not only the possibility but indeed the likelihood of systematic deception in electoral politics."

In contrast, some newer research on consultants does not characterize their impact on the public as being duplicitous at all. To the contrary, rather than reflecting efforts at manipulation that cause problems for democratic politics, the work of consultants today is more likely to be seen as activating citizens' previously held beliefs and, along the way, perhaps even raising the level of debate within the electorate.[19] This new interpretation is rooted in a closer consideration of the process that consultants usually engage in when they design the strategy and message of a campaign. Earlier research simply looked at the content of the most visible outputs produced by consultants—that is, television and radio ads and direct-mail pieces—and assumed a sleazy motive. Examining the process leading to those outputs can shed light on their effects because it can help to reveal motive.

Although the literature dealing with political consultants generally lacks theory, some recent developments speak to the effects that consultants may have on the electorate. Specifically, Medvic's (2001; 2006) theory of *deliberate priming* brings together ideas from various fields to identify what consultants actually do when they develop a strategy and message for a campaign. Central to Medvic's argument, as noted before, is an understanding of the process that consultants go through to develop a message that they wish to communicate to potential voters. At the heart of this process is public opinion research. Critics would argue that a reliance on polling is in and of itself dangerous because consultants simply end up using the data to tell candidates what position they should take on issues (that is, candidates are poll driven). The process described by Medvic, however, is different and more subtle. Instead of using polling to take the pulse of the electorate in the sense of finding out what policy positions most citizens hold, consultants seek "to determine which issues are most salient, both actually and potentially to voters" (Medvic 2001, 49). Note that Medvic stops short of the problematic aspects of critics' claims and contends that the central goal of polling is simply to identify issues that are salient, not modal issue positions; specifically, "[c]onsultants in the early stages of a campaign help candidates understand how, but not where, to position themselves" on an imaginary opinion spectrum in the electorate (Medvic 2001, 50).

Ideally, the results of early research conducted by a campaign "should have identified the most salient issues in the election, as well as issues of potential salience, and should have uncovered the effects of the various ways that those issues could be framed. In addition, the best (and worst) characteristics of the candidate should have been explored and the weaknesses of the opponent pinpointed" (Medvic 2001, 51). This information is then used by the campaign in deciding the best way for the candidate to communicate with the public. "Polling helps reveal the most beneficial approach to communicating the candidate's case for his/her election" (Medvic 2006, 20). In other words, specific messages are tested through survey research to identify how a candidate can best talk about the position(s) he or she already holds.

Candidates obviously cannot talk about every issue they might like to over the course of a campaign; a majority of the public simply does not have sufficient time for, or interest in, that kind of detailed policy discussion. Rather, candidates must choose a subset of issues on which to focus in their communications, and consultants are hired to help them with this task. The crux of the theory of deliberate priming is that "campaigns emphasize certain topics with the intention of altering the criteria that voters use for candidate evaluation" (Medvic 2001, 51).

In a sense, then, consultants are indeed the "issue choosers" that their critics describe. The missing piece of the puzzle is the *process* that consultants go through to determine the content of their ads and mail pieces. As the theory of deliberate priming suggests, consultants help candidates pick issues on which to campaign that will give them a competitive advantage over their opponent; in doing so, they naturally try to choose issues that will give their candidate the best chance to win on election day (for exceptions, see Damore 2004). This follows from Petrocik's (1996) theory of *issue ownership*, which tells us that candidates will emphasize different issues because the public views their party as being better able to handle that issue than the other party.[20] Based on survey data, Petrocik outlined a series of issues that are "owned" by Democrats and Republicans. For example, Democrats tend to own issues having to do with social welfare and the environment, while Republicans own issues related to national defense, foreign policy, and taxes. Thus, the process that consultants go through in developing a message for a campaign is all about issues—but not just any issue or set of issues. Consultants select issues for the campaign to focus on that are salient to the public *and* on which their candidate has an advantage over the opponent. As Medvic (2006, 27) explained:

> Every candidate has an advantage in particular policy areas and/or on specific character traits. Professional campaign operatives are brought into a campaign to determine what those issues/traits are, which of them their client should emphasize and how they should be framed. Those issues/traits upon which there is a distinction between the candidates and which voters regard as high priorities are likely to get emphasized in an attempt to have voters utilize those issues/traits in making a decision between candidates.

It is critical to keep in mind that this is usually done before any television ads or direct-mail pieces have been developed. Consequently, those who maintain that consultants have a manipulative effect on the public begin their critique too late in the process, by focusing on the point at which electronic and print communications are created.

One might still believe, of course, that it is misleading or somehow detrimental to the public when candidates' campaigns merely pick and choose from the full set of issues that could potentially be important to voters. Yet I have argued elsewhere (Dulio 2004) that the process by which consultants help candidates identify issues and then discuss those issues in a certain way is beneficial to the public for two reasons. First, it forces candidates and campaigns to focus on issues that are important to the members of the electorate. It would do no one any good if a candidate for office talked about issues that the public did not care about or was not interested in. For example, assume a candidate has deeply held opinions about issues such as the environment, taxes, health care reform, homeland security, and abortion. Also assume that, through polling, it is learned that the public cares or is interested mainly in homeland security, health care reform, and taxes. The electorate would not be well served if the candidate spent a large amount of time talking about abortion and the environment or another set of issues. Conducting research that allows candidates to focus on issues that the public cares about only serves to further the overall public interest. A second advantage of deliberate priming is that, by focusing on issues the public cares about, campaigns (with the help of consultants) can elevate the level of debate and give potential voters more of what they are looking for. If, for example, the candidates in a race learn through their polling that the electorate is focused primarily on the issues noted above—homeland security, health care reform, and taxes—it is likely that the Democrat will focus on health care reform because that is an issue on which Democrats traditionally have an advantage over their Republican rivals. By the same token, it is likely that the Republican will stress the remaining two issues (for similar reasons of competitive advantage).[21] However, because the two sides are talking about different issues, there will likely be pressure either from the press or from voters themselves to address issues that each would prefer to avoid. As the theories of issue ownership and deliberate priming make clear, each candidate, with the help of his or her consultants, will make an effort to define the turf on which the campaign will be waged; specifically, the candidate will try to talk primarily about issues that benefit them (or perhaps their party). The strategic nature and importance of the consultants' presence lies in the fact that the campaign that does the best job of having the campaign waged on its turf is often the one that ends up winning on election day.

Consultants' Effects on Campaigns

While studies that explore the effects of consultants on parties, voters, or the electoral process as a whole lack a clear consensus, the academic literature leaves little doubt about the tangible impact that consultants can have on campaigns. There are two broad streams of research focusing on two of the mainstays of any campaign: success in fundraising and success at the ballot box on election day. Every study that has examined the question of consultants' effects on fundraising and vote share has reached the same conclusion, specifically, that campaigns run by professionals tend to raise more money and garner more votes than do amateur-run campaigns.

Efforts to investigate such questions are a fairly recent development in the political science literature, largely because the empirical data needed for serious hypothesis testing have been difficult to come by. This was certainly true in the days prior to the explosive growth of professional consulting, when Kelley (1956, 205) observed that "there are few data for evaluating, with anything like scientific accuracy, particular propaganda techniques, and certainly not for the assessment of the effectiveness of 'public relations' in general." In fact, many interesting hypotheses in political science were originally difficult to test because of a lack of reliable data sources at the time. Yet even as matters improved (often dramatically) in other areas of the discipline, the same was not true for those who wished to explore the consequences of consultant activity in campaigns. As recently as the late 1980s, Petracca (1989, 11) described the situation as follows:

> Despite the meteoric rise to prominence of political consultants in American political campaigns, political scientists have devoted surprisingly little attention to their analysis. . . . This analytic silence may be attributed to a number of factors. First, compared to voters, PACs [political action committees], or interest groups, consultants are far more difficult to study. There are no readily available data sources to either identify consultants or document their activities. Second, the considerable variation in what it means to "consult" in the activities of professional consultants makes it difficult to identify the essence of consultancy. Finally, many scholars who study elections do so by studying voters. As a result our attention has moved away from the analysis of electoral institutions in which consultants now play such a commanding role.

Petracca's observations remained accurate until scholars in the field began to develop new data sets more appropriate to the task at hand. The first systematic attempts to understand the role of consultants in campaigns were limited, however, by the fact that they frequently relied on opinion surveys of consultants themselves.[22] While these studies certainly were of value in that they allowed us to know more about the attitudes and beliefs of campaign professionals, they still were unable to test directly hypotheses regarding consultants' effectiveness. Subsequent research has gone further, especially by centering on congressional races in which hundreds of candidates run in each election cycle—and for which at least some requisite data are available. In particular, the *dependent* variables for the two lines of inquiry noted above (money raised and votes received) can be measured using data compiled by the Federal Election Commission (FEC) in all federal races.

Unfortunately, it remains difficult to capture the *independent* (or explanatory) variable of greatest interest: the level of consultant involvement in a campaign. One might reasonably assume that federal candidates' FEC reports, in which they detail how their money was spent during the campaign, would provide the kind of information researchers need to measure consultant activity—which consultant(s) worked for each candidate, what service(s) they provided, and how much they were paid, for example. The problem is that the FEC's reporting requirements are rather limited. When preparing their FEC-required lists of fees paid, candidates' campaigns typically enter "consulting," or some other vague description that tells us little or nothing about actual work performed; as a result, the data are unreliable for discerning precisely what consultants have provided in terms of strategic advice or campaign services. This limitation, coupled with the fact that each report for each candidate can be hundreds of pages long, means that the FEC is not an ideal source of data for empirical research.

Scholars have therefore had to find other ways of measuring the presence of consultants in campaigns. This concept, despite some objections, is described in the literature as "campaign professionalization," and, as noted above, those who study its effects on candidates' fundraising and vote share have used a number of different indicators. Whatever their approach, however, they all reach essentially the same conclusion, which is that professionalized campaigns fare better than campaigns that do not use professional consultants.

Studies that look specifically at fundraising find that consultants have a positive and sometimes dramatic effect on the ability of candidates to raise money. According to Herrnson (1992, 866), "campaign professionalism influences the resource allocations of political parties, PACs, and individuals, and increases the campaign receipts of congressional candidates" (see also Medvic 2001). While this particular analysis showed that both incumbents and non-incumbents running for the U.S. House in 1984 increased their take from parties and PACs by hiring more professionals, individual contributors seemed to respond favorably only to a higher level of professionalism in incumbent campaigns. In a later study of House races in 1992, however, Herrnson (2000) found that professionalized campaigns, for incumbents and challengers alike, raised larger amounts of money from individuals.[23] Put simply, the presence of consultants signals to potential donors that the race is likely to be competitive. As a result,

> deciding whether to hire professional political consultants or to field an amateur campaign organization can have a major impact on a House candidate's fundraising prospects. The implications . . . are clear: it is important

to put together a high-quality professional campaign organization and let party committees, PACs, and individuals know about it. A professional campaign organization can greatly enhance a candidate's ability to raise money. This, in turn, can improve the candidate's prospects for electoral success (Herrnson 1992, 867).

Testing the latter proposition, Medvic and Lenart (1997) discovered that the presence as well as the actual number of consultants had a significant and positive impact on share of the vote received by challenger and open-seat candidates in the 1992 U.S. House races (incumbents were excluded from their analysis); this basic result is consistent through a number of other studies as well (see Herrnson 2000; Medvic 2000, 2001). Interestingly, and contrary to the pattern for fundraising reported in the preceding paragraph, it appears that incumbents do *not* invariably benefit from hiring political consultants. As the professionalism of challenger campaigns increases, the chance of winning grows accordingly. But with incumbents, candidates "who are involved in the most competitive elections usually put together the most professional campaign organizations, raise the most money"—and, typically, compile win-loss records that "are not as good as those of incumbents who face lower levels of competition and who do not feel the need to wage costly, highly professional campaigns" (Herrnson 2000, 85).[24]

Our understanding of this dynamic is enhanced further by research that asks questions about the importance of different *types* of consultants on candidates' election day totals. For example, "What effect do pollsters, media handlers, voter contact specialists, and generalists have? Do pollsters matter most, as [the theory of deliberate priming] would suggest? Or does another type of consultant appear to be more useful to candidates?" (Medvic 2001, 104). Medvic's results show that pollsters are the most valuable type of consultant for challengers but not for incumbents, perhaps for the same reason that incumbents seem to benefit less from using consultants in the first place (because those who do so are often facing a more spirited challenge than are those who do not).[25]

Studies such as these make an important contribution to the way we think about the role of consultants in campaigns. According to Medvic and Lenart (1997, 74), they have "quantified the influence of political professionals on election outcomes and have, therefore, avoided an anecdotal analysis of the question at hand," which was a limitation of the earlier research that reached its conclusions based on speculation and conjecture. Yet the initial work done in any field is likely to spur further investigations that ask similar questions in different ways, or attempt to challenge assumptions made by the researchers who came before. The topic of consultant influence is no different in this regard.

In my own study of consultants, I have challenged the belief expressed by both Medvic and Herrnson that consultants should be considered in the same light as any other campaign resource, and that differentiating among the consultants that candidates hire is unimportant. Medvic (2000, 93), for example, concluded that "a candidate's decision about whether or not to hire a consultant is more important than the decision about whether to hire Consultant A or Consultant B." Indeed, "[j]ust as artistic talent cannot be quantified, one cannot begin to quantify savvy on the part of a consultant. It is an unusual talent" (Johnson-Cartee and Copeland 1997a, 1). I have argued, however, that distinctions can and should be made among the individual consultants hired by candidates' campaigns. Specifically, consultants who are better known in political circles should have a greater impact on candidate fundraising than those who are less well known, and consultants who are at the top of their profession (that is, who are most effective at what they do) should deliver more votes on election day than those with fewer skills (Dulio 2004).[26] In other words, we must keep in mind that political consulting is an art at least as much as it is a science.

My research indicates that differences do exist among consultants, and that those differences have implications for fundraising and vote share. First, candidates who hire well-known consultants are able, on average, to attract more party and PAC money than are those who do not; that is, having a professional campaign organization assist with fundraising helps by confirming the viability of a campaign, but hiring the "right" consultants helps even more. In addition, I found that challengers who employ the most capable consultants (as determined by their peers) tend to receive more votes on election day—a finding that implies some consultants really do perform their jobs better than others. Interestingly, the opposite relationship was found for incumbents; when incumbents hire consultants who are identified as some of the best in the business, they tend to do worse than when they are assisted by either no consultant at all or by consultants with a less stellar reputation.

At first glance, this finding would seem to reinforce the idea that incumbents do not benefit in any systematic way from using consultants (Herrnson 2000; Medvic 2000, 2001), even when those they use are, arguably, the best available. It is worth noting, however, that incumbents facing races that are expected to be extremely competitive are the ones who usually hire the most highly regarded consultants precisely because they realize that they need the best help they can find. As I have written elsewhere,

When facing a tough challenge, [incumbents] need, more than ever, to develop a strong strategy, theme, and message, and to deliver that message effectively and efficiently. They turn to the best consultants to help them do one thing—return to the House as a member of the next Congress. Although other incumbents may be trying to increase their share of the vote to scare off potential challengers two years down the road, embattled incumbents worry only about winning. For those who are almost guaranteed a victory, it does not really matter who they hire (as Medvic [2001] suggests). However, for those who are in a difficult race, they need the best and they hire the best. Therefore, the impact of the most effective consultants may not be measurable in terms of vote percentage. It may be better measured in terms of simple victory (Dulio 2004, 162).

In sum, although the evidence is clear that consultants make a difference in candidates' campaigns by delivering more fundraising dollars and more votes on election day, consultants are not all-powerful and they cannot get just any candidate elected. Simply hiring a consultant does not guarantee victory. One has only to examine the star-studded team of consultants assembled by the Clinton or McCain presidential campaigns in 2008. Some of the best consultants in the industry were advising these candidates, and yet they did not win. In fact, the consultants in both campaigns received some blame for the lack of success. In the primary, the Clinton consultants fought among themselves over what strategy or tactic to employ (*Newsweek* 2008; Langley and Chozick 2008). In the general election, the McCain team simply did not run a sound campaign. According to one report, it "often seemed to make missteps and lurch from moment to moment in search of a consistent strategy and message" (Nagourney, Rutenberg, and Zeleny 2008). The presence of consultants, then, is not a magic potion that can turn any candidate who hires them into an elected public official.

New Directions for Research on Consultants

Scholars have hit only the tip of the iceberg with their work on professional consultants, and there are several important and interesting directions in which they might choose to take their research in the future. The relationships between campaign professionalism and both fundraising and electoral success seem clear: consultants, on average, help candidates raise more money and garner more votes. What is less understood is *how* consultants do this. More research is needed on the ways in which consultants make decisions, especially in terms of how strategies are developed within the context of an individual campaign. In other words, we know that the services provided by consultants (polling, television and radio ads, direct mail, grassroots mobilization, and the like) do matter in campaigns. What we know less about is how consultants make those services matter. A few case studies have attempted to capture this process (Thurber 2002), and some research has begun to investigate systematically how consultants make decisions in campaigns (R. Garrett 2009; Waismel-Manor 2005), but more is needed. We also would benefit from knowing how different consultants approach their craft, and from seeking to understand how consultants adapt to changes in the electoral context.

THE POLITICAL PROFESSIONALS RESPOND

Ron Faucheux

Political scientists and Hollywood filmmakers have something in common: they both have trouble grasping the impact of political consultants. For years, movies have enlarged on and embellished the role of campaign consultant. From *The Candidate* in 1972 to *Power* in 1986 to *Wag the Dog* in 1997, campaign consultants have been portrayed as calculating puppet masters, expert at manipulating candidates—and democracy itself—with crafty TV ads riddled with hidden messages, improbable polls identifying the concerns of left-handed Lithuanians in Idaho, and garish bumper stickers featuring psychology-driven color schemes. But in the end, neither Hollywood nor the Ivory Tower gets it right. Hollywood's inaccurate portrayals, along with academia's unanswered questions, have led to three fundamental misconceptions about the role of political consultants—misconceptions that are perpetuated by insiders who benefit from and outsiders who are fascinated by the image of behind-the-scenes campaign maestros conducting the electoral process like a symphony orchestra.

The first misconception: Consultants tell candidates what to do, and the candidates do it.

To be a consultant or a candidate, or to have watched either closely in action, is to know better. The reality is that the biggest complaint of consultants is that their clients *don't* listen to them. This truth is customarily downplayed, both on film and in the scholarly literature. It contradicts the dramatic depiction of the conniving, string-pulling consultant who directs compliant, scripted clients right onto the Capitol steps or into the White House.

From my own experience, both as a candidate and a consultant, I can attest to the fact that candidates frequently resist advice—something that can cause tension within campaign decision structures. This tension is not always unhealthy, however. In many cases, candidates have both better instincts and better information. They're closer to the ground, so to speak, and often have more of a "gut" feel for the shifting mood of the electorate. What candidates mostly *do* lack, and what consultants can provide, are two qualities absolutely essential to modern campaigns: *objectivity* and *technical proficiency.* The campaign consulting business was largely created to assist politicians in the planning of strategy and the handling of communications and research techniques, all of which require specific expertise. How candidates relate to consultants, and the extent to which they follow consultants' advice, differs from campaign to campaign. It's one thing to surrender one's schedule; it's something else to surrender one's soul. When candidates blindly rely on consultants to *determine* who they are and what they stand for—as opposed to simply *presenting* who they are and what they stand for—the process is subverted and democracy is damaged.

A candidate who would do or say whatever a consultant told him or her to—especially when contrary to his or her own good sense and fundamental beliefs—would be the true conniver. After all, on election day it is the candidate's name on the ballot, not the consultant's. Campaigns advance democracy only when they accurately reflect the views of the people actually running for office and honestly inform voters about the kind of elected officials they will become. When there is a disconnect between how a candidate is *positioned* during a campaign and how an officeholder *governs* after the election, public trust is undermined. Some consultants, of course, are willing to work for any candidate no matter how weak of mind or will, just for the money. They are the exception. Most consultants would have no respect for a client who was a mindless puppet and would accordingly give him or her a wide berth. Like the voters they hope to sway, political consultants are partial to candidates with purpose and principle. They want to use their consulting skills—which they naturally regard very highly—in service of something worthwhile for the country, not to mention profitable for their business. Thus, it is not when candidates follow their own convictions and ideals that a consultant becomes frustrated—rather, it is when candidates try to micromanage tactics or base important decisions on temporary emotions.

The second misconception: Campaign consultants have uniform impact on campaigns.

General strategists, pollsters, and media consultants do not always see things the same way or speak with one voice when advising candidates. To the contrary, they often must fight one another to have an impact on strategic decisions. Sometimes internal disagreements consume campaigns. Just look at Hillary Clinton's unsuccessful 2008 presidential campaign, for example. Stories of infighting among her top command are now legend.[1]

So how do you measure the influence of consultants when one of them is telling the candidate to immediately attack the opposition, another says to wait two weeks, and a third says don't attack at all? What is the impact of conflicted counsel? Clearly, even in such fractious situations consultant teams exert influence by framing choices and arguing their respective cases. But, ultimately, the candidate or campaign manager[2] must make the call. The impact of "the consultants" on that call is difficult to measure. The reality is that more than a few candidates and office-holders do not especially trust consultants and doubt the quality of their advice. In some instances, candidates have cause for skepticism. And in others, candidates are merely reacting to unwelcome advice that challenges their own skewed notions of reality. The old adage that candidates credit their own brilliance when they win and blame consultants when they lose is based on an element of truth. But so is that other old adage, the one where *consultants* credit their own brilliance when they win and blame *candidates* when they lose.

The third misconception: All consultants are created equal.

Like butchers, bakers, and candlestick makers, consultants are not all the same. And that goes for both specialization and competence. There are generalists, and there are specialists. There are those who plot strategy, and those who implement it. There are those who sell advice, and those who sell products (software, signs, bumper stickers) and services (ad production, Web site design, photography). Moreover, as in any occupation or profession, there are the good and the bad. Some consultants have wide experience; others, not so much. Some know what they're doing; others, not a clue.

Complicating life for political scientists who study this topic is the large number of actors who assume the role of consultant on the campaign stage, even though they are not technically consultants, according to Dulio's sensible definition—"an individual or firm that provides campaign services on a fee-for-service basis during an election cycle for more than one candidate, political party, organized interest group, or initiative and referendum campaign for more than one election cycle." Campaign managers, for example, are usually full-time staff but often do the work of consultants, from providing strategic advice to editing TV spot scripts, from analyzing polling data to targeting mail pieces. In addition to campaign staff, there are others, formally and informally—volunteer fundraisers, elected officials, party officials, candidates' spouses—who overlap the consultant's role. How do we dissect these parts? How do we measure impact?

When the role and influence of campaign consultants is analyzed, there tends to be a common assumption that they serve campaigns with some measure of competence. It is evident by their track records that many consultants know what they're doing—and do it well. But there are also consultants, even in major campaigns, who don't know what they're doing and end up pulling campaigns in the wrong direction. Some of them get fired along the way. This mixed bag is not easily subject to rigorous analysis. There are quacks in campaign consulting just as there are in other occupations. How scholars judge consultants' impact on the campaigns they run—or run into the ground—is a tricky assignment.

While the best and most useful consultants give clients honest and candid advice, others simply tell candidates what they want to hear. The latter are good news merchants who underscore the view that the candidate is always right. How useful is their advice? What impact do they have on campaigns? Today, just about anybody can play the "Republican Strategist" or the "Democratic Strategist" on television, particularly on cable talk shows. But when so-called strategists hawk themselves as real consultants and sign up actual clients (even though they've never run a campaign or made a major strategic decision in a campaign), it often spells trouble. It also complicates the answer to one of the central questions posed by Dulio: By hiring consultants, do candidates tend to receive more votes than they otherwise would?

It's true that political consulting lacks many of the typical characteristics of a profession. There are no regulatory barriers to entry. There is no licensure, testing, required training, or accepted competency standards. There certainly isn't a stable career ladder that can get you where you want to go or that equitably rewards hard work, knowledge, and experience. It may be a jungle out there, but there are nevertheless implied standards that hold behavior in check. Admittedly, these yardsticks are not universally understood, even-handedly applied, consistently self-policed, or readily accessible to empirical measurement, but they are present.

Campaign ads and messages that are sloppy and deceitful speak poorly not only of the consultants who devise them but of the candidates who approve them. Additionally, there is often a political price to pay for this kind of work. True, there is no Board for the Licensing of Campaign Consultants to levy fines and penalties. Nor is there a cause of action for political malpractice. But there are, nonetheless, fierce competitive pressures, considerations of reputation, and the glare of public attention that set informal but highly important commercial and ethical boundaries. Unlike most other occupations, the routine work of consultants is subject to intense public scrutiny. Everything produced by a campaign is scanned for errors and omissions and placed under the powerful microscopes of opposition researchers. Reporters apply truth tests and pundits assess effectiveness. Despite the scrutiny, what outsiders see of how campaigns are run, especially below the presidential level, is rarely more than a glimpse. Campaigns are structured to protect and serve candidates, first and foremost. As such, public disclosures, leaks, and press reports about how campaigns operate are frequently based on self-interest, often shaded and distorted, and thereby difficult for scholars to accurately assess.

The research that Dulio cites has partially pulled back the curtain on the work of consultants. It has made some sense of how this assorted, individualistic, and inscrutable group impacts the political process. But the task of those who study campaign consultants is not an easy one. That is why fundamental questions remain unanswered, and why many of the right questions have yet to be asked. It is also why further study is needed—study that discards one-size-fits-all images and takes into account the messy truths and troublesome contradictions that Hollywood filmmakers gloss over and the Ivory Tower has yet to sort out. Good luck to those who attempt it.

---

[1]For example, see www.vanityfair.com/politics/features/2008/08/clinton200808.

[2]Campaign managers should not be considered consultants for purposes of analysis. Campaign managers are staff and, as such, work full time for one campaign. Consultants come in and out of campaigns as needed; they usually have multiple clients and operate out of their own offices.

Notes

1. Although some disagreement exists over who the first political consultants were, many observers identify Clem Whitaker and Leone Baxter as the trailblazers who established the consulting industry when they formed Campaigns, Inc., in 1933 (Mitchell 1992). Others point as far back as ancient Rome and Greece, where individuals such as Quintus Cicero provided advice to office seekers about canvassing voters and other tactics (DeVries 1989; Medvic 1997). Still others, focusing only on the United States, contend that the Federalists and Anti-Federalists could be considered the first consultants, given the types of tactics they used during the battle over ratification of the Constitution, tactics that included placement of advertisements in newspapers and get-out-the-vote efforts (Dulio 2004).

2. There are, of course, other areas in which consultants have been purported to have an impact on campaigns in the United States. Some critics claim that professional consultants are behind many of the ills plaguing U.S. elections, including increasing campaigns costs, negative advertising and campaigning, and wrestling control of campaigns away from candidates. I believe that each one of these claims can be easily refuted and have argued as much elsewhere (Dulio 2004; Dulio and Nelson 2005). I limit the present review of the literature on consultants' effects in campaigns to areas that are less clear-cut and more important to the foundations of elections.

3. Four examples of older studies are Nimmo (2001; this is a reprint of work first published in 1970), Sabato (1981), Petracca (1989), and Herrnson (1992). More recent works that use the professional moniker include Dulio (2004); Thurber and Nelson (2000); Plasser (2000); Gibson and Römmele (2001); and Farrell, Kolodny, and Medvic (2001).

4. Also of note is the International Association of Political Consultants (IAPC), which describes itself as "a professional global organization of senior political and public affairs advisers dedicated to fostering democracy throughout the world." See www .iapc.org.

5. By this, I mean that running a campaign is not equivalent to plugging numbers into a formula and getting the same answer every time. Rather, political dynamics change from race to race, and the unique elements of each dictate how a campaign is won or lost. What constitutes a successful strategy for a Republican candidate in Texas, for example, may differ from that for a Republican candidate for the same office in Massachusetts.

6. Scammell refers here to an exportable model that can be used across campaigns—the sort of knowledge that would make campaigning more science than art through widely accepted practices, strategies, and tactics. The "how-to" literature, however, "shows campaigning to be largely undeveloped in any theoretical sense and the sources of campaigners' ideas [to be] predominantly political folk wisdom. There is little evidence of any overt influence of social science research in the war room" (Scammell 1998, 269).

7. I have more to say on the division of labor in campaigns below.

8. When regulation does come to the campaign world, it leads to resistance—not only from consultants. One need look no further than the challenges to the Bipartisan Campaign Reform Act of 2002 (also known as McCain-Feingold after its chief sponsors in the U.S. Senate). This attempt to regulate was challenged by all sides of the debate (see Corrado, Mann, and Potter 2003).

9. As Grossmann noted, the Graduate School of Political Management (GSPM) at George Washington University is one of these. But there are others, including programs at Yale University, American University, the University of Florida, and the University of Akron. In addition, training programs are offered by national and state parties and by private companies such as *Politics* magazine, the trade publication for consultants.

10. Two topics *not* covered here are the internationalization of consulting and the impact of consultants in initiative and referenda campaigns, both of which have seen tremendous growth in recent years. For excellent work on the internationalization of consulting, see Johnson (2009); Bowler and Farrell (1992, 2000); Farrell (1998); Plasser (2000); Plasser and Plasser (2002); Scammell (1998); Swanson and Mancini (1996). For insights into the role of consultants in initiative and referenda campaigns, see Bowler, Donovan, and Fernandez (1996); Magleby and Patterson (1998, 2000); McCuan and Stambough (2005). Some of the work that I review also discusses the consulting industry in general and how it has grown over time; for more on these topics, see Dulio (2004); Johnson (2000, 2001, 2009); Kelley (1956); Nimmo (1970, 2001); Rosenbloom (1973); Sabato (1981); Thurber, Nelson, and Dulio (2000b).

11. For more on party resurgence, see Aldrich (1995); Menefee-Libey (2000).

12. See Herrnson (1988); Kolodny and Logan (1998).

13. See Dulio (2004); Dulio and Nelson (2005); Dulio and Thurber (2003); Kolodny and Dulio (2003).

14. I want to emphasize again that not all consultants who work in campaigns, and who produce or provide services to candidates, engage in this sort of activity. Professional consultants can be divided into several categories, for example: (1) strategist, (2) specialist, and (3) vendor (see Johnson 2000)—only some of whom participate in spreading campaign messages. The ones who do perform these duties are most often the pollster (helping to design the message that will be communicated), as well as the media consultant and direct-mail specialist. Others (fundraisers, for example) are not engaged in communication, and it would therefore be a stretch to assume that they are in a position to have a direct effect on potential voters.

15. The latter is very difficult, of course, and Mellman warns that campaigns are in trouble if they need to change minds to produce enough votes to win on election day.

16. See Druckman, Jacobs, and Ostermeier (2004); Iyengar (1987); Iyengar and Kinder (1987); Krosnick and Brannon (1993); Jacobs and Shapiro (1994); Valentino, Hutchings, and White (2002); Zaller (1992). Not surprisingly, these messages can have different effects on different people (Zaller 1992).

17. For example, see Johnson-Cartee and Copeland (1997b); Petracca (1989); Sabato (1981).

18. Even so, Stevenson could not resist the idea of using television ads during his 1952 presidential campaign (though he did refuse to appear in them).

19. This is not to say that one cannot find examples of campaign communications that were designed to manipulate, deceive, or confuse. In my experience, however, these examples are the exception rather than the rule. Unfortunately, the "routine" (nonduplicitous) work done by the vast majority of political consultants receives less attention than the relatively few instances of deceit that so trouble their critics.

20. See also Damore (2004); Petrocik, Benoit, and Hansen (2003); Abbe et al. (2003); Spiliotes and Vavreck (2002); Sulkin and Evans (2006); Sulkin, Moriarty, and Hefner (2007); Sides (2006).

21. See the issue ownership literature cited above, which details the advantages on such issues for the parties.

22. Many research projects have used surveys to provide enlightening information about how consultants view themselves and their role within the system of campaigning in the United States. These questions, however, are not the topic of the discussion here. Interested readers are encouraged to see, for example, Dulio (2004); Dulio and Nelson (2005); Kolodny (2000); Kolodny and Logan (1998); Luntz (1988); Petracca (1989); Petracca and Wierioch (1988); Swint (1998); Thurber, Nelson, and Dulio (2000b).

23. This particular study was essentially descriptive and did not involve the sort of careful multivariate analysis used in Herrnson (1992).

24. See also Medvic (2000, 2001); chapter 5 in this volume. Further complicating matters, Medvic (2001) found that the presence of consultants generally helped Democratic incumbents but not Republican incumbents.

25. See also Medvic and Lenart (1997), who found that "only pollsters significantly affected challengers' vote totals while open-seat candidates gained votes by using media and mail consultants as well" (74).

26. Visibility and effectiveness were peer-determined, based on a questionnaire administered to consultants themselves. For details regarding measurement, operationalization, and the general design of this study, see chapter 6 in Dulio (2004).

12 Scandal, Corruption, and Campaign Ethics

Beth A. Rosenson

Extramarital affairs, lying, bribery charges, and lesser conflict-of-interest scandals seem to pop up in every election season, forcing many candidates and their campaigns to devote substantial energy to minimizing the damage. In the candidate-centered context of American elections, those running for office must differentiate themselves from their opponents, in both primary and general elections, in ways that go beyond party label. One way to do so is by raising charges of corruption or other improprieties. And even if candidates themselves do not bring scandals to the attention of the media, journalists may uncover them from other sources. Because journalists consider scandals highly newsworthy, they will always be part of the electoral landscape.

Sometimes scandals take center stage. They can put an end to a campaign long before election day, as when Gary Hart withdrew from the race for the Democratic presidential nomination in 1987 after reports surfaced of an extramarital affair, or when New York governor Elliot Spitzer resigned in 2007 following revelations of his involvement with a high-priced call girl. Under such circumstances, a campaign may calculate that a scandal is simply too difficult to overcome and make the decision not to fight. Or the candidate may stay in the race but fail to garner enough votes to win.[1] In some cases, however, accused politicians are able to weather scandals that initially appear to present a substantial threat, sometimes remaining in office for decades afterwards. Ted Kennedy continued to serve as U.S. senator from Massachusetts after the 1969 Chappaquiddick incident, in which a woman who was a passenger in his car died after he drove the car off a bridge and failed to notify authorities for ten hours. Massachusetts voters reelected Kennedy enthusiastically up until his death in 2009. Similarly, Bill Clinton's job approval ratings remained high even after the Monica Lewinsky affair and the resulting impeachment proceedings in Congress. In the 1989 so-called Keating Five scandal, John McCain (along with four other senators) was investigated by the Senate Ethics Committee for improperly intervening before federal regulators on behalf of a savings-and-loan operator. McCain successfully ran for reelection and continues to represent Arizona in the Senate (Thompson 1995).

Why do scandals cause serious damage to some campaigns but not to others? Whether, and to what extent, a scandal weakens a candidate depends on a variety of factors that numerous studies have examined. These include:

- the nature and extent of the alleged offense;
- the account the candidate gives of his or her behavior;
- whether voters and the accused candidate share partisanship and policy preferences;
- how heavily voters weigh character and scandal in their overall candidate evaluation; and
- the political context in which the campaign takes place, such as the state of the economy.

Whether or not a campaign can overcome corruption charges or other scandals depends both on the actions accused (and accusing) candidates take and on how different voters interpret the candidates' actions. Citizens vary in their responses to scandal charges, for example, based on their income, partisanship, level of political involvement, gender, and race.

Examining what scholars have to say about how voters respond to scandals can help campaigns devise successful responses in the event their clients are targeted. It can also help campaigns decide, as they contemplate levying charges against their opponents, whether such attacks are likely to prove fruitful. As we will see, airing charges does not always work, while fending off charges frequently does. In this chapter, I first examine research on the aggregate effect of scandal and corruption charges on candidates' decisions to retire and on their fates in primaries and general elections. Next I consider why it is that so many accused candidates win when they do stay in the race. This involves a consideration of how different types of voters process scandal information and how scandals factor into voters' overall candidate evaluations. I then review research on the effectiveness of varying "accounts" by charged candidates (which are most and least likely to work?) and, finally, look at research on when airing scandal charges is likely to succeed and when it is likely to fall flat or even backfire. I conclude with suggestions for future research.

Scandals and Retirement

In many cases, candidates decide that it is not worth it to stay in the race and fight a scandal charge. This frequently happens because party leaders pressure the accused to withdraw to avoid a broader negative impact on the party beyond the potential fallout for the individual candidate (M. Gross 2009; Sonner and Wilcox 1999). In the U.S. Senate, members who were the subject of official ethics investigations from 1789 to 2000 often chose to resign, even when the Ethics Committee cleared them of the charges (Roberds 2003–2004). In fact, member resignation was the most common outcome of such investigations. In some cases, the senators knew they were likely to be expelled by the full chamber for their behavior, as with Harrison Williams (D-N.J.), who was found guilty in the 1981 ABSCAM bribery case and sentenced to prison. Bob Packwood (R-Ore.) resigned in 1996 rather than face the possibility of expulsion for sexual harassment and evidence tampering (Roberds 2003–2004). Similarly, a study of the U.S. House found that corruption scandals occurring between 1968 and 1990 led members in virtually every election cycle to step down (Peters and Welch 1980; Welch and Hibbing 1997).

Several studies have examined the impact of the House Bank scandal, which broke in 1991 (Groseclose and Krehbiel 1994; Jacobson and Dimock 1994; Stewart 1994). Members who were revealed to have written overdrafts on their House bank accounts (analogous to receiving an interest-free loan, which banks do not offer to ordinary citizens) were significantly more likely to retire than were other members of the House, presumably because they calculated that voters might punish them at the polls. This calculation proved to be grounded in reality. While many members who had written overdrafts did opt to run again and were reelected, involvement in the scandal contributed to both primary and general election defeats in several instances (Banducci and Karp 1994; Jacobson and Dimock 1994). The survival rate was 80 percent in the general election for members with more than one hundred overdrafts, compared with 94 percent for members with fewer overdrafts and 98 percent for members with none. In other words, those who were heavily involved in the scandal were 18 percent less likely to be reelected than those who were not involved at all. And yet, four out of five of the worst "offenders" were reelected. This last point raises the question: Why do so many politicians who are charged with scandals, including widely publicized ones, survive when they choose to fight? Was the House Bank scandal unusual? Do voters care more about other types of scandals, such as those involving adultery or bribery?

Choosing to Fight: Explaining Electoral Victory in the Face of Scandal

Research that uses quantitative methods to analyze the effects of scandal on vote totals shows that scandals clearly reduce incumbent vote percentages. This happens in both U.S. Senate (Abramowitz and Segal 1992) and U.S. House elections (Peters and Welch 1980; Welch and Hibbing 1997). Nonetheless, as with the House Bank scandal, the average vote loss for an accused incumbent is not large; most of them still win. For example, a pair of studies looking at the electoral impact of corruption charges in U.S House general elections between 1968–1978 (Peters and Welch 1980) and 1982–1990 (Welch and Hibbing 1997) showed that the accused incumbent lost on average between six and thirteen percentage points from the vote total that would have been predicted on the basis of other considerations such as prior partisan vote in the district and the number of years in office.

These two studies (the first examined 81 cases; the second, 116) identified a range of scandals that were combined under the general category of "corruption," including morals charges, bribery, minor conflicts of interest, abuse of congressional prerogatives (the franking privilege, overseas travel), and campaign finance violations. Some of the cases involved formal legal action, such as indictment or conviction, while others did not. Peters and Welch (1980), whose research focused on the 1970s, reported that some charges (for example, conflict of interest charges that did not rise to the level of bribery) had no effect on members of either party. However, Welch and Hibbing (1997) found that *every* type of charge they examined had a significant negative impact on the vote in the 1980s. For both decades, morals charges had the strongest effect of any type of corruption charge, leading in the 1970s to a 22 percent decline in the vote for an accused Democratic incumbent and a 15 percent drop for an accused Republican, and in the 1980s to a 13 percent drop in the vote total for both parties.

Both of these studies also indicated that corruption charges had the greatest impact in general, versus primary, elections. This may occur because scandals provide a greater incentive for the opposing party to field quality challengers than for the candidate's own party to mount a challenge from within. In the 1980s, one-fourth of the corruption-charged House incumbents running in the general election were defeated, compared to fewer than 3 percent of non-charged incumbents; this was roughly comparable to the 30 percent defeat rate for charged incumbents in the 1970s.[2] Democrats were punished more for corruption charges than Republicans in the 1970s; by contrast, accused Republicans paid a higher price in the 1980s, losing on average 13 percent of the vote compared with 6 percent for Democrats.[3]

Surprisingly, Welch and Hibbing (1997) discovered that corruption charges in which there was formal action, either by a court of law or the House ethics committee, were associated with a smaller vote loss than those involving no formal action. Perhaps the airing of charges in the "informal" setting provided by the media gives an accused candidate less chance to make his or her case compared with an official proceeding. Ethics committee investigations are also notoriously nonpunitive, typically letting members off with a "slap on the wrist," for example, a verbal rebuke or reprimand (Rosenson 2005). When charges are aired only in the media, however, there is no "official" censure, thereby opening up accused incumbents to a more substantial sanction—one imposed by the voters. This does not mean that formal action cannot hurt the accused, of course, especially when it involves felony indictment or conviction (for example, bribery or extortion charges). One study examined only those cases in which members of Congress were formally charged and found that indictments, convictions, and ethics committee sanctions from the 1960s through the 1980s were all highly likely to result in the electoral defeat of congressional incumbents (Kirby 1985). Even so, elected officials often are able to survive corruption charges. One reason is that incumbents accused of corruption or scandal tend to have greater than average seniority (Peters and Welch 1980; Stewart 1994). These members, who typically win by large margins, are able to withstand a 10 or even 20 percent loss of votes much better than junior colleagues who have built up less constituent goodwill over the years.

Turning to the Senate, Abramowitz and Segal (1992) looked at the effects of scandals and controversies on incumbents' vote percentages in both primary and general elections. "Scandals" were defined as allegations in the media of illegal activities (such as perjury, fraud, or an arrest for drunk driving), while "controversies" involved incidents reported by the media that raised concerns about an incumbent's honesty or judgment (such as "personal eccentricities" or "excessive foreign travel"). In primaries from 1978–1988, neither scandals nor controversies reduced incumbent vote totals once the critical factor of campaign spending was controlled for. However, in the general elections for all contested Senate races from 1974–1986, senators involved in a scandal lost an average of seven percentage points in their vote totals, with other factors held constant; controversies were associated with a loss of three percentage points.

Research on the impact of corruption charges on election outcomes has certain key limitations, most notably the fact that it is based on data that are now quite dated and apply exclusively to congressional elections. Further, these studies consider voter behavior in the aggregate, calculating the correlation between charges and overall vote totals—statistics that can tell us only so much about how individual voters process scandal charges, which voters care the most (or least) about scandals and corruption, and what factors voters weigh against corruption in arriving at their vote decision. To understand why three-quarters of accused incumbents win reelection, we need to look more closely at the individual voter's decision-making process.

Who Cares About Corruption and Scandals?

The common wisdom, for which there is some empirical support, is that certain types of voters—especially those who are wealthier and better educated—give a higher priority to the need for "clean government," and are therefore more concerned about the issue of corruption, than others (McFarland 1984; Mowry 1951). Indeed, the membership of organized good-government groups tends to be drawn primarily from the ranks of upper-class, college-educated citizens (McFarland 1984). It is not true, however, that lower-income voters are more tolerant of corruption across the board. To the contrary, these voters tend to consider activities that they perceive as "favoritism" or deal-making more corrupt than do their higher-income counterparts (Redlawsk and McCann 2005).

In exit polling of more than six thousand voters carried out in six cities during the 2000 presidential election, Redlawsk and McCann (2005) asked respondents how corrupt they believed certain activities to be. These activities were broken into two main categories: the first involved clear lawbreaking (for example, bribery or placing someone on the government payroll who did no work), while the second involved favoritism or "privileged access" to government (such as an official supporting a tax break that largely benefited his wealthy backers, or recommending an unemployed friend for a government job). There was variation in how citizens of different backgrounds reasoned about corruption. Those who were concerned about corruption-as-lawbreaking (most likely to see actions in this category as "very" corrupt) were disproportionately well-educated, higher-income, white, female, older, and politically conservative. Thus, candidates charged with lawbreaking risk alienating a larger number of voters from these demographic groups.

When it came to activities that constitute "favoritism" or privileged access to government, however, those most critical were lower-income and less-educated voters, nonwhites, women, and the elderly. While the elderly and female voters were more critical than young and male voters about *both* types of corruption, the impact of income, wealth, and race was reversed for the two categories.

This suggests that behavior seen as "just politics" by many wealthier citizens is deemed more objectionable by poorer citizens, who usually reap little benefit from such activities. A candidate accused of behavior that involves showing favoritism or granting special access is therefore likely to face stronger condemnation by a different segment of the electorate than a candidate who is charged with breaking the law.

Partisan differences also exist in how voters respond to corruption and scandal. Republicans seem to give greater weight to morality charges, presumably because they tend to be more morally conservative and because their party leaders "prime" voters to weigh moral values heavily when evaluating candidates. ("Priming" refers to the attempts by political actors, including the media, to influence the criteria that citizens use to make political evaluations; see Druckman, Jacobs, and Ostermeier 2004; also chapter 7 in this volume.) Consider, for example, the responses of voters to the 1983 congressional page scandal. The U.S. House Ethics Committee investigated two members, Daniel Crane (R-Ill.) and Gerry Studds (D-Mass.), for their involvement with seventeen-year-old pages; in the end, both members were censured by the full House (Congressional Quarterly 1992). Crane admitted to a consensual affair with a female page, apologized, and was defeated in the subsequent general election. Studds admitted to a consensual affair with a male page and a "serious error in judgment" (*Time* 1983)—and was reelected another seven times until his retirement. It seems likely that a key factor in the divergent outcomes was the differing weight attached to the morality charges by two different constituencies: one predominantly Republican and morally conservative, the other mostly Democratic, liberal, and relatively tolerant of homosexuality and illicit sexual behavior.

Less anecdotal research also shows Republicans to be at least somewhat more responsive to morality charges and to character attacks in general. In a 2002 national survey, R. Sam Garrett and his colleagues (2006) discovered that Republicans were more accepting of candidates bringing up personal issues, including charges of immorality, during a campaign. The difference was small, however, with 74 percent of Democrats and 68 percent of Republicans saying it was "clearly unacceptable" for a campaign to focus "primarily on the negative personal characteristics of an opponent, rather than on issues" (Garrett, Herrnson, and Thurber 2006, 213). The language of the survey is important to keep in mind here, since voters may be not be as put off by campaigns that focus only *partially* on the negative qualities of an opponent. For example, if a campaign devoted 90 percent of its communication to attacking the opponent on personal qualities, this could lead to voter backlash more readily than a campaign that devoted only 25 percent of its communication to such attacks.

Weighing Corruption and Scandal Against Other Factors

Beyond differences in how voters from different demographic and partisan groups perceive corruption, experimental studies and surveys show that voters in general weigh scandal and corruption charges against other factors when evaluating a candidate. Voters who have heard allegations of corruption often "trade off" those charges against, for example, a candidate's policy positions and perceived competence, or the state of the economy (Fackler and Lin 1995; McCurley and Mondak 1995; Rundquist, Strom, and Peters 1977; Sonner and Wilcox 1999; Stoker 1993; Zaller 1998). Since the era of party machines, some American politicians have managed to stay in office for years despite being perceived as untrustworthy, dishonest, and corrupt (Benson 1978; Johnston 1982). Classic examples of this are Gov. Huey Long of Louisiana and Mayor James Curley of Boston, who once was elected to the local board of aldermen while serving a prison sentence for fraud.

West and Stewart (2003) offer a "teeter-totter" model of public opinion whereby voters balance competing candidate qualities, specifically, honesty and leadership. Even officials who are widely viewed as guilty of corruption can be rated highly on job performance and retained in office, as long as their perceived leadership skills counterbalance the perceived lack of integrity. McCurley and Mondak (1995) and Mondak (1995a) arrive at much the same conclusion in their study of voters' evaluations of U.S. House incumbents: both "competence" and "integrity" influenced how voters felt about candidates and shaped their vote preference. "Competence" refers to effectiveness and ability to get the job done, while "integrity" refers to a candidate having a "moral sense of right and wrong" (McCurley and Mondak 1995, 865). These two dimensions appear to be distinct in the minds of many voters; indeed, assessments of the competency and integrity of House members from 1976–1992 were only moderately correlated (at .38; see McCurley and Mondak 1995). This means that many respondents rated members relatively high on one dimension but lower on the other.

A 2001 survey in Providence, Rhode Island, conducted shortly after city mayor Buddy Cianci was indicted on bribery and other charges, showed that only 22 percent of registered voters thought Cianci was an honest person (West and Stewart 2003). Yet 70 percent believed that he had provided strong leadership for the city. Even among those who said he was dishonest, a higher percentage rated his job performance as "good" than rated it "not so good." Clearly, voters evaluate politicians along different dimensions, and honesty and leadership are separable considerations for many. Even though women, the well-off, whites, independents, and middle-aged voters were particularly likely to think Cianci was guilty, many still rated him high on job performance. Reflecting this, assessments about his job performance were predicted by people's beliefs about his leadership and management skills, but *not* by beliefs about his honesty. Similarly, Bill Clinton maintained job approval ratings above 60 percent after the Lewinsky scandal broke, despite the fact that 58 percent of Americans believed that he was not honest or trustworthy (West and Stewart 2003). Thus, many Americans compartmentalize their evaluations of personal integrity, on the one hand, and their evaluations of competence and leadership, on the other.

One reason why Cianci and Clinton were able to maintain popular support despite being widely perceived as dishonest was that they both challenged the public prosecutors appointed to handle their cases, thereby turning the scandal (to some degree) against those who had brought the charges. This is one way that skilled "rogue" politicians can succeed in keeping the public on their side—that is, by making their prosecutors, not their personal conduct, the issue. Especially when an accused politician possesses leadership skills or a charismatic personality, combining these advantages with opponents who are politically inept can help them to weather the scandal.

More generally, voters balance a host of competing concerns against scandal or corruption charges when they evaluate candidates, trading off corruption against other qualities they may value more highly (Rundquist, Strom, and Peters 1977). In a 1972–1973 experimental study, undergraduate political science students received information about two candidates in a hypothetical congressional election. The information included the position of each candidate's party on domestic and foreign policy issues—specifically, two issues (government regulation of business and Vietnam) on which the two parties clearly differed at the time. In addition, subjects were told that one candidate had engaged in alleged illegal activities and received undue financial gain while holding a previous elected position in the state assembly. Asked to cast a ballot, students tended to choose the "corrupt" candidate if they were closer to that candidate on the issues. Unlike the machine era, when "trading" between voters and politicians involved the exchange of material goods such as jobs or housing, corrupt candidates today can engage voters in trading based on policy appeals alone, even where the policies may not have a clear material dimension.

The case of Bill Clinton provides an excellent illustration of such trading. Right after the Lewinsky scandal broke, Clinton's job performance and personal ratings both took a hit. But his job approval scores rebounded after the president delivered his State of the Union address shortly afterwards. Nearly thirty-seven million homes tuned into the broadcast to hear Clinton talk about the strong economy and emphasize his policy positions, positions with which a majority of Americans agreed (Sonner and Wilcox 1999). By the end of that week, the president's job ratings were up to about 70 percent approval, compared with 51 percent right after the Lewinsky story became public. Belief in his honesty and integrity had even risen, from 51 to 59 percent. Forty-three percent of those polled by Gallup said they were "very confident" in Clinton's abilities to carry out his duties, up from 29 percent before the speech. Throughout Clinton's trial in the Senate, both public support for his job performance and public opposition to impeachment remained strong (Sonner and Wilcox 1999).

Sonner and Wilcox (1999) and Zaller (1998) concluded that voters traded concerns about Clinton's personal integrity against other factors, especially a strong economy and his policy stands. Clinton had staked out centrist positions on issues like welfare reform, a balanced budget, crime, and the minimum wage that appealed broadly to the public. Although polls conducted during the scandal said two-thirds of the public disliked Clinton as a person, more than 60 percent said they approved of his policies (Sonner and Wilcox 1999). His State of the Union emphasized a "record of peace, prosperity, and [policy] moderation" (Zaller 1998, 185). This helped to lower the weight given to the scandal in people's minds.

Switching (or trying to switch) the focus onto policy and away from potentially damaging character charges is therefore an important option for campaigns to consider. As noted earlier, priming plays a key role here. An important lesson for accused candidates and their campaigns is that to the extent they can prime voters to give greater consideration to policy positions, past candidate accomplishments, or other positive candidate qualities, they can help defuse the power of scandal. Priming does not work equally well with all voters, of course, although this cuts two ways: campaigns' efforts to prime voters to consider factors other than scandal may fail, but so too may the efforts of campaigns seeking to prime voters to weigh a given scandal heavily in their candidate assessments.

In particular, voters' partisanship and the degree to which they care about issues (their "issue orientation") affect the way that they process scandals and the weight they attach to them in evaluating candidates. Using national survey data, Stoker (1993) examined voters' support for presidential candidate Gary Hart after news of his extramarital affair broke. The evidence confirmed the finding of other scholars that shared partisanship with voters can help a politician who is accused of wrongdoing (Chanley et al. 1994; Dimock and Jacobson 1995; Gonzales et al. 1995). From a social-psychological perspective, shared partisanship reduces social distance, and lower social distance makes it more likely that someone will give another person the benefit of the doubt or err in his or her favor (Hall and Taylor 1976; Winkler and Taylor 1979).

Stoker uncovered evidence of "partisan resistance" on the part of Democrats, which limited the extent to which moral conservatism led to decreased support for Hart. Even among Democrats who considered themselves morally conservative, attitudes toward the senator did not change much in the wake of the scandal; by contrast, morally conservative Republicans became much less supportive of Hart. This suggests that partisan attachments probably muted Democrats' reaction to the information about Hart's womanizing behavior. As Zaller (1987, 1992) and others have noted, partisanship affects the reception of certain political messages and can generate resistance to uncongenial messages. Research has shown, for example, that voters' assessments of presidential character are highly influenced by partisanship (A. Campbell et al. 1960; Converse and DePeux 1962).

But partisanship alone did not guarantee Democratic support for Hart. Among Democrats who had been for Hart before the scandal, those who did not tend to think of politics in issue-based or ideological terms, and who did not base their support on programmatic criteria, reacted very negatively to the scandal—nearly as negatively as politically conservative Republicans. But Hart supporters who had a strong issue or ideological orientation to politics reacted to the scandal by becoming even *more* supportive of Hart. Whether voters cared a lot about issues and ideology thus made a big difference in how they responded to the scandal (Stoker 1993). One could conclude that the strong positive response of issue-oriented Democrats was a rationalization of their preexisting support and an example of trading of policy against scandal.

Additional evidence that voters' responses to scandal are conditioned by their preexisting feelings toward a politician emerged from Fischle's (2000) study of public response to the Clinton-Lewinsky scandal. Fischle used a panel survey that tapped the feelings of 179 North Carolina residents toward the president before and after the scandal broke. He found that respondents' perceptions of both the credibility and importance of the allegations were biased in accord with their prior feelings toward Clinton. Specifically, citizens often engaged in "motivated reasoning," in which they processed information in a selective fashion that allowed them to arrive at "congenial" conclusions consistent with their prior beliefs. People who felt positively toward Clinton before the scandal were more likely to view it as a political conspiracy, less likely to be certain that the president had engaged in impropriety, and less likely to believe that the scandal was very damaging for the country. A typical Clinton enthusiast was 49 percent certain that the scandal was a conspiracy, only 43 percent certain the charges were true, and just 35 percent satisfied that the allegations were important. By contrast, a typical Clinton detractor was 25 percent certain that the scandal was a conspiracy, 75 percent certain that the charges were true, and 70 percent satisfied that the allegations were important.[4] Thus, prior affect or feelings powerfully shaped citizens' perceptions.

Not only do preexisting feelings, partisanship, and issue-orientation affect responses to scandal, but so does a voter's level of political involvement. Early research by Converse (1962) and McGuire (1968) indicated that the most "changeable" citizens (the ones most likely to be influenced by political messages such as scandal information) are those with a *moderate* level of political involvement. Thus, the large amount of preexisting information possessed by the highly involved makes them harder to budge, while the uninvolved do not pay enough attention even to receive new information in the first place. Later scholarship, however, suggests that the impact of involvement on response to political messages is not so simple. That is, political involvement appears to interact with partisanship to influence how people respond to scandal. The curvilinear pattern, where attitude change is highest among the moderately involved, will not apply where voters' prior attachments make them particularly receptive to a message, or where the message is "congenial" given partisan attachments (Zaller 1987, 1992). Where voters are highly involved *and* predisposed by either partisanship or ideology to accept a message, increased involvement can augment or magnify attitude change (Zaller 1987). In other words, in response to a scandal about a Democrat, among Republicans the *most* involved will exhibit the strongest negative reaction. This is what Stoker (1993) found in the Gary Hart case; by contrast, the largest negative shift for Democrats occurred among the moderately involved.

This suggests that the voters who can be most easily convinced that scandal makes a candidate unappealing are highly involved voters from the opponent's party and moderately involved voters from the candidate's own party, all else equal. Similarly, campaigns trying to mount a defense against scandal should take into account the finding that shared partisanship alone is not sufficient to generate positive responses to political messages, such as a defense of alleged wrongdoing. Shared partisanship of voters is most helpful when it interacts with a high level of political expertise, less so when voters lack such expertise (Chanley et al. 1994; Zaller 1992).

Another study found that responses to scandal also are mediated by individuals' level of political information or knowledge, with those who are more informed evaluating scandal-plagued politicians differently than those who are less informed. In an experimental test, Funk (1996) examined responses to marital infidelity and tax evasion scandals involving members of Congress. The assessment that a politician was competent did not attenuate the negative effect of tax evasion on candidate evaluations by either highly informed or poorly informed respondents. But for highly informed respondents, perceived competence reduced the negative effect of a marital infidelity charge. Funk argued that levels of political information influence the processing of scandal because more knowledgeable voters are less likely to be distracted by the media circus that frequently accompanies scandals; they are better able to filter that information out and focus on what is important to them, such as a legislator's competence. Interestingly, though, the personal "warmth" of politicians did not attenuate the effects of either type of scandal examined by Funk for either highly informed or poorly informed citizens. Politicians seen as warm, but not competent, were evaluated more negatively when they were involved in an infidelity or tax evasion scandal than non-scandal-plagued politicians. Since competence seemed to mitigate the damage of marital infidelity among the highly informed, but a candidate's warmth did not, this suggests that these voters, particularly the highly informed, place greater importance on competence than on warmth when making their overall candidate evaluations.

Making the Case in Response to Scandal: What Sorts of Accounts Work Best?

Experimental research by psychologists and political scientists suggests that the type of *account* a politician offers when charged with a transgression matters. Some accounts can help, while others may actually make the situation worse. Denying responsibility, for example, or trying to diffuse responsibility onto other actors ("It was not my fault" or "I was misled") often leads to more negative evaluations of an accused politician, compared with offering no account at all (McGraw 1991). Alternatively, accounts that emphasize the constituent-service element of an act that is being called corrupt—such as giving "special access" to campaign contributors—can sometimes have a positive impact on how voters view the politician. An example of the latter occurred in the 1980s when U.S. senator Dennis DeConcini (D-Ariz.) said that he had attempted to help savings-and-loan operator Charles Keating (see above; Thompson 1995) because Keating was a major employer in Arizona and assisting him benefited the citizens of that state. In a study by Chanley and colleagues (1994), this line of reasoning helped to mitigate negative evaluations of DeConcini among experimental subjects who were exposed to various accounts (excuses and justifications) of the alleged wrongdoing. By contrast, DeConcini's initial response, in which he denied guilt and called the Senate Ethics Committee biased against him, was received less favorably.

Related research on how politicians explain unpopular decisions suggests that, in general, justifications are more effective than excuses (McGraw 1990, 1991; McGraw, Best, and Timpone 1995). "Excuses" include pleas of ignorance or trying to pass responsibility. "Justifications" assume responsibility for a questionable act but try to redefine it in a positive way, perhaps by emphasizing future benefits to constituents from an unpopular policy vote (cast by an incumbent legislator or local official) or invoking some principle such as fairness or conscience (a male candidate who did not serve in the military during the Vietnam era confronting charges that he was a draft dodger by reference to principles of conscience and morality associated with opposition to war). In many cases, however, it is difficult if not impossible to come up with a plausible justification for alleged corruption or scandal based on principles or benefits; in those instances a candidate must, by necessity, fall back on less convincing accounts. For example, the experimental study by Chanley and colleagues (1994) looked at the effectiveness of various accounts given by U.S. senator David Durenberger (R-Minn.) when he was accused in 1988 of violating Senate limits on outside income and improperly taking reimbursement from taxpayers for living expenses. Among Durenberger's accounts were denial, invoking ignorance of the law, and offering to reimburse the Senate. There was no higher principle or clear constituent benefit from his actions to which he could refer, and, consequently, none of his actions reduced the negative impact of the charges against him.[5]

There are other types of accounts that can either mitigate the damage to a candidate's image or make matters worse. For example, if a candidate accused of scandalous behavior can convince constituents that his or her actions were unintentional, he or she may lead voters to assign less blame and generate more favorable evaluations (Gonzales et al. 1995). U.S. representative Charles Rangel (D-N.Y.) was investigated in 2008–2009 by the House Ethics Committee for failing to report $75,000 in income derived from renting his Caribbean villa on either congressional disclosure forms or state and federal tax filings. Rangel claimed that he had been unaware that income had been generated, since no checks were actually received and proceeds from the rental were credited toward paying down the congressman's mortgage rather than flowing to him directly; he also said that the developer of the property did not send annual financial statements to property owners (Lee 2008). Although the outcome of Rangel's case had not yet been determined as this chapter was being written, similar accounts have sometimes been effective for candidates in the past.

It is also important to consider a candidate's degree of political power in assessing how different accounts are likely to play with voters. For example, where candidates offer a contentious account (justifications or refusals of responsibility, as opposed to concessions), those who are perceived as powerful appear to be evaluated more favorably than their less influential counterparts. Seniority or power seems to help accused politicians weather the storm, as voters consider the value of such qualities when factoring scandal into their overall candidate evaluation. However, even relatively low-power politicians can occasionally succeed with contentious accounts in the face of scandal. Gonzales and colleagues (1995, 146), for example, found that where candidates start out making concessions but later become more defensive and contentious, they can win points for demonstrating "gumption and intestinal fortitude."[6]

Some candidates choose simply to admit wrongdoing and appeal to the compassion and understanding of their constituents. There is relatively little research on admission of guilt as a type of account, compared with the work that has been done on justifications, excuses, and denials. The limited research that exists suggests that this route can yield positive results, particularly if the media respond sympathetically to the candidate saying he knows that he did something wrong and is sorry. For example, a candidate for the California State Senate went public in 2005 to reveal an extramarital affair early in the campaign season. Analysis of the news stories that ran showed the tone of the reporting to be positive, rather than neutral or negative (Rosenson 2008). Reporters and editors covering the campaign seemed to appreciate the candidate's honesty. However, too much "sharing" by the candidate can be perceived as inappropriate, leading to a media backlash, as with South Carolina governor

Mark Sanford's 2009 press conference during which he admitted guilt over an extramarital affair and then offered in detail his feelings for his mistress.

Raising Scandal and Corruption Charges: When Does It Work Best?

The research on accounts of alleged wrongdoing focuses mainly on how a candidate should best *respond* to the charges to temper negative evaluations. What does scholarly research tell us about the candidate who initially airs, or later disseminates, such charges *against* an opponent, through direct mail, debates, or other communication with voters? Several studies suggest that airing scandal charges can fall flat or even have backlash effects against the campaigns that make them an issue (Kaid 2006; Sonner and Wilcox 1999; West and Stewart 2003; Zaller 1998). A 1996 survey, for example, found that 43 percent of respondents felt that negative campaigning featuring character attacks is unethical (Kaid, McKinney, and Tedesco 2000). Indeed, when negative campaigning is effective, it tends to work best when it centers on issues rather than on character (Kaid 2006).[7]

Even if voters do not object to the substance of a character-based attack, they may nonetheless have doubts about the credibility of a particular source, whether it is the opposing candidate, a prosecutor, a private citizen, or someone else (Rundquist, Strom, and Peters 1977; Sonner and Wilcox 1999; Zaller 1998). For example, many voters did not believe Paula Jones's claim made during the 1992 presidential campaign that she had engaged in a sexual relationship with Bill Clinton; at least in some quarters, Jones was seen as "motivated by a desire for financial gain and as a pawn in the hands of Republican activists" (Sonner and Wilcox 1999, 557). And even if voters believe the charges, they may take them less seriously if they are aired by a weak challenger or by a prosecutor who is believed to be highly partisan or overzealous. For example, 58 percent of Americans disapproved of the methods used by special prosecutor Kenneth Starr in his investigation during the Clinton-Lewinsky scandal, and 60 percent characterized the investigation as partisan (Sonner and Wilcox 1999). This hurt Starr's legitimacy and helped Clinton.[8] The public also viewed the House Republican leadership's aggressive pushing of impeachment proceedings with suspicion, and the GOP suffered for it in the 1998 midterm elections (Sonner and Wilcox 1999).

Political theorist Dennis Thompson has elaborated guidelines for when it is most justified and convincing to air information about the personal lives of politicians or their misbehavior, such as adultery or lawbreaking (Thompson 1987). Although his work is not intended as a guide for campaigns, but rather as an exercise in identifying reasons for invading politicians' privacy, it is nevertheless instructive. Thompson's basic suggestion is that it is justifiable to disclose information about actions that might be considered private when a compelling argument can be made that the particular behavior affects job performance. In other words, if a campaign can successfully make the case that a public official's behavior has already affected his or her job performance—or that it *could* do so in the future—then it is justifiable to air the charges. Voters are more likely to take those charges seriously, and not reject them, if they can see some connection to performance. And practically speaking, it helps the party airing the charges if it can sever the compartmentalization of personal integrity from competence on the job that seems to characterize the way voters evaluate politicians (McCurley and Mondak 1995).

For example, Thompson suggests that if a candidate for attorney general belongs to a country club that discriminates against African Americans, it is justifiable to make this public because the attorney general is the official charged with promoting equal protection under the law. His or her private behavior arguably affects his or her ability to do the job. It is also justifiable to publicize an intimate activity such as an affair, Thompson argues, if the affair involves abuse of office, as when U.S. representative Wayne Hays (D-Ohio) famously put his mistress on the House payroll in the 1970s even though she later admitted that she did not even know how to type. Again, it is a matter of linking personal integrity to job performance and showing that what may at first seem like a private matter actually has direct implications for the carrying out of public service.

Thompson also suggests that it is justifiable to reveal information such as a candidate's arrest for drunken driving if it can be argued that the action is a part of a *pattern* of questionable behavior, not just an isolated incident. Also, if a morality charge can be linked to a charge of hypocrisy (for example, if a candidate has ceaselessly promoted "family values" while conducting several extramarital affairs), it is justifiable to make this public since hypocrisy arguably affects future job performance; that is, if a candidate says one thing but does another, it is harder to trust that the candidate will always do what he or she promises once in office.

Directions for Future Research

We know a fair amount about the ways scandals and corruption affect candidates and their campaigns, but many questions remain. Additional research in several areas would help to illuminate the nuances of these effects, clarify whether the effects demonstrated in earlier periods still apply, and highlight the role of the media in the process of conveying scandal and corruption information to the public. For example, more experimental studies that ask people to respond to different types of accounts by candidates accused of wrongdoing would be useful in exploring what happens when a candidate offers a simple admission of guilt rather than a more complex explanation. Further, what happens when the accused candidate shows varying degrees and types of emotion (tears, anger) in answering charges? Do voters respond to the emotional component of an account, to the informational content, or to both? Does crying humanize a candidate, or does it just make that candidate appear weak? Are there differences by gender?

As noted earlier, most comprehensive aggregate-level studies of how scandal and corruption affect election outcomes use data that are decades old. Looking at more recent cases—and also at state and local candidates, not just members of Congress—is necessary to determine whether voters today evaluate certain types of charges differently than in the past. For example, do morality charges have less impact as a result of their having become a more common feature of the political landscape? Also, what sorts of scandals attract the most attention, and the most sustained attention, from the media? Which types of scandals or alleged corruption are *journalists* most or least likely to forgive? These last two questions suggest a potentially fruitful direction for new research on scandals and campaigns, specifically, what is the intermediary role of the media in explaining how scandals affect voters? Scholars need to examine more closely the quantity and tone of media coverage, as these factors will almost certainly shape the impact of a scandal on voters. For example, if the media deem a scandal to be unimportant or quash it entirely, it would seem unlikely for it to have much effect on a campaign. At the other extreme, is there a saturation point at which extended media coverage actually benefits an accused candidate?

With regard to the media's intermediary role, researchers also might look at the amount of time or space that journalists give accused candidates to state their case in their own words and see if that makes a difference. And, of course, we need to keep in mind that voters get their political information, including scandal information, from a broader range of sources than ever before. How does the information source affect voters' responses to a given incident of scandal or corruption? Does receiving information about a scandal from a "biased" outlet such as Fox News magnify voters' response relative to if the information came from a more neutral source? Finally, when does turning the tables and criticizing the media for airing scandal charges work best, and when does such a response strategy fail? Addressing these questions will help to expand our understanding of the varied and subtle effects of scandal on political campaigns.

THE POLITICAL PROFESSIONALS RESPOND

Susan B. Casey

The first lesson one learns living in the world of politicians is that every person who runs for public office is but a mere mortal. Everyone has lived a life filled with experiences, relationships, deeds, and secrets. And human frailty being what it is, somewhere along life's path most mere mortals make mistakes, cross lines they wish they hadn't crossed, fail to live up to their own or others' expectations, and sometimes do not tell the whole truth. And, sadly, modern campaigns being what they are, with the proven efficacy of opposition research and negative campaigning, it is standard political strategy to try to unearth and then use some tidbit of scandal that might undo your opponent.

If you run for high office, it is not so much *if*, but *when*. Charges of wrong-doing or personal indiscretion will surface. And when they do, the question becomes: Can the candidacy survive? Will the charge or rumor or attack ad take center stage for a day or two and then disappear? Or will it sprout legs, start running, and ultimately define the candidacy and overshadow all else? We've all seen (and some of us have experienced firsthand) campaigns hit by scandal. Sometimes a campaign rolls right on, the scandal causing barely a blip; sometimes it never recovers. What makes the difference? Why is it that some scandals derail a candidacy and others do not?

These are the nightmare-inducing questions that keep campaign practitioners awake late at night. Trying to make some sense of the impact that scandals and charges of corruption have on a politician's electoral fortunes is much more than an academic exercise. Rosenson's analysis relies on data and scholarship, and does a good job of laying out the terrain to be considered, with her focus on policy differences, partisanship, and the state of the economy, as well as the five factors that play a role in determining the impact of such charges on a candidacy. And she gets it more than partially right.

However, as I try to provide a slightly different take on the matter, totally uninformed by scholarship, I am continually drawn to the phrase, "Well, it depends." It depends first of all on what kind of scandal we are talking about, and whether the scandals or charges are violations in one's public life or sins in one's private life. It sometimes, but not always, depends on whether a crime has been committed, though the assumption that charges of illegality are always more troublesome than charges of sinfulness might be a false one.

Take the case of former U.S. representative William Jefferson (D-La.). In 2006, investigators found $90,000 in cash, nicely wrapped in aluminum foil, in his home freezer. There were even pictures to go with the story! It was enough to eventually (three years later) get Jefferson convicted of bribery, racketeering, and money laundering—but not enough, at least initially, to prevent his being reelected.[1] Then again, this was Louisiana, where former governors Huey Long and Edward Edwards and an accompanying cast of veritable outlaws thrived as elected officials. These shady characters were accepted, often celebrated, for very public unethical, immoral, and illegal behaviors that would have ended political careers anywhere but Louisiana. Or Chicago. Or Providence, Rhode Island. Or New Jersey. Or New York City. But I digress. . . .

The nature of the scandal does matter, whether or not the charge reaches the level of a crime. Charges that appear to be obscure procedural or legal technicalities (conflict of interest, bank overdrafts, influence peddling, campaign finance violations, accepting travel and gifts), or that are debatably just a shade over the line from what is generally acceptable, simply cannot be compared to charges involving sex, drugs, or rock and roll. Stained blue dresses, fake hiking trips to sneak across the border to meet your soul mate, kinky high-priced call girls, and hand signals under public toilet stalls bear little resemblance to breaches of seemingly arcane rules and regulations.

Whatever type of scandal, the impact on electoral survivability also depends on other factors. It depends, for example, on how far from accepted or expected behavior the misbehavior is. It depends on the political culture, tradition, and history of the candidate's state or community, and on voters' expectations regarding the ethics and behavior of their political leaders. It depends on the decade, reflecting ever-evolving moral standards and changing technological means for playing gotcha. It depends on the media: the intensity of its investigatory zeal and budget for same, the conflicts between journalistic styles of straight-news reportage and analytical commentary, the length of the news cycle as multiple stories are covered (sometimes including multiple scandals competing for attention), and the development of new media technologies that provide sound and images instantaneously. It depends on the amount of political money available, and on the sophistication and effectiveness of specific tactics used by opponents or independent groups in their attempt to derail an accused candidate's campaign.

In addition to all of the "it depends" considerations, the following might be good predictors of whether or not a candidacy will be able to survive scandal, especially one of the more salacious ones:

- whether or not there are pictures;
- the *ick* factor, as when some behavior crosses a barrier of accepted decency, going from simply disappointing to absolutely disgusting;

- the *hypocrisy* factor, as when the political figure appears to be guilty of applying a different standard of behavior to his or her own actions than he or she demands of others; and
- how well or badly the candidate and the campaign handle it.

Jack Germond, a highly respected reporter with the *Baltimore Sun,* covered national politics for four decades. Whatever the scandal, charge, crisis, mistake, or sin, his take was almost always the same: it didn't much matter the nature of what happened or any of the other "it depends" factors—instead, it was how the candidate and the campaign handled what happened that would make the difference in how serious the damage would be to a candidacy.

When engulfed in a major campaign scandal, it is like being hit by a tsunami. It is certainly difficult to imagine in the midst of it that one has the power to control one's fate. But Germond may be right that what comes *after* is what matters, for good or ill. Having facts on your side helps. Being able to quickly disprove a negative helps. If in your response you look like a liar, or a snake, or a hypocrite, or just plain silly, you are doomed. If you fight back, stand your ground, and are able to turn the finger on those who are after you, you may have a chance.

Sometimes scandals and crises provide an opportunity for candidates to show what they are made of, and many pass the test. They fight back, hard. They change the subject. They admit making a mistake, and that admission shows strength. They apologize to all, shouldering responsibility. They acknowledge the need to make amends. They offer another powerful narrative. They prove they can take a punch and are stronger for it, or at least not defeated by it. They show strength of character that can counterbalance whatever questions of character are being raised.

Bill Clinton survived after his team did all of these things following the Gennifer Flowers tsunami during his 1992 presidential primary campaign, from aggressive denial to admitting to problems in his marriage while at the same time providing a picture of the candidate holding hands with his wife on *60 Minutes.*[2] Clinton showed character and provided an alternative narrative, one of a fighter who could be counted on to never give up, and by so doing he provided a more compelling message and a more powerful indication of character than did the actual fact that he might (wink, wink) have strayed. He didn't pretend to be holier than thou; he may even have been a cad. But he made people believe that he would fight for them. In contrast, in 1988 Democrat Gary Hart did none of these things, and his candidacy did not survive. Hart believed it was none of anyone's damn business, but at the time didn't say so to the press. He also didn't admit making mistakes. He didn't apologize. He didn't really fight back in any meaningful way. And there were pictures.[3]

San Francisco mayor Gavin Newsom was caught in a swirl of scandal a few years ago, admitting to an affair with the wife of his top aide. I doubt that voters approved of his behavior (even though the mayor was in the process of divorcing his own wife at the time), but there were no pictures, no icky details, no hypocrisy or excuses, and the voters seemed to understand and forgive. As Sen. Dianne Feinstein (D-Calif.) said at the time, "We all make mistakes" (Marinucci 2007).

Newsom stayed on as mayor, and in 2009 was a candidate for governor until weak fundraising (not scandal) forced him out of the race.[4] I suspect that South Carolina governor Mark Sanford's admission in 2009 to an affair will not end well for him, however. Pictures matter, either real ones or the images that his own words and weird story may conjure. Sanford pretended to be hiking on the Appalachian Trail when in fact he was slinking off to Rio to be with his "soul mate." And his blubbering, too-much-information press conference left an impression that makes me want to avert my eyes each time his name is mentioned. The ick and hypocrisy factors (given his well-known advocacy of strong Christian values) might very well be his political undoing.[5]

When scandal hits, what comes after could matter a whole lot. To optimize the chance of electoral success, I would recommend the following:

- Be ready. Do opposition research on your own candidate, and have both the facts and alternative versions of the facts at your fingertips.
- Act fast. Provide information quickly and as completely as possible, but not too much and not the icky stuff (see Mark Sanford).
- Fight back. Provide alternative interpretation, alternative message about character and judgment, an alternative narrative. Minimize, obfuscate, raise doubts about the seriousness or unacceptability of the charge.
- Own up. Admit and apologize and pledge to do better.
- Move on. Don't wallow. Stop answering questions. Go back to work. Cross your fingers.

---

[1] Jefferson lost to Republican Joseph Cao in 2008; see www.cnn.com/2008/POLITICS/12/06/louisiana.congress.

[2] See www.washingtonpost.com/wp-srv/politics/special/clinton/frenzy/clinton.htm.

[3] See www.unc.edu/~pmeyer/Hart/hartarticle.html.

[4] See http://blogs.abcnews.com/george/2009/10/sf-mayor-gavin-newsom-dropping-out-of-ca-governors-race.html.

[5] A personal cost has already been paid. Sanford's wife filed for divorce in December 2009 (see Brown 2009).

Notes

1. Consider the case of former U.S. representative Phil Crane (R-Ill.), who lost his seat in 2004 after thirty-six years in office. During that campaign, the Democratic Congressional Campaign Committee sent out direct mail dubbing Crane the "junket king," with photos of the congressman on privately sponsored trips to Antigua and Scotland. Crane's acceptance of free trips from a wide range of industries with an interest in government policy might be viewed as something of a "mini-scandal"—that is, a relatively minor conflict of interest not rising to the level of a Watergate or Iran-contra. But while the scandal alone probably did not do Crane in, political analysts concluded that it contributed to his narrow loss, as Democratic challenger Melissa Bean was able to frame the scandal within a broader portrayal of the incumbent as an out-of-touch pol who had been in office too long. Combined with redistricting that left Crane with a much less conservative constituency than had been the case previously, and a lackluster effort by the candidate himself, the scandal helped propel Bean to victory. See Chase and Bush (2004); *Washington Post* (2004).

2. For the 1980s, Welch and Hibbing (1997) reported that just 4 percent of accused incumbents lost their primary, though this figure was nonetheless higher than the 1 percent primary defeat rate for nonaccused incumbents.

3. The authors fail to offer a compelling explanation for this result; while it is provocative, more research is needed to identify the mechanism by which corruption may affect one party differently than the other.

4. In this study, respondents were asked to classify their certainty about conspiracy, perceived truthfulness of the charges, and perceived importance within a specified range (for example 0–25 percent certain, 26–50 percent certain, and so on).

5. Knowing what types of accounts are plausible in the face of a particular scandal (as well as what kind of account the candidate prefers to offer) allows campaigns to assess whether or not it makes sense for a candidate to run in the first place, as Durenberger did. In some cases, even where a principle can be referenced to explain behavior, it may not resonate with the relevant constituency (for example, citing conscience as a reason for avoiding service in a district that is home to a large number of military personnel or retirees). Faced with such circumstances, the candidate may conclude that it is better to withdraw from the race altogether.

6. The case used in the experimental study by Gonzales and colleagues (1995, 146) involved a state senator accused of accepting the free use of a lobbyist's luxury condo. The fictitious senator first admitted to poor judgment and said he was sorry; later, though, he stated that he would not be influenced by the gift, said people should worry about officials who "squander the *taxpayers'* money," and suggested that many senators had received similar gifts [emphasis in original]. A real-life parallel is the case of U.S. senator David Vitter (R-La.), who issued a public apology but refused to resign from office following revelation of his involvement with a prostitution ring in Washington, D.C. When asked in a "telephone town hall conference" why he did not follow the example of former New York governor Elliot Spitzer, who resigned in 2008 under similar circumstances, Vitter insisted that "[a]nybody who looks at the two cases will see that there is an enormous difference between . . . them. The people that are trying to draw comparisons to the two cases are people who've never agreed with me on important issues like immigration and other things" (Jordan 2008). As of this writing, Vitter's political fate remained uncertain.

7. The effectiveness of negative advertising is discussed more fully in chapter 6.

8. Another example of how scandal may not gain much traction when exploited by a weak opponent is the case of U.S. representative Barney Frank (D-Mass.). In 1990, Frank was accused both of allowing his apartment to be used for prostitution by a man he had met through an ad in a gay newspaper and of using official stationery to write a letter to the man's probation officer. Although the House Ethics Committee found no evidence that Frank knew his apartment was being used for prostitution, Frank was still reprimanded by the full House (Congressional Quarterly 1992). However, the campaign that was attempting to exploit the scandal was a weak one, mounted on behalf of an opponent with little political experience and weak debating skills (in sharp contrast to the sharp-tongued incumbent). Frank won reelection with 66 percent of the vote that year, in part because voters did not seem to take the challenger's campaign very seriously. Further, as with the Clinton scandal, Frank benefited from his policy positions, which mirrored those of voters in his liberal district much more than did the positions of his conservative Republican opponent. This assessment is based on my experience as a reporter for a community newspaper in Massachusetts (the *Newton Graphic*) at the time this scandal broke. I covered the Frank campaign, including a debate with his opponent, John Soto.

13 A View From the Trenches

David B. Hill

A former university faculty colleague, now departed from the profession despite great success, frequently took delight in needling political science, describing it as the most insecure of academic disciplines. One argument that he often used to buttress his case was that we are so lacking in self-confidence about our empirical qualifications that we have to put the word "science" into our discipline's name just to reassure ourselves and others of the credibility of our work. Only a handful of our academic departments—Princeton and Virginia come to mind—are satisfied to be simply a Department of Politics. And even at those institutions, I'd be willing to bet that most faculty members self-identify as political scientists—that is, as assumed experts in the sciences of political phenomena. In the interest of consistency, my friend referred to himself simply as a "pothole counter," owing to his research agenda that tried to make systematic observations about municipal service distribution patterns in urban areas. His work was even published on more than one occasion by the *American Political Science Review,* so whether he accepted it or not, he was probably a scientist himself.

I suspect that there are many political consultants working in the trenches who share my former colleague's lack of enthusiasm for the notion that there is a science of campaign politics. By science, I mean a systematic body of knowledge that delineates cause-and-effect relationships, allowing those with such knowledge to make predictive and prescriptive declarations about political events. Some of the consultants' commentaries that appear in this volume attest to practitioners' skepticism about political science. But most consultants, armed with a little more knowledge of the history and philosophy of science, would recognize that they are closer to scientist status than they imagine. Indeed, the consultant community shares many qualities that are usually recognized as scientific. There is, for example, a systematic body of lay knowledge about campaigns and politics that seems like science, even if consultants don't describe it as such. A U.S. senator once told me that after talking with many consultants, he had concluded that their work is largely a "series of war stories."

This is a crude way of describing our current body of knowledge. Just as a panel of experienced U.S. Army master sergeants can tell you something about the science of war-fighting based on their accumulated knowledge, most political consultants can make observations about campaigning that apply across a variety of contexts and, thus, can be considered scientific.

Political consulting is also very prescriptive and predictive, as some sciences tend to be. Ask a political consultant about a particular race and there is a good chance that he or she will start saying things about what the campaign "should have done" or "should do" in the future. Consultants didn't get their reputations for being the "doctors of democracy" without justification.

Political consulting also incorporates enough systematic methodology and research to bolster its credentials as a science. Examples of experimental and quasi-experimental science are abundant in the consulting trade. Pollsters routinely split-sample two versions of a question in order to compare reactions to two related concepts, randomly assigning half their sample to version A and the other half to version B. It's a great way to decide, for example, whether to describe your candidate's latest policy white paper as "smart" or "intelligent" in campaign communications. Similarly, direct mailers do sophisticated trial tests of fundraising letters to help them decide whether a short 1–2 page version would bring in more donations than an alternative 9–10 page version. Ad-makers run two versions of an ad through dial-testing focus groups, comparing A/B versions of soundtracks, voice talents, fonts, or even camera shots. Data miners spider through news clip databases and campaign finance reports, employing complex algorithms in a search for useful "dirt" on an opponent. Media planners rely on sophisticated models and databases to make the broadest and deepest media buy, targeted at the right voters, all at the lowest possible cost. Micro-targeters explore previously undocumented relationships, such as between auto registration data and voter preferences. The systematic knowledge and high-tech methods underlying all of these efforts certainly look and feel a lot like scientific inquiry.

Political consulting also shows evidence of science in its cultivation of "community" for sharing knowledge. While some consultants are very proprietary, secretive, and even solitary and isolationist in the practice of their trade, there is a growing community of "campaign scientists" who seem drawn to publishing descriptions of their work and making systematic observations about how campaigns work. Trade magazines, postelection conferences, and even books like this one reflect a growing sense that the knowledge we have accumulated needs to be shared and tested in conversations with colleagues. That's very much what scientific communities do.

The development that most convinces me that campaign consulting is becoming a science is the number of relatively well-defined "laws" that are obeyed by the campaigning community. By law, I mean a conclusion that is validated by inductive reasoning based on repeated observation. Inside campaigns, we may not formally refer to these conclusions as laws, but they nevertheless constitute rules of the road that we tend to observe, even if our response to a stop sign is sometimes a half-hearted rolling stop rather than the full-and-complete version that statutes insist upon. Our consulting rules of the road are based on true and broadly accepted descriptions of the political world that describe cause-and-effect relationships associated with at least three distinct campaign phenomena: *political timing, prohibitions,* and *penalties.*

There are many timing rules in politics. Just as a state's statutes dictate which driver goes first if two cars arrive at the four-way stop at the same moment, politics has rules about political career starts and stops. Some laws regarding career ladders say you have to take one or another path when seeking public office. Run for local office before seeking a legislative seat or the electorate will reject your candidacy. Run for a cabinet office before running for governor to improve your prospects for election. Every state has its norms and folkways. In some states, it makes sense for a wealthy and successful business executive to start a political career running for governor. In others, this is frowned upon. Ask a local political consultant for systematic knowledge on this matter. In some states you must finish your term before seeking another, higher office. In others, it is thought best to resign to run. Carpetbagging is a similar phenomenon, with state-to-state variations in the law. An Arkansan can run for U.S. senator from New York and win, but a New Yorker could never (successfully) do the same in Arkansas. Social scientific laws are not the only ones limited by context, of course. Laws in the hard sciences suffer the same fate. Laws discovered here on Earth, for example, in the presence of gravity, are not necessarily applicable in the gravity-free environment of outer space. It's the same in politics. Laws about politics may be proven false when extrapolated to a different time and place, but they can still maintain the status of law in the proper circumstance.

Some laws describing *political* behavior are based on in-depth understanding of moral or ethical principles that shape *social* behavior. In 1996, it was "Bob Dole's turn" to be the GOP nominee for president. Republicans seem to have a profound normative sense that candidates who run and lose with some distinction should go to the front of the line in the next election. Everyone knew he would lose to Bill Clinton, and there were other choices that might have been more competitive, but Dole got the nomination in 1996 because he had previously run, albeit unsuccessfully, in 1980 and 1988, thereby putting him first in line at the next opportunity. The social scientist must be thoroughly familiar with norms like this to articulate laws that will accurately describe or predict electoral behavior that is likely to occur in similar circumstances.

Some timing laws involve campaign advertising. I once knew a candidate whose science said "no one pays attention to politics until after the World Series." He KNEW this based on prior personal observation and subsequently was devout in his assurance that earlier ads were useless. Others say that you don't advertise until Labor Day or that you advertise first, whenever that is. Some say that if your opponent advertises, you must respond in like manner (same-size ad buy) immediately or risk losing. Some say you must attack an opponent only after an attack *by* that opponent, lest you be criticized for negative campaigning. Others say you attack first to extract the greatest benefit from the volley. Ask a panel of political consultants a battery of questions about these sorts of timing issues and you may find 70–80 percent consensus, or better. Where such a high degree of consensus exists about matters of timing (or prohibitions or penalties; see below), you don't have the equivalent of the laws of physics; but when such valences exist, you certainly have something more powerful and useful than simple rules of thumb.

For many consultants, however, it must be emphasized that "campaign laws" don't hinge upon consensus among peers and colleagues. Some consultants, based simply on their own personal observations about causes and effects in campaigns, construct a set of hypotheses that harden into self-proclaimed "laws." Again, this parallels the scientific process. Charles Darwin didn't establish his laws of natural selection until he had personally observed the natural record and substantiated his hypotheses. The process of making his theory of evolution a scientific law is still not complete—some scientists still challenge it—but the process is far enough along that most biologists think of it as law. Many political beliefs are at a similar stage of progression; they have ardent advocates who say they are laws.

Using these notions about how campaign laws develop and are defined, we can also say that political consultants have laws of *prohibition*. When the topic arises, I always think of a conference I once attended in South Florida. A presumed expert on judicial races said that there was "only one thing" you could never do and still get elected judge—have a DUI conviction. Some of us in attendance had consulted for candidates for other offices that secured election in spite of having an earlier DUI, so we questioned the presenter's science. He came back strong and convinced me of the validity of his observation, at least in the case of judges. Consultants have other negative laws: you can't beat an incumbent unless you outspend him or her. Or, you can't attack a woman. Or, you can't win without a geographic or ideological base. The list is long. Again, not everyone would subscribe to these laws or rules or maxims, whatever you want to call them, but enough do agree that it's fair to use such terms indicating that there is a widespread consensus.

There are solid hypotheses regarding *penalties* (or sanctions) as well. A candidate caught in a lie or other indiscretion must apologize publicly or face consequences. A candidate who attacks first will suffer a loss of support. An attack unrebutted becomes an attacked accepted, with resulting negative consequences. Spend too much money too early in a campaign cycle and you'll suffer a lack of funds at the end when competitive resources are critical. Once you go on TV with paid advertising, you must stay on the air or risk losing whatever advantage your initial TV ads create. Fail to articulate a reason for running and your campaign will go nowhere. Fail to ask a donor for the right amount of money and you won't get the check.

These are more than summaries of conventional wisdom. They are often truisms that accurately describe predictable cause-and-effect relationships in the campaign realm. Follow the scientifically validated and tested prescriptions or risk the consequences. To be sure, there are disagreements within our community. But what science doesn't involve disagreement? The scientific furors over climate change, causes of cancer, and the origins of the universe itself are familiar reminders that even the so-called hard sciences are not completely free from disagreements and controversies.

As someone who has played roles on both sides of the line that divides political science from politics, I can say further that there are some things consultants know only dimly about politics and political consulting that are on the cusp of science, but could benefit from the sort of investigative rigor that political scientists bring to their inquiries. For this to occur, however, academic political scientists need to consider how their efforts differ from those of campaign scientists. A glimpse of this difference can be gleaned from the mind of C. S. Lewis. The Oxford don and Christian man of letters once wrote an essay, "Meditation in a Tool Shed," that distinguished between "looking at" and "looking along" something. He offered a simple example to illustrate his meaning:

> A young man meets a girl. The whole world looks different when he sees her. Her voice reminds him of something he has been trying to remember all his life, and ten minutes casual chat with her is more precious than all the

favours that all other women in the world could grant. He is, as they say, "in love." Now comes a scientist and describes this young man's experience from the outside. For him it is all an affair of the young man's genes and a recognized biological stimulus. That is the difference between looking *along* the sexual impulse and looking *at* it.

When you have got into the habit of making this distinction you will find examples of it all day long. The mathematician sits thinking, and to him it seems that he is contemplating timeless and spaceless truths about quantity. But the cerebral physiologist, if he could look inside the mathematician's head, would find nothing timeless and spaceless there—only tiny movements in the grey matter. The savage dances in ecstasy at midnight before Nyonga and feels with every muscle that his dance is helping to bring the new green crops and the spring rain and the babies. The anthropologist, observing that savage, records that he is performing a fertility ritual of the type so-and-so. . . .

As soon as you have grasped this simple distinction, it raises a question. You get one experience of a thing when you look along it and another when you look at it. Which is the "true" or "valid" experience? Which tells you most about the thing? (Lewis 1970, 212–213; emphasis in original)

Lewis's distinction seems to have some relevance to modern-day political science in its quest to better understand the electoral process. Most academics seem to be merely looking *at* campaigns and elections. Yet by looking *along* the object of their analysis, they might make unexpected progress in theory building and relationship discovery. I am not sure that either approach, by itself, gives us a superior insight into campaigns and how they work. But unless political scientists can add looking *along* to their repertoire, their understanding will necessarily remain incomplete.

The question, then, is how can one look along campaigns and elections? I would suggest several strategies. My first admonition is to move beyond the safe confines of the academy to the trenches of political conflict. In research parlance, more political scientists should become participant observers. Fortunately, in this day and age, that's not hard to do. Scholars would seldom need to take a leave of absence to see, hear, and experience the insides of a campaign. To the contrary, narcissistic political consultants have allowed their "insider" and "secret" deliberations about politics to be portrayed in theaters (as in *The War Room* and its fictional counterpart, *Primary Colors*), in books (as in Ray Strother's 2003 memoir, *Falling Up:*

How a Redneck Helped Invent Political Consulting, or most anything written by James Carville), on the Sunday television talk shows (*Meet the Press, This Week,* and *Face the Nation*), and more recently in blogs and other Web-based communications. Some skeptics might wonder whether these open, public forums provide any meaningful insight into real campaign decision making and strategy. I can enthusiastically say they do. Most consultants (to a greater degree than candidates) act pretty much the same in private as they do in public. Sure, a consultant knows there are certain politically incorrect things you can't say on television, but, for the most part, what you see is what you get.

In this regard, let me raise a topic that, while at the heart of political campaigning, is seldom rigorously investigated by political scientists. What I refer to are "talking points," the public embodiment of campaign message development and discipline.[1] The most effective campaigns are those that consistently apply their chosen talking points from start to finish. Accordingly, many hours are spent poring over polls and focus group transcripts to find the best talking points, with numerous criteria being applied to assess their possible value. For example:

- Do they energize the base of core supporters?
- Do they persuade undecided voters?
- Do they cross-pressure the opposition's supporters?
- Are they easy to understand?
- Do they build an unassailable wall of logic?
- Are they credible and believable?
- Can they be easily learned and repeated by surrogates?

I have had more than one consultant tell me that they think of elections as being like a courtroom, where voters are the jury. The campaign's talking points are analogous to the opening statement, presentation of evidence, and closing statements—and if these elements can persuade a jury, they can win an election. Some consultants believe, then, that there is a logical foundation to winning campaigns, and exploring that logic through an analysis of talking points would be something best undertaken by participant observers. Academics might worry that such an approach would produce little more than a series of idiosyncratic, qualitative case studies that could not be generalized to anything larger—a concern that obviously would have merit if the participant observer didn't use these studies as a fertile field for the propagation of new theories that could be tested through larger and more comprehensive empirical research projects of broader generalizability. However, it is just this sort of propagation that I expect to occur.

Another possible avenue for advancing campaign research is also qualitative in nature: the in-depth interview. Following almost every election cycle, I receive one or two mail or Web-based surveys from academics asking me about some aspect of the campaign process. Unfortunately, most of these surveys seem to have been written by people who never spent any time working inside real politics or campaigns. The words chosen to describe things, the syntax, the colloquialisms, and nearly everything else scream academia rather than politics. I sometimes find that the questions are so far off the mark that it is nearly impossible to fashion a response. On occasion, I have tried and tried to answer a question, only to chuck the survey into the trash because I assume that anyone who would write a question like that could never understand my answer anyway.

Rather than writing surveys, or at least prior to writing surveys, it might be useful for a researcher to do some in-depth interviews; these could even be done by telephone, if necessary. Each interview might consist of five or six general questions that could be posed during the course of interviews of perhaps thirty to forty-five minutes in length. The advantage of this format is that the researcher would encounter the natural language of the campaign participant (candidate, manager, consultant, donor, or volunteer) while having an opportunity to hear his or her questions parsed and reworded to fit the reality that he or she seeks to understand.

As with case studies, a by-product of in-depth interview encounters might be the discovery of new, testable notions about how politics works. When I changed careers from political science to political consulting, I was surprised to find a fairly robust sense of the "science" of politics (even if it was never called that) outside the academic arena. As a junior university professor, I was frequently struck by the almost impossible nature of quantifying a true knowledge and understanding of politics. In the consulting trade, however, I routinely encountered other consultants who had rendered in their minds a coherent and often detailed scientific theory of how campaigns work. Further, most of these consultants have continued to refine and validate their theories as they moved along through their professional careers.

One consultant with whom I have worked maintains that everything in an election is about likeability. Nothing else matters—not party, not money, and not issues. (I am simplifying somewhat here, obviously.) What is truly important is which candidate is most likeable. Now, you may not think winning elections could be so simple, but someone who makes his living doing campaigns believes that. It is an elegant and testable notion about politics, and, as such, it is worth examining and refining. What constitutes likeability? Are there limits to inducing competitive likeability? How does likeability trump (or reinforce) other voting factors? The questions surrounding this small theory of campaigns and election outcomes could consume a researcher's lifetime.

Skeptics may contend that the consultant's "science of politics" is too often merely anecdotal and devoid of systematic truth. My own experiences lead me to believe that more than a little reality can be found in much of what passes for conventional wisdom inside the campaigner community. There are axioms about the bloc voting of African Americans, for example, that are invariably confirmed from one campaign to the next. There are assumptions about the role of money that are proven anew in each subsequent electoral cycle. And there are rules of thumb about analyses of polls that I have seen validated time and again. But only if these rules of thumb are tested more systematically and woven into larger scientific theories—tasks more suited to political scientists, will they make significant contributions to our understanding of political behavior.

To provide some examples of campaigner notions that political scientists might help refine, let me share a few of the real-world rules of thumb about polling. There is, for example, the "what you see is what you get" rule, which has several variants. The first time I encountered it was in the South twenty-five years ago. The rule postulated that Republicans would get none of the undecided vote identified by preelection polls; thus, if the final poll showed a Republican leading 46 percent to 42 percent, with 12 percent undecided, the Republican would lose by approximately 46 percent to 54 percent. The logic here was that if historically Democratic-leaning southern voters had not decided to vote Republican a week before the election, the prospects for an eleventh-hour conversion were remote. As the South has become more Republican in its long-term partisanship, things have changed substantially. Nevertheless, the "what you see is what you get" rule has several contemporary corollaries. One of these postulates is that, in issue referenda, the final poll's "Yes" vote typically is what the "Yes" side gets on election day; in other words, the undecided vote in the final poll usually ends up voting "No" by an overwhelming margin. A similar rule holds for incumbents. That is, entrenched officeholders running for reelection seldom get much of the undecided vote. If you have not decided to reelect an incumbent a week before the election, chances are that you'll end up supporting the challenger.

Another pollster rule of thumb is that preelection polls exaggerate crossover voting. For example, preelection surveys frequently show Republican candidates getting a larger share of the African-American vote (often 15–20 percent) than they actually receive on election day. I've learned to expect 95 percent of African Americans to vote for the Democrat, no matter what the preelection polls say. This is referred to as the "coming home" principle, whereby most voters who lean toward defection for a time, earlier in the campaign, eventually return to their own partisan preference.

There are both obvious and elusive explanations for familiar informal rules like these, yet little systematic work has been done to find empirical support and theoretical foundations for those explanations. Regarding the African-American vote, we know that the early poll defectors are younger, better educated, and more affluent than Democrats who remain loyal to their party's candidate all along. Yet after some early dalliance with possibly voting Republican, why do these young, high-status blacks return to their Democratic roots? This is just one of numerous phenomena routinely observed by consultants that could benefit from the analysis of political scientists.

In general, the "looking along" research strategies I am suggesting are more qualitative than quantitative. Qualitative studies are more likely than their number-crunching counterparts to yield theory-building insights and perspectives on the nature of electoral politics. This is not to say that quantitative studies aren't useful. But until political scientists formulate smarter and more elegant theories of how campaigns and elections work, the progress of quantitative research will be limited accordingly. And where quantitative studies *are* used, they would benefit from a more direct approach to the discovery process. It seems that political scientists are trained to prefer inference and deduction over direct inquiry. For example, if an investigator seeks to understand why candidates or their consultants do certain things, they could look at their actions and infer or deduce certain conclusions; thus, if I want to know whether consultants think that early advertising is useful, I could study patterns of spending over the course of a campaign. Alternatively, and more directly, I could ask campaign decision makers when they spend their money, and why. It is just so simple, yet some researchers undoubtedly would have trouble trusting the result—perhaps because of a suspicion that they will be misled by their research subjects. Whatever the source of their misgivings, they should not be afraid of asking a direct question and getting a direct answer.

A final shortcoming of academic campaign research is that it draws so deeply on the electoral behavior literature that approaches campaigns from a voter perspective. Although it is useful to examine campaigns and elections through the prism of voter behavior, this is not always how practitioners approach the topic. It may be useful to consider an example from the world of sports to make the point here. There are numerous occasions when a losing college or professional sports program hires a new coach to turn things around. Sometimes the new coach is able to win with the same players his predecessor lost with, and sometimes he induces fans to attend games and wear certain colors when his predecessor couldn't even fill the seats, much less influence wardrobe. This is how many consultants see political campaigns. Just because Consultant A couldn't get a minority-party candidate elected in a state does not mean that Consultant B cannot do so. Even though Consultant A and Consultant B may have the same knowledge and understanding of voter behavior in a state, this doesn't mean their strategies and tactics will be identical, even for the same candidate. Coaching matters. Consultants matter. This is true even when voters and players remain the same. So merely understanding elections from a voter perspective leaves half of the equation blank.

Notes

1. I would be remiss if I failed to mention that my longtime friend at Stanford University, Shanto Iyengar, has begun to take a closer look at talking points in his study of "framing" in politics; see Iyengar (2005). In his essay, Iyengar drew on George Lakoff's *Don't Think of an Elephant!* (2004) to explore the possibilities and limitations related to a candidate's and party's ability to frame messages for voters. Lakoff developed his thoughts on this topic further in a more recent volume, *The Political Mind* (2008), as did Drew Westen in *The Political Brain* (2007).

References

Abbe, Owen G., Jay Goodliffe, Paul S. Herrnson, and Kelly D. Patterson. 2003. "Agenda setting in congressional elections: The impact of issues and campaigns on voting behavior." *Political Research Quarterly* 56: 419–430.

Abramowitz, Alan I. 1988. "Explaining Senate election outcomes." *American Political Science Review* 82: 385–403.

_____. 1991. "Incumbency, campaign spending, and the decline of competition in U.S. House elections." *Journal of Politics* 53: 34–56.

_____. 2004. "Terrorism, gay marriage, and incumbency: Explaining the Republican victory in the 2004 presidential election." *The Forum* 2(4), article 3. www.bepress.com/forum.

_____. 2008. "Forecasting the 2008 presidential election with the time-for-change model." *PS: Political Science & Politics* 41: 691–695.

Abramowitz, Alan I., and Kyle Saunders. 2005. "Why can't we just get along? The reality of a polarized America." *The Forum* 3(2), article 1. www.bepress.com/forum.

Abramowitz, Alan I., and Jeffrey A. Segal. 1986. "Determinants of the outcomes of U.S. Senate elections." *Journal of Politics* 48: 433–439.

_____. 1992. *Senate Elections.* Ann Arbor: University of Michigan Press.

Abramson, Paul R., and William Claggett. 2001. "Recruitment and political participation." *Political Research Quarterly* 54: 905–916.

Adkins, Randall E., and David A. Dulio, eds. 2010. *Cases in congressional campaigns: Incumbents playing defense.* New York: Routledge.

Ahlstrom, Sydney E. 1972. *A religious history of the American people.* New Haven: Yale University Press.

Aldrich, John A. 1995. *Why parties? The origin and transformation of political parties in America.* Chicago: University of Chicago Press.

Alexander, Brad. 2005. "Good money and bad money: Do funding sources affect electoral outcomes?" *Political Research Quarterly* 58: 353–358.

Allen, Mike. 2008. "Zogby won't duplicate poll." *Politico,* November 20. www.politico.com/news/stories/1108/15829.html.

Allsop, Dee, and Herbert F. Weisberg. 1988. "Measuring change in party identification in an election campaign." *American Journal of Political Science* 32: 996–1017.

Allswang, John M. 2000. *The initiative and referendum in California, 1898–1998.* Stanford: Stanford University Press.

Alterman, Eric. 2008. "Out of print: The death and life of the American newspaper." *The New Yorker,* March 31. www.newyorker.com/reporting/2008/03/31/080331fa_fact_alterman.

Althaus, Scott L. 2003. *Collective preferences in democratic politics: Opinion surveys and the will of the people.* New York: Cambridge University Press.

Althaus, Scott L., Peter F. Nardulli, and Daron R. Shaw. 2001. "Campaign effects on presidential voting, 1992–2000." Paper presented at the annual meeting of the American Political Science Association, August 30–September 2, San Francisco.

_____. 2002. "Candidate appearances in presidential elections, 1972–2000." *Political Communication* 19: 49–72.

Alvarez, R. Michael. 1997. *Information and elections.* Ann Arbor: University of Michigan Press.

Alvarez, R. Michael, Asa Hopkins, and Betsy Sinclair. 2010. "Mobilizing Pasadena

Democrats: Measuring the effects of partisan campaign contacts." *Journal of Politics* 72: 31–44.

American Civil Liberties Union. 2008. "Foreign intelligence surveillance act (FISA)," February 5 (press release). www.aclu.org/national-security/foreign-intelligence-surveillance-act-fisa.

American Political Science Association. 2005. "Symposium on the 2004 presidential vote forecasts." *PS: Political Science & Politics* 38: 23–40.

Ansolabehere, Stephen, and Alan Gerber. 1994. "The mismeasure of campaign spending: Evidence from the 1990 U.S. House elections." *Journal of Politics* 56: 1106–1118.

Ansolabehere, Stephen, and Shanto Iyengar. 1995. *Going negative: How political advertisements shrink and polarize the electorate.* New York: Free Press.

_____. 1996. "Can the press monitor campaign advertising?" *Harvard International Journal of Press/Politics* 1: 72–86.

Ansolabehere, Stephen D., Shanto Iyengar, and Adam Simon. 1999. "Replicating experiments using aggregate and survey data: The case of negative advertising and turnout." *American Political Science Review* 93: 901–909.

Ansolabehere, Stephen, Shanto Iyengar, Adam Simon, and Nicholas Valentino. 1994. "Does attack advertising demobilize the electorate?" *American Political Science Review* 88: 829–838.

Ansolabehere, Stephen, James M. Snyder Jr., and Charles Stewart III. 2001. "Candidate positioning in U.S. House elections." *American Journal of Political Science* 45: 136–159.

Arceneaux, Kevin. 2006. "Do campaigns help voters learn? A cross-national analysis." *British Journal of Political Science* 36: 159–173.

_____. 2007. "I'm asking for your support: The effects of personally delivered campaign messages on voting decisions and opinion formation." *Quarterly Journal of Political Science* 2: 43–65.

_____. 2008. "Can partisan cues diminish democratic accountability?" *Political Behavior* 30: 139–160.

Arceneaux, Kevin, and Robin Kolodny. 2009a. "Educating the least informed: Group endorsements in a grassroots campaign." *American Journal of Political Science* 53: 755–770.

_____. 2009b. "The effect of grassroots campaigning on issue preferences and issue salience." *Journal of Elections, Public Opinion & Parties* 19: 235–249.

Arceneaux, Kevin, Thad Kousser, and Megan Mullin. 2009. "Get out the vote by mail? Evidence from a natural/field experiment." Unpublished working paper, Social Science Research Network. http://ssrn.com/abstract=1404027.

Arceneaux, Kevin, and David W. Nickerson. 2009. "Who is mobilized to vote? A reanalysis of 11 field experiments." *American Journal of Political Science* 53: 1–16.

_____. 2010. "Comparing negative and positive campaign messages: Evidence from two field experiments." *American Politics Research* 38: 54–83.

Ashworth, S. 2006. "Campaign finance and voter welfare with entrenched incumbents." *American Political Science Review* 100: 55–68.

Associated Press. 2008. "Obama's pastor Reverend Wright says the media used him as a weapon." *New York Daily News,* November 7. www.nydailynews.com/news/politics/2008/11/07/2008–11–07_obamas_pastor_reverend_wright_says_the_m.html#ixzz00lPiEZPB.

Atkin, Charles, and Gary Heald. 1976. "Effects of political advertising." *Public Opinion Quarterly* 40: 216–228.

Austen-Smith, David. 1987. "Interest groups, campaign contributions and probabilistic voting." *Public Choice* 54: 123–139.

Bailey, Michael A., Ronald Faucheux, Paul S. Herrnson, and Clyde Wilcox, eds. 2000. *Campaigns and elections: Contemporary case studies.* Washington, D.C.: CQ Press.

Balz, Dan, and Jon Cohen. 2009. "Public option gains support: Clear majority now backs plan." *Washington Post,* October 20. www.washingtonpost.com/wp-dyn/content/article/2009/10/19/AR2009101902451.html.

Balz, Dan, and Haynes Johnson. 2009. *The battle for America 2008: The story of an extraordinary election.* New York: Viking.

Banducci, Susan A., and Jeffrey A. Karp. 1994. "Electoral consequences of scandal and reapportionment in the 1992 House elections." *American Politics Quarterly* 22: 3–26.

Bardwell, Kedron. 2005. "Reevaluating spending in gubernatorial races: Job approval as a baseline for spending effects." *Political Research Quarterly* 58: 97–105.

Bartels, Larry M. 1993. "Messages received: The political impact of media exposure." *American Political Science Review* 87: 267–285.

_____. 1996. "Uninformed votes: Information effects in presidential elections." *American Journal of Political Science* 40: 194–230.

_____. 2000. "Partisanship and voting behavior, 1952–1996." *American Journal of Political Science* 44: 35–50.

Basil, Michael, Caroline Schooler, and Byron Reeves. 1991. "Positive and negative political advertising: Effectiveness of ads and perceptions of candidates." In *Television and political advertising,* Vol. 1: *Psychological processes,* ed. Frank A. Biocca, 245–262. Hillsdale, N.J.: Lawrence Erlbaum.

Baum, Matthew A., and Tim Groeling. 2008. "New media and the polarization of American political discourse." *Political Communication* 25: 345–365.

Baumgartner, Jody C., and Jonathan S. Morris. 2006. "The *Daily Show* effect: Candidate evaluations, efficacy, and American youth." *American Politics Research* 34: 341–367.

_____. 2010. "MyFaceTube politics: Social networking Web sites and political engagement of young adults." *Social Science Computer Review* (forthcoming).

Bellantoni, Christina. 2009. "GOP surpasses Dems on Twitter." *Washington Times,* February 17. http://www3.washington times.com/news/2009/feb/17/gop-jumps-on-tech-bandwagon-to-rival-obama/print.

Bennett, Courtney. 1997. "Assessing the impact of ad watches on the strategic decision-making process: A comparative analysis of ad watches in the 1992 and 1996 presidential elections." *American Behavioral Scientist* 40: 1161–1182.

Bennett, Stephen Earl. 1996. "Know-nothings revisited again." *Political Behavior* 18: 219–233.

_____. 2003. "Is the public's ignorance of politics trivial?" *Critical Review* 15: 307–337.

Benoit, William L., Glenn J. Hansen, and Rebecca M. Verser. 2003. "A meta-analysis of the effects of viewing U.S. presidential debates." *Communication Monographs* 70: 335–350.

Benson, George C. S. 1978. *Political corruption in America.* Lexington, Mass.: D.C. Heath.

Berelson, Bernard R., Paul F. Lazarsfeld, and William N. McPhee. 1954. *Voting: A study of opinion formation in a presidential campaign.* Chicago: University of Chicago Press.

Bernstein, Carl, and Bob Woodward. 1974. *All the president's men.* New York: Simon and Schuster.

Beyle, Thad L. 1986. "The cost of becoming governor." *Journal of State Government* 59: 95–101.

Bialik, Carl. 2008. "Zogby's misleading poll of Obama voters." *Wall Street Journal,* November 20. http://blogs.wsj.com/ numbersguy/zogbys-misleading-poll-of-obama-voters-459.

Bimber, Bruce A. 1998. "The Internet and political transformation: Populism, community, and accelerated pluralism." *Polity* 31: 133–160.

Bimber, Bruce A., and Richard Davis. 2003. *Campaigning online: The Internet in U.S. elections.* New York: Oxford University Press.

Bishop, George F. 2005. *The illusion of public opinion: Fact and artifact in American public opinion polls.* Lanham, Md.: Rowman and Littlefield.

Bishop, George F., Robert W. Oldendick, and Alfred J. Tuchfarber. 1978. "The presidential debates as a device for increasing the 'rationality' of electoral behavior." In *The presidential debates: Media, electoral, and policy perspectives,* ed. George F. Bishop, Robert G. Meadow, and Marilyn Jackson-Beeck, 179–196. New York: Praeger.

Blondheim, Menahem. 1994. *News over the wires: The telegraph and the flow of public information in America, 1844–1897.* Cambridge, Mass.: Harvard University Press.

Blumenthal, Mark. 2007. "I'm competing with the margin of error." *Pollster.com,* January 31. www.pollster.com/blogs/im_competing_with_the_margin_o.php.

Blumler, Jay G., and Elihu Katz, eds. 1974. *The uses of mass communications: Current perspectives on gratifications research.* Beverly Hills, Calif.: Sage.

Boatright, Robert G. 2009. "Campaign finance in the 2008 election." In *The American Elections of 2008,* ed. Janet M. Box-Steffensmeier and Steven E. Schier, 138–160. Lanham, Md.: Rowman and Littlefield.

Boehmke, Frederick J. 2002. "The effect of direct democracy on the size and diversity of state interest group populations." *Journal of Politics* 64: 827–844.

_____. 2005. "The initiative process and interest group attention to legislative activity." Paper presented at the 2005 University of California Center for the Study of Democracy/USC-Caltech Center for the Study of Law and Politics/Initiative and Referendum Institute conference, Newport Beach, Calif.

Bohne, Maik, Alicia Kolar Prevost, and James A. Thurber. 2009. "Campaign consultants and political parties today." In *Routledge Handbook of Political Management,* ed. Dennis W. Johnson, 497–508. New York: Routledge.

Bond, Jon R., Cary Covington, and Richard Fleisher. 1985. "Explaining challenger quality in congressional elections." *Journal of Politics* 47: 510–529.

Born, Richard. 1990. "Surge and decline, negative voting, and the midterm loss phenomenon: A simultaneous choice analysis." *American Journal of Political Science* 34: 615–645.

Boudreau, Cheryl. 2009. "Closing the gap: When do cues eliminate differences between sophisticated and unsophisticated citizens?" *Journal of Politics* 71: 964–976.

Bowler, Shaun, and Todd Donovan. 1994. "Information and opinion change on ballot propositions." *Political Behavior* 16: 411–435.

_____. 1998. *Demanding choices: Opinion, voting, and direct democracy.* Ann Arbor: University of Michigan Press.

_____. 2002. "Democracy, institutions and attitudes about citizen influence on government." *British Journal of Political Science* 32: 371–390.

Bowler, Shaun, Todd Donovan, and Ken Fernandez. 1996. "The growth of the political marketing industry and the California initiative process." *European Journal of Marketing* 30: 173–185.

Bowler, Shaun, Todd Donovan, and Trudi Happ. 1992. "Ballot propositions and information costs: Direct democracy and the fatigued voter." *Western Political Quarterly* 45: 559–568.

Bowler, Shaun, and David M. Farrell. 1992. *Electoral strategies and political marketing.* New York: St. Martin's.

_____. 2000. "The internationalization of campaign consultancy." In *Campaign warriors: Political consultants in elections,* ed. James A. Thurber and Candice J. Nelson, 153–174. Washington, D.C.: Brookings Institution Press.

Box-Steffensmeier, Janet M. 1996. "A dynamic analysis of the role of war chests in campaign strategy." *American Journal of Political Science* 40: 352–371.

Brader, Ted. 2006. *Campaigning for hearts and minds: How emotional appeals in political ads work.* Chicago: University of Chicago Press.

Branton, Regina P. 2003. "Examining individual-level voting behavior on state ballot propositions." *Political Research Quarterly* 56: 367–377.

Brewer, Mark D. 2005. "The rise of partisanship and the expansion of partisan conflict within the American electorate." *Political Research Quarterly* 58: 219–229.

Brians, Craig Leonard, and Martin P. Wattenberg. 1996. "Campaign issue knowledge and salience: Comparing reception from TV commercials, TV news, and newspapers." *American Journal of Political Science* 40: 172–193.

Broder, David S. 1971. *The party's over: The failure of politics in America.* New York: Harper and Row.

_____. 1997. "Initiative fever still grips California." *Denver Post,* August 15, B7.

_____. 2000. *Democracy derailed: Initiative campaigns and the power of money.* New York: Harcourt.

Brody, Richard A., and Benjamin I. Page. 1973. "Indifference, alienation, and rational decisions: The effects of candidate evaluations on turnout and the vote." *Public Choice* 15: 1–17.

Brooks, Deborah. 2006. "The resilient voter: Moving toward closure in the debate over negative campaigning and turnout." *Journal of Politics* 68: 684–696.

Brown, Robbie. 2009. "Sanford's wife files for divorce." *New York Times,* December 11. www.nytimes.com/2009/12/12/us/12sanford.html.

Brown, Ronald E., and Monica L. Wolford. 1994. "Religious resources and African-American political action." *National Political Science Review* 4: 30–48.

Browning, Rufus P., Dale Rogers Marshall, and David H. Tabb, eds. 1997. *Racial politics in American cities,* 2nd ed. New York: Longman.

Burden, Barry C. 2004. "An alternative account of the 2004 presidential election." *The Forum* 2(4), article 2. www.bepress.com/forum.

Burton, Michael John, and Daniel M. Shea. 2003. *Campaign mode: Strategic vision in congressional elections.* Lanham, Md.: Rowman and Littlefield.

Caldeira, Gregory A., Samuel C. Patterson, and Gregory A. Markko. 1985. "The mobilization of voters in congressional elections." *Journal of Politics* 47: 490–509.

Calderone, Michael. 2009. "Limbaugh wishes Wilson hadn't apologized." *Politico,* September 10. www.politico.com/blogs/michaelcalderone/0909/Limbaugh_wishes_Wilson_hadnt_apologized.html.

Calhoun-Brown, Allison. 1996. "African American churches and political mobilization: The psychological impact of organizational resources." *Journal of Politics* 58: 935–953.

Camobreco, John F. 1998. "Preferences, fiscal policies, and the initiative process." *Journal of Politics* 60: 819–829.

Campaign Finance Institute. 2008. "Independent expenditures in the 2008 election." www.cfinst.org/federal/parties/ieDSCC.aspx.

Campbell, Angus, Philip E. Converse, Warren E. Miller, and Donald E. Stokes. 1960. *The American voter.* New York: Wiley.

Campbell, Angus, Gerald Gurin, and Warren E. Miller. 1954. *The voter decides.* Evanston: Row, Peterson.

Campbell, James E. 2000. *The American campaign: U.S. presidential campaigns and the national vote.* College Station: Texas A&M University Press.

_____. 2001a. "The referendum that didn't happen: The forecasts of the 2000 presidential election." *PS: Political Science & Politics* 34: 33–38.

_____. 2001b. "When have presidential campaigns decided election outcomes?" *American Politics Research* 29: 437–460.

_____. 2003. "The stagnation of congressional elections." In *Life after reform: When the Bipartisan Campaign Reform Act meets politics,* ed. Michael J. Malbin, 141–158. Lanham, Md.: Rowman and Littlefield.

_____. 2008. "The trial-heat forecast of the 2008 presidential vote: Performance and value considerations in an open-seat election." *PS: Political Science & Politics* 41: 697–701.

_____. 2009. "The 2008 campaign and the forecasts derailed." *PS: Political Science & Politics* 42: 19–20.

Campbell, James E., Lynna L. Cherry, and Kenneth A. Wink. 1992. "The convention bump." *American Politics Quarterly* 20: 287–307.

Campbell, James E., and James C. Garand, eds. 2000. *Before the vote: Forecasting American national elections.* Thousand Oaks, Calif.: Sage.

Campbell, James E., and Michael S. Lewis-Beck. 2008. "U.S. presidential election forecasting: An introduction." *International Journal of Forecasting* 24: 189–192.

Cao, Xiaoxia. 2008. "Political comedy shows and knowledge about primary campaigns: The moderating effects of age and education." *Mass Communication and Society* 11: 43–61.

Caplan, Bryan. 2007. *The myth of the rational voter: Why democracies choose bad policies.* Princeton: Princeton University Press.

Cappella, Joseph N., and Kathleen Hall Jamieson. 1994. "Broadcast adwatch effects." *Communication Research* 21: 342–365.

_____. 1997. *Spiral of cynicism: The press and the public good.* Oxford: Oxford University Press.

Cardy, Emily Arthur. 2005. "An experimental field study of the GOTV and persuasion effects of partisan direct mail and phone calls." *Annals of the American Academy of Political and Social Science* 601: 28–40.

Carey, James W. 2002. "American journalism on, before, and after September 11." In *Journalism after September 11,* ed. Barbie Zelizer and Stuart Allen, 71–90. New York: Routledge.

Carey, John M., Richard G. Niemi, and Lynda W. Powell. 2000. "Incumbency and the probability of reelection in state legislative elections." *Journal of Politics* 62: 671–700.

Carsey, Thomas M. 2000. *Campaign dynamics: The race for governor.* Ann Arbor: University of Michigan Press.

Center for the Study of Elections and Democracy. 2009a. "Democrats exploit newfound individual donor advantage and superior voter mobilization efforts as part of a dramatic change election," June 23 (press release). http://csed.byu.edu/Assets/Monograph%20Executive%20Summary%202008_2.pdf.

_____. 2009b. "Campaign donor survey: Women, online donors, and youth explain Obama's small donor fundraising success," June 23 (press release). http://csed.byu.edu/Assets/Donor%20Survey%20Press%20Release%202008_4.pdf.

Chadwick, Andrew. 2006. *Internet politics: States, citizens, and new communication technologies.* New York: Oxford University Press.

_____. 2007. "Digital network repertoires and organizational hybridity." *Political Communication* 24: 283–301.

_____. 2009. "Web 2.0: New challenges for the study of E-democracy in an era of informational exuberance." *I/S: Journal of Law and Policy for the Information Society* 5: 9–41.

Chaffee, Steven H., and Jack Dennis. 1979. "Presidential debates: An assessment." In *The past and future of presidential debates,* ed. Austin Ranney, 75–101. Washington, D.C.: American Enterprise Institute.

Chambers, Simone. 2001. "Constitutional referendums and democratic deliberation." In *Referendum democracy: Citizens, elites and deliberation in referendum campaigns,* ed. Matthew Mendelsohn and Andrew Parkin, 231–255. New York: Palgrave Macmillan.

Chang, Chingching. 2001. "The impacts of emotion elicited by print political advertising on candidate evaluation." *Media Psychology* 3: 91–118.

_____. 2003. "Party bias in political-advertising processing: Results from an experiment involving the 1998 Taipei mayoral election." *Journal of Advertising* 32: 55–67.

Chanley, Virginia, John L. Sullivan, Marti Hope Gonzalez, and Margaret Bull Kovera. 1994. "Lust and avarice in politics: Damage control by four politicians accused of wrongdoing (or, politics as usual)." *American Politics Quarterly* 22: 297–333.

Chase, John, and Rudolph Bush. 2004. "Junket mail spoofs Crane trips." *Chicago Tribune,* October 27, Metro Section, 3.

Chávez, Lydia. 1998. *The color bind: California's battle to end affirmative action.* Berkeley: University of California Press.

Cillizza, Chris. 2008. "Obama campaign will use six consulting 'teams.'" *Washington Post,* June 4. http://voices.washington

post.com/thefix/eye-on-2008/obama-will-use-six-consulting.html.

Citrin, Jack, Beth Reingold, and Evelyn Walters. 1990. "The 'official English' movement and the symbolic politics of language in the United States." *Western Political Quarterly* 43: 535–559.

Clinton, Joshua D., and Scott Ashworth. 2007. "Does advertising exposure affect turnout?" *Quarterly Journal of Political Science* 2: 27–41.

Clinton, Joshua D., and John S. Lapinski. 2004. "'Targeted' advertising and voter turnout: An experimental study of the 2000 presidential election." *Journal of Politics* 66: 69–96.

Clinton, Joshua D., and Andrew Owen. 2006. "An experimental investigation of advertising persuasiveness: Is impact in the eye of the beholder?" Paper presented at the 2006 annual meeting of the Canadian Political Science Association, Toronto.

Coate, Stephen. 2004a. "Pareto-improving campaign finance policy." *American Economic Review* 94: 628–655.

_____. 2004b. "Political competition with campaign contributions and informative advertising." *Journal of the European Economic Association* 2: 772–804.

Coleman, John J., and Paul F. Manna. 2000. "Congressional campaign spending and the quality of democracy." *Journal of Politics* 62: 757–789.

Colvile, Robert. 2008. "Barack Obama's grassroots campaign was unprecedented." *Telegraph.co.uk*, November 6. www.telegraph.co.uk/comment/personal-view/3563300/Barack-Obamas-grassroots-campaign-was-unprecedented.html.

Congressional Quarterly. 1992. "Congressional ethics: History, facts, and controversy." Washington D.C.: CQ Press.

Conover, Pamela Johnston, and Stanley Feldman. 1981. "The origins and meaning of liberal/conservative self-identifications." *American Journal of Political Science* 25: 617–645.

Converse, Philip E. 1962. "Information flow and the stability of partisan attitudes." *Public Opinion Quarterly* 26: 578–599.

_____. 1964. "The nature of belief systems in mass publics." In *Ideology and discontent,* ed. David E. Apter, 206–261. New York: Free Press.

_____. 1975. "Public opinion and voting behavior." In *Handbook of political science,* Vol. 4, ed. Fred I. Greenstein and Nelson W. Polsby, 75–169. Reading, Mass.: Addison-Wesley.

_____. 2000. "Assessing the capacity of mass electorates." *Annual Review of Political Science* 3: 331–353.

Converse, Philip E., and George DePeux. 1962. "Politicization of the electorate in the U.S. and France." *Public Opinion Quarterly* 26: 1–23.

Copeland, Gary W. 1983. "Activating voters in congressional elections." *Political Behavior* 5: 391–401.

Corrado, Anthony. 1996. "Elections in cyberspace: Prospects and problems." In *Elections in cyberspace: Toward a new era in American politics,* ed. Anthony Corrado and Charles M. Firestone, 1–31. Washington, D.C.: Aspen Institute.

Corrado, Anthony, Thomas E. Mann, Daniel R. Ortiz, and Trevor Potter, eds. 2005. *The new campaign finance sourcebook.* Washington, D.C.: Brookings Institution Press.

Corrado, Anthony, Thomas E. Mann, Daniel R. Ortiz, Trevor Potter, and Frank J. Sorauf, eds. 1997. *Campaign finance reform: A sourcebook.* Washington, D.C.: Brookings Institution Press.

Corrado, Anthony, Thomas E. Mann, and Trevor Potter, eds. 2003. *Inside the campaign finance battle: Court testimony on the new reforms.* Washington, D.C.: Brookings Institution Press.

Craig, Stephen C., James G. Kane, and Jason Gainous. 2005. "Issue-related learning in a gubernatorial campaign: A panel study." *Political Communication* 22: 483–503.

Craig, Stephen C., Amie Kreppel, and James G. Kane. 2001. "Public opinion and support for direct democracy: A grassroots perspective." In *Referendum democracy: Citizens, elites and deliberation in referendum campaigns,* ed. Matthew Mendelsohn and Andrew Parkin, 25–46. New York: Palgrave Macmillan.

Cronin, Thomas E. 1989. *Direct democracy: The politics of initiative, referendum, and recall.* Cambridge, Mass.: Harvard University Press.

Crotty, William J., and Gary C. Jacobson. 1980. *American parties in decline.* Boston: Little, Brown.

D'Alessio, Dave, and Mike Allen. 2000. "Media bias in presidential elections: A meta-analysis." *Journal of Communication* 50: 133–156.

Dalton, Russell J. 1984. "Cognitive mobilization and partisan dealignment in advanced industrial democracies." *Journal of Politics* 46: 264–284.

———. 2008. *Citizen politics: Public opinion and political parties in advanced industrial democracies,* 5th ed. Washington, D.C.: CQ Press.

Damore, David F. 2004. "The dynamics of issue ownership in presidential campaigns." *Political Research Quarterly* 57: 391–397.

Dao, James. 2004. "Same-sex marriage issue key to some GOP races." *New York Times,* November 4, A4.

Davis, Richard, Jody C. Baumgartner, Peter L. Francia, and Jonathan S. Morris. 2008. "The Internet in U.S. election campaigns." In *Routledge Handbook of Internet Politics,* ed. Andrew Chadwick and Philip N. Howard, 13–24. New York: Routledge.

Dawson, Michael C., Ronald E. Brown, and Richard L. Allen. 1990. "Racial belief systems, religious guidance, and African-American political participation." *National Political Science Review* 2: 22–44.

Delli Carpini, Michael X., and Scott Keeter. 1996. *What Americans know about politics and why it matters.* New Haven: Yale University Press.

Devitt, James. 1997. "Framing politicians: The transformation of candidate arguments in presidential campaign news coverage, 1980, 1988, 1992, and 1996." *American Behavioral Scientist* 40: 1139–1160.

Devlin, L. Patrick. 1989. "Contrasts in presidential campaign commercials of 1988." *American Behavioral Scientist* 32: 389–414.

DeVries, Walter. 1989. "American campaign consulting: Trends and concerns." *PS: Political Science & Politics* 22: 21–25.

DeVries, Walter, and Lance Tarrance Jr. 1972. *The ticket-splitter: A new force in American politics.* Grand Rapids, Mich.: Eerdmans.

Dewey, John. 1927. *The public and its problems.* New York: Holt.

DiClerico, Robert E. 2000. *Political parties, campaigns, and elections.* Upper Saddle River, N.J.: Prentice Hall.

DiMaggio, Paul, Eszter Hargittai, W. Russell Neuman, and John P. Robinson. 2001. "Social implications of the Internet." *Annual Review of Sociology* 27: 307–336.

Dimock, Michael A., April Clark, and Juliana Menasce Horowitz. 2008. "Campaign dynamics and the swing vote in the 2004 election." In *The swing voter in American politics,* ed. William G. Mayer, 58–74. Washington, D.C.: Brookings Institution Press.

Dimock, Michael A., and Gary C. Jacobson. 1995. "Checks and choices: The House bank scandal's impact on voters in 1992." *Journal of Politics* 57: 1143–1159.

Djupe, Paul A., and David A. M. Peterson. 2002. "The impact of negative campaigning: Evidence from the 1998 senatorial primaries." *Political Research Quarterly* 55: 845–860.

Donovan, Todd, Christopher Z. Mooney, and Daniel A. Smith. 2009. *State and local politics: Institutions and reform.* Belmont, Calif.: Cengage Learning Wadsworth.

Donovan, Todd, and Joseph R. Snipp. 1994. "Support for legislative term limitations in California: Group representation, partisanship, and campaign information." *Journal of Politics* 56: 492–501.

Donovan, Todd, Caroline J. Tolbert, and Daniel A. Smith. 2008. "Priming presidential votes by direct democracy." *Journal of Politics* 70: 1217–1231.

———. 2009. "Political engagement, mobilization, and direct democracy." *Public Opinion Quarterly* 73: 98–118.

Dow, Jay K. 2009. "Gender differences in political knowledge: Distinguishing characteristics-based and returns-based differences." *Political Behavior* 31: 117–136.

Downs, Anthony. 1957. *An economic theory of democracy.* New York: Harper.

Druckman, James N. 2004. "Priming the vote: Campaign effects in a U.S. Senate election." *Political Psychology* 25: 577–594.

Druckman, James N., Lawrence R. Jacobs, and Eric Ostermeier. 2004. "Candidate strategies to prime issues and image." *Journal of Politics* 66: 1180–1202.

Druckman, James N., Martin J. Kifer, and Michael Parkin. 2007. "The technological development of congressional candidate Web sites: How and why candidates use Web innovations." *Social Science Computer Review* 25: 425–442.

———. 2009a. "Campaign communications in U.S. congressional elections." *American Political Science Review* 103: 343–366.

———. 2009b. "Timeless strategy meets new medium: Going negative on congressional campaign websites, 2002–2006." Paper presented at the 2009 annual meeting of the American Political Science Association, Toronto.

Duch, Raymond M., Harvey D. Palmer, and Christopher J. Anderson. 2000. "Heterogeneity in perceptions of national economic conditions." *American Journal of Political Science* 44: 635–652.

Dulio, David A. 2004. *For better or worse? How political consultants are changing elections in America.* Albany: State University of New York Press.

Dulio, David A., and Candice J. Nelson. 2005. *Vital signs: Perspectives on the health of American campaigning.* Washington, D.C.: Brookings Institution Press.

Dulio, David A., and James A. Thurber. 2003. "The symbiotic relationship between political parties and political consultants: Partners past, present, and future." In *The state of the parties: The changing role of contemporary American parties,* 4th ed., ed. John C. Green and Rick Farmer, 215–224. Lanham, Md.: Rowman and Littlefield.

Dyck, Joshua J. 2009. "Initiated distrust: Direct democracy and trust in government." *American Politics Research* 37: 539–568.

Dyck, Joshua J., and Edward L. Lascher Jr. 2009. "Direct democracy and political efficacy reconsidered." *Political Behavior* 31: 401–427.

Eldersveld, Samuel J. 1956. "Experimental propaganda techniques and voting behavior." *American Political Science Review* 50: 154–165.

Eldersveld, Samuel J., and Richard W. Dodge. 1954. "Personal contact or mail propaganda? An experiment in voting turnout and attitude changes." In *Public opinion and propaganda: A book of readings,* ed. Daniel Katz, Dorwin Cartwright, Samuel Eldersveld, and Alfred M. Lee, 532–542. New York: Dryden.

Elliot, Philip. 2009. "Rep. Wilson: No second apology for 'You lie' words." *San Francisco Chronicle,* September 13. www.sfgate.com/cgi-bin/article.cgi?f=/n/a/2009/09/10/national/a134748D31.DTL.

Ellis, Richard J. 2002. *Democratic delusions: The initiative process in America.* Lawrence: University Press of Kansas.

Entman, Robert M. 1993. "Framing: Toward clarification of a fractured paradigm." *Journal of Communication* 43: 51–58.

Erickson, Stephanie. 2003. "Wage issue could shape vote." *Orlando Sentinel,* September 22, B1.

Erikson, Robert S., and Thomas R. Palfrey. 1998. "Campaign spending and incumbency: An alternative simultaneous equations approach." *Journal of Politics* 60: 355–373.

———. 2000. "Equilibria in campaign spending games: Theory and data." *American Political Science Review* 94: 595–609.

Everson, David H. 1981. "The effects of initiatives on voter turnout: A comparative state analysis." *Western Political Quarterly* 34: 415–425.

Faber, Ronald J., and M. Claire Storey. 1984. "Recall of information from political advertising." *Journal of Advertising* 13: 39–44.

Fackler, Tim, and Tse-min Lin. 1995. "Political corruption and presidential elections, 1929–1992." *Journal of Politics* 57: 971–993.

Fallows, James. 1996. *Breaking the news: How the media undermine American democracy.* New York: Pantheon.

Farrell, David M. 1996. "Campaign strategies and tactics." In *Comparing democracies: Elections and voting in global perspective,* ed. Lawrence LeDuc, Richard G. Niemi, and Pippa Norris, 158–181. Thousand Oaks, Calif.: Sage.

——. 1998. "Political consultancy overseas: The internationalization of campaign consultancy." *PS: Political Science & Politics* 31: 171–178.

Farrell, David M., Robin Kolodny, and Stephen Medvic. 2001. "Parties and campaign professionals in a digital age: Political consultants in the United States and their counterparts overseas." *Harvard International Journal of Press/ Politics* 6: 11–30.

Farrell, Henry, and Daniel W. Drezner. 2008. "The power and politics of blogs." *Public Choice* 134: 15–30.

Finkel, Steven E. 1993. "Reexamining the 'minimal effects' model in recent presidential campaigns." *Journal of Politics* 55: 1–21.

Finkel, Steven E., and John G. Geer. 1998. "A spot check: Casting doubt on the demobilizing effect of attack advertising." *American Journal of Political Science* 42: 573–595.

Fiorina, Morris P. 1981. *Retrospective voting in American national elections.* New Haven: Yale University Press.

——. 2002. "Parties and partisanship: A 40-year retrospective." *Political Behavior* 24: 93–115.

Fischle, Mark. 2000. "Mass response to the Lewinsky scandal: Motivated reasoning or Bayesian updating?" *Political Psychology* 21: 135–159.

Fisher, Dana R. 2006. *Activism, inc.: How the outsourcing of grassroots campaigns is strangling progressive politics in America.* Stanford: Stanford University Press.

——. 2008. "From the bottom-up: Using the internet to mobilize campaign participation." Published by the Publius Project at the Berkman Center for Internet & Society at Harvard University, December 10. http://publius.cc.

——. 2009. "Harnessing technology to mobilize the ground war." Paper presented at the 2009 annual meeting of the American Sociological Association, San Francisco.

Fitzgerald, Mary. 2008. "Two Davids behind Obama's Goliath of a campaign." *Irish Times,* November 7. www.irishtimes .com/newspaper/opinion/2008/1107/ 1225925540012.html.

Fox News. 2009. "Obama 'green jobs' adviser Van Jones resigns amid controversy." *FoxNews.com,* September 6. www.fox news.com/politics/elections/2009/09/06/ obama-green-jobs-adviser-van-jones-resigns-amid-controversy.

Franklin, Charles H. 1991. "Eschewing obfuscation? Campaigns and the perception of U.S. Senate incumbents." *American Political Science Review* 85: 1193–1214.

Frantzich, Stephen. 2002. "Watching the watchers." *Harvard International Journal of Press/Politics* 7: 34–57.

Franz, Michael M. 2008. *Choices and changes: Interest groups in the electoral process.* Philadelphia: Temple University Press.

Franz, Michael M., and Travis N. Ridout. 2007. "Does political advertising persuade?" *Political Behavior* 29: 465–491.

——. 2010. "Political advertising and persuasion in the 2004 and 2008 presidential elections." *American Politics Research* 38 (2): 303–329.

Franz, Michael M., Paul B. Freedman, Kenneth M. Goldstein, and Travis N. Ridout. 2008a. *Campaign advertising and American democracy.* Philadelphia: Temple University Press.

——. 2008b. "Understanding the effect of political ads on voter turnout: A response to Krasno and Green." *Journal of Politics* 70: 262–268.

Frazier, E. Franklin. 1963. *The Negro church in America.* New York: Shocken Books.

Freedman, Paul, Michael Franz, and Kenneth Goldstein. 2004. "Campaign advertising and democratic citizenship." *American Journal of Political Science* 48: 723–741.

Freedman, Paul, and Ken Goldstein. 1999. "Measuring media exposure and the effects of negative campaign ads." *American Journal of Political Science* 43: 1189–1208.

Freeman, Jo. 1986. "The political culture of the Democratic and Republican parties." *Political Science Quarterly* 101: 327–356.

Freidson, Eliot. 2001. *Professionalism, the third logic: On the practice of knowledge.* Chicago: University of Chicago Press.

Fridkin, Kim L., and Patrick J. Kenney. 2004. "Do negative messages work? The impact of negativity on citizens' evaluations of candidates." *American Politics Research* 32: 570–605.

———. 2008. "The dimensions of negative messages." *American Politics Research* 36: 694–723.

Fridkin, Kim L., Patrick J. Kenney, Sarah Allen Gershon, Karen Shafer, and Gina Serignese Woodall. 2007. "Capturing the power of a campaign event: The 2004 presidential debate in Tempe." *Journal of Politics* 69: 770–785.

Fritz, Sara, and Dwight Morris. 1992. *Handbook of campaign spending: Money in the 1990 congressional races.* Washington, D.C.: CQ Press.

Fulk, Elizabeth. 2004. "State ballot initiatives may play large role in '04 elections; candidates ignore them 'at their own peril,' pollster says." *The Hill,* September 23. http://thehill.com/homenews/news/10979-state-ballot-initiatives-may-play-large-role-in-04-elections.

Funk, Carolyn L. 1996. "The impact of scandal on candidate evaluations: An experimental test of the role of candidate traits." *Political Behavior* 18: 1–24.

———. 1997. "Implications of political expertise in candidate trait evaluations." *Political Research Quarterly* 50: 675–697.

Gallup, George. 1977. "Support for Panama treaties increases with knowledge." *Gallup Report,* October 23 (press release). www.jimmycarterlibrary.org/documents/panama/document11.pdf.

Galston, William A. 2001. "Political knowledge, political engagement, and civic education." *Annual Review of Political Science* 4: 217–234.

Gamble, Barbara S. 1997. "Putting civil rights to a popular vote." *American Journal of Political Science* 41: 245–269.

Ganz, Marshall. 2009. "Organizing Obama: Campaign, organizing, movement." Paper presented at the 2009 annual meeting of the American Sociological Association, San Francisco.

Garramone, Gina M. 1984. "Voter responses to negative political ads." *Journalism Quarterly* 61: 250–259.

———. 1985. "Effects of negative political advertising: The roles of sponsor and rebuttal." *Journal of Broadcasting and Electronic Media* 29: 147–159.

Garrett, Elizabeth. 2004. "Democracy in the wake of the California recall." *University of Pennsylvania Law Review* 153: 239–284.

Garrett, Elizabeth, and Daniel A. Smith. 2005. "Veiled political actors and campaign disclosure laws in direct democracy." *Election Law Journal* 4: 295–328.

Garrett, R. Sam. 2009. *Campaign crises: Detours on the road to Congress.* Boulder, Colo.: Lynne Rienner.

Garrett, R. Sam, Paul S. Herrnson, and James A. Thurber. 2006. "Perspectives on Campaign Ethics." In *The Electoral Challenge: Theory Meets Practice,* ed. Stephen C. Craig, 203–225.

Gartner Newsroom. 2009. "Gartner says newspaper publishers are not doing enough to take advantage of the social power of their readers." *Gartner.com,* March 25. www.gartner.com/it/page.jsp?id=919612.

Geer, John G. 1988. "The effects of presidential debates on the electorate's preferences for candidates." *American Politics Quarterly* 16: 486–501.

———. 1998. "Campaigns, party competition, and political advertising." In *Politicians and party politics,* ed. John G. Geer, 186–217. Baltimore: Johns Hopkins University Press.

———. 2000. "Assessing attack advertising: A silver lining." In *Campaign reform: Insights and evidence,* ed. Larry M. Bartels and Lynn Vavrek, 62–78. Ann Arbor: University of Michigan Press.

———. 2006. *In defense of negativity: Attack ads in presidential campaigns.* Chicago: University of Chicago Press.

Geer, John G., and James H. Geer. 2003. "Remembering attack ads: An experimental investigation of radio." *Political Behavior* 25: 69–95.

Geer, John G., and Richard R. Lau. 2005. "Filling in the blanks: A new method for estimating campaign effects." *British Journal of Political Science* 36: 269–290.

Geiger, Seth F., and Byron Reeves. 1991. "The effects of visual structure and content emphasis on the evaluation and memory for political candidates." In *Television and political advertising,* Vol. 1: *Psychological processes,* ed. Frank Biocca, 125–143. Hillsdale, N.J.: Lawrence Erlbaum.

Gelman, Andrew, and Gary King. 1993. "Why are American presidential election campaign polls so variable when votes are so predictable?" *British Journal of Political Science* 23: 409–451.

Gerber, Alan S. 1998. "Estimating the effect of campaign spending on Senate election outcomes using instrumental variables." *American Political Science Review* 92: 401–411.

Gerber, Alan S., and Donald P. Green. 2000a. "The effect of a nonpartisan get-out-the-vote drive: An experimental study of leafletting." *Journal of Politics* 62: 846–857.

———. 2000b. "The effects of canvassing, telephone calls, and direct mail on voter turnout: A field experiment." *American Political Science Review* 94: 653–663.

———. 2001. "Do phone calls increase voter turnout? A field experiment." *Public Opinion Quarterly* 65: 75–85.

———. 2005. "Do phone calls increase voter turnout? An update." *Annals of the American Academy of Political and Social Science* 601: 142–154.

Gerber, Alan S., Donald P. Green, and Matthew N. Green. 2003. "Partisan mail and voter turnout: Results from randomized field experiments." *Electoral Studies* 22: 563–579.

Gerber, Elisabeth R. 1996. "Legislative response to the threat of popular initiatives." *American Journal of Political Science* 40: 99–128.

———. 1999. *The populist paradox: Interest group influence and the promise of direct legislation.* Princeton: Princeton University Press.

Gerber, Elisabeth R., and Arthur Lupia. 1995. "Campaign competition and policy responsiveness in direct legislation elections." *Political Behavior* 17: 287–306.

Gerber, Elisabeth R., Arthur Lupia, Mathew D. McCubbins, and D. Roderick Kiewiet. 2001. *Stealing the initiative: How state government responds to direct democracy.* Upper Saddle River, N.J.: Prentice Hall.

Gershtenson, Joseph. 2003. "Mobilization strategies of the Democrats and Republicans, 1956–2000." *Political Research Quarterly* 56: 293–308.

Gertner, Jon. 2004. "The very, very personal is the political." *New York Times,* February 15. www.nytimes.com/2004/02/15/magazine/15VOTERS.html.

Gibson, Rachel K., and Andrea Römmele. 2001. "Changing campaign communications: A party-centered theory of professionalized campaigning." *Harvard International Journal of Press/Politics* 6: 31–43.

Gierzynski, Anthony, and David A. Breaux. 1993. "Money and the party vote in state House elections." *Legislative Studies Quarterly* 18: 515–533.

Gierzynski, Anthony, Paul Kleppner, and James Lewis. 1998. "Money or the machine: Money and votes in Chicago aldermanic elections." *American Politics Quarterly* 26: 160–173.

Gilens, Martin. 2001. "Political ignorance and collective policy preferences." *American Political Science Review* 95: 379–396.

Gimpel, James G., Karen M. Kaufmann, and Shanna Pearson-Merkowitz. 2007. "Battleground states versus blackout states: The behavioral implications of modern presidential campaigns." *Journal of Politics* 69: 786–797.

Glantz, Stanton A., Alan I. Abramowitz, and Michael P. Burkart. 1976. "Elections outcomes: Whose money matters?" *Journal of Politics* 38: 1033–1038.

Godbout, Jean-François, and Éric Bélanger. 2007. "Economic voting and political sophistication in the United States: A reassessment." *Political Research Quarterly* 60: 541–554.

Godwin, R. Kenneth. 1988. *One billion dollars of influence: The direct marketing of politics.* Chatham, N.J.: Chatham House.

Goidel, Robert K., and Donald A. Gross. 1994. "A systems approach to campaign finance in U.S. House elections." *American Politics Quarterly* 22: 125–153.

Goidel, Robert K., Donald A. Gross, and Todd G. Shields. 1999. *Money matters: Consequences of campaign finance reform in U.S. House elections.* Lanham, Md.: Rowman and Littlefield.

Golan, Guy, and Wayne Wanta. 2001. "Second-level agenda setting in the New Hampshire primary: A comparison of coverage in three newspapers and public perceptions of candidates." *Journalism and Mass Communication Quarterly* 78: 247–259.

Goldenberg, Edie N., Michael W. Traugott, and Frank R. Baumgartner. 1986. "Preemptive and reactive spending in U.S. House races." *Political Behavior* 8: 3–20.

Goldman, Julianna, and Michael Tackett. 2008. "Obama sealed win by taking biggest risks, making fewest errors." *Bloomberg.com,* November 4. www .bloomberg.com/apps/news?pid= 20601087&refer=home&sid=ac CoBJXeBvU8.

Goldstein, Kenneth M. 2004. "What did they see and when did they see it: Measuring the volume, tone, and targeting of television advertising in the 2000 presidential election." In *The medium and the message: Television advertising and American elections,* ed. Kenneth M. Goldstein and Patricia Strach, 27–42. Upper Saddle River, N.J.: Prentice Hall.

Goldstein, Kenneth M., and Paul Freedman. 2000. "New evidence for new arguments: Money and advertising in the 1996 Senate elections." *Journal of Politics* 62: 1087–1108.

_____. 2002a. "Campaign advertising and voter turnout: New evidence for a stimulation effect." *Journal of Politics* 64: 721–740.

_____. 2002b. "Lessons learned: Campaign advertising in the 2000 elections." *Political Communication* 19: 5–28.

Goldstein, Kenneth M., and Travis N. Ridout. 2002. "The politics of participation: Mobilization and turnout over time." *Political Behavior* 24: 3–29.

Gomez, Brad T., and J. Matthew Wilson. 2003. "Causal attribution and economic voting in American congressional elections." *Political Research Quarterly* 56: 271–282.

_____. 2006. "Cognitive heterogeneity and economic voting: A comparative analysis of four democratic electorates." *American Journal of Political Science* 50: 127–145.

Gonzales, Marti Hope, Margaret Bull Kovera, John L. Sullivan, and Virginia Chanley. 1995. "Private reactions to public transgressions: Predictors of evaluative responses to allegations of political misconduct." *Personality and Social Psychology Bulletin* 21: 136–148.

Goodliffe, Jay. 2001. "The effect of war chests on challenger entry in U.S. House elections." *American Journal of Political Science* 45: 830–844.

_____. 2004. "War chests as precautionary savings." *Political Behavior* 26: 289–315.

Goren, Paul. 1997. "Political expertise and issue voting in presidential elections." *Political Research Quarterly* 50: 387–412.

Gosnell, Harold F. 1926. "An experiment in the stimulation of voting." *American Political Science Review* 20: 869–874.

_____. 1927. *Getting out the vote: An experiment in the stimulation of voting.* Chicago: University of Chicago Press.

_____. 1948. *Democracy: The threshold of freedom.* New York: Ronald Press.

_____. 1950. "Does campaigning make a difference?" *Public Opinion Quarterly* 14: 413–418.

_____. 1968 [1938]. *Machine politics: Chicago model.* Chicago: University of Chicago Press.

Goss, Kristin A., and Michael T. Heaney. 2010. "Organizing women *as women:* Hybridity and grassroots collective action in the 21st century." *Perspectives on Politics* 8: 27–52.

Graber, Doris A. 1987. "Framing election news broadcasts: News context and its

impact on the 1984 presidential election."
Social Science Quarterly 68: 552–568.

———. 1993. *Mass media and American politics*, 4th ed. Washington, D.C.: CQ Press.

———. 2001. *Processing politics: Learning from television in the Internet age.* Chicago: University of Chicago Press.

———. 2010. *Mass media and American politics*, 8th ed. Washington, D.C.: CQ Press.

Grace, Francie. 2006. "Simpsons outpace U.S. Constitution." *CBSNews.com*, March 1. www.cbsnews.com/stories/2006/03/01/politics/main1356854.shtml.

Grafstein, Robert. 2009. "The puzzle of weak pocketbook voting." *Journal of Theoretical Politics* 21: 451–482.

Green, Donald P. 2004. "Mobilizing African-American voters using direct mail and commercial phone banks: A field experiment." *Political Research Quarterly* 57: 245–255.

Green, Donald P., and Alan S. Gerber. 2008. *Get out the vote! How to increase voter turnout,* 2nd ed. Washington, D.C.: Brookings Institution Press.

Green, Donald P., Alan S. Gerber, and David W. Nickerson. 2003. "Getting out the vote in local elections: Results from six door-to-door canvassing experiments." *Journal of Politics* 65: 1083–1096.

Green, Donald Philip, and Jonathan S. Krasno. 1988. "Salvation for the spendthrift incumbent: Reestimating the effects of campaign spending in House elections." *American Journal of Political Science* 32: 884–907.

———. 1990. "Rebuttal to Jacobson's 'New evidence for old arguments.'" *American Journal of Political Science* 34: 363–372.

Green, Donald, Bradley Palmquist, and Eric Schickler. 2002. *Partisan hearts and minds: Political parties and the social identities of voters.* New Haven: Yale University Press.

Green, John C., James L. Guth, Corwin E. Smidt, and Lyman A. Kellstedt. 1996. *Religion and the culture wars: Dispatches from the front.* New York: Rowman and Littlefield.

Green, John C., Mark J. Rozell, and Clyde Wilcox, eds. 2003. *The Christian right in American politics: Marching to the millennium.* Washington, D.C.: Georgetown University Press.

Greene, William H. 2008. *Econometric analysis*, 6th ed. Upper Saddle River, N.J.: Prentice Hall.

Grey, Lawrence. 2007. *How to win a local election: A complete step-by-step guide,* 3rd ed. Lanham, Md.: M. Evans.

Groseclose, Timothy, and Keith Krehbiel. 1994. "Golden parachutes, rubber checks, and strategic retirements from the 102nd House." *American Journal of Political Science* 38: 75–99.

Gross, Donald A., and Robert K. Goidel. 2003. *The states of campaign finance reform.* Columbus: Ohio State University Press.

Gross, Matt. 2009. "Scandal, party government, and retirements from the House of Representatives, 1978–2006." Unpublished working paper, University of Tennessee–Knoxville.

Grossmann, Matt. 2009. "Going pro? Political campaign consulting and the professional model." *Journal of Political Marketing* 8: 81–104.

Gueorguieva, Vassia. 2008. "Voters, MySpace, and YouTube: The impact of alternative communication channels on the 2006 election cycle and beyond." *Social Science Computer Review* 26: 288–300.

Gulati, Girish J. "Jeff," and Christine B. Williams. 2009. "Congressional candidates' use of YouTube in 2008: Its frequency and rationale." Paper presented at the annual conference of the *Journal of Information Technology and Politics:* YouTube and the 2008 Election Cycle in the United States, Amherst, Mass., April 16–17. http://scholarworks.umass.edu/jitpc2009/1.

Guth, James L., Lyman A. Kellstedt, John C. Green, and Corwin E. Smidt. 2002. "A distant thunder? Religious mobilization in the 2000 elections." In *Interest Group Politics,* 6th ed., ed. Allan J. Cigler and Burdett A. Loomis, 161–184. Washington, D.C.: CQ Press.

———. 2007. "Getting the spirit: Religious and partisan mobilization in the 2004 elections." In *Interest Group Politics,* 7th ed., ed. Allan J. Cigler and Burdett A. Loomis, 157–181. Washington, D.C.: CQ Press.

Ha, Shang E., and Dean S. Karlan. 2009. "Get-out-the-vote phone calls: Does quality matter?" *American Politics Research* 37: 353–369.

Hadwiger, David. 1992. "Money, turnout, and ballot measure success in California cities." *Western Political Quarterly* 45: 539–547.

Hajnal, Zoltan L., Elisabeth R. Gerber, and Hugh Louch. 2002. "Minorities and direct legislation: Evidence from California ballot proposition elections." *Journal of Politics* 64: 154–177.

Hajnal, Zoltan L., and Paul G. Lewis. 2003. "Municipal institutions and voter turnout in local elections." *Urban Affairs Review* 38: 645–668.

Hall, J. A., and S. E. Taylor. 1976. "When love is blind: Maintaining idealized images of one's spouse." *Human Relations* 29: 751–761.

Harfoush, Rahaf. 2009. *Yes we did! An inside look at how social media built the Obama brand.* Berkeley, Calif.: New Riders Press.

Harper, Max. 2009. "Uploading hope: An inside view of Obama's HQ new media video team." Keynote presentation at the annual conference of the *Journal of Information Technology and Politics:* YouTube and the 2008 Election Cycle in the United States, Amherst, Mass., April 16–17. http://youtubeandthe2008election.hosted.panopto.com/CourseCast/Viewer/Default.aspx?id=c1dd49a4–0471–4048–9488–23e947f4ece2.

Harris, Frederick C. 1999. *Something within: Religion in African-American political activism.* New York: Oxford University Press.

Hasen, Richard L. 2000. "Parties take the initiative (and vice versa)." *Columbia Law Review* 100: 731–752.

_____. 2005. "Rethinking the unconstitutionality of contribution and expenditure limits in ballot measure campaigns." *Southern California Law Review* 78: 885–925.

Heaney, Michael T. 2008. "Blogging Congress: Technological change and the politics of the congressional press galleries." *PS: Political Science and Politics* 41: 422–426.

Hero, Rodney E., and Caroline J. Tolbert. 2004. "Minority voices and citizen attitudes about government responsiveness in the American states: Do social and institutional context matter?" *British Journal of Political Science* 34: 109–121.

Herr, J. Paul. 2002. "The impact of campaign appearances in the 1996 election." *Journal of Politics* 64: 904–913.

Herrnson, Paul S. 1988. *Party campaigning in the 1980s.* Cambridge, Mass.: Harvard University Press.

_____. 1992. "Campaign professionalism and fundraising in congressional elections." *Journal of Politics* 54: 859–870.

_____. 2000. "Hired guns and House races: Campaign professionals in House elections." In *Campaign warriors: Political consultants in elections,* ed. James A. Thurber and Candice J. Nelson, 65–90. Washington, D.C.: Brookings Institution Press.

_____. 2001. *Playing hardball: Campaigning for the U.S. Congress.* Upper Saddle River, N.J.: Prentice Hall.

_____. 2004. *Congressional elections: Campaigning at home and in Washington,* 4th ed. Washington, D.C.: CQ Press.

Herrnson, Paul S., and Diana Dwyre. 1999. "Party issue advocacy in congressional election campaigns." In *The state of the parties: The changing role of contemporary American parties,* 3rd ed., ed. John C. Green and Daniel M. Shea, 86–104. Lanham, Md.: Rowman and Littlefield.

Hershey, Marjorie Randon. 2008. *Party politics in America,* 13th ed. New York: Longman.

Hetherington, Marc J. 2001. "Resurgent mass partisanship: The role of elite polarization." *American Political Science Review* 95: 619–631.

_____. 2005. *Why trust matters: Declining political trust and the demise of American liberalism.* Princeton: Princeton University Press.

Hibbing, John R., and Elizabeth Theiss-Morse. 1995. *Congress as public enemy: Public attitudes toward American political institutions.* Cambridge: Cambridge University Press.

———, eds. 2001. *What is it about government that Americans dislike?* New York: Cambridge University Press.

Hiebert, Ray, Robert Jones, Ernest Lotito, and John Lorenz, eds. 1971. *The political image merchants: Strategies in the new politics.* Washington, D.C.: Acropolis Books.

Highton, Benjamin. 2009. "Revisiting the relationship between educational attainment and political sophistication." *Journal of Politics* 71: 1564–1576.

Hill, David, and Seth C. McKee. 2005. "The electoral college, mobilization, and turnout in the 2000 presidential election." *American Politics Research* 33: 700–725.

Hillygus, D. Sunshine. 2005. "Campaign effects and the dynamics of turnout intention in election 2000." *Journal of Politics* 67: 50–68.

Hillygus, D. Sunshine, and Simon Jackman. 2003. "Voter decision making in Election 2000: Campaign effects, partisan activation, and the Clinton legacy." *American Journal of Political Science* 47: 583–596.

Hillygus, D. Sunshine, and J. Quin Monson. 2008. "The ground campaign: The strategy and influence of direct communications in the 2004 presidential election." Unpublished working paper, Harvard University.

Hillygus, D. Sunshine, and Todd G. Shields. 2008. *The persuadable voter: Wedge issues in presidential campaigns.* Princeton: Princeton University Press.

Hindman, Matthew. 2005. "The real lessons of Howard Dean: Reflections on the first digital campaign." *Perspectives on Politics* 3: 121–128.

Hitchon, Jacqueline C., and Chingching Chang. 1995. "Effects of gender schematic processing on the reception of political commercials for men and women candidates." *Communication Research* 22: 430–458.

Hochschild, Jennifer L. 2001. "Where you stand depends on what you see: Connections among values, perceptions of fact, and political prescriptions." In *Citizens and politics: Perspectives from political psychology,* ed. James H. Kuklinski, 313–340. New York: Cambridge University Press.

Hogan, Robert E. 1999. "Campaign and contextual influences on voter participation in state legislative elections." *American Politics Quarterly* 27: 403–433.

———. 2004. "Challenger emergence, incumbent success, and electoral accountability in state legislative elections." *Journal of Politics* 66: 1283–1303.

Holbrook, Allyson L., Jon A. Krosnick, Penny S. Visser, Wendi L. Gardner, and John T. Cacioppo. 2001. "Attitudes toward presidential candidates and political parties: Initial optimism, inertial first impressions, and a focus on flaws." *American Journal of Political Science* 45: 930–950.

Holbrook, Thomas M. 1994. "Campaigns, national conditions, and U.S. presidential elections." *American Journal of Political Science* 38: 973–998.

———. 1996. *Do campaigns matter?* Thousand Oaks, Calif.: Sage.

———. 1999. "Political learning from presidential debates." *Political Behavior* 21: 67–89.

———. 2001. "Forecasting with mixed economic signals: A cautionary tale." *PS: Political Science & Politics* 34: 39–44.

———. 2002a. "Did the whistle-stop campaign matter?" *PS: Political Science & Politics* 35: 59–66.

———. 2002b. "Presidential campaigns and the knowledge gap." *Political Communication* 19: 437–454.

———. 2008. "Incumbency, national conditions, and the 2008 presidential election." *PS: Political Science & Politics* 41: 709–712.

———. 2010. "Forecasting U.S. presidential elections." In *The Oxford Handbook of American Elections and Political Behavior,* ed. Jan E. Leighley. Oxford: Oxford University Press (forthcoming).

Holbrook, Thomas M., and Scott D. McClurg. 2005. "The mobilization of core supporters: Campaigns, turnout, and electoral composition in United States presidential elections." *American Journal of Political Science* 49: 689–703.

Hollihan, Thomas A. 2009. *Uncivil wars: Political campaigns in a media age,* 2nd ed. New York: Bedford/St. Martins.

_____. 2010. "Barack Obama and America's journey: Implicit and explicit arguments about race." In *The functions of argument and social context: Selected papers from the NCA/AFA Conference on Argumentation,* ed. Dennis Gouran. Washington, D.C.: National Communication Association (forthcoming).

Holman, Craig B., and Luke P. McLoughlin. 2001. "Buying time 2000: Television advertising in the 2000 federal elections." Report prepared for the Brennan Center for Justice at New York University School of Law.

Houser, Daniel, and Thomas Stratmann. 2008. "Selling favors in the lab: Experiments on campaign finance reform." *Public Choice* 136: 215–239.

Huber, Gregory A., and Kevin Arceneaux. 2007. "Identifying the persuasive effects of presidential advertising." *American Journal of Political Science* 51: 957–977.

Huckfeldt, Robert. 1986. *Politics in context: Assimilation and conflict in urban neighborhoods.* New York: Agathon Press.

Huckfeldt, Robert, Eric Plutzer, and John Sprague. 1993. "Alternative contexts of political behavior: Churches, neighborhoods, and individuals." *Journal of Politics* 55: 365–381.

Huckfeldt, Robert, and John Sprague. 1991. "Discussant effects on vote choice: Intimacy, structure, and interdependence." *Journal of Politics* 53: 122–158.

_____. 1992. "Political parties and electoral mobilization: Political structure, social structure, and the party canvass." *American Political Science Review* 86: 70–86.

_____. 1995. *Citizens, politics, and social communication: Information and influence in an election campaign.* New York: Cambridge University Press.

Huffington, Arianna. 2008. Remarks made at the Web 2.0 Summit, San Francisco, November 7. www.web2summit.com/web2008/public/schedule/detail/5066.

Hutchings, Vincent L. 2003. *Public opinion and democratic accountability: How citizens learn about politics.* Princeton: Princeton University Press.

Inglehart, Ronald. 1990. *Culture shift in advanced industrial society.* Princeton: Princeton University Press.

Institute for Politics, Democracy, and the Internet. 2008. "Best practices for political advertising online." Unpublished report prepared for the Graduate School of Political Management, George Washington University.

Institute of Politics, John F. Kennedy School of Government, and Harvard University, eds. 2005. *Campaign for president: The managers look at 2004.* Lanham, Md.: Rowman and Littlefield.

Iyengar, Shanto. 1987. "Television news and citizens' explanations of national affairs." *American Political Science Review* 81: 815–831.

_____. 1990. "Shortcuts to political knowledge: The role of selective attention and accessibility." In *Information and democratic processes,* ed. John A. Ferejohn and James H. Kuklinski, 160–185. Urbana: University of Illinois Press.

_____. 1996. "Framing responsibility for political issues." *Annals of the American Academy of Political and Social Science* 546: 59–70.

_____. 2005. "Speaking of values: The framing of American politics." *The Forum* 3(3), article 7. www.bepress.com/forum.

Iyengar, Shanto, Simon Jackman, and Kyu Hahn. 2008. "Polarization in less than thirty seconds: Continuous monitoring of voter response to campaign advertising." Paper presented at the 2008 annual meeting of the Midwest Political Science Association, Chicago.

Iyengar, Shanto, and Donald R. Kinder. 1987. *News that matters: Television and American opinion.* Chicago: University of Chicago Press.

Iyengar, Shanto, Helmut Norpoth, and Kyu S. Hahn. 2004. "Consumer demand for election news: The horserace sells." *Journal of Politics* 66: 157–175.

Iyengar, Shanto, and Adam F. Simon. 2000. "New perspectives and evidence on political communication and campaign effects." *Annual Review of Psychology* 51: 149–169.

Jackson, Robert A. 1996. "The mobilization of congressional electorates." *Legislative Studies Quarterly* 21: 425–445.

_____. 1997. "The mobilization of U.S. state electorates in the 1988 and 1990 elections." *Journal of Politics* 59: 520–537.

_____. 2002. "Gubernatorial and senatorial campaign mobilization of voters." *Political Research Quarterly* 55: 825–844.

Jacobs, Lawrence R., and Robert Y. Shapiro. 1994. "Issues, candidate image, and priming: The use of private polls in Kennedy's 1960 presidential campaign." *American Political Science Review* 88: 527–540.

Jacobson, Gary C. 1975. "The impact of broadcast campaigning on electoral outcomes." *Journal of Politics* 37: 769–793.

_____. 1978. "The effects of campaign spending in congressional elections." *American Political Science Review* 72: 469–491.

_____. 1980. *Money in congressional elections.* New Haven: Yale University Press.

_____. 1985. "Money and votes reconsidered: Congressional elections, 1972–1982." *Public Choice* 47: 7–62.

_____. 1987. "Enough is too much: Money and competition in House elections, 1972–1984." In *Elections in America,* ed. Kay Lehman Schlozman, 173–195. Winchester, Mass.: Allen and Unwin.

_____. 1989. "Strategic politicians and the dynamics of U.S. House elections, 1946–86." *American Political Science Review* 83: 773–793.

_____. 1990. "The effects of campaign spending in House elections: New evidence for old arguments." *American Journal of Political Science* 34: 334–362.

_____. 1993. "You can't beat somebody with nobody: Trends in partisan opposition." In *Controversies in voting behavior,* 3rd ed., ed. Richard G. Niemi and Herbert F. Weisberg, 241–267. Washington, D.C.: CQ Press.

_____. 1999. "The effect of the AFL-CIO's 'voter education' campaigns on the 1996 House elections." *Journal of Politics* 61: 185–194.

_____. 2001. *The politics of congressional elections,* 5th ed. New York: Longman.

_____. 2004. *The politics of congressional elections,* 6th ed. New York: Longman.

_____. 2009. *The politics of congressional elections,* 7th ed. New York: Longman.

Jacobson, Gary C., and Michael A. Dimock. 1994. "Checking out: The effects of bank overdrafts on the 1992 House elections." *American Journal of Political Science* 38: 601–624.

Jacobson, Gary C., and Samuel Kernell. 1983. *Strategy and choice in congressional elections,* 2nd ed. New Haven: Yale University Press.

Jacoby, Susan. 2008. *The age of American unreason.* New York: Pantheon.

Jamieson, Kathleen Hall, Paul Waldman, and Susan Sherr. 2000. "Eliminate the negative? Categories of analysis for political advertisements." In *Crowded airwaves: Campaign advertising in elections,* ed. James A. Thurber, Candice J. Nelson, and David A. Dulio, 44–64. Washington D.C.: Brookings Institution Press.

Janowitz, Morris, and Dwaine Marvick. 1964 [1956]. *Competitive pressure and democratic consent: An interpretation of the 1952 presidential election,* 2nd ed. Chicago: Quadrangle Books.

Jasperson, Amy E., and David P. Fan. 2002. "An aggregate examination of the backlash effect in political advertising: The case of the 1996 U.S. Senate race in Minnesota." *Journal of Advertising* 31: 1–12.

Jerit, Jennifer. 2009. "Understanding the knowledge gap: The role of experts and journalists." *Journal of Politics* 71: 442–456.

Jerit, Jennifer, Jason Barabas, and Toby Bolsen. 2006. "Citizens, knowledge, and the information environment." *American Journal of Political Science* 50: 266–282.

Johnson, Dennis W. 2000. "The business of political consulting." In *Campaign warriors: Political consultants in elections,* ed. James A. Thurber and Candice J.

Nelson, 37–52. Washington, D.C.: Brookings Institution Press.

———. 2001. *No place for amateurs: How political consultants are reshaping American democracy.* London: Routledge.

———. 2007. *No place for amateurs: How political consultants are reshaping American democracy,* 2nd ed. London: Routledge.

———, ed. 2009. *Routledge Handbook of Political Management.* London: Routledge.

Johnson-Cartee, Karen S., and Gary Copeland. 1997a. *Inside political campaigns: Theory and practice.* Westport, Conn.: Praeger.

———. 1997b. *Manipulation of the American voter: Political campaign commercials.* Westport, Conn.: Praeger.

Johnston, Michael. 1982. *Political corruption and public policy in America.* Monterey, Calif.: Brooks-Cole.

Johnston, Richard, Michael G. Hagen, and Kathleen Hall Jamieson. 2004. *The 2000 presidential election and the foundations of party politics.* Cambridge: Cambridge University Press.

Jones, Jeffrey M. 1998. "Does bringing out the candidate bring out the votes? The effects of nominee campaigning in presidential elections." *American Politics Quarterly* 26: 395–419.

Jordan, Scott. 2008. "The Vitter Phone Call." *The* [Baton Rouge, La.] *Independent Weekly,* March 18. www.theind.com/index.php?option=com_content&task=view&id=2204&Itemid=1&ed=1013.

Journalism.org. 2004. "The state of the news media 2004: An annual report on American journalism." www.stateofthemedia.org/2004/narrative_newspapers_audience.asp?cat=3&media=2.

———. 2008. "Winning the media campaign: How the press reported the 2008 general election." October 22. www.journalism.org/node/13307.

———. 2009. "The state of the news media 2009: An annual report on American journalism." www.stateofthemedia.org/2009/narrative_newspapers_audience.php?cat=2&media=4.

Just, Marion R., Ann N. Crigler, Dean E. Alger, Timothy E. Cook, Montague Kern, and Darrell M. West. 1996. *Crosstalk: Citizens, candidates, and the media in a presidential campaign.* Chicago: University of Chicago Press.

Kahn, Kim Fridkin, and John G. Geer. 1994. "Creating impressions: An experimental investigation of political advertising on television." *Political Behavior* 16: 93–116.

Kahn, Kim Fridkin, and Patrick J. Kenney. 1999. "Do negative campaigns mobilize or suppress turnout? Clarifying the relationship between negativity and participation." *American Political Science Review* 93: 877–889.

———. 2000. "How negative campaigning enhances knowledge of Senate elections." In *Crowded airwaves: Campaign advertising in elections,* ed. James A. Thurber, Candice J. Nelson, and David A. Dulio, 65–95. Washington, D.C.: Brookings Institution Press.

———. 2004. *No holds barred: Negativity in U.S. Senate campaigns.* Upper Saddle River, N.J.: Pearson.

Kaid, Lynda Lee. 1997. "Effects of the television spots on images of Dole and Clinton." *American Behavioral Scientist* 40: 1085–1094.

———. 2006. "Political advertising." In *The electoral challenge: Theory meets practice,* ed. Stephen C. Craig, 79–96. Washington, D.C: CQ Press.

Kaid, Lynda Lee, and John Boydston. 1987. "An experimental study of the effectiveness of negative political advertisements." *Communication Quarterly* 35: 193–201.

Kaid, Lynda Lee, and Anne Johnston. 2001. *Videostyle in presidential campaigns: Style and content of televised political advertising.* Westport, Conn.: Praeger.

Kaid, Lynda Lee, Mitchell S. McKinney, and John C. Tedesco. 2000. *Civic dialogue in the 1996 presidential campaign: Candidate, media, and public voices.* Cresskill, N.J.: Hampton Press.

Kaid, Lynda Lee, and John C. Tedesco. 1999. "Tracking voter reactions to the television advertising." In *The electronic election: Perspectives on the 1996 campaign communication,* ed. Lynda Lee Kaid and Dianne G. Bystrom, 233–245. Mahwah, N.J.: Lawrence Erlbaum.

Karabell, Zachary. 2000. *The last campaign: How Harry Truman won the 1948 election.* New York: Knopf.

Karp, Jeffrey A. 1998. "The influence of elite endorsements in initiative campaigns." In *Citizens as legislators: Direct democracy in the United States,* ed. Shaun Bowler, Todd Donovan, and Caroline J. Tolbert, 149–165. Columbus: Ohio State University Press.

Karpf, David. 2009. "Macaca moments reconsidered . . . YouTube effects or netroots effects?" Paper presented at the annual conference of the *Journal of Information Technology and Politics:* YouTube and the 2008 Election Cycle in the United States, Amherst, Mass., April 16–17. http://scholarworks.umass.edu/jitpc2009/1.

Kaye, Kate. 2009. Campaign '08: A turning point for digital media. CreateSpace.

Keith, Bruce E., David B. Magleby, Candice J. Nelson, Elizabeth Orr, Mark C. Westlye, and Raymond E. Wolfinger. 1992. *The myth of the independent voter.* Berkeley: University of California Press.

Kelley, Stanley, Jr. 1956. *Professional public relations and political power.* Baltimore: Johns Hopkins University Press.

Kenny, Christopher B. 1992. "Political participation and effects from the social environment." *American Journal of Political Science* 36: 259–267.

Kenny, Christopher B., and Michael McBurnett. 1992. "A dynamic model of the effect of campaign spending on congressional vote choice." *American Journal of Political Science* 36: 923–937.

———. 1994. "An individual-level multi-equation model of expenditure effects in contested House elections." *American Political Science Review* 88: 699–707.

———. 1997. "Up close and personal: Campaign contact and candidate spending in U.S. House elections." *Political Research Quarterly* 50: 75–96.

Key, V. O., Jr. 1942. *Politics, parties, and pressure groups.* New York: Crowell.

———. 1966. *The responsible electorate: Rationality in presidential voting, 1936–1960.* Cambridge, Mass.: Belknap Press of Harvard University Press.

Kiely, Kathy. 2009. "Presidential press conferences: Obama beating Bush 23–10." *USA Today,* June 16. http://content.usatoday.com/topics/post/People/Politicians,+Government+Officials,+Strategists/Executive/George+W.+Bush/68173381.blog/1.

Kiewiet, D. Roderick. 1983. *Macroeconomics and micropolitics: The electoral effects of economic issues.* Chicago: University of Chicago Press.

Kim, Hak Ryang. 2004. *Winning campaign strategies: Methodologies and in-depth guide.* Columbus, Ohio: Camst.

Kim, Young Mei. 2009. "Issue publics in the new information environment: Selectivity, domain specificity, and extremity." *Communication Research* 36: 254–284.

Kimball, David C. 2008. "Interest groups in the 2008 presidential election: The barking dog that didn't bite." *The Forum* 6(4), article 2. www.bepress.com/forum.

Kinder, Donald R., Gordon S. Adams, and Paul W. Gronke. 1989. "Economics and politics in the 1984 American presidential election." *American Journal of Political Science* 33: 491–515.

Kinder, Donald R., and D. Roderick Kiewiet. 1979. "Economic discontent and political behavior: The role of personal grievances and collective economic judgments in congressional voting." *American Journal of Political Science* 23: 495–527.

———. 1981. "Sociotropic politics: The American case." *British Journal of Political Science* 11: 129–161.

King, David C., and Richard E. Matland. 2003. "Sex and the Grand Old Party: An experimental investigation of the effect of candidate sex on support for a Republican candidate." *American Politics Research* 31: 595–612.

King, James D. 2001. "Incumbent popularity and vote choice in gubernatorial elections." *Journal of Politics* 63: 585–597.

Kirby, James C. 1985. "The Role of the Electorate in Congressional Ethics." In *Representation and responsibility: Exploring legislative ethics,* ed. Bruce Jennings and Daniel Callahan, 29–37. New York: Plenum Press.

Klapper, Joseph T. 1960. *The effects of mass communication.* New York: Free Press.

Klotz, Robert J. 2003. *The politics of Internet communication.* Lanham, Md.: Rowman and Littlefield.

_____. 2007. "Internet campaigning for grassroots and astroturf support." *Social Science Computer Review* 25: 3–12.

_____. 2009. "The sidetracked 2008 YouTube Senate campaign." Paper presented at the annual conference of the *Journal of Information Technology and Politics:* YouTube and the 2008 Election Cycle in the United States, Amherst, Mass., April 16–17. http://scholarworks.umass.edu/jitpc2009/1.

Koch, Jeffrey W. 2002. "Gender stereotypes and citizens' impressions of House candidates' ideological orientations." *American Journal of Political Science* 46: 453–462.

_____. 2008. "Campaign advertisements' impact on voter certainty and knowledge of House candidates' ideological positions." *Political Research Quarterly* 61: 609–621.

Koger, Gregory, Seth Masket, and Hans Noel. 2009. "Partisan webs: Information exchange and party networks." *British Journal of Political Science* 39: 633–653.

_____. 2010. "Cooperative party factions in American politics." *American Politics Research* 38: 33–53.

Kolodny, Robin. 2000. "Electoral partnerships: Political consultants and political parties." In *Campaign warriors: Political consultants in elections,* ed. James A. Thurber and Candice J. Nelson, 110–132. Washington, D.C.: Brookings Institution Press.

Kolodny, Robin, and David A. Dulio. 2003. "Political party adaptation in U.S. congressional elections: Why political parties use coordinated expenditures to hire political consultants." *Party Politics* 9: 729–746.

Kolodny, Robin, and Angela Logan. 1998. "Political consultants and the extension of party goals." *PS: Political Science & Politics* 31: 155–159.

Koster, Josh. 2009. "Long-tail nanotargeting." *Politics,* February, 22–26.

Kramer, Gerald H. 1970. "The effects of precinct-level canvassing on voter behavior." *Public Opinion Quarterly* 34: 560–572.

_____. 1971. "Short-term fluctuations in U.S. voting behavior, 1896–1964." *American Political Science Review* 65: 131–143.

Krasno, Jonathan S., and Donald P. Green. 2008. "Do televised presidential ads increase voter turnout? Evidence from a natural experiment." *Journal of Politics* 70: 245–261.

Krebs, Timothy B. 1998. "The determinants of candidates' vote share and the advantages of incumbency in city council elections." *American Journal of Political Science* 42: 921–935.

Kreiss, Daniel. 2009a. "Developing the 'good citizen': Digital artifacts, peer networks, and formal organization during the 2003–2004 Howard Dean campaign." *Journal of Information Technology and Politics* 6: 281–297.

_____. 2009b. "Institutional contexts of use of new media in electoral politics: From Howard Dean to Barack Obama." Paper presented at the 2009 annual meeting of the American Sociological Association, San Francisco.

_____. 2009c. "The whole world is networking: Crafting networked politics from Howard Dean to Barack Obama." Paper presented at the 2009 annual meeting of the Society for Social Studies of Science, Washington, D.C.

Krosnick, Jon A. 1990. "Government policy and citizen passion: A study of issue publics in contemporary America." *Political Behavior* 12: 59–92.

Krosnick, Jon A., and Laura A. Brannon. 1993. "The impact of the Gulf War on the ingredients of presidential evaluations: Multidimensional effects of political involvement." *American Political Science Review* 87: 963–975.

Kuklinski, James H., and Norman L. Hurley. 1994. "On hearing and interpreting political messages: A cautionary tale of citizen cue-taking." *Journal of Politics* 56: 729–751.

Kuklinski, James H., and Paul J. Quirk. 2000. "Reconsidering the rational public:

Cognition, heuristics, and mass opinion." In *Elements of reason: Cognition, choice, and the bounds of rationality,* ed. Arthur Lupia, Matthew D. McCubbins, and Samuel L. Popkin, 153–182. New York: Cambridge University Press.

Kuklinski, James H., Paul J. Quirk, Jennifer Jerit, David Schwieder, and Robert F. Rich. 2000. "Misinformation and the currency of democratic citizenship." *Journal of Politics* 62: 790–816.

Kull, Steven. 2004. "Public perceptions of the foreign policy positions of the presidential candidates." Report issued by the Program on International Policy Attitudes at the University of Maryland, September 29. www.pipa.org/OnlineReports/FP_MakingProcess/CandidateFPPercep_Sept04/CandidateFPPercep_Sept04_rpt.pdf.

Kurtz, Howard. 2005. "Online nude photos are latest chapter in Jeff Gannon saga." *Washington Post,* February 16. www.washingtonpost.com/wp-dyn/articles/A27730–2005Feb15.html.

Lacey, Robert J. 2005. "The electoral allure of direct democracy: The effect of initiative salience on voting, 1990–1996." *State Politics and Policy Quarterly* 5: 168–181.

Ladd, Everett Carll, Jr., with Charles D. Hadley. 1978. *Transformations of the American party system: Political coalitions from the New Deal to the 1970s,* 2nd ed. New York: Norton.

Lakoff, George. 2004. *Don't think of an elephant! Know your values and frame the debate.* White River Junction, Vt.: Chelsea Green Publishing.

_____. 2008. *The political mind: Why you can't understand 21st-century American politics with an 18th-century brain.* New York: Viking.

Langley, Monica, and Amy Chozick. 2008. "Clinton team seeks to calm turmoil." *Wall Street Journal,* February 14. http://online.wsj.com/article/SB12029 5209438666989.html?mod=hpp_us_ pageone.

La Raja, Raymond J. 2008. *Small change: Money, political parties, and campaign finance reform.* Ann Arbor: University of Michigan Press.

Lascher, Edward L., Jr., Michael G. Hagen, and Steven A. Rochlin. 1996. "Gun behind the door? Ballot initiatives, state policies and public opinion." *Journal of Politics* 58: 760–775.

Lasswell, Harold D. 1927. "The theory of political propaganda." *American Political Science Review* 21: 627–631.

Lau, Richard R. 1985. "Two explanations for negativity effects in political behavior." *American Journal of Political Science* 29: 119–138.

Lau, Richard R., David J. Andersen, and David P. Redlawsk. 2008. "An exploration of correct voting in recent U.S. presidential elections." *American Journal of Political Science* 52: 395–411.

Lau, Richard R., and Gerald M. Pomper. 2001. "Effects of negative campaigning on turnout in U.S. Senate elections, 1988–1998." *Journal of Politics* 63: 804–819.

_____. 2004. *Negative campaigning: An analysis of U.S. Senate elections.* Lanham, Md.: Rowman and Littlefield.

Lau, Richard R., and David P. Redlawsk. 1997. "Voting correctly." *American Political Science Review* 91: 585–598.

Lau, Richard R., and Lee Sigelman. 2000. "Effectiveness of political advertising." In *Crowded airwaves: Campaign advertising in elections,* ed. James A. Thurber, Candice J. Nelson, and David A. Dulio, 10–43. Washington, D.C.: Brookings Institution Press.

Lau, Richard R., Lee Sigelman, and Ivy Brown Rovner. 2007. "The effects of negative political campaigns: A Meta-analytic reassessment." *Journal of Politics* 69: 1176–1209.

Lau, Richard R., Lee Sigelman, Caroline Heldman, and Paul Babbitt. 1999. "The effects of negative political advertisements: A meta-analytic assessment." *American Political Science Review* 93: 851–875.

Lawton, L. Dale, and Paul Freedman. 2001. "Beyond negativity: Advertising effects in the 2000 Virginia senate race." Paper presented at the 2001 annual meeting of the Midwest Political Science Association, Chicago.

Lazarsfeld, Paul F. 1944. "The election is over." *Public Opinion Quarterly* 8: 317–330.

Lazarsfeld, Paul F., Bernard Berelson, and Hazel Gaudet. 1944. *The people's choice: How the voter makes up his mind in a presidential campaign.* New York: Duell, Sloan and Pearce.

———. 1948. *The people's choice: How the voter makes up his mind in a presidential compaign,* 2d ed. New York: Columbia University Press.

Lee, Christopher. 2008. "Rangel says he didn't know of loan terms." *Washington Post,* September 6.

Leighley, Jan E. 2001. *Strength in numbers? The political mobilization of racial and ethnic minorities.* Princeton: Princeton University Press.

———. 2004. *Mass media and politics: A social science perspective.* Boston: Houghton-Mifflin.

Lemert, James B. 1993. "Do televised presidential debates help inform voters?" *Journal of Broadcasting & Electronic Media* 37: 83–94.

Lemert, James B., Wayne Wanta, and Tien-Tsung Lee. 1999. "Party identification and negative advertising in a U.S. Senate election." *Journal of Communication* 49: 123–134.

Levine, Peter, and Mark Hugo Lopez. 2005. "What we should know about the effectiveness of campaigns but don't." *Annals of the American Academy of Political and Social Science* 601: 180–191.

Lewis, C. S. 1970. "Meditation in a toolshed." In *God in the dock: Essays on theology and ethics,* by C. S. Lewis, ed. Walter Hooper, 212–215. Grand Rapids, Mich.: Eerdmans. Originally published in *The Coventry Evening Telegraph,* July 17, 1945, 4.

Lewis-Beck, Michael S. 1988. "Economics and the American voter: Past, present, and future." *Political Behavior* 10: 5–21.

———. 2005. "Election forecasting: Principles and practice." *British Journal of Politics and International Relations* 7: 145–164.

Lewis-Beck, Michael S., and Tom W. Rice. 1992. *Forecasting elections.* Washington, D.C.: CQ Press.

Lewis-Beck, Michael S., and Charles Tien. 2008. "The job of president and the jobs model forecast: Obama for '08?" *PS: Political Science & Politics* 41: 687–690.

Limbaugh, Rush. 2009. "From kids on bus to Kanye West: Race rules all in Obama's America." *The Rush Limbaugh Show,* September 15. www.rushlimbaugh.com/home/daily/site_091509/content/01125106.guest.html.

Lipinski, Daniel, and Gregory Neddenriep. 2004. "Using 'new' media to get 'old' media coverage: How members of Congress utilize their Web sites to court journalists." *Harvard International Journal of Press/Politics* 9: 7–21.

Lipset, Seymour Martin. 1996. *American exceptionalism: A double-edged sword.* New York: Norton.

Los Angeles Times. 2003. "Democracy run amok, or running smoothly?" *Los Angeles Times,* July 29, B14.

———. 2009a. "As boycott continues, Glenn Beck's audience swells." *Los Angeles Times,* August 27. http://latimesblogs.latimes.com/showtracker/2009/08/as-boycott-continues-glenn-becks-audience-swells.html?cid=6a00d8341c630a53ef0120a57d7d05970c.

———. 2009b. "South Carolina Rep. Joe Wilson yells 'You lie' to the president." *Los Angeles Times,* September 10. http://latimesblogs.latimes.com/comments_blog/2009/09/south-carolina-joe-wilson-liar-president-barack-obama.html.

Lowenstein, Daniel H. 1982. "Campaign spending and ballot propositions: Recent experience, public choice theory and the First Amendment." *UCLA Law Review* 29: 505–641.

Lowy, Joan. 2004. "DNC: Dems, GOP push ballot measures to influence voters." *Naples News,* July 29. www.naplesnews.com/npdn/news/article/0,2071,NPDN_14940_3071424,00.html.

Luntz, Frank I. 1988. *Candidates, consultants, and campaigns: The style and substance of American electioneering.* New York: Basil Blackwell.

Luo, Michael. 2009. "Small online contributions add up to huge fund-raising edge for Obama. *New York Times,* February 20. www.nytimes.com/2008/02/20/us/politics/20Obama.html?scp=1&sq=&st=nyt.

Lupia, Arthur. 1994. "Shortcuts versus encyclopedias: Information and voting behavior in California insurance reform elections." *American Political Science Review* 88: 63–76.

———. 2001. "Dumber than chimps? An assessment of direct democracy voters." In *Dangerous democracy? The battle over ballot initiatives in America,* ed. Larry J. Sabato, Howard R. Ernst, and Bruce A. Larson, 66–70. Lanham, Md.: Rowman and Littlefield.

Lupia, Arthur, and John G. Matsusaka. 2004. "Direct democracy: New approaches to old questions." *Annual Review of Political Science* 7: 463–482.

Luskin, Robert C. 1990. "Explaining political sophistication." *Political Behavior* 12: 331–361.

Magleby, David B. 1984. *Direct legislation: Voting on ballot propositions in the United States.* Baltimore: Johns Hopkins University Press.

———. 1989. "Opinion formation and opinion change in ballot proposition campaigns." In *Manipulating public opinion: Essays on public opinion as a dependent variable,* ed. Michael Margolis and Gary A. Mauser, 95–115. Pacific Grove, Calif.: Brooks/Cole.

———. 2004. "The impact of issue advocacy and party soft money electioneering." In *The medium and the message: Television advertising and American elections,* ed. Kenneth M. Goldstein and Patricia Strach, 84–104. Upper Saddle River, N.J.: Prentice Hall.

Magleby, David B., and J. Quin Monson, eds. 2004. *The last hurrah? Soft money and issue advocacy in the 2002 congressional elections.* Washington, D.C.: Brookings Institution Press.

Magleby, David B., and Kelly D. Patterson. 1998. "Consultants and direct democracy." *PS: Political Science & Politics* 31: 160–169.

———. 2000. "Campaign consultants and direct democracy: Politics of citizen control." In *Campaign warriors: Political consultants in elections,* ed. James A. Thurber and Candice J. Nelson, 133–152. Washington, D.C.: Brookings Institution Press.

———, eds. 2008. *The battle for Congress: Iraq, scandal, and campaign finance in the 2006 election.* Boulder, Colo.: Paradigm Publishers.

Malbin, Michael J., ed. 2003. *Life after reform: When the Bipartisan Campaign Reform Act meets politics.* Lanham, Md.: Rowman and Littlefield.

Malbin, Michael J., and Thomas L. Gais. 1998. *The day after reform: Sobering campaign finance lessons from the American states.* Albany, N.Y.: Rockefeller Institute Press.

Mann, Thomas E., and Raymond E. Wolfinger. 1980. "Candidates and parties in congressional elections." *American Political Science Review* 74: 617–632.

Marcus, George E., and Michael B. MacKuen. 1993. "Anxiety, enthusiasm, and the vote: The emotional underpinnings of learning and involvement during presidential campaigns." *American Political Science Review* 87: 672–685.

Marcus, George E., W. Russell Neuman, and Michael MacKuen. 2000. *Affective intelligence and political judgment.* Chicago: University of Chicago Press.

Marinucci, Carla. 2007. "Sex scandal a serious obstacle to mayor's hopes for higher office." *San Francisco Chronicle,* February 2. http://articles.sfgate.com/2007-02-02/news/17230653_1_ruby-rippey-tourk-alex-tourk-new som-s-affair.

Markus, Gregory B. 1988. "The impact of personal and national economic conditions on the presidential vote: A pooled cross-sectional analysis." *American Journal of Political Science* 32: 137–154.

———. 1992. "The impact of personal and national economic conditions on presidential voting, 1956–1988." *American Journal of Political Science* 36: 829–834.

Markus, Gregory B., and Philip E. Converse. 1979. "A dynamic simultaneous equation model of electoral choice." *American Political Science Review* 73: 1055–1070.

Martin, Paul S. 2004. "Inside the black box of negative campaign effects: Three reasons why negative campaigns mobilize." *Political Psychology* 25: 545–562.

Masket, Seth E., Michael T. Heaney, Joanne M. Miller, and Dara Z. Strolovitch. 2009. "Networking the parties: A comparative study of Democratic and Republican national convention delegates in 2008." Paper presented at the State of the Parties Conference, Ray C. Bliss Institute of Applied Politics, University of Akron, October 15–16. www .uakron.edu/bliss/docs/Networking_ the_Parties.pdf.

Matsusaka, John G. 2004. *For the many or the few: The initiative, public policy, and American democracy.* Chicago: University of Chicago Press.

Mayer, William G. 1996. "In defense of negative campaigning." *Political Science Quarterly* 111: 437–455.

_____. 2007. "The swing voter in American presidential elections." *American Politics Research* 35: 358–388.

_____, ed. 2008. *The swing voter in American politics.* Washington, D.C.: Brookings Institution Press.

Mayhew, David R. 1974a. *Congress: The electoral connection.* New Haven: Yale University Press.

_____. 1974b. "Congressional elections: The case of the vanishing marginals." *Polity* 6: 295–317.

McClurg, Scott D. 2004. "Indirect mobilization: The social consequences of party contacts in an election campaign." *American Politics Research* 32: 406–443.

McCombs, M. E., and D. L. Shaw. 1972. "The agenda-setting functions of mass media." *Public Opinion Quarterly* 36: 176–185.

McCuan, David, Shaun Bowler, Todd Donovan, and Ken Fernandez. 1998. "California's political warriors: Campaign professionals and the initiative process." In *Citizens as legislators: Direct democracy in the United States,* ed. Shaun Bowler, Todd Donovan, and Caroline J. Tolbert, 55–79. Columbus: Ohio State University Press.

McCuan, David, and Stephen Stambough. 2005. *Initiative-centered politics: The new politics of direct democracy.* Durham, N.C.: Carolina Academic Press.

McCurley, Carl, and Jeffrey J. Mondak. 1995. "Inspected by #1184063113: The influence of incumbents' competence and integrity in U.S. House elections."

American Journal of Political Science 39: 864–885.

McFarland, Andrew S. 1984. *Common cause: Lobbying in the public interest.* Chatham, N.J.: Chatham House.

McGerr, Michael E. 2003. *A fierce discontent: The rise and fall of the Progressive Movement in America, 1870–1920.* New York: Free Press.

McGraw, Kathleen M. 1990. "Avoiding blame: An experimental investigation of political excuses and justifications." *British Journal of Political Science* 20: 119–131.

_____. 1991. "Managing blame: An experimental test of the effects of political accounts." *American Political Science Review* 85: 1133–1157.

McGraw, Kathleen M., Samuel Best, and Richard Timpone. 1995. "'What they say or what they do?' The impact of elite explanation and policy outcomes on public opinion." *American Journal of Political Science* 39: 53–74.

McGuire, W. J. 1968. "Personality and susceptibility to social influence." In *Handbook of personality theory and research,* ed. E. F. Borgatta and W. W. Lambert, 1130–1187. Chicago: Rand McNally.

McNulty, John E. 2005. "Phone-based GOTV—What's on the line? Field experiments with varied partisan components, 2002–2003." *Annals of the American Academy of Political and Social Science* 601: 41–65.

Medvic, Stephen K. 1997. *Is there a spin doctor in the House? The impact of political consultants in congressional campaigns.* Ph.D. dissertation, Purdue University.

_____. 1998. "The effectiveness of political consultants as a campaign resource." *PS: Political Science & Politics* 31: 150–154.

_____. 2000. "Professionalization in congressional campaigns." In *Campaign warriors: Political consultants in elections,* ed. James A. Thurber and Candice J. Nelson, 91–109. Washington, D.C.: Brookings Institution Press.

_____. 2001. *Political consultants in U.S. congressional elections.* Columbus: Ohio State University Press.

_____. 2003. "Professional political consultants: An operational definition." *Politics* 23: 119–127.

_____. 2006. "Understanding campaign strategy: 'Deliberate priming' and the role of professional political consultants." *Journal of Political Marketing* 5: 11–32.

_____. 2010. *Campaigns and elections: Players and processes.* Boston: Wadsworth.

Medvic, Stephen K., and Silvo Lenart. 1997. "The influence of political consultants in the 1992 congressional elections." *Legislative Studies Quarterly* 22: 61–77.

Meirick, Patrick. 2002. "Cognitive responses to negative and comparative political advertising." *Journal of Advertising* 31: 49–62.

Mendelsohn, Matthew, and Fred Cutler. 2000. "The effect of referendums on democratic citizens: Information, politicization, efficacy and tolerance." *British Journal of Political Science* 30: 685–701.

Mendelsohn, Matthew, and Andrew Parkin, eds. 2001. *Referendum democracy: Citizens, elites and deliberation in referendum campaigns.* New York: Palgrave Macmillan.

Menefee-Libey, David B. 2000. *The triumph of campaign-centered politics.* New York: Chatham House.

Mercurio, John. 2002. "Lott apologizes for Thurmond comment." *CNN.com,* December 10. archives.cnn.com/2002/ALLPOLITICS/12/09/lott.comment.

Merritt, Sharyne. 1984. "Negative political advertising: Some empirical findings." *Journal of Advertising* 13: 27–38.

Michelson, Melissa R. 2003. "Getting out the Latino vote: How door-to-door canvassing influences voter turnout in rural central California." *Political Behavior* 25: 247–263.

_____. 2005. "Meeting the challenge of Latino voter mobilization." *Annals of the American Academy of Political and Social Science* 601: 85–101.

Michelson, Melissa R., and Herbert Villa Jr. 2003. "Mobilizing the Latino youth vote." Presented at the 2003 annual meeting of the Western Political Science Association, Denver.

Milbank, Dana, and Dan Balz. 2005. "O come, all ye faithful." *Washington Post,* January 16. www.washingtonpost.com/wp-dyn/articles/A12611–2005Jan15.html.

Miller, Arthur H., and Michael MacKuen. 1979. "Informing the electorate: A national study." In *The great debates: Carter vs. Ford, 1976,* ed. Sidney Kraus, 269–297. Bloomington: Indiana University Press.

Miller, Joanne M., and Jon A. Krosnick. 2000. "News media impact on the ingredients of presidential evaluations: Politically knowledgeable citizens are guided by a trusted source." *American Journal of Political Science* 44: 301–315.

Miller, Melissa K., and Shannon K. Orr. 2008. "Experimenting with a 'third way' in political knowledge estimation." *Public Opinion Quarterly* 72: 768–780.

Mitchell, Greg. 1992. *The campaign of the century: Upton Sinclair's race for governor of California and the birth of media politics.* New York: Random House.

Mondak, Jeffrey J. 1995a. "Competence, integrity, and the electoral success of congressional incumbents." *Journal of Politics* 57: 1043–1069.

_____. 1995b. *Nothing to read: Newspapers and elections in a social experiment.* Ann Arbor: University of Michigan Press.

_____. 2000. "Reconsidering the measurement of political knowledge." *Political Analysis* 8: 57–82.

_____. 2001. "Developing valid knowledge scales." *American Journal of Political Science* 45: 224–238.

Mondak, Jeffrey J., and Mary R. Anderson. 2004. "The knowledge gap: A reexamination of gender-based differences in political knowledge." *Journal of Politics* 66 (May): 492–512.

Moore, David W. 1987. "Political campaigns and the knowledge-gap hypothesis." *Public Opinion Quarterly* 51: 186–200.

Morris, Dwight, and Murielle E. Gamache. 1994. *Gold-plated politics: The 1992 congressional races.* Washington, D.C.: CQ Press.

Mott, Frank Luther. 1962. *American journalism: A history: 1690–1960,* 3rd ed. New York: Macmillan.

Mowry, George E. 1951. *The California Progressives*. Berkeley: University of California Press.

Mullins, K. J. 2009. "Online newspaper readership grows." *Digital Journal*, April 23. www.digitaljournal.com/article/271436.

Munro, William Bennett, ed. 1912. *The initiative, referendum and recall*. New York: Appleton.

Murray, Mark. 2009. "Steele blasts Carter for comment." *MSNBC.com*, September 16. http://firstread.msnbc.msn.com/archive/2009/09/16/2071356.aspx.

Mutz, Diana C. 1994. "Contextualizing personal experience: The role of mass media." *Journal of Politics* 56: 689–714.

Nadeau, Richard, Neil Nevitte, Elisabeth Gidengil, and André Blais. 2008. "Election campaigns as information campaigns: Who learns what and does it matter?" *Political Communication* 25: 229–248.

Nagourney, Adam, Jim Rutenberg, and Jeff Zeleny. 2008. "Nearly flawless run is credited in victory." *New York Times*, November 5. www.nytimes.com/2008/11/05/world/americas/05iht-05recon.17541362.html.

Neuman, W. Russell. 1986. *The paradox of mass politics: Knowledge and opinion in the American electorate*. Cambridge, Mass.: Harvard University Press.

Neuman, W. Russell, Marion R. Just, and Ann N. Crigler. 1992. *Common knowledge: News and the construction of political meaning*. Chicago: University of Chicago Press.

New York Times. 2004. "Transcript of President Bush's speech." www.nytimes.com/2004/11/03/politics/campaign/03cnd-bush-text.html.

———. 2009. "House vote of disapproval on Rep. Joe Wilson." *New York Times*, September 15. www.nytimes.com/aponline/2009/09/15/us/politics/AP-US-House-RollCall-Heckling.html?_r=1.

Newsom, Gavin. 2008. Remarks made at the Web 2.0 Summit, San Francisco, California, November 7. www.web2summit.com/web2008/public/schedule/detail/5066.

Newsweek. 2008. "How he did it." *Newsweek*, November 5. www.newsweek.com/id/167582.

Nicholson, Stephen P. 2003. "The political environment and ballot proposition awareness." *American Journal of Political Science* 47: 403–410.

———. 2005. *Voting the agenda: Candidates, elections, and ballot propositions*. Princeton: Princeton University Press.

Nickerson, David W. 2005. "Partisan mobilization using volunteer phone banks and door hangers." *Annals of the American Academy of Political and Social Science* 601: 10–27.

———. 2006. "Volunteer phone calls can increase turnout: Evidence from eight field experiments." *American Politics Research* 34: 271–292.

———. 2007. "Quality is job one: Professional and volunteer voter mobilization calls." *American Journal of Political Science* 51: 269–282.

———. 2008. "Is voting contagious? Evidence from two field experiments." *American Political Science Review* 102: 49–57.

Nickerson, David W., Ryan D. Friedrichs, and David C. King. 2006. "Partisan mobilization campaigns in the field: Results from a statewide turnout experiment in Michigan." *Political Research Quarterly* 59: 85–97.

Nie, Norman H., Sidney Verba, and John R. Petrocik. 1976. *The changing American voter*. Cambridge, Mass.: Harvard University Press.

Nimmo, Dan. 1970. *The political persuaders: The techniques of modern election campaigns*. Englewood Cliffs, N.J.: Prentice Hall.

———. 2001. *The political persuaders: The techniques of modern election campaigns*, 2nd ed. New Brunswick, N.J.: Transaction Publishers.

Niven, David. 2001. "The limits of mobilization: Turnout evidence from state House primaries." *Political Behavior* 23: 335–350.

———. 2004. "The mobilization solution? Face-to-face contact and voter turnout in a municipal election." *Journal of Politics* 66: 868–884.

_____. 2006. "A field experiment on the effects of negative campaign mail on voter turnout in a municipal election." *Political Research Quarterly* 59: 203–210.

Nohria, N., and R. Eccles. 2000. "Face-to-face: Making network organizations work." In *Technology, organizations and innovation: Critical perspectives on business and management,* ed. David Preece, Ian McLoughlin, and Patrick Dawson, 1659–1681. New York: Routledge.

Norquist, Grover. 1993. "Prelude to a landslide: How Republicans will sweep the Congress." *Policy Review* (fall): 30–36.

Norris, Pippa, and David Sanders. 2003. "Message or medium? Campaign learning during the 2001 British general election." *Political Communication* 20: 233–262.

Obama, Barack H. 1995. *Dreams from my father: A story of race and inheritance.* New York: Random House.

O'Neill, Tip, with William Novak. 1987. *Man of the House: The life and political memoirs of Speaker Tip O'Neill.* New York: Random House.

Orr, Jimmy. 2009. "Jimmy Carter: Racism behind Joe Wilson outburst." *Christian Science Monitor,* September 16. http://features.csmonitor.com/politics/2009/09/16/jimmy-carter-racism-behind-joe-wilson-outburst.

O'Shaughnessy, Nicholas J. 1990. *The phenomenon of political marketing.* New York: St. Martin's.

Overby, Marvin L., and Jay Barth. 2006. "Radio advertising in American political campaigns: The persistence, importance, and effects of narrowcasting." *American Politics Research* 34 (4): 451–478.

Page, Benjamin I. 1978. *Choices and echoes in presidential elections: Rational man and electoral democracy.* Chicago: University of Chicago Press.

Page, Benjamin I., and Calvin C. Jones. 1979. "Reciprocal effects of policy preferences, party loyalties and the vote." *American Political Science Review* 73: 1071–1089.

Page, Benjamin I., Robert Y. Shapiro, and Glenn R. Dempsey. 1987. "What moves public opinion?" *American Political Science Review* 81: 23–43.

Panagopoulous, Costas, and Peter W. Wielhouwer. 2008. "The ground war 2000–2004: Strategic targeting in grassroots campaigns." *Presidential Studies Quarterly* 38: 347–362.

Pappu, Sridhar. 2007. "In S.C., Obama seeks a spiritual awakening." *Washinton Post,* October 29. www.washingtonpost.com/wp-dyn/content/article/2007/10/28/AR2007102801466.html?hpid%3Dtopnews&sub=AR.

Parry, Janine, Jay Barth, Martha Kropf, and E. Terrence Jones. 2008. "Mobilizing the seldom voter: Campaign contact and effects in high-profile elections." *Political Behavior* 30: 97–113.

Partin, Randall W. 2001. "Campaign intensity and voter information: A look at gubernatorial contests." *American Politics Research* 29: 115–140.

_____. 2002. "Assessing the impact of campaign spending in governors' races." *Political Research Quarterly* 55: 213–233.

Patterson, Samuel C. 1982. "Campaign spending in contests for governor." *Western Political Quarterly* 35: 457–477.

Patterson, Samuel C., and Gregory A. Caldeira. 1983. "Getting out the vote: Participation in gubernatorial elections." *American Political Science Review* 77: 675–689.

Patterson, Thomas E. 2002. *The vanishing voter: Public involvement in an age of uncertainty.* New York: Knopf.

_____. 2006. "Voter competence." In *The electoral challenge: Theory meets practice,* ed. Stephen C. Craig, 39–57. Washington, D.C.: CQ Press.

Patterson, Thomas E., and Robert D. McClure. 1976. *The unseeing eye: The myth of television power in national politics.* New York: Putnam's.

Peele, Gillian. 1982. "Campaign consultants." *Electoral Studies* 1: 355–362.

Peer, Limor, and Mary Nesbitt. 2004. "An analysis of content in 52 U.S. daily newspapers: Summary report," July.

www.readership.org/new_readers/data/
content_analysis.pdf.

Perlmutter, David D. 2008. "Political blogging and campaign 2008: A round-
table." *International Journal of Press/
Politics* 13: 160–170.

Perloff, Richard M. 1998. *Political communi-
cation: Politics, press, and public in
America*. Mahwah, N.J.: Lawrence
Erlbaum.

Peters, John G., and Susan Welch. 1980. "The
effects of charges of corruption on voting behavior in congressional elections."
American Political Science Review 74:
697–708.

Petracca, Mark P. 1989. "Political consultants
and democratic governance." *PS: Political Science & Politics* 22: 11–14.

Petracca, Mark P., and Courtney Wierioch.
1988. "Consultant democracy: The
activities and attitudes of American
political consultants." Paper presented
at the 1988 annual meeting of the
Midwest Political Science Association,
Chicago, April 14–16.

Petrocik, John R. 1996. "Issue ownership
in presidential elections, with a 1980
case study." *American Journal of Political Science* 40: 825–850.

Petrocik, John R., William L. Benoit, and
Glenn J. Hansen. 2003. "Issue ownership and presidential campaigning,
1952–2000." *Political Science Quarterly*
118: 599–626.

Pew Research Center for the People and the
Press. 2001. "Why Americans aren't
stirred by campaign finance reform."
March 27. http://people-press.org/
commentary/?analysisid=1.

———. 2007. "Public knowledge of current
affairs little changed by news and information revolutions: What Americans
know: 1989–2007." April 15. http://peo
ple-press.org/report/319/public-knowl
edge-of-current-affairs-little-changed-
by-news-and-information-revolutions.

———. 2008. "Who knows news? What you
read or view matters, but not your politics." October 15. http://pewresearch
.org/pubs/993/who-knows-news-what-
you-read-or-view-matters-but-not-
your-politics.

———. 2009a. "No decline in belief that
Obama is a Muslim." April 1. http://
pewre search.org/pubs/1176/obama-
muslim-opinion-not-changed.

———. 2009b. "What does the public
know?" October 14. http://pewresearch
.org/pubs/1378/political-news-iq-quiz.

Pfau, Michael, R. Lance Holbert, Erin Alison
Szabo, and Kelly Kaminski. 2002.
"Issue-advocacy versus candidate
advertising: Effects on candidate preferences and democratic process." *Journal of Communication* 52: 301–315.

Pfau, Michael, Henry C. Kenski, Michael
Nitz, and John Sorenson. 1989. "Use of
the attack message strategy in political
campaign communication." Paper presented at the 1989 annual meeting of
the Speech Communication Association, San Francisco.

Pfau, Michael, David Park, R. Lance Holbert,
and Jaeho Cho. 2001. "The effects of
party- and PAC-sponsored issue advertising and the potential of inoculation
to combat its impact on the democratic
process." *American Behavioral Scientist*
44: 2379–2397.

Pfau, Michael, Roxanne Parrott, and Bridget
Lindquist. 1992. "An expectancy theory
explanation of the effectiveness of
political attack television spots: A case
study." *Journal of Applied Communication Research* 20: 235–253.

Pinderhughes, Dianne M. 1992. "The role of
African American political organiza-
tions in the mobilization of voters." In
*From exclusion to inclusion: The long
struggle for African American political
power*, ed. Ralph C. Gomes and Linda
Faye Williams, 35–52. New York:
Greenwood.

Pinkleton, Bruce E. 1997. "The effects of
negative comparative political advertising on candidate evaluations and
advertising evaluations: An exploration." *Journal of Advertising* 26: 19–29.

———. 1998. "Effects of print comparative
political advertising on political decision-making and participation." *Journal of Communication* 48: 24–36.

Pirch, Kevin A. 2008. "Bloggers at the gates:
Ned Lamont, blogs, and the rise of

insurgent candidates." *Social Science Computer Review* 26: 275–287.

Plasser, Fritz. 2000. "American campaign techniques worldwide." *Harvard International Journal of Press/Politics* 5: 33–54.

Plasser, Fritz, and Gunda Plasser. 2002. *Global political campaigning: A worldwide analysis of campaign professionals and their practices.* Westport, Conn.: Praeger.

Plouffe, David. 2009. *The audacity to win: The inside story and lessons of Barack Obama's historic victory.* New York: Viking.

Popkin, Samuel L. 1991. *The reasoning voter: Communication and persuasion in presidential campaigns.* Chicago: University of Chicago Press.

———. 1992. "Campaigns that matter." In *Under the watchful eye: Managing presidential campaigns in the television era,* ed. Mathew D. McCubbins, 153–170. Washington, D.C.: CQ Press.

———. 1994. *The reasoning voter: Communication and persuasion in presidential campaigns,* 2nd ed. Chicago: University of Chicago Press.

Powell, G. Bingham, Jr., and Guy D. Whitten. 1993. "A cross-national analysis of economic voting: Taking account of the political context." *American Journal of Political Science* 37: 391–414.

Prat, Andrea. 2002. "Campaign advertising and voter welfare." *Review of Economic Studies* 69: 999–1017.

Preston, Michael B., Lenneal J. Henderson Jr., and Paul Puryear, eds. 1982. *The new black politics: The search for political power.* New York: Longman.

Price, Vincent, Clarissa David, Brian Goldthorpe, Marci McCoy Roth, and Joseph N. Cappella. 2006. "Locating the issue public: The multi-dimensional nature of engagement with health care reform." *Political Behavior* 28: 33–63.

Price, Vincent, and John Zaller. 1993. "Who gets the news? Alternative measures of news reception and their implications for research." *Public Opinion Quarterly* 57: 133–164.

Prior, Markus. 2009. "The immensely inflated news audience: Assessing bias in self-reported news exposure." *Public Opinion Quarterly* 73: 130–143.

Prior, Markus, and Arthur Lupia. 2008. "Money, time, and political knowledge: Distinguishing quick recall and political learning skills." *American Journal of Political Science* 52: 169–183.

Putnam, Robert D. 2000. *Bowling alone: The collapse and revival of American community.* New York: Simon and Schuster.

Rackaway, Chapman. 2007. "Trickle-down technology? The use of computing and network technology in state legislative campaigns." *Social Science Computer Review* 25: 466–483.

Rahn, Wendy M. 1993. "The role of partisan stereotypes in information processing about political candidates." *American Journal of Political Science* 37: 472–496.

Rainey, James. 2009. "Anti-Obama rants take on new ferocity." *Los Angeles Times,* August 26. www.latimes.com/news/nationworld/nation/healthcare/la-et-onthemedia26–2009aug26,0,4419688.column.

Rapoport, Ronald B., Kira Allman, Daniel Maliniak, and Lonna Rae Atkeson. 2009. "The Internet-ilization of American parties: The implications of the Unity 08 effort." Paper presented at the State of the Parties Conference, Ray C. Bliss Institute of Applied Politics, University of Akron, Ohio, October 15–16. www.uakron.edu/bliss/docs/Rapoport finalfinal_akron_paper_2009_DM_editsrbr.pdf.

Rapoport, Ronald B., Kelly L. Metcalf, and Jon A. Hartman. 1989. "Candidate traits and voter inferences: An experimental study." *Journal of Politics* 51: 917–932.

Redlawsk, David P., and James A. McCann. 2005. "Popular interpretations of 'corruption' and their partisan consequences." *Political Behavior* 27: 261–283.

Reichley, A. James. 1992. *The life of the parties: A history of American political parties.* New York: Free Press.

Reinsch, Paul. 1912. "The initiative and referendum." *Proceedings of the Academy of Political Science in the City of New York* 3: 155–161.

Richardson, Glenn W., Jr. 2008. *Pulp politics: How political advertising tells the stories of American politics*, 2nd ed. Lanham, Md.: Rowman and Littlefield.

Ridout, Travis N. 2009. "Campaign microtargeting and the relevance of the televised political ad." *The Forum* 7(2), article 5. www.bepress.com/forum.

Riker, William H. 1989. "Why negative campaigning is rational." Paper presented at the 1989 annual meeting of the American Political Science Association, Atlanta, Ga.

Rivlin, Joel. 2008. "On the air: Advertising in 2004 as a window on the 2008 presidential general election." *The Forum* 5(4), article 7. www.bepress.com/forum.

Roberds, Stephen C. 2003–2004. "Do congressional ethics committees matter? U.S. Senate ethics cases, 1789–2000." *Public Integrity* 6: 25–38.

Robinson, John P., and Mark R. Levy. 1986. *The main source: Learning from television news*. Beverly Hills, Calif.: Sage.

Rogers, Everett M., James W. Dearing, and Dorine Bregman. 1993. "The anatomy of agenda-setting research." *Journal of Communication* 43: 68–84.

Rosenbloom, David Lee. 1973. *The election men: Professional campaign managers and American democracy*. New York: Quadrangle Books.

Rosenson, Beth A. 2005. "The congressional ethics investigations of Wright, Gingrich and DeLay: Beyond a 'partisan ethics wars' interpretation." Paper presented at the 2005 annual meetings of the American Political Science Association, Washington, D.C.

———. 2008. "Media coverage of state legislatures: Assessing quantity, content, and tone." Paper presented at the 2008 annual meeting of the American Political Science Association, Boston, Mass.

Rosenstone, Steven J., and John Mark Hansen. 1993. *Mobilization, participation, and democracy in America*. New York: Macmillan.

Rother, Larry, and Liz Robbins. 2008. "Joe in the spotlight." *New York Times*, October 16. http://thecaucus.blogs.nytimes.com/2008/10/16/joe-in-the-spotlight.

Rove, Karl. 2008. "How the president-elect did it." *Wall Street Journal*, November 6. http://online.wsj.com/article/SB122593304225103509.html.

Rundquist, Barry S., Gerald S. Strom, and John G. Peters. 1977. "Corrupt politicians and their electoral support: Some empirical observations." *American Political Science Review* 71: 954–963.

Rutenberg, Jim, and Kate Zernike. 2004. "Going negative: When it works." *New York Times*, August 22. http://www.nytimes.com/2004/08/22/weekinreview/22zern2.html.

Saad, Lydia. 2006. "Political corruption is bipartisan PR problem." Report issued by the Gallup News Service, January 5. www.gallup.com/poll/20731/Political-Corruption-Bipartisan-Problem.aspx.

———. 2009. "More Americans plugged into political news." Report issued by the Gallup News Service, September 28. www.gallup.com/poll/123203/Americans-Plugged-Into-Political-News.aspx#1.

Sabato, Larry J. 1981. *The rise of political consultants: New ways of winning elections*. New York: Basic Books.

———. 1988. *The party's just begun: Shaping political parties for America's future*. Glenview, Ill.: Scott, Foresman.

Sabato, Larry J., Mark Stencel, and S. Robert Lichter. 2000. *Peep show: Media and politics in an age of scandal*. Lanham, Md: Rowman and Littlefield.

Salmore, Barbara G., and Stephen A. Salmore. 1989. *Candidates, parties, and campaigns: Electoral politics in America*, 2nd ed. Washington, D.C.: CQ Press.

Savage, Charlie, and Alan Wirzbicki. 2005. "White House–friendly reporter under scrutiny." *The Boston Globe*, February 2. www.boston.com/news/nation/washington/articles/2005/02/02/white_house_friendly_reporter_under_scrutiny.

Scammell, Margaret. 1998. "The wisdom of the war room: U.S. campaigning and Americanization." *Media, Culture & Society* 20: 251–275.

Schenck-Hamlin, William J., David E. Procter, and Deborah J. Rumsey. 2000.

"The influence of negative advertising frames on political cynicism and politician accountability." *Human Communication Research* 26: 53–74.

Schlozman, Daniel, and Ian Yohai. 2008. "How initiatives don't always make citizens: Ballot initiatives in the American states, 1978–2004." *Political Behavior* 30: 469–489

Schlozman, Kay Lehman, Sidney Verba, and Henry E. Brady. 2009. "The weapon of the strong? Participatory inequality and the Internet revolution." Paper presented at the 2009 annual meeting of the Midwest Political Science Association, Chicago.

Schrag, Peter. 1998. *Paradise lost: California's experience, America's future.* New York: New Press.

Schweitzer, Eva J. 2009. "Attack politics on the Internet: Comparing German and American E-campaigns." Paper presented at the 2009 annual meeting of the American Political Science Association, Toronto.

Sears, David O., and Jack Citrin. 1982. *Tax revolt: Something for nothing in California.* Cambridge, Mass.: Harvard University Press.

Semiatin, Richard. 2004. *Campaigns in the 21st century.* Boston: McGraw Hill.

Shaer, Matthew. 2009. "Sarah Palin wades back into the 'death panel' debate." *Christian Science Monitor,* September 9. http://features.csmonitor.com/politics/2009/09/09/sarah-palin-wades-back-into-the-death-panel-debate.

Shapiro, Michael A., and Robert H. Rieger. 1992. "Comparing positive and negative political advertising on radio." *Journalism Quarterly* 69: 135–145.

Shaw, Catherine M. 2010. *The campaign manager: Running and winning local elections,* 4th ed. Boulder, Colo.: Westview.

Shaw, Daron R. 1999a. "A study of presidential campaign event effects from 1952 to 1992." *Journal of Politics* 61: 387–422.

———. 1999b. "The effect of TV ads and candidate appearances on statewide presidential votes, 1988–96." *American Political Science Review* 93: 345–361.

———. 1999c. "The impact of news media favorability and candidate events in presidential campaigns." *Political Communication* 16: 183–202.

———. 2006. *The race to 270: The electoral college and the campaign strategies of 2000 and 2004.* Chicago: University of Chicago Press.

Shaw, David. 1996. "Critics of media cynicism point a finger at television." *Los Angeles Times,* April 19, A1, A21–22.

Shea, Daniel M., and Michael John Burton. 2001. *Campaign craft: The strategies, tactics, and art of political campaign management,* revised and updated ed. Westport, Conn.: Praeger.

Shenkman, Rick. 2008. *Just how stupid are we? Facing the truth about the American voter.* New York: Basic Books.

Shepard, Scott. 2008. "A look at the insiders in the 'age of Obama.'" *Atlanta Journal Constitution,* November 12. www.ajc.com/news/content/shared/news/stories/2008/11/OBAMA_INNER_CIRCLE12_1STLD_COX.html.

Shepherd, Ben. 2009. "Newspapers online—the real dilemma." *Talking Digital,* June 8. http://talkingdigital.wordpress.com/2009/06/08/newspapers-online-the-real-dilemma.

Shepsle, Kenneth A. 1972. "The strategy of ambiguity: Uncertainty and electoral competition." *American Political Science Review* 66: 555–568.

Sides, John. 2006. "The origins of campaign agendas." *British Journal of Political Science* 36: 407–436.

———. n.d. "The importance of interaction in campaigns." Unpublished working paper, George Washington University.

Siemaszko, Corky. 2009. "Advertisers continue to abandon Glenn Beck after pundit had called President Obama a 'racist.'" *New York Daily News,* September 3. www.nydailynews.com/money/2009/09/03/2009–09–03_advertisers_.html.

Sigelman, Lee, and David Bullock. 1991. "Candidates, issues, horse races, and hoopla: Presidential campaign coverage, 1888–1988." *American Politics Quarterly* 19: 5–32.

Sigelman, Lee, and Mark Kugler. 2003. "Why is research on the effects of negative campaigning so inconclusive? Understanding citizens' perceptions of negativity." *Journal of Politics* 65: 142–160.

Silva, Mark. 2008. "Bush encounters: By numbers." *The Swamp*, April 10. www.swamppolitics.com/news/politics/blog/2008/04/bush_encounters_by_numbers.html.

Silver, Nate. 2008. "Zogby engages in apparent push polling for right-wing website." *FiveThirtyEight.com*, November 18. www.fivethirtyeight.com/2008/11/zogby-engages-in-apparent-push-polling.html.

Skaperdas, Stergios, and Bernard Grofman. 1995. "Modeling negative campaigning." *American Political Science Review* 89: 49–61.

Smith, Aaron. 2009. "The Internet's role in campaign 2008." Report prepared for the Pew Internet and American Life Project, Washington, D.C. www.pewinternet.org/~/media//Files/Reports/2009/The_Internets_Role_in_Campaign_2008.pdf.

Smith, Aaron, Kay Lehman Schlozman, Sidney Verba, and Henry Brady. 2009. "The Internet and civic engagement." Report prepared for the Pew Internet and American Life Project, Washington, D.C. www.pewinternet.org/Reports/2009/15—The-Internet-and-Civic-Engagement.aspx.

Smith, Culver H. 1977. *The press, politics, and patronage.* Athens, Ga.: University of Georgia Press.

Smith, Daniel A. 1998. *Tax crusaders and the politics of direct democracy.* New York: Routledge.

_____. 2001a. "Campaign financing of ballot initiatives in the American states." In *Dangerous democracy: The battle over ballot initiatives in America,* ed. Larry J. Sabato, Howard R. Ernst, and Bruce A. Larson, 71–90. Lanham, Md.: Rowman and Littlefield.

_____. 2001b. "Special interests and direct democracy: An historical glance." In *The battle over citizen lawmaking: A collection of essays,* ed. M. Dane Waters,

59–72. Durham, N.C.: Carolina Academic Press.

_____. 2001c. "Homeward bound? Micro-level legislative responsiveness to ballot initiatives." *State Politics and Policy Quarterly* 1: 50–61.

_____. 2004. "Peeling away the populist rhetoric: Toward a taxonomy of anti-tax ballot initiatives." *Public Budgeting and Finance* 24: 88–110.

_____. 2008. "Was Rove right? Ohio's gay marriage ban and the 2004 presidential election." In *Direct Democracy's Impact on American Political Institutions,* ed. Shaun Bowler and Amihai Glazer, 21–34. New York: Palgrave Macmillan.

_____. 2009. "Financing ballot measures in the U.S." In *Financing referendum campaigns,* ed. Karin Gilland Lutz and Simon Hug, 39–61. New York: Palgrave Macmillan.

Smith, Daniel A., Matthew DeSantis, and Jason Kassel. 2006. "Same-sex marriage ballot measures and the 2004 presidential election." *State and Local Government Review* 38: 78–91.

Smith, Daniel A., and Dustin Fridkin. 2008. "Delegating direct democracy: Interparty legislative competition and the adoption of the initiative in the American states." *American Political Science Review* 102: 333–350.

Smith, Daniel A., and Joseph Lubinski. 2002. "Direct democracy during the Progressive Era: A crack in the populist veneer?" *Journal of Policy History* 14: 349–383.

Smith, Daniel A., and Caroline J. Tolbert. 2001. "The initiative to party: Partisanship and ballot initiatives in California." *Party Politics* 7: 738–757.

_____. 2004. *Educated by initiative: The effects of direct democracy on citizens and political organizations in the American states.* Ann Arbor: University of Michigan Press.

_____. 2007. "The instrumental and educative effects of ballot measures: Research on direct democracy in the American states." *State Politics and Policy Quarterly* 4: 417–445.

_____. 2010. "Direct democracy, opinion formation, and candidate choice." *Public Opinion Quarterly* (forthcoming).

Smith, Eric R. A. N. 1989. *The unchanging American voter*. Berkeley: University of California Press.

Smith, Mark A. 2001. "The contingent effects of ballot initiatives and candidate races on turnout." *American Journal of Political Science* 45: 700–706.

_____. 2002. "Ballot initiatives and the democratic citizen." *Journal of Politics* 64: 892–903.

Sonner, Molly W., and Clyde Wilcox. 1999. "Forgiving and forgetting: Public support for Bill Clinton during the Lewinsky scandal." *PS: Political Science & Politics* 32: 554–557.

Soraghan, Mike, and Jared Allen. 2009. "Pelosi halts effort to sanction Wilson." *The Hill,* September 10. http://thehill .com/homenews/house/58115-dems-may-move-to-censure-wilson?page=6.

Sorauf, Frank J. 1988. *Money in American Elections*. Glenview, Ill.: Scott, Foresman.

Sosnik, Douglas B., Matthew J. Dowd, and Ron Fournier. 2006. *Applebee's America: How successful political, business, and religious leaders connect with the new American community.* New York: Simon and Schuster.

Spiliotes, Constantine J., and Lynn Vavreck. 2002. "Campaign advertising: Partisan convergence or divergence?" *Journal of Politics* 64: 249–261.

Squire, Peverill. 1992. "Challenger profile and gubernatorial elections." *Western Political Quarterly* 45: 125–142.

Star, Michael. 2008. "Jon's got game." *New York Post,* September 25. www.nypost .com/p/entertainment/tv/jon_got_game_ARuthNhfEW09txbCOTBNkO.

Stelter, Brian. 2009. "Fox's volley with Obama intensifying." *New York Times,* October 11. www.nytimes.com/2009/10/12/business/media/12fox.html?pagewanted=all.

Stevens, Daniel. 2005. "Separate and unequal effects: Information, political sophistication and negative advertising." *Political Research Quarterly* 58: 413–425.

Stewart, Charles H., III. 1994. "Let's go fly a kite: Correlates of involvement in the House bank scandal." *Legislative Studies Quarterly* 19: 521–535.

Stimson, James A. 1999. *Public opinion in America: Moods, cycles, and swings,* 2nd ed. Boulder, Colo.: Westview.

_____. 2004. *Tides of consent: How public opinion shapes American politics.* Cambridge: Cambridge University Press.

Stoker, Laura. 1993. "Judging presidential character: The demise of Gary Hart." *Political Behavior* 15: 193–223.

Stonecash, Jeffrey M. 2008. "Swing voters in subnational campaigns." In *The Swing Voter in American Politics,* ed. William G. Mayer, 102–111. Washington, D.C.: Brookings Institution Press.

Strachan, J. Cherie. 2003. *High-tech grass roots: The professionalization of local elections.* Lanham, Md.: Rowman and Littlefield.

Stratmann, Thomas. 2005. "Some talk: Money in politics. A (partial) review of the literature." *Public Choice* 124: 135–156.

Strother, Raymond D. 2003. *Falling up: How a redneck helped invent political consulting.* Baton Rouge: Louisiana State University Press.

Stroud, Natalie Jomini. 2008. "Media use and political predispositions: Revisiting the concept of selective exposure." *Political Behavior* 30: 341–366.

Sturgis, Patrick, Nick Allum, and Patten Smith. 2008. "An experiment on the measurement of political knowledge in surveys." *Public Opinion Quarterly* 85: 90–102.

Sulkin, Tracy, and Jillian Evans. 2006. "Dynamics of diffusion: Aggregate patterns in congressional campaign agendas." *American Politics Research* 34: 505–534.

Sulkin, Tracy, Cortney M. Moriarty, and Veronica Hefner. 2007. "Congressional candidates' issue agendas on- and off-line." *Harvard International Journal of Press/Politics* 12: 63–79.

Sullivan, John L., John H. Aldrich, Eugene Borgida, and Wendy Rahn. 1990. "Candidate appraisal and human nature: Man and superman in the 1984 election." *Political Psychology* 11: 459–484.

Swanson, David L., and Paolo Mancini, eds. 1996. *Politics, media, and modern democracy: An international study of innovations in electoral campaigning and their consequences.* Westport, Conn.: Praeger.

Sweet, Lynn. 2008. "What's next for David Axelrod?" *Chicago Sun Times,* November 2. http://www.suntimes.com/news/sweet/1254879,CST-NWS-sweet02.article.

Swint, Kerwin C. 1998. *Political consultants and negative campaigning: The secrets of the pros.* Lanham, Md.: University Press of America.

Tedesco, John C., and Lynda Lee Kaid. 2003. "Style and effects of the Bush and Gore spots." In *The Millennium Election: Communication in the 2000 Campaigns,* ed. Lynda Lee Kaid, John C. Tedesco, Dianne G. Bystrom, and Mitchell S. McKinney, 5–16. Lanham, Md.: Rowman and Littlefield.

Tedesco, John C., Lynda Lee Kaid, and Lori M. McKinnon. 2000. "Network adwatches: Policing the 1996 primary and general election presidential ads." *Journal of Broadcasting and Electronic Media* 44: 541–555.

The Big E. 2009. "MN-SEN: Some inside scoop on how Franken knew he was going to win." *Daily Kos,* November 23. www.dailykos.com/story/2009/11/23/807232/-MN-SEN:some-inside-scoop-on-how-Franken-knew-he-was-going-to-win.

Thomas, Scott J. 1989. "Do incumbent expenditures matter?" *Journal of Politics* 51: 965–976.

Thompson, Dennis F. 1987. *Political ethics and public office.* Cambridge, Mass.: Harvard University Press.

_____. 1995. *Ethics in Congress: From individual to institutional corruption.* Washington, D.C.: Brookings Institution Press.

Thrush, Glenn. 2009. "58 percent of GOP not sure/doubt Obama born in U.S." *Politico,* July 31. www.politico.com/blogs/glennthrush/0709/58_of_GOP_not_suredont_beleive_Obama_born_in_US.html?showall.

Thrush, Glenn, and Martin Kady II. 2009. "GOP seizes on terror issue." *Politico,* December 29. www.politico.com/news/stories/1209/31016.html.

Thurber, James A. 1998. "The study of campaign consultants: A subfield in search of theory." *PS: Political Science & Politics* 31: 145–149.

_____. 2002. "From campaigning to lobbying." In *Shades of gray: Perspectives on campaign ethics,* ed. Candice J. Nelson, David A. Dulio, and Stephen K. Medvic, 151–170. Washington, D.C.: Brookings Institution Press.

Thurber, James A., and Candice J. Nelson, eds. 2000. *Campaign warriors: Political consultants in elections.* Washington, D.C.: Brookings Institution Press.

_____. 2004. *Campaigns and elections American style,* 2nd ed. Boulder, Colo.: Westview.

_____. 2010. *Campaigns and elections American style,* 3rd ed. Boulder, Colo.: Westview (forthcoming).

Thurber, James A., Candice J. Nelson, and David A. Dulio, eds. 2000a. *Crowded airwaves: Campaign advertising in elections.* Washington, D.C.: Brookings Institution Press.

_____. 2000b. "Portrait of campaign consultants." In *Campaign warriors: Political consultants in elections,* ed. James A. Thurber and Candice J. Nelson, 10–36. Washington, D.C.: Brookings Institution Press.

Time. 1983. "Housecleaning." *Time,* July 25. www.time.com/time/magazine/article/0,9171,953990,00.html.

Tolbert, Caroline J. 2003. "Direct democracy and institutional realignment in the American states." *Political Science Quarterly* 118: 467–489.

Tolbert, Caroline J., John A. Grummel, and Daniel A. Smith. 2001. "The effects of ballot initiatives on voter turnout in the American states." *American Politics Research* 29: 625–648.

Tolbert, Caroline J., and Rodney E. Hero. 1996. "Race/ethnicity and direct democracy: An analysis of California's illegal immigration initiative." *Journal of Politics* 58: 806–818.

Tolbert, Caroline J., Daniel H. Lowenstein, and Todd Donovan. 1998. "Election law and rules for using initiatives." In *Citizens as legislators: Direct democracy in the United States,* ed. Shaun Bowler,

Todd Donovan, and Caroline J. Tolbert, 27–54. Columbus: Ohio State University Press.

Tolbert, Caroline J., Ramona S. McNeal, and Daniel A. Smith. 2003. "Enhancing civic engagement: The effect of direct democracy on political participation and knowledge." *State Politics and Policy Quarterly* 3: 23–41.

Tolbert, Caroline J. and Daniel A. Smith. 2005. "The educative effects of ballot initiatives on voter turnout." *American Politics Research* 33: 283–309.

Tolbert, Caroline J., Daniel A. Smith, and John C. Green. 2009. "Strategic voting and legislative redistricting reform: District and statewide representational winners and losers." *Political Research Quarterly* 62: 92–109.

Tomz, Michael, and Robert P. Van Houweling. 2009. "The electoral implications of candidate ambiguity." *American Political Science Review* 103: 83–98.

Trippi, Joe. 2004. *The revolution will not be televised: Democracy, the Internet, and the overthrow of everything.* New York: Regan Books.

Trish, Barbara. 2009. "Organizing for America." Paper presented at the State of the Parties Conference, Ray C. Bliss Institute of Applied Politics, University of Akron, October 15–16. www.uakron .edu/bliss/docs/Trishpaper.final.pdf.

Troy, Gil. 1996. *See how they ran: The changing role of the presidential candidate,* revised and expanded ed. Cambridge, Mass.: Harvard University Press.

Tufte, Edward R. 1975. "Determinants of the outcomes of midterm congressional elections." *American Political Science Review* 69: 812–826.

———. 1978. *Political control of the economy.* Princeton: Princeton University Press.

Tyson, Gerald S. 1999. "GOTV: Get out the vote." In *The Manship School guide to political communication,* ed. David T. Perlmutter, 131–136. Baton Rouge: Louisiana State University Press.

Ulferts, Alisa. 2003. "Lawmakers want hard road for initiatives." *St. Petersburg Times,* December 9. www.sptimes .com/2003/12/09/State/Lawmakers_ want_hard_r.shtml.

Utz, Sonja. 2009. "The (potential) benefits of campaigning via social network sites." *Journal of Computer-Mediated Communication* 14: 221–243.

Vaccari, Cristian. 2008. "From the air to the ground: The Internet in the 2004 U.S. presidential campaign." *New Media and Society* 10: 647–665.

Valentino, Nicholas A., Vincent L. Hutchings, and Ismail K. White. 2002. "Cues that matter: How political ads prime racial attitudes during campaigns." *American Political Science Review* 96: 75–90.

Valentino, Nicholas A., Vincent L. Hutchings, and Dmitri Williams. 2004. "The impact of political advertising on knowledge, internet information seeking, and candidate preference." *Journal of Communication* 54: 337–354.

Van Dunk, Emily. 1997. "Challenger quality in state legislative elections." *Political Research Quarterly* 50: 793–807.

Vargas, Jose Antonio. 2008. "Obama raised half a billion online." *Washington Post,* November 20. http://voices.washing tonpost.com/44/2008/11/20/obama_ raised_half_a_billion_on.html.

Vaughn, Stephen L., ed. 2008. *Encyclopedia of American journalism.* New York: Routledge.

Vavreck, Lynn. 2009. *The message matters: The economy and presidential campaigns.* Princeton: Princeton University Press.

Verba, Sidney, Nancy Burns, and Kay Lehman Schlozman. 1997. "Knowing and caring about politics: Gender and political engagement." *Journal of Politics* 59: 1051–1072.

Verba, Sidney, Kay Lehman Schlozman, and Henry E. Brady. 1995. *Voice and equality: Civic voluntarism in American politics.* Cambridge, Mass.: Harvard University Press.

Waismel-Manor, Israel Sergio. 2005. *Making up their minds: Knowledge, learning and decision-making among campaign consultants.* Unpublished dissertation, Cornell University.

Wallison, Peter J., and Joel M. Gora. 2009. *Better parties, better government: A realistic program for campaign finance reform.* Washington, D.C: American Enterprise Institute.

Wallsten, Kevin. 2009. "'Yes we can': How online viewership, blog discussion, campaign statements and mainstream media coverage produced a viral video phenomenon." Paper presented at the annual conference of the *Journal of Information Technology and Politics:* YouTube and the 2008 Election Cycle in the United States, Amherst, Mass., April 16–17. http://scholarworks .umass.edu/jitpc2009/1.

Walton, Hanes, Jr., ed. 1994. *Black politics and black political behavior: A linkage analysis.* Westport, Conn.: Praeger.

Washington Post. 2004. "New representatives: Profiles of non-incumbent winners." *Washington Post,* November 3, A36.

Waters, M. Dane. 2003. *Initiative and referendum almanac.* Durham, N.C.: Carolina Academic Press.

Watson, Robert P., and Colton C. Campbell, eds. 2003. *Campaigns and elections: Issues, concepts, cases.* Boulder, Colo.: Lynne Rienner.

Wattenberg, Martin P. 1991. *The rise of candidate-centered politics: Presidential elections of the 1980s.* Cambridge, Mass.: Harvard University Press.

———. 1998. *The decline of American political parties, 1952–1996.* Cambridge, Mass.: Harvard University Press.

Wattenberg, Martin P., and Craig Leonard Brians. 1999. "Negative campaign advertising: Demobilizer or mobilizer?" *American Political Science Review* 93: 891–899.

Weaver, David, and Dan Drew. 2001. "Voter learning and interest in the 2000 presidential election: Did the media matter?" *Journalism and Mass Communication Quarterly* 78: 787–798.

Weisberg, Herbert F., and Jerrold G. Rusk. 1970. "Dimensions of candidate evaluation." *American Political Science Review* 64: 1167–1185.

Weiss, Jeffrey. 2008. "Listen to and read the whole 'God damn America' sermon by the Reverend Jeremiah Wright." *Dallas Morning News,* March 27. http://reli gionblog.dallasnews.com/archives/ 2008/03/listen-and-read-to-the-whole-g .html.

Weissman, Stephan R., and Ruth Hassan. 2005. "BCRA and the 527 Groups." In *The election after reform: Money, politics, and the bipartisan campaign reform act,* ed. Michael J. Malbin, 79–111. Lanham, Md.: Rowman and Littlefield.

Welch, Susan, and John R. Hibbing. 1997. "The effects of charges of corruption on voting behavior in congressional elections, 1982–1990." *Journal of Politics* 59: 226–239.

Wenzel, James, Todd Donovan, and Shaun Bowler. 1998. "Direct democracy and minorities: Changing attitudes about minorities targeted by initiatives." In *Citizens as legislators: Direct democracy in the United States,* ed. Shaun Bowler, Todd Donovan, and Caroline J. Tolbert, 228–248. Columbus: Ohio State University Press.

West, Darrell M. 2009. *Air wars: Television advertising in election campaigns, 1952– 2008,* 5th ed. Washington, D.C.: CQ Press.

West, Darrell M., and Katherine Stewart. 2003. "Popular rogues: Citizen opinion about political corruption." *New England Journal of Public Policy* 18: 171–181.

Westen, Drew. 2007. *The political brain: The role of emotion in deciding the fate of the nation.* New York: Public Affairs.

White, John Kenneth, and Daniel M. Shea. 2004. *New party politics: From Jefferson and Hamilton to the information age,* 2nd ed. Belmont, Calif.: Wadsworth.

Wielhouwer, Peter W. 1999. "The mobilization of campaign activists by the party canvass." *American Politics Quarterly* 27: 177–200.

———. 2000. "Releasing the fetters: Parties and the mobilization of the African-American electorate." *Journal of Politics* 62: 206–222.

———. 2003. "In search of Lincoln's perfect list: Targeting in grassroots campaigns." *American Politics Research* 31: 632–669.

———. 2006. "Grassroots mobilization." In *The Electoral Challenge: Theory Meets Practice,* ed. Stephen C. Craig, 163–182. Washington, D.C.: CQ Press.

———. 2009. "Religion and American political participation." In *The Oxford handbook of religion and American politics,* ed. Corwin E. Smidt, Lyman A. Kellstedt, and James L. Guth, 394–426. New York: Oxford University Press.

Wielhouwer, Peter W., and Brad Lockerbie. 1994. "Party contacting and political participation, 1952–90." *American Journal of Political Science* 38: 211–229.

Wilcox, Clyde. 2008. "Internet fundraising in 2008: A new model?" *The Forum* 6(1), article 6. www.bepress.com/forum.

Wilkinson, Mike, and Nathan Hurst. 2008. "Dailies reveal unique delivery changes." *Detroit News,* December 17. www.detnews.com/apps/pbcs.dll/article?AID=/20081217/METRO/812170368.

Williams, Christine B., and Girish J. "Jeff" Gulati. 2009. "Social networks in political campaigns: Facebook and congressional elections 2006, 2008." Paper presented at the 2009 annual meeting of the American Political Science Association, Toronto.

Winkler, J., and S. E. Taylor. 1979. "Preference, expectations, and attributional bias: Two field studies." *Journal of Applied Social Psychology* 2: 183–197.

Winograd, Morley, and Michael Hais. 2008. *Millennial Makeover: MySpace, YouTube, and the Future of American Politics.* New Brunswick, N.J.: Rutgers University Press.

Wlezien, Christopher. 1995. "The public as thermostat: Dynamics of preferences for spending." *American Journal of Political Science* 39: 981–1000.

———. 2001. "On forecasting the presidential vote." *PS: Political Science and Politics* 34: 25–31.

Wlezien, Christopher, and Robert S. Erikson. 2002. "The timeline of presidential election campaigns." *Journal of Politics* 64: 969–993.

Wolak, Jennifer. 2006. "The consequences of presidential battleground strategies for citizen engagement." *Political Research Quarterly* 59: 353–361.

Wong, Janelle S. 2005. "Mobilizing Asian American voters: A field experiment." *Annals of the American Academy of Political and Social Science* 601: 102–114.

Xenos, Michael A., and Amy B. Becker. 2009. "Moments of Zen: Effects of *The Daily Show* on information seeking and political learning." *Political Communication* 26: 317–332.

Zaller, John R. 1987. "The diffusion of political attitudes." *Journal of Personality and Social Psychology* 53: 821–833.

———. 1992. *The nature and origins of mass opinion.* Cambridge: Cambridge University Press.

———. 1996. "The myth of massive media impact revived: New support for a discredited idea." In *Political persuasion and attitude change,* ed. Diana C. Mutz, Paul M. Sniderman, and Richard A. Brody, 17–78. Ann Arbor: University of Michigan Press.

———. 1998. "Monica Lewinsky's contribution to political science." *PS: Political Science & Politics* 31: 182–189.

Zeleny, Jeff. 2009a. "Health debate fails to ignite Obama's grass roots." *New York Times,* August 15. www.nytimes.com/2009/08/15/health/policy/15ground.html?_r=2&hp.

———. 2009b. "Thousands rally in capital to protest big government." *New York Times,* September 12. www.nytimes.com/2009/09/13/us/politics/13protestweb.html?_r=2&scp=3&sq=Tea%20Party&st=Search.

Zhang, Weiwu, Thomas J. Johnson, Trent Seltzer, and Shannon L. Bichard. 2010. "The revolution will be networked: The influence of social networking sites on political attitudes and behavior." *Social Science Computer Review* (forthcoming).

Zhao, Xinshu, and Glen L. Bleske. 1998. "Horse-race polls and audience issue learning." *Harvard International Journal of Press/Politics* 3: 13–34.

Zhao, Xinshu, and Steven H. Chaffee. 1995. "Campaign advertisements versus television news as sources of political issue information." *Public Opinion Quarterly* 59: 41–65.

Zogby International. 2008. "Zogby poll: Almost no Obama voters ace election test." November 18 (press release). www.zogby.com/news/ReadNews.cfm?ID=1642.

Zukin, Cliff, and Robin Snyder. 1984. "Passive learning: When the media environment is the message." *Public Opinion Quarterly* 48: 629–638.